Faces of History

DONALD R. KELLEY

Faces of History

HISTORICAL INQUIRY FROM HERODOTUS TO HERDER

Yale University Press
New Haven &
London

Published with assistance from the Louis Stern Memorial Fund.

Set in Sabon type by Keystone Typesetting, Inc.

Printed in the United States of America by BookCrafters, Chelsea, Michigan.

Library of Congress Cataloging-in-Publication Data
Kelley, Donald R., 1931–
    Faces of history : historical inquiry from Herodotus to Herder / Donald R. Kelley.
      p cm.
    Includes bibliographical references and index.
    ISBN 0–300–07308–9 (cloth : alk. paper). —
ISBN 0–300–07558–8 (pbk. : alk. paper)
     1. History — Philosophy. 2. Historicism. I. Title.
D16.8.K37 1998
901–dc21
                                    98–10979
                                       CIP

A catalogue record for this book is available from the British Library.

To Paul Kristeller, and in memory of Myron Gilmore,
Felix Gilbert, Hans Baron, and Jack Hexter

Man vergilt einem Lehrer schlecht
wenn man immer der Schüler bleibt.

Contents

Preface

History has been written in many times and places, under many conditions, for many purposes, and from many points of view. A history of "history" itself can be written with reference to all of these variables, including the psychology, social status, political standpoint, and cultural environment of particular historians; but it can also be written in the phenomenological terms of the historical genre itself and the surviving values which have become part of the basic vocabulary and mentality of historians. The most familiar of these values are claims of truth, accuracy, relevance, explanatory power, literary skill, political or philosophical utility, and scholarly or popular acceptance. Of course these terms can themselves be understood not only as constant intellectual qualities but also as cultural constructions, political positions, or literary topoi, and yet — as history shows — they preserve meanings beyond particular historical contexts.

The premise of this latter, largely "internalist" approach is not that of an author positioned somehow behind the surviving texts but that of a reader — a reader for whom works of historiographical tradition are in one sense "taken out of context" (as if they could remain in some original context still tied to authorial intention) and yet in another sense are set in the only context accessible to the reader, that of an evanescent present. For readers, all histories are contemporary; to this extent Collingwood's maxim surely applies. As readers, none of us has been present at the birth of a work, nor can we reproduce that conjectural authorial condition except through the conceptual resources and rhetorical devices of this same historiographical tradition in its current state.

This book not only accepts this irremediable hermeneutical condition of reading histories but insists on the value of establishing meaning from and for a contemporary standpoint. Herodotus, Thucydides, and their successors wrote for posterity—and for the time being we *are* this posterity. This book offers one person's view of the history of history as it can be assembled from currently available primary texts and secondary commentaries; it is not the chronicle of a literary process but an interpretation of what retrospectively appears as an intellectual tradition and even (for some readers), a canon. This is a subject which has occupied many of my working and leisure hours since undergraduate days, and having published detailed studies in several areas of European historical thought and writing, I have decided to attempt a synthesis on the basis of studies begun, if memory serves, with a senior thesis on Lord Acton (if not with my sophomore study of Collingwood's *Idea of History*) and pursued in a number of books and articles published in the intervening years. I do not always agree with the author of many of these earlier writings, but I continue to rely in many ways on his line of inquiry and judgments.

I began back then with the notion (for which I hardly needed Collingwood's authorization) that history was a form of inquiry—not the end or object but the beginning of an intellectual project. Many years of study have reinforced that view, conceived in Herodotean innocence, although I have had to consider the many answers to the question "What is history?" which presume to give larger meanings or even closure to the lines of questioning opened by Herodotus and his successors. These often elaborate answers are also part of the story of Western historical writing over the past two and a half millennia (and, *ante litteram,* much more), but none of them nullifies the Herodotean and Collingwoodian idea that history is fundamentally an endless inquiry into the human condition. This is especially true for the remoter reaches of the Western past, which (rather than contemporary history) is my main concern here.

I have learned much since my first naive epiphany and have been deeply impressed, over almost five decades, by debates in philosophy, the human sciences (sociology and then anthropology), and literary criticism, which have shaped my ideas about the theory and practice of history and especially about its limitations. I remain skeptical about the possibility of getting "behind the back of language," as Gadamer put it, or of finding an Archimedean point beyond the confines of culture (however we may define it). Culture is an ocean in which we swim, and, despite the efforts of study and the wonders of technology, we remain—at least we historians remain—fish and not oceanographers.

In any case this awareness of our hermeneutical predicament seems appropriate to a practicing historian, especially one writing about the history of this practice and some of the theories behind it. I do not pretend that this standpoint is, in a disciplinary way, any less conventional than that of philosophers, literary theorists, or even ethnomethodologists, but it does seem to me essential for my purpose, which is to tell one historian's story about the tradition of historical inquiry on the basis of texts linked semantically to the idea of "history" as "we" of the present understand it. The study of history does not move the world, though it may move people, and I hope this approach offers, if not remedies, at least some measure of self-understanding.

Forgetting is an essential part of effective memory (as Gadamer has noted) and an essential part of living (I would add); but methodological amnesia is not something for historians, the curators of anamnesis, to cultivate. Practitioners of "new histories," successors to the Moderns of the early modern period, have advantages over the old and outmoded, but historical perspective requires that we remember the prior, pioneering efforts of the Ancients. "Boerhave is more useful than Hippocrates, Newton than all of antiquity, and Tasso than Homer," remarked Voltaire, that most fervent of Moderns—"*sed gloria primis.*" Or, if not glory, then historical appreciation, for this is also part of what used to be called wisdom.

The essential purpose of this book is to present a critical survey and interpretation of the Western tradition of historical inquiry and writing from Herodotus and Thucydides down to the masterworks of the eighteenth century and the beginnings of "scientific history" in the nineteenth. It concerns many of the major and minor works and a number of themes and issues which have informed the practice and theory of historiography over some twenty-five centuries and across a variety of cultures, including our own. Among these topics are questions of historical truth and utility, methods of interpretation and criticism, narrative and monographic forms, relations of history to myth and poetry, the origins of peoples and nations, the chronology and the auxiliary sciences, and, ante litteram, the philosophy of history. Throughout the survey the principal faces of history are kept in mind, especially the antiquarian and cultural interests of Herodotus, the contemporary political analysis of Thucydides, and the universal chronicle of Eusebius, which drew together pagan and Christian views of the past—all of which have left their imprint on modern conceptions and practices of history and its meanings.

The work was conceived, in its last incarnation, as a companion piece to my anthology *Versions of History from Antiquity to the Enlightenment* (1991); but although it follows a similar design, it extends far beyond the selection of texts and themes assembled there. I have not reproduced, but have drawn on, some of my earlier writings, some republished in two collections, *History, Law, and the Human Sciences* (1984) and *The Writing of History and the Study of Law* (1997). I use English translations of primary texts when available; the others are mine, and I note (*VH*) those which are included in the aforementioned *Versions of History*. I use Eduard Fueter's classic *Geschichte der neueren Historiographie* (1936) and, more cautiously, James Westfall Thompson's collaborative *A History of Historical Writing* (1943). My own bibliographical notes are far from exhaustive, but they are up-to-date as of 1997.

I began listing my debts for this project in my first book, *Foundations of Modern Historical Scholarship: Language, Law, and History in the French Renaissance* (1970), and since then they have increased beyond numbering. In the last stages of work I am especially grateful to the members of the Folger Library seminar "Encounters with Antiquity," which I directed in the spring of 1994; to the Institute for Advanced Study, Princeton, which in 1996–97 again gave haven from some academic commitments; and to many colleagues, including Peter Paret, Daniel Woolf, David Sacks, Joseph Levine, and especially Anthony Grafton, who gave an absolutely Scaligerian critique of the manuscript, saving me from many errors, suggesting improvements, and sending me off in more directions than I could safely take.

Some of these directions have been taken by Bonnie Smith, who has been in this same terrain of European historiography (and has finished her book simultaneously with mine), though in a later period, from a different standpoint, through a different line of questioning, and with a different gallery of portraits; we, too, represent two different "faces of history." Living, traveling, and working together, we often cross paths intellectually as well, but it is a testimony to the richness, variety, and complexity of that foreign country which is the past that we continue to find unsuspected and unexamined aspects of historical studies. For the past twenty years Bonnie has been, for me, the one constant in the world of historical and historiographical flux; without her I would never have journeyed so far or seen so much.

Mythistory

That which was from the beginning . . . write we unto you, that your joy may
be full.
—I John 1.1

"History," Michel de Certeau writes, "is probably our myth."[1] According to an old and familiar story, history emerged from myth and purged itself
gradually of legendary features until it gained full enlightenment in the age of
Machiavelli and Guicciardini—or perhaps Voltaire and Gibbon, or perhaps
Mommsen and Ranke, or perhaps the "new" economic, social, and cultural
histories of this century, and so on. Or maybe, as Certeau suggests and Hans
Blumenberg argues, not. "Sceptical doubt . . . is a malady which can never be
radically cured," David Hume remarked, and the same can be said (with or
without the pathological conceit) about history as well as myth; for we cannot
see beyond our deepest prejudices, nor can we quite write history without
them.[2] The Enlightenment was defeated by historicism, Hans Blumenberg
believes, while historicism has itself lost its hegemonic status among many
moderns and postmoderns.[3] Yet we continue to "historicize," following Fredric Jameson's para-Marxist admonition, for the enlightenment, or perhaps
comfort, that history still offers.[4] Paralleling the reflexive process of "work on
myth," this seems most appropriate for the study of history itself, which is one
of the latest, if not the last, of Western mythical constructions by which we try
to make sense of the largely unknown and perhaps ultimately unknowable
world beyond our small cultural horizons.

Two Faces of History

In the National Museum of Naples there is a striking Janus-faced double herm of Herodotus and Thucydides, heads back to back and looking in opposite directions.[5] The two busts of the sculpture were separated in early modern times but were rejoined in the eighteenth century, when they passed from the Farnese family to the Neapolitan museum. Herodotus and Thucydides were both investigators of the Hellenic past, both spectators of the dramatic events of fifth-century B.C. Greek civilization, so why are they situated so close together and yet seem poles apart in their spectations and so, perhaps, speculations? Is it not because they have different ways of looking at history and represent two distinct faces of history in its formative stage? So at least it seems from the retrospective view taken here.

The study of history is always renewing itself, but it is nonetheless, unavoidably but also appropriately, bound to its past. Herodotus was a man of very broad horizons, though they were not our horizons, and he might have been surprised by his posterity. Self-consciously though he began his pathbreaking "inquiries" (*historie*), he could hardly know that he was initiating a literary genre, a canon, and ultimately a discipline which, two millennia later, would become the basis of a science and a profession. We know this, however, and cannot forget it; and it is naive to pretend that we are *not* reading Herodotus's work in the light of this later tradition. Whatever meaning Herodotus intended to express and to communicate, the face of history displayed in his book is revealed fully only in what we would call its reception and the ancients called its "fortune" — *habent sua fortuna libelli* — that is, its interpretive history across many centuries and cultures and in many guises, whether as the work of the "father of history" or of the "father of lies," both of which titles were bestowed on Herodotus.[6] History has always been located in the realm of opinion, between poles of truth and falsehood, certainty and probability, and so it has indeed followed the fortunes of Herodotus, his reputation, and his *History*.[7]

The second founding figure in the Western tradition of historiography displays to us an altogether different countenance. Like Herodotus, Thucydides was fascinated by war and its causes, but his line of questioning was quite different. He was a practical and committed man of affairs and not a cosmopolitan and compulsive tourist like Herodotus; and so he deliberately confined himself to immediate or directly remembered experience, rejecting "mythistory" and devoting himself to the task of explaining events in terms of causes, immediate and underlying, and the actions and motives of political and military participants like himself in the historical process.[8] (This is one reason why he has often been preferred by historians who take politics and war as the essence of historical inquiry.) As Herodotus allowed his curiosity to range across many cultural frontiers, from civilization to barbarism, from myth to ascertainable fact, so Thucydides turned to his local horizons and the Peloponnesian wars, the terrible predicament in which he was involved and of which he was, finally, a victim. He had no time for antiquarian or anthropological inquiry, swept up as he was in *l'histoire événementielle* and the fate of his community — and of course his own fate.

Clio has shown more than two faces, of course; but the paradigms established by these first two devotees of the muse of history have persisted, in a complex and kaleidoscopic way, for almost twenty-five centuries. On the one hand is the tradition of what by the eighteenth century was called "cultural history," which concerns itself with all aspects of human experience, spiritual as well as material, private as well as public, female as well as male, and with the myths and mysteries of remote antiquity as well as current crises. On the other hand is the concern for the headline events of political and military history, questions of material interests, agency, and power and the causal factors underlying conspicuous changes in public affairs. On one hand, history as a broad and open-ended field of human "inquiry," and on the other, history as a process to be enclosed in, or reduced to, familiar explanatory factors, and perhaps even (if the lessons were well learned) to be controlled.

As a term and concept, history is, in European perspective, a Greek creation, but of course this is not to deny that there have been historical practices ante litteram, and here we enter a minefield of conflicting ideas, interpretations, and interests. The difficulty arises from the question of what qualifies, retrospectively, as "history."[9] At one extreme are the literal-minded scholars who would exclude even Herodotus's "inquiries" on the grounds that they do not fit modern prescriptions of historical methods; at the other extreme are those who would include under this rubric a whole range of pre-Herodotean and extra-Greek writing. Myth, epic poetry, lists of priests and kings, chronography, and other identifiable genres all become potential forms of history before "history," and many of these indeed provided Herodotus with materials or models. However, this semantic problem is itself at bottom a question of historical inquiry; and *history*, as the term will be employed here, includes older usages over the entire semantic life of the term, concept, and practices which have accumulated under the rubric *historia* and its vernacular offspring. History, therefore, is the subject of a self-forming canon to which authors may apply but into which they gain admission only later, and often posthumously.[10]

By definition, such canons are formed only retrospectively. Scholars used to speak of "precursors" (following the old German fascination with *Vorläufer* or *Vorbereiter*), and it is only in this sense of belated recognition that this awkward notion — a "proleptic" fallacy, as it has been regarded — makes sense.[11] So Thucydides is a precursor of Polybius, Guicciardini, and Ranke in the sense not that he somehow foresaw or aspired to found a school of pragmatic, political history but only that over the centuries a sympathetic readership — followership — interpreted his work in this way and tried to imitate and to emulate it; and so Herodotus is a precursor of Dionysius of Halicarnassus, Voltaire, and Karl Lamprecht for the same retrospectively argued reasons. Obviously, the historiographical canon is much more complex than this. Yet in a long perspective, and so from a great distance, the two faces of Herodotus and Thucydides represent two poles of historiographical interest, as can be seen not only in scholarly practice but also in methodological debates between scholars of very different persuasions — between present-minded historians and pedantic "antiquarians," for example, or between what J. R. Green called "drum and trumpet history" and the richer and more diffuse concerns of social, cultural, and intellectual historians who have followed Herodotus's gaze.[12]

There is another way of looking at this polarization, one that attends to the different strategies of narrative and analytical history — history which tells a story, with or without a point, and history which poses a question, whether answerable or not. In antiquity this distinction is blurred, for Herodotus's curiosity takes the form of stories (*logoi*), whereas Thucydides' narrative is devoted mainly to the question of the causes and progression of the Peloponnesian wars. Study problems, not periods, Lord Acton famously advised; but of course historians must do some of both. Nevertheless, the nature of the questions to be asked does commit the writer to some more or less specific strategy. Seeking the causes of a bitter armed conflict does tend toward a kind of reductionism which privileges factors of power and human agency, whereas inquiring into the mysteries of ancient and "barbarian" culture avoids the narrowness and closure implied by explanatory narrative and opens a path of inquiry leading beyond the familiar landmarks of the historian's experience and culture.

One large question that intrudes itself in this binocular view concerns the relation of history to biography and autobiography, which from early antiquity down to Bacon and indeed to Macaulay have been regarded as legitimate forms of historical writing. The forms of biographical writing are manifold — lives of "famous men," princes and popes, saints and martyrs, philosophers and men (and women) of letters — and enormously influential in the canon of Western historical writing.[13] Plutarchian (chronological) and Suetonian (systematic) efforts at life writing constitute not only a genre but also an ingredient in mainstream historiography, suggesting a private and moral dimension and yet being central to ideas of historical change, the role played by individual motives, and the relevance of private life to the office of the historian. And this debate, too, goes on.

Historians indeed look in different directions and employ different strategies for their various projects; yet, retrospectively viewed, they do form a community transcending time and local cultures. From the fifteenth century, scholars spoke of a Republic of Letters joining European authors not only with one another across national and confessional boundaries but also with their medieval and modern colleagues, whom they saw in effect as colleagues engaged in the same effort of learning and criticism. Within this republic, the province inhabited by writers of history has a more specific shape, defined as it is by a common (and commonly debated) method, common purposes, and of course a common genealogy going back in particular to the Greek fathers. The state of the art and (from the sixteenth century) the science of history was expressed in literary forms (history universal and local, general and specialized, and so on) but also in discussions about the theory of history. There were of course, disagreements, but they were carried on in a single semantic field generated by the Greco-Roman writing and conceptualization of history in the Herodoto-Thucydidean sense. Here appear the faces of history familiar to most of us.

Contexts of History

The writing of history has been carried on in many different cultural contexts, within many institutional frameworks, and under many ideological pressures — in many specific "scenes of inquiry," as Nicholas Jardine calls them.[14] One result is that old-fashioned *Quellenforschung* — determining which historians are repeated by another — is in some ways subordinate to contextual, or extratextual, considerations.[15] Thucydides, for example, was conspicuously and painfully the product of a political "crisis," and his work cannot be extricated from his own intense and ultimately tragic experiences. By contrast, Herodotus seems to be a disinterested and self-decontextualized traveler, led by curiosity and driven by literary ambition, who passed through many scenes without being much shaped by them; but his work, too, can surely be re-contextualized with closer attention to his various experiences and predicaments. All the successors — "postcursors" they might be called — of Herodotus and Thucydides have likewise to be understood in terms of their own ages and social environments, which of course differ so radically as to make one wonder whether they can really be regarded as members of the same community engaged in the same effort.

My assumption, or hypothesis, is that indeed they can, at least if one is concerned with history in the sense of the fortune rather than the composition of historical works. Pre-textual "history" is fascinating, but (like oral literature in general) it is largely conjectural and irrelevant to questions of communication and interpretation even in the case of works of unproblematical status and intention. Whatever messages authors may have wanted to send, the messages received are construed in different times, places, and circumstances. What Paul Ricoeur has called the "semantic autonomy of the text" entails a cutting of the umbilical cord of authorship and authorial intent and a concern with the altogether different meanings of books once they have set out on their own careers.[16] Although we can hardly help being curious about the real—the historical—Herodotus and Thucydides, we have little more than their words; and yet what was it, after all, that inspired our interest in the first place? The historians behind the words, like the thoughts between the lines, are truly beyond our grasp—and here mostly beside the point. For present purposes, let our motto be that of the epigraph composed by Erasmus for the medal of his features cast by Quentin Metsys: it was an interesting portrait no doubt, but "the writings will show the better picture."[17] Many authors down to Proust and after have entered similar pleas, and this seems to be a reasonable rule for reading most histories.

The histories that we read have been written in worlds that are not only different but even in some ways incommensurable, and yet they have been accommodated to a single intellectual community. What illustrates the coherence of the Western tradition and canon of historical writing is above all the conventions of language shared by those who more or less deliberately followed the lead of Herodotus, Thucydides, and their epigones and critics. Even in our foreshortened, postmodern world not all traditional meanings are lost in translation. This is what I mean by "semantic field"—a shared discourse that makes possible what Gadamer calls "an experience of tradition" and a hermeneutical "fusion of horizons" in which meaning reappears in renewed forms.[18] So we return to the works themselves—not, however, the works merely as conceived by authors in the remote and inaccessible specificity of their minds but also the works as they were "published," sent out into the world, studied, translated, summarized, read, and misread by generations of readers, critics, and imitators and thereby introduced to new scenes and contexts and so—following the shift of perspective suggested by reception theory and reception history—new meanings.[19]

Over its long career the term *history* has acquired fundamental ambiguities all too often overlooked by historians. *History* may refer directly to the past, that is, to things done in the past ("what really happened," in the words of Lucian, repeated by Ranke); to the study or recollection of such things (history as "the life of memory," in Cicero's much-quoted phrase); to the historical narrative of these things (the "art of history"), which indeed need not be "past" at all; or to the meaning of the past (history as the "mistress of life," in another Ciceronian topos), which survives in the modern form of an idealized history which "shows" this or that — or does not show, as in the cynical observation that "the only thing one learns from history is that no one ever learns from it."[20] There may be as many definitions of history as there are historians, but again the notion of a single, static definition is unhistorical in the extreme, and an understanding of the term and concept of history can be unfolded only in an extensive study of its fortunes and usages in a variety of contexts such as I offer here.

The Concept of History

There are three general questions which must be asked about the art of history, indeed have been asked over the entire career of Western historiography, and these concern its scope, its method, and its purpose. The question of scope involves subject matter, chronology, geography, and historical evidence, that is, materials remembered and orally or scribally transmitted which historians judge to be worthy of note or heuristically useful. The question of method involves the means of gathering this information, making sense of it, and rendering it into written form to transmit to a reading public. The question of purpose involves the utility claimed for the study of history and what later came to be called the philosophy of history. Each of these matters may be projected on a small or a large scale — local or global, specialized or general, long or short term — but every historian has some sense of the horizons within which historical inquiry is carried on, the materials it employs, the form in which it is cast, and the end it has in view.

History need not be tied to chronology, but in modern times it has come into alliance with temporal sequence and by extension with antiquarian curiosity and what Bruno Neveu has called "archaeolatry" — parallel, perhaps, to the more speculative quest for origins which Eric Voegelin has termed "historiogenesis."[21] The assumption that history is situated in a very long time span, including an extended period of prehistory, has informed historical consciousness ever since Herodotus, who reported on the immense antiquity of Egyptian dynasties. Like epic poets, historians have always been fascinated with the question of origins, of first causes, which usually meant the founding of particular national traditions. Within the Judeo-Christian tradition the narrative usually begins not *ab urbe* but *ab orbe condita* — not from the start of a dynasty but from the creation of the universe; but in effect this, too, represents the beginning of a national tradition. The science of chronology, from Eusebius to Archbishop Ussher (and religious fundamentalists of today), evolved within this parochial time frame as a result of the effort to determine the parallel, synchronic progression of histories Jewish and Gentile, Christian and pagan; and it remained generally unchallenged until the sixteenth century, when speculations arose about non- and pre-Adamic peoples, especially because of encounters with the New World. Yet within this expanded and problematized framework, historians continued to project the story of humanity back into a "natural history" and toward questions of geogony and cosmogony.

The shape of human space, like that of human time, has changed profoundly over the centuries, since the relatively small Hellenic world explored by Herodotus, and historical study has expanded accordingly. The theater of Herodotean history was the bloody conjunction of three continents (southeastern Europe, Asia Minor, and northwestern Africa); the "universal history" of Polybius was largely that of Roman imperial conquest and appetite; that of the Christian church looked beyond the Greco-Roman *oecumene* to other parts of creation. From Herodotus to present historians, Christians as well as pagans have been bound to a self-defining binocular vision dividing humanity into spheres of civilization and barbarism — the We and the Other — which is itself a product of the horizon structure of historical inquiry and a premise of its geographical limitations.[22] So history has always been "geohistory" (in the coinage of Bodin preserved by Fernand Braudel), and historians have always tried to correlate observed human behavior with its environment, including the natural and social contexts that locate and discriminate it from other parts of humanity. In a time-honored conceit, history is played out in a vast "theater of nature," in which historians, like all human beings, are at once actors and spectators — and, moreover, critics and, betimes, judges.[23] The insight of modern science which, rejecting fictions of objectivity, situates the observer in the process of scientific investigation was a premise of historical inquiry from the beginning.

Historical time and space are open-ended. What about the substance of historical inquiry? Again, there seems to be no end to the varieties of human experience that furnish materials for the historian's craft; to the human historian there was, in the words of Terence, "nothing alien." Again, too, there seems to be a conventional dualism which derives from the horizon structure

of human perception, namely, the distinction between the private and pu
spheres — between family, personal relations, and domestic economy in th
center of life, on the one hand, and the world of the agora and forum, of law,
politics, and war, on the other. Thus history ranges from the "pragmatic"
focus of Polybius on matters of power to the anecdotal interests of Procopius
in his "secret history" of Justinian and Theodora — from headlines to the gos-
sip pages, from high (or low) politics to low (or high) culture. So the interests
of history have ranged from cradle to grave (and beyond), circled around the
clock, and extended from hearth and bedroom to the furthest reaches of exploration and colonization, the only limits being those of heuristics — the accessibility of sources — and of the historian's imagination. From the beginning
too, then, there was potential for what Henri Berr called *l'histoire totale*,
which included things that might not be significant but were at least, as Paul
Veyne has argued, "interesting," for whatever reason.[24]

This brings up the endlessly discussed question of historical method, which
was considered quite self-consciously by Herodotus, but less so by Thucydides, and which was elaborated in connection with rhetoric as well as in the art
of historiography. The first concern of history — its "first law," according to
Cicero — was to tell the truth and to mix in nothing that was false.[25] Herodotus displayed unprecedented, if irregular, sophistication in extracting truth
from oral sources and separating it from the incredible; Thucydides made his
task easier by discounting the possibility of determining the truth of most
ancient times — and indeed the relevance of such matters. This theme was also
taken up by the rhetoricians to emphasize the difference between history and
poetry, although Cicero and others admitted that the poets were the first
historians. For many later scholars, however, Herodotus was altogether too
credulous, and for some he became the prototype of the gullible, if not men-
dacious, historian. The debate between admirers and detractors of Herodotus
has continued from the time of Plutarch down to the present; and the division
between skeptics and presentists on the one hand and mythographers, antiquarians, and crusaders for "heritage" on the other was over the Herodoto-
Thucydidean legacy — a struggle that has contributed not only to interdisciplinary methods but also to cultural and lately women's history and gender
studies.[26]

"Method" implied, or came to imply, not only the techniques of historical
inquiry and judgment but also the communication of the results to a reading
(rather than a listening) public. Here again the function of rhetoric was essential, to the extent indeed that the art of history was virtually identified with the
art of oratory, which was likewise to be explanatory, persuasive, and didactic.[27] Like philosophy, history concerned itself with questions of cause and

...he level of particularity rather than generality, as Aristotle
... connection the art of history came to be associated not
...arts of poetry and rhetoric but also with moral philosophy,
...aimed, as indeed it was by Herodotus's follower Dionysius
...at history was "philosophy teaching by example" — which
...phasis from the writing to the reading of history.[28] In
modern times this imperialist notion was extended, with the reinforcement of
Polybius's pragmatic history, from moral to political philosophy; and history — as in Jean Bodin's famous *Method for the Easy Comprehension of
History* of 1566 — was elevated from the status of "art" to that of "science," or
rather, "above all sciences."[29]

The Language of History

History, term and concept, has passed through, and gathered meaning
from, many radically different authorial contexts, ranging from the poets,
logographers, and annalists of antiquity to postmodern professors of new
(and even newer) historical forms in the high-tech environment of late ty-
pographical and early electronic culture; and it is one of the tasks of the
historian of historiography to explore and to specify the cultural environments and moments which have situated historical works and their authors.
Yet there are other contexts, diachronic as well as synchronic, which have
occupied these authors and which also deserve attention — factors of *longue
durée* that attach to terms and concepts and that produce, in retrospect, certain semantic continuities which historiographical practice and theory have
reinforced. To some extent we are still speaking the language, if not thinking
the thoughts, of Herodotus and Thucydides — although the questions we put,
and the answers we expect, are our own.

Of the themes which have survived profound changes in language, culture,
knowledge, ideology, and human values, the most essential is the idea of truth.
Every historian claims to tell the truth, as contrasted with error, fable, fiction,
or excessive credulity; and every historian, while claiming truth for his own,
seldom hesitates to deny it to others. But, to rephrase Pilate's question, what
does *truth* mean? Educated men were skeptical about the possibility of truth
before Pilate asked his famous question — and would not (as Bacon remarked)
stay for an answer. In retrospect we see that there are many answers. *Aletheia,
veritas, la vérité, die Wahrheit,* Truth certainly had different natures and histories, although their meanings may seem to converge in a single ideal. For the
Greeks, according to Marcel Detienne, *Aletheia* was something very different
from *truth* in the light of modern Western science, since it suggested not an

objective finding but rather a special view limited to a quasi-priestly elite, such as the devotees of the muse Clio.[30] Yet did not such an idea survive also in the nineteenth century, when truth could also be regarded as a monopoly of the learned and the licensed (an overwhelmingly male community until modern times)?[31] Nor has there ever been any lack of Pilates around to cast doubt on the ideal of truth in any sense. It nevertheless seems clear that even historical "truth" is not a static value; for truth, too, even in a "scientific" context, "has its fortune."[32]

Historians live, speak, write, and are read in time, but they have never agreed on a definition of this dimension. The experience of time passing cannot be captured except in language, whose tense structure, however, offers a poor vehicle for representing individual actions and experiences or the memory or anticipation thereof. How much more problematic is the representation of events or experiences only recorded or reported at second- or thirdhand or inferred from other evidence? For historians, in fact, past events are ever "present," the tense in which we speak, write, listen, read, and, of course, remember; and the deployment of past tenses is a linguistic strategy for giving the illusion of time passing. Much the same may be said of subjectivity and point of view, which are set by language (first, second, and third person).[33] An illusion of objectivity, like that of pastness, can be achieved only through use of the passive voice and other lip-serving ways of depersonalizing narrative. The historian is like a point in space-time — though to be sure a moving point — and only language makes it possible to reach out in imagination and rhetoric into past, future, and whatever lies beyond immediate experience. This, too, is a condition of historical inquiry and interpretation.

One consequence of this hermeneutical condition is the continuing interplay and confrontation between "antiquity" and "modernity" — a temporalized version of the "I and the Thou," or We and the Other. Fathers and sons, Ancients and Moderns, Moderns and Postmoderns, and other dualities formed on a generational or genealogical, a pedagogical or polemical, model give both continuity and dynamism to history. Sons learn from fathers, Moderns from Ancients, even Postmoderns from Moderns, and learn *history* in particular, but younger generations also break and perhaps do battle with the older, so that neither the course nor the interpretation of history can be regular. History is not merely a lesson to be learned but also an argument to be played out, not merely a legacy to be received but also a war to be waged — and *la lutte continue.*

History is often regarded as a form of memory, but this nice identification creates more problems than it solves.[34] We each of us are familiar with our own memories and those of others — until we forget — but what does "memory" mean in a collective sense? And just where does this memory reside? In the remains and records of human activity or in the act of historiographical poesis that gives shape and meaning to these traces of the past? In any case memory is selective; it is not a simple process of recording or retrieval but a way of commemorating or memorializing certain phenomena within some system of meaning, which itself changes in time.

There is another common denominator of historians over the centuries, and this is the medium of the written, and later the printed, word. What has been argued about the impact of printing applies also to scribal culture—that it encourages a sense of historical distance through the juxtaposition of disparate texts in a single moment of time.[35] In any case writing—the keeping of records and the historiographical interpretation thereof—becomes an aide-mémoire that takes on a life of its own and a career in time. Historians can no longer simply invoke their muse but must, looking back, pass judgment on their sources and, looking ahead, consider the ways of influencing their readers and perhaps (as Thucydides hoped) a more distant posterity. It was in this connection that history became assimilated to rhetoric and to "literature" in a sense that was specific as well as general—moral and aesthetic as well as formal, whence the discussions of prescribed "rules" for a conventionalized *ars historiographica* and an image of the ideal historian educated for his scribal calling, whatever the circumstances.[36]

The last big question faced (or avoided) by historians is that of purpose: What is the good of studying the past? Once again the range of answers appears to remain constant over a long period of time. History preserves or celebrates the memory of notable events or persons, characteristically those of a national tradition, and so it is in one incarnation a figurative form of genealogy. Detached from such parochial concerns, history may claim a didactic function as a source of particular moral or political lessons, usually on the grounds that human nature is at bottom, despite differing customs and beliefs, much the same. But history also teaches that such lessons are not learned and certainly not agreed upon, and so a broader justification has been envisioned—namely, that history is a form of self-knowledge, or the search for self-knowledge, which is not satisfied with tribal complacencies and which does not expect neat answers to specific questions.[37] It is a form of wisdom—knowledge of things human and divine, as Ancients and Moderns, pagans and Christians, have written—which is a way of extending human horizons backward and forward in time and beyond local experience and concerns. For these aspirations it will continue to be subject to skepticism, but it will likewise always be renewed by feelings of nostalgia, curiosity, or anxiety. To this extent, it will always be part of the human condition.

One illusion, or at least conventional posture, that I want to avoid is the notion of a large gap between historians and the bygone ages they study. To be sure the past is a foreign country—more foreign than we can hope to know, even an absolute alterity—but it is not a country we really visit, not even in memory, except in the sense that imagination is a form of memory. To be sure, too, people "do things differently there," but all we have are the records and remains of these doings; and in making sense of these records and remains, we are incorrigible romantics, if not antiromantics. This, I take it, is what Gadamer's famous "fusion of horizons" must mean to historians: not that we somehow retrieve or rethink the cultural past (in the sense of Romantic hermeneutics or Crocean-Collingwoodian empathy) but rather that we express it through its traces in our own terms and thus give it our own meanings (semantically overlapping, we assume, with those of our predecessors). Like Herodotus and Thucydides, and fortunately with their help, we look out over our own horizons, at our own points of time, in our own directions, to envision in our own way the faces of history.

History before "History"

"History" began with Herodotus, as far as we know; but of course the practice, in various forms, antedated the theory and terminology of inquiry into the past. As Herodotus himself noted, the Egyptians were the best historians of any nation he knew. Scholars agree, though with many conditions and quibbles, that there was an "idea of history in the Ancient Near East" as well as forms of "collective memory"; and they have supplied many examples of historical inquiry and interpretation produced in the earliest documented stages of civilization.[38] Cultural parochialism, in history as well as philosophy and science, has tended to make Greece the starting point for the story of the human condition in time; and indeed the character of Western education and scholarship, as well as the languages of Western tradition, have reinforced this tendency. Yet even the Greeks knew that, if they were not quite the "children" of the famous remark Plato quoted from an Egyptian priest, they were deeply indebted to their Asian and African antecedents.[39] And this awareness has been broadened and deepened by modern investigations into pre-Hellenic civilizations, including some not known to the Greeks.

There were certain questions in which all Near Eastern civilizations were interested—the origins of the universe, their own gods, the genealogies of their rulers, victories over their enemies, and life after death—and these interests are reflected in surviving monuments and records from the third and even fourth millennia B.C. The king lists of the Egyptians and Sumerians took of necessity a chronological form and included other information, including disasters both natural and human — floods and military defeats.[40] Egyptian records date from the middle of the third millennium B.C., beginning with the famous inscriptions of the Palermo stone, one of six surviving fragments of a great slab containing regnal lists projected back into the mid–fourth millennium. The Sumerian king lists, dating from the late third millennium, disclose a mythical past extending back a quarter-million years to the time when "kingship descended from heaven." Egyptian history, too, as indicated by the pyramids and other monuments, as well as by later annals, passed through periods of gods and demigods before entering into human stages. So the social memory embodied in architectural and funereal remains was joined to myth as the basis of scribal efforts to preserve this memory and to endorse these myths. And all of this material was scrutinized, or legitimized, by more self-conscious historians, most notably, for Egypt, the third-century B.C. priest Manetho, whose summary of tradition has continued to dominate Egyptology.[41]

The general pattern can be seen as the transformation of list into chronology and the broadening of chronology into full-fledged history, which reviewed tradition and accommodated, in one way or another, the accumulation of myth that had been shaped by poets. The initial motives for interest in history, aside from those of a material and practical character, were above all a fascination with death and an afterlife. Egyptian pyramids, the most imposing product of this obsession, succeeded indeed in preserving the memory of the pharaohs that they were, as "houses of death," built to protect. Such monuments were also designed to legitimize the institutions of kingship, including the incessant practices of war and slavery.

Another protohistorical genre was instructional literature, which dates also from the mid–third millennium B.C. The earliest example is the instruction given by the king's son Hardjedef to his own son, exhorting him to prosper, seek "well-watered fields," take a wife, have a son, and follow the customs of his ancestors. "The house of death is for life," he writes, urging that the funerary priest be honored above even family.[42] The "Instruction of Ptahhotep" (late third or early second millennium) recommends that "the ways of the ancestors, who have listened to the gods," be followed, "so that strife may be banned from the people." Obey custom, he advises, for "no one is born wise." And in conclusion,

> If you listen to my sayings,
> All your affairs will go forward;
> In their truth resides their value,
> Their memory goes on in the speech of men,

Because of the worth of their precepts;
If every word is carried on,
They will not perish in the land. . . .
It is good to speak to posterity,
It will listen to it.[43]

"Copy your fathers, your ancestors," urges another manual, this one from the sixteenth century B.C.:

See, their words endure in books,
Open, read them, copy their knowledge,
He who is taught becomes skilled.[44]

From the beginning, protohistorians and historians inherited the concerns and values of such backward-looking men of pious commitment. Like the builders and recorders, they devoted themselves to a similar memorialization of the illustrious dead and the mighty deeds they had wrought, occasionally turning to more mundane and material matters underlying power and politics; and like the authors of the wisdom literature, they claimed to have important lessons to teach not only their readers but also posterity: *Historia magistra vitae.*

In Greek culture there was a variety of pre-Herodotean, protohistoriographical forms of writing, especially genealogy, geography and ethnography, and horography, or local history. A significant change of attitude toward the remote past is marked by the famous words of Hecataeus, who remarked in his *Genealogies* that "what I write here is the account which I consider to be true, for the stories of the Greeks are numerous and in my opinion ridiculous."[45] This attitude was shared by Hecataeus's younger contemporary Herodotus, who may also have drawn on the work of the older genealogist and geographer. Chronology was the special concern of another contemporary writer, Hellanicus, who attempted to make a comparative study of the chronologies of Greek and barbarian nations, though unfortunately he was not able to extricate this project from the mythical materials with which he, like Hecataeus and Herodotus, worked.

History and Myth

In *The Corsican Brothers,* Alexander Dumas tells the story of twins who were joined at birth but then separated first physically and then geographically for most of their lives. Spiritually, however, they remained attached, felt each other's joys, fears, and pains until finally, in their last years, they were reunited. From a certain standpoint this tale can be seen as symbolic of the intertwined careers of myth and history. Born of memory — of the union between Zeus and the Titan Mnemosyne — myth and history were severed at the dawn of critical consciousness and thenceforth led separate lives, history going on to intellectual and political glory and myth becoming, for many, a term of abuse and censure. Yet they remained linked in a number of ways, just as (alleged) truth and lies are linked.[46] In various periods history produced its own myths, whether acknowledged or not, while myth has often been taken as the expression of a higher poetic or even religious truth. In our own century some scholars have tried to bring about the reunion of these squabbling siblings, asserting that myth has a historical face and that history has not been quite the promoter of absolute truth which it so often claimed to be. As myth once passed for history, now history may indeed be "our myth."

Like history, myth can be understood as a form of memory, or commemoration, designed to make sense of and give shape to the past — or respect to the dead.[47] But over the generations historians have looked on this past with different eyes. Older scholars such as J. B. Bury, Felix Jacoby, and Chester G. Starr have minimized the connections between the two. Herodotus and Thucydides "were not the first to chronicle human events, but they were the first to apply criticism," as Bury declared in his Harvard lectures. "And that means, they originated history."[48] Of course Bury had a very strict idea of the nature of history — "a science, no more, no less" — leaving little room for criticism of historical science itself. It is undeniable as well as tautological that, as Momigliano wrote, "there was no Herodotus before Herodotus."[49] Yet in historiographical as well as epic tradition, there were, as Acton remarked, "brave men who wrote before Agamemnon"[50] — historians before the storied pioneers, uncritical no doubt, but then so were Herodotus and Thucydides.

In Greek history the gods and demigods preceded human agents, and as Cicero and others believed, the poets were the first historians. Four hundred years before his time, Herodotus declared, "Homer and Hesiod were the first to compose genealogies and give the gods their epithets, to allot them their several offices and occupations, and disclose their forms."[51] Did Herodotus believe these myths? Perhaps not; it is hard to tell from his cautious statements, and "belief" is as slippery a concept as "truth."[52] In any case myths were matters to be reported, as historians from Herodotus and Livy to George Grote assumed. Nor could they be separated from some underlying "reality"; they are not, as J.-P. Vernant puts it, saying "something else."[53] B. G. Niebuhr aspired to open the "many-colored veil" of poetry cast over "historical truth," but a later generation became doubtful of this noble dream.[54] To pretend to recreate the true picture of Greek life behind a "curtain" of ancient myth was nothing more than speculation, Grote argued (perhaps in the spirit of Herodotus), for "the curtain *is* the picture," and myth represented "the entire mental stock of the Greeks" and so the very substance of history.[55]

Some myths are old, if not prehistorical, such as the superiority of race or national culture; others are of more recent vintage, such as the myth of the end of all myth—the end of the "Enlightenment Project" and its offspring, the "noble dream" of objectivity. Postmodern critics like Jean-François Lyotard might include, under the rubric of myth, such outmoded "metanarratives" as humanism and liberalism. So history continues to be, in Blumenberg's terms, "work on myth."[56] Yet historians, no matter how much they may try to distance their activity from myth, share the same interpretive tradition. This is archetypically true of Homer, or whatever the answer is to the "Homeric question," in the sense not only that the poet inquired into the same Hellenic past as Herodotus did but also, more specifically, that, as Bury admitted, following Dionysius of Halicarnassus, "Homer was the literary master of Herodotus."[57] Homer was a maker of fables, but he was also a source of many-formed wisdom that was human as well as "divine." According to tradition, he was a theologian as well as a poet.[58] Yet he remained aware of his human status and dependence on his muse; otherwise, "hard were it for me, as though I were a god, to tell the tale of all these things." Only the muses, through the gods, "know all things," Homer acknowledged, "whereas we hear but a rumour and know not anything."[59] But as G. M. Trevelyan famously urged against the scientific, or scientistic, hubris of J. B. Bury, "Clio [is] a Muse." (Or was it an illocutionary pun: "Clio, amuse!"?)[60]

After Homer in the interpretive tradition comes Hesiod, who likewise displayed a human face behind the muse-ridden posture of the *poeta-theologus.* Hesiod turned his human curiosity to the genealogy of the gods and to questions of moral order in the universe.[61] In retrospect the myth of five races set down in the *Theogony,* whether or not it has Near Eastern sources, represents a sort of philosophy or prehistory. "The Greek theogonist," writes Jacob Burckhardt, "represents the moment at which the nation desired and received a coherent form for its boundless wealth of myth."[62] Hesiod imagines a succession of races in descending order: golden, silver, bronze, and the "demigods," preceding his own deplorable iron age. The golden age, founded on justice and free of toil, disease, and old age, was spoiled by Pandora and the hubris of Prometheus, who brought fire but also civilization, with all its evils as well as benefits. After this, history entered into its sublunar, stadial processes of generation and corruption, which produced matter less suitable for poetry than for the prosaic attitude of Herodotus and his following.

Historians after Herodotus were increasingly hostile to the mythical context from which their projects had apparently emerged. But as T. S. Eliot asked,

"Where is the wisdom we have lost in truth?"[63] —which indeed is the grounds for Aristotle's famous argument that poetry is more philosophical than history.[64] It was the habit of historians to invert this distinction and make a virtue of the concreteness and particularity of historical truth. This was the argument of Lorenzo Valla, as it would be for champions of nineteenth-century historicism, and in more recent times it can be found in the distinction between the "idiographic" nature of the human sciences and the "nomothetic" character of the natural sciences.[65] Here, too, the faces of Herodotus and Thucydides can be seen, inquiring into the particular experiences of their culture and that of others.

A question for modern historians has been how to restore myth to a historical condition —how to retrieve the reality from behind the tales of "once upon a time." There have been many theories of myth since the Renaissance, but as Martin Nilsson remarks, "No literature has so quickly gone out of date as the numerous writings on mythology."[66] This has often been grounds for skepticism. Many Greeks besides Thucydides were doubtful about deciphering the meaning of myth. Myth was perhaps a form of truth, and "yet the gods have not revealed all things to men from the beginning," declared Xenophanes, and so "no man knows, or ever will know, the truth about the gods."[67] According to Marcel Detienne, myth was a creation of the mythographers; it is reflected in the texts that we read, but there is no "original text" and so, as Blumenberg believes, no "original myth."[68] As Martin Nilsson has also written, "The historical aspect of Greek mythology and especially the mythical chronology are products of the systematizing of the myths by the poets and still more the product of rationalization by the logographers."[69]

But may one not say much the same thing about history —or at any rate about the interpretations of history that seek meaning behind the texts and remains of human action? For an analogy one might think of the *Enigma Variations,* by Edward Elgar. Historians, like mythographers, produce elaborations of an unstated theme, a theme which must be assumed but which is forever inaccessible and must always fail to achieve a consensus. History may be the "mistress of life," but she is a fickle one. Yet we continue to pursue her —and the pursuit still begins with Herodotus and Thucydides. History is more than a series of footnotes to these seminal figures, but it can never forget their foundational efforts.

Greek Horizons

History is philosophy teaching by example.
— Dionysius of Halicarnassus

To introduce Herodotus, I made use of the Janus image that represents him gazing into an unspecified and unfocused distance and toward, perhaps, a posterity that looks back at him; to examine Herodotean history, however, I want to look at him from the standpoint of this posterity, or at least its most recent stage.[1] What Herodotus was in the pristine condition of his own experiences is a matter of antiquarian debate, but the reception and interpretation of his work, which was "published" and so separated from its creator more than twenty-four centuries ago, is something for readers, critics, and historians to discover and rediscover. The aim here is to observe Herodotus in hindsight — in a rear-view mirror, as it were, which may distort the features of the "father of history" but which is the best we can do from our latter-day and fast-changing perspective.

Herodotus

Herodotus, "gift of Hera," was born in Halicarnassus in 484 B.C. and, from what can be deduced from his book, lived a largely uncommitted life of traveling, interviewing, and lecturing in the period between the first Peloponnesian and the second "great" war chronicled by Thucydides. He journeyed as far north as Scythia and also into Asia Minor and Egypt, perhaps as far as

1,700 miles both north-south and east-west. He died in about 428, not long after he published the book that came to be called his *History*. Antiquarian inquiry has thrown some light on the career of Herodotus; but for posterity, and for present purposes, the man must be identified with the book, which has been transmitted in fairly reliable manuscript tradition, despite the fanciful naming of sections by an early editor (and followed in the Aldine edition) after the nine Greek muses — from Clio, muse of history itself, to Calliope (fair speech) — all of them being daughters of Mnemosyne (memory).[2] The extent to which it is a unified work of art rather than a collection of *logoi* (stories) to be read to audiences is debatable; but overall structures, as in the treatment of East versus West, are apparent, even if conscious authorial design has been exaggerated by formalist literary scholars.[3]

Many of the fundamental themes of "history" in a post-Herodotean sense appear in the very first paragraph of this "publication of the researches of Herodotus of Halicarnassus" (*Herodotou Halicarnesseos histories apodeixis*).[4] Aside from the notion of history as "inquiry," Herodotus declares his intention of preserving the memory of worthy deeds from the destructive effects of time, this being the justification for the mostly true stories which constituted much of his composition. In one fundamental way Herodotus followed the lead of Homer, and that was in posing many questions.[5] The historian followed the poet, too, in using myth and heroic deeds in his stories, though in a mode that is critical, analytical, and somewhat ironic.[6] Beyond offering entertainment, he proposed to dig deeper and to reveal the reason for the actions of both the Greeks and their enemies, focusing especially on the causes of war, which, issuing from private feuds, represented the most memorable of human actions. For this there was good and often-followed precedent: war (*polemos*) was, according to Heraclitus, the source of all things; and indeed, with questions of war guilt and the consequences of waging war, it has remained a central concern of mainstream historiography ever since.

What was the cause (*aitia*) of the feud between the Greeks and the Persians? To answer this, Herodotus reviewed the standard mythical explanations — that it was the fault of the Phoenicians, who had kidnapped some women of Argos; that this crime caused retaliation by the Greeks, who later seized Europa, daughter of the king of Crete, and later compounded this by carrying off Medea, daughter of the king of Aea; and that still later Alexander, the son of Priam, made a prize of Helen, thus initiating the epic war memorialized by Homer. For Herodotus none of these silly stories, reflecting what John Myres called a "*cherchez-la-femme* view of history," were worthy of belief.[7]

This is only the first of many instances in which Herodotus rejects legends as baseless and in violation of his conception of history. For Herodotus, history depended on one of two criteria, that it be based on testimony that was either eyewitness (*opsis*) or hearsay (*akoe*), and of course this largely disqualified the poets. He would not dispute the truth of the matter, as beyond such criteria, but was content with pointing out the one who, to his own certain knowledge, first wronged the Greeks, namely, Croesus, king of Lydia, who lusted for empire in the West and whose fate was determined by his wealth. The Croesus *logos* thus introduces Herodotus's declared purpose, which was to tell the story of the struggles between East and West, between Persians and Greeks, reaching a climax in his own time.

History had a pattern that could be explained, but it also had smaller lessons attached to this larger trajectory; for Herodotus, analysis is amplified by anecdote. The riches of Croesus were proverbial, but this was no guarantee against the insight that Herodotus offered at the beginning of his story of Croesus, "that human happiness never continues long in one stay." According to Herodotus, Solon, who was then himself on travels to Egypt and the East, tried to teach Croesus the lesson that not riches but a full life and a glorious death were the key to human happiness, and this became clear only at the end of life. This lesson was lost upon the proud Croesus until after Solon left, when the "vengeance of god" (*theou nemesis*) was set upon him in the form of the accidental death of his son, his defeat at the hands of the Persian King Cyrus, and the imprisonment in which he spent the rest of his life — a judgment that was confirmed also, as Herodotus recounts, by the oracle of Delphi.[8]

It was in connection with the Croesus, or Lydian, story, too, that Herodotus introduced the theme that gave shape and value to his narrative, which is to say, Greek culture as represented by the two preeminent Hellenic nations, the Lacedemonians and the Athenians. From its beginning the Greek nation had preserved its speech and developed its own style of communal life. In their rise to power, the Greeks, while they had embraced barbaric peoples, were confident of their superiority in cleverness and "freedom from foolish simpleness" — the familiar stereotypes of Greek cunning and rationality versus barbaric naïveté and superstition (but also, some would add, sense of history).[9] In Croesus's time Athens was emerging from tyranny and beginning to enjoy good government as well as military success as a result of the reforms of Lycurgus. Of all the Greeks, Herodotus insists, the Athenians were the cleverest and the most attached to their freedom. This theme will return with a vengeance in later stages of Herodotus's account.

In the complex narrative of the *History*, the Croesus story is followed by that of his conqueror, Cyrus; and once again Herodotus seeks to extricate the "simple truth" from the various legends (*logoi* that are not) which still circulated, relying for this effort on employing the most unbiased Persian authorities. He offers a brief discussion, based on personal knowledge (*peri auton eidos*), of Persian social, religious, and dietary customs, and remarks in particular on their sense of superiority and their centrist belief, like that of the Medes as well, "that those who are farthest off must be the most degraded of mankind."[10] This horizon structure of perception, knowledge, and expectation would itself be a fundamental premise of historical understanding.

The ethnographical essay on the Persians follows the same lines as his later discussions of other non-Greek and therefore "barbarian" nations—Egypt, Scythia, Thrace, and (though these sections are lost) Assyria.[11] In these essays Herodotus takes a comparative view and is much concerned with whether, to judge from customs and language, the peoples in question are autochthonous or from another place. Following his "historical" criteria, Herodotus is suspicious of the stories he heard and even expresses outright incredulity, for example, toward the Assyrian belief that their chief god, Bel (Zeus Belus), had appeared in the chamber of the temple built for him—"but I do not believe it."[12]

Book II of Herodotus's work—"Euterpe," muse of lyric poetry—is the famous Egyptian logos, containing a topically arranged report, diverging from Greek "opinion" (*gnome*), on his travels, impressions, and conversations, especially with the priests at Memphis, probably sometime before 430.[13] This section begins with the story of Pharaoh Psammeticus's notorious experiment with two children, which involved keeping them from hearing human language for over two years to determine what their first words would be, and thereby human language itself. *Bekos,* the first utterance of the culturally deprived children, was the word for bread (perhaps related to the English *bake*) in Phrygian, from which was inferred that they were the oldest people. Credible or not, this experiment was much discussed, repeated, and interpreted more than once over the centuries by rulers fascinated with the question of human origins (including Emperor Frederick II and King James IV of Scotland).[14] For his part Herodotus thought that there was no need for such an experiment and that, moreover, "the Egyptians . . . have existed ever since the human race began," and "no country . . . possesses so many wonders."

The Greeks owed much to the Egyptians, including the very name of Hercules, who was truly a god, Herodotus decided after visiting several temples devoted to his worship. The Greeks took the name of their Hercules, and indeed of most other gods as well as many religious practices, from the Egyptians; but the many foolish stories they told showed their ignorance of this ancient culture—his predecessor Hecataeus has also remarked on "the many and ridiculous" stories of the Greeks—and it was part of his mission to enlighten them. Not that he had opinions about prehistorical origins, for "whence the gods severally sprang, whether or no they had existed from all eternity, what forms they bore — these are questions of which the Greeks knew nothing until the other day, so to speak. For Homer and Hesiod . . . lived but 400 years before my time, as I believe."[15] For the first part of this assertion Herodotus invoked the authority of the oracle of Dodona; for Homer and Hesiod he reported his own opinion; but he deferred especially to the Egyptians, who (in embarrassing contrast to the short-sighted Greeks) were deeply concerned with royal genealogy, burial rites, embalming, and other aspects of their past, as well as the afterlife.

Herodotus commented on the extreme antiquity claimed by the Egyptian priests — some 341 generations, which added up (counting three generations per century) to 11,340 years.[16] Herodotus's predecessor, the geographer and genealogist Hecataeus (for whom Herodotus showed less respect than he did for Homer), had been told the same story when he had boasted to the priests of his own divine pedigree, going back a mere sixteen generations. Herodotus reports on these traditions without offering personal judgment. However, he was mightily impressed when the priests read from a papyrus king list the names of 330 pharaohs succeeding Menes (who himself had succeeded the gods) and even preferred their version of the story of Helen of Troy. The Egyptians, Herodotus argued, "devoting themselves, as they do, far more than any other people in the world, to the preservation of past actions, are the best skilled in history of any men that I have ever met."[17] Compared with them, as Plato also suggested, the Greeks were indeed children.

Did Herodotus believe the tall tales of the Egyptians — not to mention those of the Greeks?[18] Ancient critics often charged him with mendacity and "malignity," and yet there is another side to his work. Readers "are free to accept [Egyptian stories] as history," Herodotus wrote. "For my own part, I propose to myself through my whole work faithfully to record the traditions of the several nations."[19] Later he generalized this disclaimer: "For myself, my duty is to report all that I have said, but I am not obliged to believe it all alike — a remark which may be understood to apply to my whole History."[20] This is the face of the Herodotus, the honest and objective historian, who came to be admired by Cicero and others as the father of history, by John Myres as the father of anthropology as well, and by Arnaldo Momigliano as a pioneer who, extending intellectual horizons in time as well as space, "guid[ed] historical research toward the exploration of the unknown and of the forgotten."[21]

Book III ("Thalia," muse of comedy) continues the story of Persian expansion, beginning with the conquest of Egypt (525 B.C.) by Cambyses, son of Cyrus. Herodotus here corrects the Egyptians for claiming Cambyses as their own in order to claim relationship with the house of their conqueror. He recounts the descent of Cambyses into madness and uses it to teach another lesson about one of the premises of his *History*. Cambyses must have been raving mad to make sport of the religious customs of the people, Herodotus argues, for people always prefer their own customs, or laws (*nomoi*), to those of any others in the world. The poet Pindar was right in his judgment, Herodotus concluded: "Law is king over all" (*nomos basileus*).[22]

Darius succeeded his father, Cambyses, after the "slaughter of the Magi" — one of the many sensationalist stories ornamenting Herodotus's narrative — put an end to the temporary usurpation; and he busied himself with restoring order to the Persian Empire, reconquering Babylon, and penetrating the Mediterranean as far as southern Italy. What follows this episode is one of the classic sets of orations employed by Herodotus to argue a larger political point, in this case the ideal form of government.[23] Otanes, a supporter of Darius, argues for democracy and "equality before the law," recalling the despotism of the mad Cambyses, and votes to put the people above monarchy. A second speaker, Megabyzus, speaks up for oligarchy, in which only the worthiest would have political authority. Darius supports monarchy, partly because it is in keeping with tradition, partly because it means the rule of "the very best man in the state"; and it is his argument that finally wins the prize, which is nothing less than the empire of his father.[24]

Book IV ("Melpomene," muse of tragedy) contains the further adventures of Darius, including two major stories concerning the expeditions into Scythia and into Libya, and it provokes more puzzling questions about Herodotus's aims, perceptions, and "representations." Scythia, on the northern edge of Herodotus's world, posed a sharp contrast to Egypt in the south not only geographically and climatically but also historically; for as Egypt was the oldest, so Scythia, whatever its origin, was the "youngest of all nations."[25] Egypt was bound to the Nile, moreover, but the Scythians were a nomadic people, living on the "most distant lands" (*eschatiai*), displaying a barbarism to contrast with the familiar culture at the starting point of Herodotus's researches.[26] For Herodotus, Scythia was as remote in cultural space as Egypt, in the way described by its priests, was in cultural time. In the words of François de Hartog, the Scythians represented the "imaginary autochthonous being," the "imaginary nomad," constituting the absolute Other of Herodotus's ethnocentric, if intellectually expansionist and imperialistic, inquiries.[27] They were made more barbarous and more "other" by their "extreme hatred of all foreign customs, particularly of those in use among the Greeks."[28] This was shown by the murder of Anacharsis, committed, Herodotus said, "on account of his attachment to foreign customs, and the intercourse which he held with the Greeks." Such were the people whom Darius vainly tried to conquer, and Herodotus to understand.

The following books — V ("Terpsichore," muse of the dance), VI ("Erato," muse of love poetry), and VII ("Polymnia," muse of sacred poetry) — treat the Ionian revolt in the generation before Herodotus's birth; the main causes of Athenian policy, including the democratic revolution of Cleisthenes; the battle of Marathon (490), with accompanying prodigies; and the efforts of Darius's son Xerxes to "pass through Europe from one end to the other" and to take revenge against the Greeks, with accompanying speeches. The concomitant rise of Athens, described by Herodotus in exquisite and digressive detail, demonstrated "not from this instance only, but from many everywhere, that freedom is an excellent thing."[29] Darius came to hate this little democratic nemesis which blocked his way to empire, as Romans came later to hate Carthage; and Xerxes carried on his father's obsession with a vengeance, beginning with the battle of Thermopylae (480).

For Herodotus fate presided over this disaster, of which he no doubt had personal memories, but there was human choice, too. At one point in the deliberations he has Xerxes, "full of wrath," declare: "So now retreat is on both sides impossible, and the choice lies between doing and suffering injury; either our empire must pass under the dominion of the Greeks, or their land become the prey of the Persians; for there is no middle course left in this quarrel."[30] So Herodotus gives dramatic shape to the tragedy, long in the making, which arose from the human motives — glory, greed, vengeance — underlying the wars that shaped the human condition and preoccupied poets and historians alike. He did stop for smaller human emotions, allowing Xerxes a prebattle scene in which he wept for "the shortness of man's life" and grieved at the thought that in a century not one of the gigantic host at Salamis would still be alive.[31] But then, of course, he — Xerxes, but also Herodotus — returned to the business at hand, that is, the coming slaughter, and to the preordained tragedy.

This was the moment of Greek glory and the triumph of Greek culture, and here Herodotus qualifies his praise of Athenian liberty by associating it with the force of law and custom which defined and gave strength to all nations. It was because of their freedom that the Greeks were singly as brave as any, but it was because of their collective values that they were bravest of all when fighting in a body. As Herodotus put it (in words he attributes to a counselor of Xerxes), "For though [the Lacedemonians] be free men, they are not in all respects free; Law is the master whom they own, and this master they fear more than your [Xerxes'] subjects fear you. . . . [This law] requires them to stand firm, and either to conquer or to die."[32] As they competed in the Olympic games only for honor — something which the Persians could not understand — so they fought in war not for greed but for glory.[33] Law was indeed, as Pindar had taught, "king over all." In this crucial instance it strengthened the will of the Athenians, who had "withstood the barbarians" and who therefore, Herodotus concluded, might well be regarded as "the saviours of Greece."[34]

Book VIII ("Urania," muse of astronomy) gives the story of the battle of Salamis (480), along with speeches on both sides, reported or constructed by Herodotus, one of them by Artemisia, Queen of Halicarnassus.[35] Although (according to Herodotus) she advised against the plan, she joined the Persians and shared the defeat in the narrow straits of Salamis, one result being that the five-year-old Herodotus, who (as Myres imagines) may have seen the returning ships, was taken into exile and to his own historiographical calling. On the advice again of Artemisia, Xerxes then returned home, leaving the Greeks to divide the spoils and to celebrate victory. In this section Herodotus represents the Athenians, this time in a speech to a Macedonian ambassador, as celebrating the special virtues which underlay the recent victory by refusing an alliance and by declaring that their love of liberty was such that they would never come to terms with the barbarians.

The occasion for this declaration, the maneuverings of the Persian military leader Mardonius and Alexander of Macedonia, formed the background to a new Persian invasion and the battle of Platea (479) and was the subject of the last book ("Calliope") of Herodotus's *History.* After the victory of the Greeks, the Persians departed, the wiser for their misfortunes, as Herodotus hoped, and leaving the Greeks, at least for a time, to enjoy the fruits of victory, freedom, and law and perhaps, like Herodotus, to reflect on the causes of this great war.

Though Herodotus was concerned with his own time, his major contribution to the historical enterprise that he symbolically set in motion was opening up a new "historical space," or rather extending this historical space into "mythical space," which was made possible by the Egyptian memory, which he accepted as a way of criticizing Greek tradition.[36] For Herodotus most of the Greek gods originated with the barbarians, just as (centuries later) Diogenes Laertius would suggest for Greek philosophy.[37] In these ways Greek philosophy and myth were projected back into the "time of the gods" and so humanized, historicized, and brought into the arena of rational and historical inquiry.

Yet Herodotus was not as original as the vagaries of literary survival might suggest. Aside from influences from epic poetry and (more problematic) Ionian science, he drew on traditions of genealogy, mythography, logography (writings of uncritical prose recorders), chronography, and horography (city annals).[38] To this may be added works with ethnographical implications such as the Hippocratic work *Air, Waters, Places*.[39] Most important of all (so important that it has drawn charges of plagiarism) was the work of Hecataeus, who may have traveled even more widely than Herodotus and who expressed similar critical standards and a desire to separate work from fiction. Hecataeus's critical genealogy illustrates another effort to join the "times of men" and the "times of the gods."

Not that still earlier writers—including Homer and Hesiod—had not claimed to speak the truth, but they had operated with very different notions of experience and evidence. Such pre-Herodotean anticipators of "history," like the mute forerunners of Homer, survive in fragments at best and do not figure much in later tradition; given such obscurity around the question of paternity, Herodotus must indeed, for practical purposes, be taken as the "father" of historical practice as it has developed over the past two and a half millennia. In this perspective it was Herodotus who expanded the horizons of human experience in both space and time. Following Hecataeus, he explored the three continents of ancient knowledge and, if only through rumor and legend, pushed his inquiries to the "edges of the earth."[40] Following the poets as well as the prose-writing logographers, he also tried to plumb the depths of the past back to at least its human origins. As a pioneer, he could escape neither the myths and misconceptions of his time nor the reproaches of ancient critics. Nor was he safe from the charges of modern scholars and commentators, who measured him by the imperious standards of nineteenth-century historical science.

Herodotus has had his detractors—from Plutarch's attack on his "malice," and Juan Luis Vives's charge that he was the father not of history but of lies, down to the *Quellenforschung* and hypercriticism of modern classicists—and it is surely true that he does not measure up to the standards of the modern "science of history."[41] Recently, a German scholar has revived these charges with reference to Herodotus's false, or imaginative, employment of the citation of sources and has gone so far as to cast doubt on the factuality of many of Herodotus's travels, including the Egyptian visit.[42] For Detlev Fehling, Herodotus told his stories, and finally wrote them, within a threefold horizon, of which the inner ring encompasses his own experiences, the second circle contains what he learned by hearsay, and the outer area is relegated to matters of speculation. In all areas, however, Herodotus's work was dominated by literary invention and perhaps the strategies of "lying literature," which depends on the amassing of detail, the invocation of authorities, and manipulation of materials. Such criticism surely undermines (further) the authority of

Herodotus as a "source," but it hardly affects his paternity as far as the canon of history is concerned, though it may cast further doubt on the historiographical enterprise itself. How many historians, professing fidelity to truth and yet reaching out for a larger audience and posterity, can survive centuries of such scrutiny?

In any case, Herodotus's work was, from a modern standpoint, *primum in genere,* and its value is more appreciated than ever today — not so much for the gripping narrative of memorable military actions as for the interstitial background investigations of geography (or mythogeography) customs, religious practices, myths, and questions of national origins, which established a continuing tradition of social and cultural history. Momigliano concluded, perhaps wishfully, that he is more appreciated today than Thucydides, who is his only serious rival as a founder of the study of history as understood and appreciated by us moderns, or postmoderns.

Thucydides

Thucydides has been represented as looking in a very different direction than Herodotus, and indeed this is a view reinforced by Thucydides himself and by critics and admirers of both him and Herodotus over the centuries. The judgment of R. G. Collingwood is extreme but not untypical: "Thucydides is not the successor of Herodotus in historical thought but the man in whom the historical thought of Herodotus was overlaid and smothered beneath antihistorical motives."[43] Thucydides is perhaps more of a human presence than Herodotus, at least as far as biographical data are concerned, but again mine is not a quest for the historical Thucydides as he might have been behind the writings which he left or as the political and military efforts might suggest. What is of interest here is mainly his work, the *History of the Peloponnesian Wars* — the famous "possession for the ages" that Thucydides envisioned as the fate of his literary effort — as well as its reception, both readings and misreadings, and the meanings it suggests from a modern retrospective.

Thucydides, born sometime after 460, was a generation older than Herodotus, and though his experience was more direct, his horizons were much smaller. He began his history of the wars between Athens and the Spartan alliance in 431, just as Herodotus was in the last stages of his work and the last years of his life. Thucydides survived the great plague in Athens in 429 and later served as a general in the war. Dismissed in 424, he went into exile for twenty years to his estate in Thrace, returning in 404 to continue his *History of the Peloponnesian Wars,* which breaks off in 411 (to be continued by Xenophon), with nine years left in the war, and he died a few years after the war at the hands of an assassin.

With Thucydides we move, historiographically speaking, into a very different world even though he overlapped Herodotus chronologically, shared the same culture, and was concerned with some of the same problems. While Herodotus made "inquiries," Thucydides never spoke of his lifework in terms of such *historie* but rather as a project of "writing" (*syngraphe*). Like Herodotus, Thucydides was fascinated with the causes of war and prized liberty and other Greek political values, but otherwise his strategies were very different. While Herodotus took all of the knowable world and tradition as his subject, Thucydides was content for the most part with the immediate experience of his own generation and of the Greek wars, which he hyperbolically claimed, in the first sentence of his composition and in what would become a topos of historical prefaces, to be "more worthy of relation than any that had preceded it," locating the greatest transformation in the history of Hellas.[44] Moreover, whereas Herodotus devoted time to subjects of human interest, such as the culture and religion of barbarians, Thucydides preferred to attend to the political and military aspects of Athenian imperialism, which he surveyed and analyzed for purposes of instruction and edification.[45]

Most of Thucydides' *History* is devoted to the events of the twenty-year war between Athens and the Greek alliance, in which he took part; only Book I (1–23), the section usually called the "archaeology," discusses the more remote historical period. In fact Thucydides deprecates this antiquarian effort on the grounds that few happenings before his own time were either significant or accessible. Consequently, his account, which avoids matters of myth and antiquities and even manages to marginalize Homer and the Trojan War, is quite generalized and designed largely to furnish background to his main story. Much more than Herodotus, and certainly poets and chroniclers, who reflected the passions of the moment, Thucydides distrusted hearsay evidence and relied either on eyewitness testimony or on "what others saw for me"; and he tried in particular to stick to the spirit, if not always the letter, of the many speeches (a Herodotean device, too) which he reported in order to reveal the motives and emotions underlying the wars.[46]

In olden times (*ta paleia*) the Greeks were weak, divided into separate tribes, inclined to piracy, and incapable of such collective action as mounting a respectable expedition against an enemy. Thucydides' special concern was the question of economic motivation and power, especially sea power, and the recent emergence of Greek states from such weakness into a condition of commercial wealth, seafaring prowess, and military strength. Like Herodotus, he was interested in priority and paternity, but he disagreed about the founder of sea power, bestowing on Minos the honor of being the earliest naval pioneer, while for Herodotus, "Polycrates . . . was the first of mere human birth who conceived the design of gaining the empire of the sea."[47] For Thucydides, a thorough modernist in this regard, the Homeric precedent was of small importance. Agamemnon had attained a position of leadership in the Trojan War through superior strength, but he and the other Greeks were hampered by a lack of money, and it was only in recent times that the Greeks had progressed far enough economically to wage war either effectively or memorably. In any case this strength, concluded Thucydides, was the underlying cause (*prophasis*) of the conflict which he undertook to analyze.[48]

Thucydides, in the words which he put into the mouth of Pericles in an oration given to honor the Athenian dead in the first year of the war, resumed this theme by arguing that the immediate ancestors of the Athenians deserved more praise then the earlier members of this tradition for the present height of political achievement.[49] The reason for this success was the extraordinary constitution (*politeia*) which the Athenians had constructed, making possible the sort of freedom that Herodotus had also celebrated and representing the Athenian state as a model for all of Greece. The brazen chauvinism of Pericles paraded the human motives, including those of Thucydides, underlying the wars which persisted for two more decades and which shaped and almost destroyed his world. The speech also reflected Thucydides' assumption that it was human thinking and deliberation and decisions that constituted the essence of historical explanation in the short term.

In another important sense, the historical practice of Thucydides contrasted with that of Herodotus. Limiting his vision to the polis, its nature, its growth, and the threats to its survival, Thucydides had a much narrower conception of human thought and action. While Herodotus came to his conclusions on the basis of cross-cultural inquiries and a sort of comparative ethnography, Thucydides, drawing upon Hippocratic medicine, took a largely uniformitarian view of "human nature" (*anthropeia physis*), which for him was based on self-interest, aggressiveness, and other drives that made war, too, a "natural" phenomenon.[50] (Perhaps it was this conception of human nature that drew the young Thomas Hobbes to translate the *History* of Thucydides.) Such in any case was the basis of the "intellectual revolution" which Werner Jaeger saw reflected in Thucydides' history—that "historical writing had not become political, but political thinking had become historical."[51]

Yet there is another dimension to the work of Thucydides that suggests a different line of influence, for, like Herodotus, he could not escape the literary influence of the poets and dramatists who also shaped the culture of Athens. It is a "modernist fallacy," according to Francis Cornford, to let the analytical and political surface of Thucydides' narrative overshadow its artistic features and tragic overtones.[52] For the economic motives of the actors and orators of the Peloponnesian wars were also tragic passions, like those informing the dramatic creatures of Aeschylus. Thucydides wrote as if he were a direct observer of these tragic actions, but in fact, as Cornford suggested, these were emotions recollected not in poetic tranquillity but in bitter exile, an exile that turned the actor into an artist. If Thucydides did not range widely over, he thought deeply about, the process of history. For Macaulay, Herodotus had "a simple and imaginative mind" and told tales for a relatively uncultivated audience, whereas Thucydides had a "spacious and reflecting mind," "judge[d] better of circumstances than of principles," and wrote in wartime in a political school that later included Richelieu, Mazarin, and Shaftesbury. And Macaulay, who himself preferred the company of men of power to that of men of letters, concluded that Thucydides "is the greatest historian who ever lived."[53]

Polybius

Writing more than two centuries after Herodotus and Thucydides and in the wake of many lesser historians, Polybius worked in their shadow and yet had his own distinctive claim to fame, which was his aspiration to encompass the whole world in his narrative of the rise of Rome.[54] With Herodotus he shared an interest in the "barbarian" nations that came to play a part in his story, with Thucydides a utilitarian concern for political history and its assignable causes, and with both he entertained a certain disdain for his predecessors and a professed hope to accomplish something original. Just as the epic of Rome's ascent to world dominion far surpassed the stories of the empires of the Persians and Greeks, so Polybius's own history was uniquely significant, since, he argued, "nobody else among our contemporaries has set out to write a general history."[55] Already, it seems, originality was a conventional topos in the historiographical canon.

Polybius of Megapolis (in Arcadia) was born at the turn of the second century B.C. and followed his father in a political career in the service of the Achaean League, a military federation which came to dominate Greece at the end of the third century. With his political experience, he combined a wide knowledge of philosophical, literary, and especially historical writers. He rose to the rank of general in the league and, after the defeat of Macedonia, was one of many culpable Greeks exiled to Rome. There he remained, protected by his friendship with Scipio Africanus, even after he was free to return home to Greece, although he did return on a mission to Achaea after the dissolution of the league in 146, and reportedly he traveled widely throughout the Roman world.[56] But the chief preoccupation of Polybius for over half a century, and his major legacy to the Western historiographical canon, was his *History,* which was published after his death in forty books (of which only Books I–V, most of VI, and fragments of the rest have survived).

For Polybius, Roman expansion was "an achievement which is without parallel in human history." He begins his complex narrative in 220 B.C. with the various wars in Greece, Asia, Italy, and Africa, especially the Second and Third Punic Wars; but he devotes an introduction (Books I and II) to background, starting with the first intrusion of Rome into Greece in 264 B.C. (when the history of Timaeus broke off). Polybius's was a story that could not be told from a parochial or national perspective, nor indeed according to a simple linear order; it had to be "woven" like a garment.[57] Unlike Herodotus, he declined to interrupt his story with accounts of far-off and irrelevant wonders, such as the Pillars of Hercules and the "outer sea."[58] He approached his narrative as he would a complicated campaign, keeping in sight at all times the goal of clear and rational explanation and yet stopping periodically, sometimes in the first person, to inform readers, Romans as well as Greeks, of his self-conscious literary strategies.[59] He employed the device of alternate chapters for parallel phenomena around the Mediterranean world, pausing occasionally for methodological digressions, descriptions of social, political, or geographical background, and explanatory flashbacks.[60]

Like Thucydides, Polybius reserved his "archaeology" for background, avoiding genealogies, myths, and other topics which had been treated by his predecessors; and he declared his intention (another topos) of avoiding the sensationalism of some authors who wanted "simply to produce a striking effect on their readers."[61] He limited himself therefore to "a history of actual events,"[62] though he recognized that laws and customs were essential for the understanding of any political system;[63] and he regarded questions of geography and climate as fundamental to the explanatory purposes of pragmatic history, though poorly understood by earlier Greek authors.[64] Like Thucydides, too, though in a less indulgent manner, Polybius employed speeches to reveal human motives and underlying causes of political and military actions.[65] He also made use of documentary sources, such as the texts of the treaty between the Romans and the Carthaginians, which had been preserved in his own day on bronze tablets next to the temple of Zeus on the Capitol.[66]

"Pragmatic history" (*pragmatike historia*) was Polybius's phrase for the "betterment and pleasure" and the utility which he offered in his life's work.[67] For him the purpose of history was general education and training for a political career (*politike praxis*), which more specifically included ways of coping with the terrible trials of fortune (*tyche*) and unexpected events. A knowledge of such history was essential for both private and public life, Polybius argued, whether to correct an injustice, to acquire something, to anticipate an attack, or to defend the status quo.[68] Being a good historian, however, involved more than just being a good man or good citizen, for it required that he be prepared to tell the truth at all costs, to the extent even of accusing a friend or praising an enemy. Nor should historians rely on the supernatural in their effort to make sense of the vicissitudes of human life;[69] they should stick to facts that can be verified according to standards established long before by Herodotus and Thucydides. So he took occasion to criticize the shortcomings in this regard of a number of his predecessors, including Phylarchus, Zeno, and especially Timaeus, who was ignorant of geography and practical affairs as well as documentary sources.[70] Deprived of truth, Polybius aphorized, employing the usual optical metaphor, history is like a man deprived of eyesight.[71]

Polybius has often been compared with Machiavelli because of his political realism and concern for social order, but he was too much the conservative aristocrat and moralist for the parallel to be exact. Yet like Machiavelli, Polybius believed that a science of politics was accessible through historical analysis. He was fascinated with the trajectory of history passing from past to future, the patterns described by this process, and the ways in which the historian might "penetrate to the knowledge of the causes," especially in political matters; for it was here that readers could find more specific instruction. Causal analysis was difficult, and Polybius was careful to distinguish the beginning (*arche*) from the cause (*aitia*) of something, and both from a pretext (*prophasis*).[72] Thus the beginning of Alexander's war against Persia was his crossing into Asia, but the cause had to do with his plans and preparations, and the pretext with his declared intentions.

In general Polybius frowned on the practice of historians who ascribed a causal role to fate, fortune, or the gods in historical phenomena rather than to human will or failing; yet he acknowledged that fortune played a part in the form of an external contingency—such as Xerxes' invasion of Europe—or when two contenders were evenly matched.[73] He acknowledged, moreover, that, beyond the power of human will, "all existing things are subject to decay."[74] Just as fortune had brought down the empire of the Persians, so it would do to that of the Macedonians, according to the prophecy of Demetrius of Phalerum recalled by Polybius.[75] And it remained to be seen whether the Romans, with their "inflexible determination" of will, could withstand the forces of nature and the difficulties which fortune cast before even the strongest.[76]

Polybius thought that the Romans represented a unique case, however, in part because what was a basis for reproach in other peoples was "actually the

element which holds the Roman state together" — in marked contrast to the
faithless Greeks — that is, "a scrupulous fear of the gods."[77] There were two
other more obvious reasons for Roman success: first, they had built their
empire on an unprecedentedly stable constitutional basis, and second, they
had managed to extend their political rule over the whole of the known world.
In these circumstances, too, are to be found the special value of Polybius's
history, which likewise claimed to have an extraordinary political value and
which likewise displayed a universal and a unified character.[78] Beyond the
claims of all earlier authors, Polybius could thus offer not only a political and
in this sense pragmatic history but also a truly universal history (*historia
katholike*), which, like a living organism, could not be understood except in
terms of its entire morphology.[79] For this reason, too, perhaps, Polybius was
able to compare history with the science of medicine.[80]

At the center of Polybius's explanation of Roman success was the famous
digression in Book VI, which was devoted to the Roman constitution (*politeia*) and to the political ideas which Polybius drew from it, namely, the
theory of the "mixed constitution," which was to have such an extraordinary
afterlife.[81] Adapting Aristotle's notion of three constitutional forms, Polybius
began by doubling their number, distinguishing between normal and perverted forms of each species, joining them in a process of transformation, or
revolution (*anacyclosis*), and placing them in chronological sequence. According to this "natural" progress of political development — which overrode human will, if not fortune — monarchy, emerging from one-man rule, degenerates into tyranny, aristocracy into oligarchy, and democracy into mob rule,
thus completing the cycle. It was the special virtue of the Roman constitution
that it was "so fairly and so suitably ordered and regulated through the agency
of these three elements [consul, senate, and plebs] that it was impossible even
for the Romans to declare with certainty whether the whole system was an
aristocracy, a democracy, or a monarchy."[82] The results included an unusual
balance between civic and military offices and a constitutional stability appropriate to a universal empire.

This analysis leads Polybius into speculations about the origins of civil
society and the reasons for its transformations from respect for strength to
respect for reason and justice, though periodically lapsing from civilized motives and so provoking popular reactions, civil wars, and the revolutions
which kept the cycle going. Theories of historical recurrence had wide currency in classical and even Christian antiquity.[83] In the historicizing version of
Polybius — which had an extraordinary impact on later historical and political
writers, including Machiavelli — the move is from the practice of pragmatic
and universal history to another level of conceptualization, which would come

later to be regarded as the philosophy of history. Beginning as a simple inquiry into causes and customs, the Polybian practice of history took on increasingly ambitious programs of finding larger meanings and uses, and later historians erected even grander schemes on these foundations.

Diodorus of Sicily

The dual tradition of Greek historiography derived from the perspectives and practices of Herodotus and Thucydides traces a curious downward trajectory, the followers and eclectic adapters of these two pioneers usually falling short in acumen as well as artistry, and certainly in originality, although not in rhetorical and speculative ingenuity. Between the fifth and the first centuries B.C. there had been vast increases in historical and geographical knowledge. The "edges of the earth" were extended first by Alexander's and then by the Romans' imperial expansion, and the mental horizons of classical scholars were likewise expanded in many ways. As art and science, however, historiography enjoyed a quantitative rather than a qualitative progress, at least according to modern taste and judgment.

Like Polybius, Diodorus of Sicily offers a bridge between the old civilization of Greece and the upstart power of Rome, between the age of Greek decline and the threshold of Roman imperial expansion. Born in Agyria and gaining some familiarity with the Latin language, Diodorus made his Herodotean Egyptian pilgrimage (60–57 B.C.) and lived for several years in Rome. He made other journeys in pursuit of historical information and spent, he says, thirty years on his *Historical Library*. Despite reliance on the books of earlier authors, Diodorus was more than a "mere copyist," for he had his own rhetorical strategies, lessons to teach, and opinions, which often contradicted those of his predecessors.[84] His book, which is the largest work of history that antiquity has to offer, gives an account of world history from the mythical origins of Hellenic and barbarian nations down to the time of Caesar's Gallic War; but of thirty books, only I–V (the mythic history of the Egyptians, Assyrians, Ethiopians, and Greeks) and XI–XX (from the Second Persian War to the successors of Alexander) have survived intact.

It was Diodorus's purpose, following Herodotean perspective and Polybian scope, to assemble a "universal history" (*koina historia*) from the standpoint of Rome.[85] In fact his *Library* was in large part a collection of the writings of others, including the pioneering works in this genre (now lost) by Theopompus and Ephorus, which treated "all the deeds in Hellas and the barbarian lands."[86] Following what was by then a historical cliché, reinforced by Stoic teachings, Diodorus insisted on the utility of history, which has the further advantage of not exposing readers to the distresses of direct participation in unpleasant or dangerous affairs, as (here invoking Homer) Odysseus was so painfully forced to do. Just as elderly men exceed their juniors in experience, so history offers a vicarious sort of experience that no human being could hope to accumulate. Moreover, universal history in the Polybian mode brings together all mankind in ways that perhaps providence but certainly no political conquest or organization could succeed in doing. Thus, Diodorus concluded, history is "the benefactor of all mankind."[87]

Diodoran rhetoric inflated another commonplace of historical writing, that is, Thucydides' hope of making his work a "possession of the ages," as history was represented as a means of turning time the destroyer into time the guardian of human tradition for all posterity, although (in contrast to Thucydides) through eloquence rather than impartial analysis.[88] In this way history, by the cunning deployment of language, became the distinguishing mark of civilized men over barbarians. Again following good classical precedent (Herodotean, Thucydidean, and Polybian), Diodorus tended to disparage the accomplishments of his predecessors on the grounds that they all fell short of his universal plan — neglecting the deeds of the barbarians, limiting themselves to particular traditions, confusing chronology, and overlooking significant events. It was for this reason that Diodorus settled upon his extraordinarily laborious task not of observing and reporting on events but of examining, according to his own lights, the whole historiographical tradition down to his own time. Thus Diodorus's *Library* was, despite his travels in Africa, Asia, and Europe, fashioned mainly, and admittedly, from secondary sources.[89] It is ironic that classicists, clinging as they so derivatively do to textual tradition, have not forgiven the derivative character of his work.

In the manner of many world historians down to the present century, Diodorus considered the prehistorical origins of humankind, reviewing briefly the rival theories of the eternity of the universe, defended by the Peripatetics, and that of creation in time. Whatever the correct cosmogony, Diodorus departed from the ancient notion of a golden age and described the original condition of humanity as one of misery and bestiality. Necessity and experience — in collaboration with a distinguished succession of founders, leaders, and what Kenneth Sacks calls "culture heroes" — were the teachers of primitive man, and only gradually did language and social organization, arising in different places in the world, improve these harsh conditions.[90] But this was all pre- and metahistorical speculation, and Diodorus hastened to take up his major theme, which was the human condition as preserved in memory, and more especially in writing, the privileged medium of that noble but relatively new class of men, the historiographers, to which Diodorus belonged. Poetry gives pleasure, and the codes of law demand punishment, he argued; only history offers instruction.[91]

Following Herodotus and the lessons of mythology, Diodorus locates the origins of the gods, and therefore civilization, in Egypt; and he summarizes Egyptian concepts of the beginning of the world, repeating the praises of land, climate, and the role of the Nile in Egyptian history.[92] The fabled Flood, known to Plato as well as to Hebrew tradition, was survived by the Egyptians, who afterward, struck with wonder at the stars, began the study of nature, which they first expressed in the mythical terms later adapted by the Greeks. The sun and moon — Osiris and Isis — were the ruling gods of the cosmos, and the Egyptians worshiped them even as they carried on the investigation of the heavens, the conquest of the land, the founding of cities, and other elements of human progress which, along with corresponding decadence, Diodorus recorded.[93]

Turning from mythical and prehistorical questions, Diodorus next considered fundamental questions of geography, especially the source and the mysterious rising of the Nile, which dominated Egyptian consciousness.[94] On this question Diodorus again found fault with his predecessors — Hecataeus and Cadmus being misled by myth, while Thucydides and Xenophon avoided the question entirely, and even Herodotus only guessed. Diodorus himself, who required written testimony for his conclusions, reviewed the theories of origins but left the question in doubt; and as for the swelling of the river, he preferred the common-sense notion that it was occasioned by seasonal rain.

After considering geohistorical conditions, Diodorus took up properly historical questions of politics, social structure, religion, and culture, including what he saw as the outlandish worship of animals and burial practices. Central to Egyptian civilization, as to human culture in general, was the practice of writing, and he pointed to the "sacred" as well as common scripts with which Egyptians carried on matters of government, religious worship, and education. The Egyptians were pioneers, too, in the arts of geometry, which again necessity (in the form of boundary disputes) reinforced, and of arithmetic, which was required for business operations. Not only in such arts but also in lawmaking the Egyptians were the teachers of other peoples, Diodorus believed, and especially of the Greeks.

In later books Diodorus went on in Herodotean fashion to discuss the cultures of Assyria, India, Ethiopia, and finally of Greece itself, again dwelling at length on mythology, difficult as the astonishing details of this subject were for historians. Readers who judged Hercules by contemporary (mortal) life, for example, or who required modern standards of truth, were bound to be dissatisfied, Diodorus realized (as indeed, on similar grounds, modern classicists have been dissatisfied with Diodorus's own work). Yet both historical curiosity about origins, or causes, and piety demanded that the subject be pursued.[95] In this way Diodorus gave himself license to tell once again, but this time comprehensively and critically or at least ironically, the stories of Hercules and other legendary figures who appeared in poetic tradition — which by then, of course, had also come to be written.

Dionysius of Halicarnassus

Contemporary with Diodorus was Dionysius of Halicarnassus, a rhetorician and literary critic as well as a historian and another link between the Hellenistic and Roman worlds. Dionysius came to Rome just as Caesar was putting an end to civil war, and he spent twenty-two years first learning Latin and then gathering materials for his *Romanike Archeologia,* which traced the history of Rome from its mythical origins down to the beginning of the First Punic War.[96] Of the twenty books of his *Roman Antiquities* only the first nine and parts of the next two remain. Dionysius also wrote a critique of Thucydides, although judging from his long-winded and apologetic study of the Roman conquerors of the Greeks, later scholars would regard "the tasteless Dionysius" (as Macaulay called him) as hardly worthy of comparison with his illustrious predecessor.

Dionysius begins, inevitably, with the topos of literary immortality, which had been expressed in their different ways by both Herodotus and Thucydides — that the "monuments of the mind" (*mnemeia*) should not be allowed to go to ruin with the body.[97] "Longer than deeds live words," sang Pindar, but for Dionysius, truth and justice were even better than poetry as guarantees of immortality.[98] Such a claim on posterity required, of course, the loftiest of subjects, and there was no loftier story than Rome's rise to power, Dionysius argued, following the lead of Polybius. The Assyrians were oldest but covered only a small part of Asia; the Medes ruled for just four generations; the Persians held power for two centuries but never succeeded in mastering Europe; and the life span and extent of Greek imperialism was also limited: "But Rome rules every country that is not inaccessible or uninhabited, and she rules every sea . . . ; she is the first and the only State recorded in all time that ever made the risings and the settings of the sun the boundaries of her dominion."[99] Thus are echoed the themes of the "four world monarchies," which had already been sounded by Polybius and others, and of the supremacy of Rome.

Like Diodorus, Dionysius also began with the earliest legends of Rome, a subject which earlier historians avoided because of its difficulty. Here he announced another familiar theme, that is, the ignorance of the Greeks about early history, especially that of their present masters. Nor, he continued, were the origins of Rome as ignominious a subject as some ill-informed or envious persons believed. That the early Romans were not Greek by no means diminished their heritage or certainly their achievement; the only problem was—and here is another lament that becomes commonplace in the self-promotions of historians, especially national ones—that in concentrating on deeds, the Romans had neglected words and so had not yet found a worthy historian to celebrate their accomplishments.

It was this deficiency which Dionysius, a Greek, proposed to redeem. Like Diodorus, he acknowledged the secondary sources on which he drew while proclaiming their insufficiency and uncritical character, especially in identifying the confusion of peoples that invaded Italy. Rejecting the tedious annalistic form of the local historians of Greece (*Atthides*), Dionysius employed a topical method that permitted not only the simple narrative of deeds—*histoire événementielle*—but also analysis of government, society, and culture.[100] Dionysius's work was in some ways closer to that of the Roman antiquarian Varro than the historian Livy (whose work he must have known but does not cite). According to Dionysius, sorting through various stories about national origins, the Romans were (and kept the name of) "Aborigines" until the time of the Trojan War, when they began to be called "Latins" after the eponymous king Latinus.[101] In any case the process of occupying the land and, jointly with the Pelasgians, building cities began, and never ceased.

Among the peoples that came to Italy from Greece were the Arcadians, and Dionysius pointed out that some of their religious customs had survived until his own day, although others have been forgotten and neglected by their descendants.[102] Nevertheless, such residues proved the importance of Greek culture from early times. The Arcadians may also have been the ones to introduce Greek laws, letters, and musical instruments into Italy. The dubious evidence of mythology also reports that other Greeks, led by Hercules, came to Rome and built a town on the Capitoline Hill. Despite the civilizing influence of the Greeks, the land they settled had its own character, religious beliefs, and admirable geographical qualities; and it came to be called "Italia" (after another eponymous king, Italus, who was himself a son of Hercules).[103]

This was also the time of the Trojan War, which sent Aeneas and his companions on the long journey taking them to Sicily and ending finally in Italy. There were skeptics who (pointing out the multiplicity of tombs said to hold the remains of Aeneas) denied that Aeneas ever came to Italy; but Dionysius rejected their views and followed the "most credible account," which he took to be that of Hellanicus, though he by no means rejected the testimony of Homer and other literary sources.[104] In this way Trojan elements—which were apparent in the images of Trojan gods still displayed in Dionysius's time — were joined to those of Italian Aborigines and Greeks in the founding of the Roman state, and the marriage of Aeneas and Latinus's daughter Lavinia symbolized the dual nature of the new Roman *populus*.[105]

What about the founding of the city itself? Dionysius's narrative is based on his "reading very diligently many works written by both Greek and Roman authors." He relates the various stories from this seminal but controversial prehistorical period of Roman history, including those surrounding Romulus and Remus, perhaps sons of Aeneas or perhaps not, but he does not commit himself to any of these legendary or conjectural accounts. Indeed he suggests the possibility of three separate foundings — not only one after the Trojan War and another fifteen generations later but also an original settlement in a remoter past before the coming of the Greeks.[106] As the narrative continues, Dionysius tries to separate history or probable truth from myth — or more usually, to report all variations and then let the reader choose — and, in a separate treatise, to correlate Greek and Roman chronologies, calculated according to the Olympiadic system and the problematic dating from "the founding of the city," respectively. In any case Dionysius believes that, in this first book, he has shown Rome to be not barbaric in origin but a creation of the Greeks.[107]

With his second book Dionysius turns to the question of Roman government and sets the scene through the old classical device of a speech, this one put in the mouth of Romulus, who expresses the fundamental premise of Roman government — the partnership of ruler and people, later embodied in the legendary *lex regia* — by offering the Populus Romanus the choice of the form of government to rule them. The people responded by accepting the traditional, ancestral form, which was kingship; and so, after a favorable sign from the gods, the line of Roman kings was formed by election.[108] After this divinely and socially sanctioned foundation, Romulus went on to organize the people into classes, most likely following the Athenian model, and to begin the military and political expansion that led to the greatest empire the world ever knew.

Dionysius's description of Romulus's foundational activities is both laudatory and highly idealized, as is his view of Roman religion, tolerant as it was of other customs and beliefs. Indeed Dionysius preferred the sober forms of Roman public religion to the myths of Greece, though he appreciated the uses of the latter in explaining the mysteries of nature through allegory.[109] Accompanying the order of religion was the structure of laws that Romulus set up, by which "the Romans have kept their commonwealth flourishing for many generations."[110] Included in Romulus's provisions for social order, described approvingly by Dionysius, was the absolute authority invested in the male head of family, which made the wife subordinate to her husband and which, through the *patriapotestas* (paternal power), made children virtually the slaves of the father.[111]

The second king, Numa Pompilius, reinforced the new Romulan order in many ingenious ways. He also controlled the discontents of his subjects by distributing honors to the patricians and land to the plebeians. In this way, Dionysius concluded, "He attuned the whole body of the people, like a musical instrument, to the sole consideration of the public good."[112] He was likewise adept in manipulating religion for the benefit of the state. Dionysius rejected the story that Numa had studied with Pythagoras but acknowledged that he was a virtuoso manager of religious institutions, including the festival of the sacred Terminalia (illustrating the characteristic Roman obsession with boundaries, their defense and their extension), the Vestal Virgins (although Dionysius attributed their temple to Romulus), and the special relationship which he claimed with the gods to instill fear in his credulous subjects. Not that Dionysius took a cynical view of the political value of religion, for he wholly disapproved of the so-called atheistic philosophers of his own day, who denied the role of the gods in public affairs and of course in history.[113] So Dionysius, filling in often tedious details neglected by Livy, followed the fortunes of Rome under her kings—the few interregna, the several political and military reforms, and the many wars—and praised the good old customs, including slavery and censorship, which underlay this triumphant story. He continued his narrative into the republican period, using speeches even more than his predecessors, though it is less full, if not less prolix and rhetorical, than his treatment of the earlier and more obscure periods.

Like Diodorus, and also writing several centuries after his Hellenic models, Dionysius forged a link between the Greek and Roman worlds and carried on the genre founded in the fifth century. Aspiring to combine the range and richness of Herodotus with the acumen and analytical program of Thucydides, both of these epigones produced vast, and vastly flawed, masterpieces, which were each represented as a summa of historical knowledge and as state of the historical art. The themes of Herodotus and Thucydides were great, that of Polybius greater still, but greatest of all—the historiographical hyperbole was cumulative—was the antiquarian creation of Dionysius and the encyclopedic one of Diodorus.

These epigones were eclectics, combining myth and history (even as they affected to distinguish between the two), description and analysis, considerations of curious customs and causes of change, antiquarianism and chronological narrative. Their achievements were indeed heroic, but heroic in a different sense from that of the pioneering tourist Herodotus or the tragic general

Thucydides, in whose shadow they worked. They were derivative in the sense not only that they followed the trails blazed by the founders of the historiographical canon but also that, while they traveled and used oral and material or monumental evidence, they were concerned mainly, in scholastic fashion, to gather, to summarize, to criticize, and to draw conclusions from a mass of secondary literature. In order to manage this accumulation of knowledge and opinion, they drew on the formal resources of rhetoric, especially under the influence of Isocrates, for whom learning was to be placed in the service of civic culture.[114] However, this had both disadvantages and advantages for history as intelligent inquiry and as intelligible narrative — as science and as art. In their hands the historiographical canon had advanced in quantitative and perhaps in critical and theoretical ways, but the genre of historical writing continued to be dominated (at least as we see it in retrospect) by the Janus figures and founding fathers, Herodotus and Thucydides.

The Idea of History

Neither Herodotus nor Thucydides gave much thought to the theoretical foundations of their historiographical practice. They wanted to tell the "truth" as they saw it and thus to communicate something of value to their readers, but they did not speculate, except perhaps implicitly, about larger patterns or deeper structures, or certainly the philosophical meaning of the deeds and thoughts they investigated and commented on.[115] In the course of time, however, and with the accumulation of interpretations and controversies about the recollection and literary recovery of aspects of the human past, more theoretical questions were posed by Greek authors, though seldom by practicing historians.

The study of antiquities, though part of the Herodotean agenda, was conventionally distinguished from history even though it was essential to the early stages of historical narrative. The antiquarian dimension of history in a modern sense ran a parallel course to historiography, being linked originally to the turn to words by the ancient Sophists and to writing by the tradition of scholarship culminating in the Alexandrine schools. One of Socrates' interlocutory victims, the Sophist Hippias of Elias, was the first to use the term *archaeology* in the course of explaining the attractions of his interests, which seemed so trivial to the philosopher: people "are very fond of hearing about the genealogies of heroes and men, Socrates, and the foundations of cities in ancient times and, in short, about antiquity [*archeologia*] in general."[116] In his list of Olympic winners Hippias was also perhaps a founder of Greek chronology as well as the learned study of antiquities.

Closer still to this aspect of historical study was the tradition of classical scholarship — the work of the *grammatikoi,* the *kritikoi,* and the *philologoi,* as they were variously termed. In the work of Alexandrine critics like Eratosthenes in the third century B.C., philology, which began with a concern for editing ancient texts, especially the Homeric poems, shifted from literary and stylistic to historical criticism. Eratosthenes, who was the first to call himself a philologist, was also a pioneering contributor to the auxiliary disciplines of geography and chronology, fields which were central to the emergence of the modern "science" of history in the sixteenth century.[117]

History always had a close relationship with other human sciences, of which political philosophy was most obvious. Aristotle's *Politics* presented a developmental scheme which suited historical interpretation, most evident in the interpretations of Polybius's "pragmatic history." This historical attitude is apparent especially in Aristotle's project of collecting, and analyzing comparatively on the analogy of a natural history and biology, a large number of Greek constitutions, including the *Athenian Constitution,* a work discovered later and attributed to him. In this work Aristotle moved away from the idealism of his master, Plato, toward an empirical and in a way historical conception of nature and bodies politic, which passed through their own temporal processes of generation and corruption.[118]

Another auxiliary science of history was geography, which indeed was one of the principal sources of inspiration for Herodotus as well as Hecataeus, Polybius, and other historians whose horizons extended beyond Hellas. At the turn of the first century B.C. Strabo assembled a summa of ancient geographical ideas and knowledge and their links with history.[119] He regarded his discipline as superior to that of Herodotus and Thucydides, especially in its devotion to truth. By contrast, Strabo charged, "The early historians say many things that are not true, because they were accustomed to falsehoods on account of the myths in their writings [and so they] do not agree with one another concerning the same things."[120] This was especially true of the Romans, who were in any case largely derivative of the Greeks.[121]

Yet Strabo had a deep appreciation for myth, which, like philosophy, ran parallel to history. Homer was, of course, the founder of all these fields of knowledge, including geography. It was Homer, for example, who first associated the character of men with differences in climate, and through widening experience other authors elaborated this notion. "Homer's narrative is founded on history," Strabo declared, and praised this "father of geography" for many insights, including his recognition of the all-encompassing Ocean, denying that this was a myth — not, of course, that there were not falsehoods in Homer, as there were also in Herodotus and Polybius. In general Strabo,

citing the old Greek motto about man's natural desire for knowledge, regarded myth as just the prehistorical prelude to such knowledge, after which
came "in the course of time history and our present philosophy."[122] Even in his
own day myth was not without educational, political, and geographical value,
although Strabo did deplore unfounded legends such as those surrounding the
history of Alexander.

Strabo, who wrote a continuation of Polybius's *History* (though the work
has not survived), was an admirer of the Polybian and Dionysian vision of
universal history — the Greek idea of the *oikumene* — and promoter of geography and climate as foundations of historical study. Following Hippocrates and
Posidonius, Strabo joined medical, astronomical, and geographical ideas into
a theoretical mix which produced, as Clarence Glacken has written, an "interesting discussion of the problems of the mental, linguistic, and cultural causation in ethnology and history."[123] However, the simplistic formulas of Herodotus, Thucydides, and even Polybius had become less plausible, and (as
Glacken further notes) "the accumulation of knowledge regarding the world's
peoples and their remarkable diversity put great strains on simpler causal
explanations than had been satisfactory in the past." The result was the sort of
confused eclecticism, or rather syncretism, into which philosophy was also
falling, a condition which would be reinforced and aggravated in the coming
age of religious conflicts.

In other ways, too, the art of history had begun to find a theoretical dimension, especially in the context of other fields of study. It was again Aristotle
who, more or less in passing in his *Poetics,* defined the conceptual (or perhaps
nonconceptual) status of history. His point, much discussed by later scholars,
was that history, besides being distinguished by the medium of prose, describes
something which happened, while poetry describes something which might
happen — that history treats the particular and the contingent, while poetry
treats the general and the (reasonably) possible — and so poetry is more "philosophical."[124] Amplifying this argument, Aristotle contrasts history with epic
poetry on the grounds that history is chronological, while the epic treats unified action.[125] In either case history is, because of its parochial and particular
character, subordinated to the more elevated and generalizing artistic and
conceptual pursuits of the poet and the philosopher.

If history was cast in the shadows of philosophy and poetry, however, it was
quite the opposite with the art of rhetoric, the practice of which converged
with post-Herodotean and post-Thucydidean historical writing, and the theory of which transformed the weaknesses of history into strengths. Rhetoric
and oratory dealt with specific cases, and they appealed to specific emotions.
Now, Aristotle does not take up the topic of history in his *Rhetoric,* nor does

he emphasize its specificity, arguing indeed that rhetoric considers not individuals but classes of individuals; yet the practice of rhetoric in persuading and explaining has to proceed on a more particular and local level, which means, in effect, on the level of historical experience. These implications would be drawn out much more clearly in the work of Cicero, Quintilian, and other Roman authors as well as Renaissance scholars.

In any case, the historical writing of the epigones of Herodotus and Thucydides came increasingly under the spell of rhetoric.[126] Greek public oratory, emerging in an environment of political democracy, litigation, and sophistic education touched every sort of discourse. For historians, it was especially important not only for their use of speeches but also for the efforts to increase the aesthetic appeal, persuasiveness, and didactic — especially the moral and political — value of history and for the task of coping with and criticizing the accumulated opinions of the historiographical canon. In the introduction to his history, Diodorus of Sicily had linked history more generally with the faculty of speech, which set the Greek above the barbarian and gave distinction and power to the historian.[127]

Rhetoric was associated especially with the growing concern of historians with matters of writing rather than methods of inquiry, that is, literary style, form, and moral and political judgment. These were certainly the concerns of Dionysius of Halicarnassus, who was a rhetorician as well as a historian and in this connection regarded history as "philosophy teaching by example." Dionysius devoted an essay to the faults of Thucydides on literary grounds and according to the rigid canons of rhetorical theory, although there were also analytical and conceptual implications of his criticisms. According to Dionysius, Thucydides, rising above the parochialism of "atthidography" (early chronicles of Attica) but falling short of the grand design of Herodotus, followed a confusing seasonal organization, and instead of beginning his history with the true cause of the Peloponnesian War — that is, the rise of the Athenian state — he started with the pretexts for this struggle.[128] Dionysius found fault with the speeches which Thucydides reported, or fabricated, although he admitted that the famous funeral oration of Pericles was "worthy of imitation."[129] Dionysius claimed that his main interest was in the "truth," but what mainly concerned him was Thucydides' faulty principles of selection, which omitted many important events and contained many stylistic failings, as well as with his impact on later orators, especially Demosthenes. This writerly concern with textual surfaces has dominated the literary criticism of historiography from Dionysius of Halicarnassus down to the present age of rhetorical fashion.

Another work in the genre of historiographical criticism was Plutarch's attack *On the Malice of Herodotus,* which (according to one scholar) is the first example of the "slashing review."[130] What disturbed Plutarch was Herodotus's anti-Athenian bias, or rather his failure to conceal the pro-Persian bias of the Boeotians, but even more his uncivil tendency to emphasize the faults of his protagonists while neglecting "good things"; for "it is no honest-minded writer who uses very fierce nouns and verbs in his narrative when soft ones are available."[131] According to Plutarch, Herodotus libeled not only individuals but whole nations, as when he asserted that the Persians learned "sexual intercourse with boys" and that they "practised castration before they ever saw the Aegean."[132] Plutarch multiplied such examples, showing how Herodotus, in contrast to Thucydides, regularly chose the most damaging account, seized upon the shabbiest motive, and in general composed his narrative in a reprehensible spirit of meanness and ill will.

Plutarch himself was not primarily a historian; he was a moral philosopher of the Platonic school and especially, in the eyes of posterity, a biographer, whose standards were quite different from those of the candid "inquiries" of Herodotus and his followers.[133] As Polybius had said, biography was not tied to chronology, was closer to the genre of eulogy, and was not intended to present portraits warts and all. Plutarch himself presented his *Parallel Lives* — which (like the works of Polybius, Diodorus, and Dionysius) forged a link between the Greek and Roman worlds — in a rather idealized fashion, with the intention of conveying moral examples to imitate or avoid. Plutarch also, while deploring superstition, was indulgent in his attitude toward myth, at least in the form of civil religion, as shown in the providential aspects of Roman origins and the influence of Egyptian wisdom on Pythagoras, Solon, Thales, Plato, and other Greeks who, according to legend, visited Egypt.[134]

Not that Plutarch lacked standards of truth, for his scholarship in the *Lives* was impressive, and both here and in his *Roman Questions,* which made cautious inquiry into ancient Roman religion and ritual, he was careful to distinguish between fables and "probable reasoning."[135] It was just that he associated such truth with standards of civility and correctness. So, for example, in rejecting the scandalous rumors about an affair between Pericles and his son's wife, Plutarch admitted the difficulty of making judgments about events long ago: "So very difficult a matter it is to trace and find out the truth of anything by history, when, on the one hand, those who afterwards write it find long periods of time intercepting their view, and, on the other hand, the contemporary records of any actions and lives, partly through envy and ill-will, partly through favour and flattery, pervert and distort truth."[136] In trying to sift fact from fiction, Plutarch deserves at least a small place in the canon of classical historiography.

Several ancient authors wrote treatises on history, but the only one to survive is Lucian of Samosata's *How to Write History,* written on the occasion of the Parthian war (A.D. 166) against the barbarians and the concomitant "campaign of glorification."[137] Historical writing in the second century was a popular genre but also derivative, plagiaristic, and pretentious, not to mention barren, and the satirist Lucian wrote his little work to criticize its weaknesses and excesses. He mocks contemporary historians for their inflated Homeric comparisons of the do-nothing general Lucius Verus with Achilles. On the positive side, Lucian's model is Thucydides and his ideal of making history a "possession for the ages," with Herodotus following at a distance, but for the most part Lucian's essay, following good rhetorical precedent, is devoted to commonplace prescriptions concerning style and form.

The task of the historian, according to Lucian, is to tell what happened and not to spend time in useless praise; his chief virtues are political understanding, which is a gift of nature, and literary power, which is a product of education and effort.[138] The poet, on behalf of his art, commands his material; the orator may shape it to his argumentative ends; but the historian, out of respect for the facts, must follow it and worship only Truth. He should be a stranger ("the past is a foreign country"), committed to no country, party, or patron, and although he may report myths, he should not accept them. A touch of poetry may be permitted for lofty subjects, as is the freedom to give effective order to his narrative, yet the historian, serving a different muse, must avoid flights of fancy and keep his feet on the ground. His writing must be like an undistorted mirror and, while distinguishing between virtue and vice, let the facts speak for themselves. He should write sub specie aeternitatis—like Zeus, looking impartially on Persians, Greeks, and Romans alike. In short—the maxim honored at least nominally from Lucian to Ranke and beyond—"the historian's sole task is to tell the tale as it happened." The "noble dream" of modern scientific historiography was thus already part of the idea of history embodied in the Greek canon established by Herodotus, Thucydides, their epigones, their critics, their readership, and their posterity, including the likes of us.[139]

3

Roman Foundations

History concerns deeds remote from the memory of our age.
— Cicero

Roman historical writing developed out of a deep and to some extent parochial sense of tradition and location.[1] The Romans measured time "from the founding of the city" (*ab urbe condita,* the title of Livy's national history), and for them space was centered likewise on the city, with its sacred boundary, the *pomaerium* established by Numa Pompilius, defining the city and marking a frontier defended by the god Terminus, which would be extended eventually to much of the known world.[2] In such terms Roman history was conceived and interpreted by historians and poets and by ordinary citizens, the "fathers" honoring their ancestors and their family-centered religion as well as the senatorial regime which had replaced the quasi-mythical rule of Etruscan kings. This earthly, ethnocentric sense of being and becoming was reinforced by the Roman obsession with property, civic growth, legal order, and finally imperial mastery. There was, of course, an overlay of Hellenism which Romans were never able wholly to escape. As Horace wrote, "Greece, the captive, made her savage victor captive, and brought the arts into rustic Latium."[3] And of these arts, of course, one of the most valuable was the Herodoto-Thucydido-Polybian practice of historical writing.

Archaeolatry

"Obscura est historia romana," Cicero wrote, thinking of the earliest ages of Rome.[4] From the beginning, history was obsessed with beginnings. Archaeolatry began with the poets, who exploited Greek as well as native legends, intermingling gods and kings with the Trojan émigrés and constructing interesting genealogies. But poetic origins, the "zero point of history," elude us; memory and even imagination fail us; and as Michel Serres writes, "The *Quellenforschung* never ceases."[5] Livy and his sources recount these legends without trying seriously to discredit them. "It is the privilege of antiquity to mingle divine things with human," Livy declared at the outset of his history. Yet, while limiting his vision to the human horizons defined by written sources, he, like many of his colleagues, could not refrain from commenting on prehistory and the "divine things" concealed therein.

The poets and writers of history were not the only ones to pursue archaeolatrous inquiry into the obscurities and mysteries of the Roman past and to try to excavate the accomplishments of the fathers and founders of Rome. Authors of all sorts, but especially the antiquarians and the jurists, carried on this national enterprise. Unlike the historiographers, however, these scholars were not concerned with reporting the words and deeds for purposes of pleasant narrative. The antiquarians investigated the language and culture of bygone and often forgotten ages, while the object of study of the jurists was the residues of actions preserved collectively in ancient customs, laws, and institutions.[6] Yet these scholars, too, were, in their own way, students of Roman foundations, at least as reflected in verbal behavior and juridical states of mind; and from a modern perspective they, too, deserve attention as participants in a longer and richer tradition of historical studies.

Like the writers of history, the Roman jurists believed that understanding required a return to the "origins," and so the second century B.C. jurisconsult Gaius thought that, to interpret the ancient laws, and notably those of the Twelve Tables, he had to "trace the law of the Roman people from the very beginning of the city" (*ab urbis initiis*), for "the most important part of anything is its beginning."[7] Here Gaius used the term *principle* (*principium*), equivalent to the Greek *arche,* which signified cause as well as origin. This was the premise, too, of the handbook of Gaius's contemporary Pomponius, who was also convinced that "we must account for the origin and development of law itself." Fragments of both of these classic works of Roman legal science were placed in the very first book of Justinian's *Digest,* in a place of honor second only to that of the philosophy of law and justice. Pomponius went on to offer a survey of Roman legal history parallel to the standard accounts of Livy, Dionysius of Halicarnassus, and other historians.

Pomponius's interpretation was more legalistic and quite without the literary pretensions of historical writers or their fascination with colorful legends. He contented himself with a brief mention of Romulus's legislative work and a characterization of the expulsion of the kings as the work of a "tribunician law." Pomponius also accepted the tradition which sent a committee of ten (Decemviri) on a mission to Greece to consult about the law of the Twelve Tables, which succeeded this early period of "uncertain law and custom" and which was supplemented, thenceforth, by the "actions at law" and the "civil law" of the jurists. The later social conflict was described by Pomponius in terms of a fourth source of law, that is, the decree of the commons (*plebis scita*), which arose in opposition to the senatorial laws (*senatus consulta*). To this were added the "honorary law" (*jus honorarium*) of the magistrates and the praetors, later of the constitutions of the emperors and the decisions of the jurists; and Pomponius described at length the great tradition of Roman jurists, of which he was a member. Such, with other details of administration and legal procedures, was the framework within which legal scholars told the story of Rome's rise from the founding of the city to political and juristic grandeur.

Antiquarianism was a natural companion of the disintegration of "the old Roman life," in the opinion of T. R. Glover.[8] It was perhaps nostalgia that drew Latin scholars to the question of origins, but their work was much more miscellaneous and unfocused than that of the practical-minded jurists. The model of Roman erudition was the incredibly prolific M. Terentius Varro, the most learned of all Romans, according to Quintilian. Having studied in Athens in the eclectic academy of the first century B.C., Varro also had a public career, including service under both Pompey and Caesar, before he retired to a life of study and writing, producing hundreds of volumes in science, law, and philosophy, as well as historical studies, and furnishing at least the raw materials for history. Most influential was his treatise *On the Latin Language,* which included learned and sometimes fanciful explorations in etymology and ancient vocabulary and the problem of the conflict between individual expression and collective usage.[9] Varro's *Antiquities,* which employed archival sources, was also devoted to the knowledge of "things both divine and human," a formula (*res humanae* and *res divinae*) that from Cicero's time on was applied to the notion of human wisdom (*sapientia*) in general.[10]

Another investigator of, among other things, ancient wisdom and origins — divine, human, and natural — was Aulus Gellius, a second century B.C. scholar, who studied philosophy in Athens and rhetoric in Rome and devoted himself to compiling a commonplace book based on his book learning, "rolling and unrolling many a scroll" in order to collect "flowers of history."[11] Aulus Gellius was a self-admitted pedant, and his work, the *Attic Nights* (so called because he began it in a Greek country place), treated grammar, antiquities, history, biography, philosophy, law, customs, textual criticism, literary criticism, and anecdotes about authors and friends, such as his colleague Favorinus, whom he often quotes.[12] The work, arranged in brief fragments, was a miscellany — a "paradoxography" — defiantly presented without literary ambition, philosophical depth, or even logical order; it was not intended to instruct but only, as "first fruits" of unfocused reading, to point the way thereto. Yet he claimed to despise pointless erudition, aiming at only (according to the proto-Socratic maxim of Homer) "whate'er of good and ill has come to you at home."[13]

Aulus Gellius's scribbling did hinge in many ways on an unusual antiquarian curiosity. This is evident from his citations from Ennius, Cato, and other authors now lost to view, as well as from Herodotus, Thucydides, Sallust, and other classics, and from his concern with questions of chronology, such as the dating of Homer, Hesiod, and Solon and the relative ages of Hellanicus, Herodotus, and Thucydides, who "enjoyed glory at almost the same time, and did not differ greatly in age."[14] It is illustrated even more conspicuously by his sensitivity to language and its use and abuse. To some extent this is just the pedant's or literary artist's concern for correct style (the errors to be found in even the best authors and dislike of "loquacity" and improper words), but Gellius also shows a remarkable sensitivity to the changes in language over time. For literary expression this merely suggested the rule that, while one might indeed venerate ancient ideals, one should not try to ape their linguistic usage: "Live by all means according to the manners of the past, but speak in the language of the present."[15] But for historical scholarship this also meant recovering the precise meaning of ancient words and their correct etymologies, which even Varro was known to mistake.[16] This was the basis of Gellius's philological researches, which attempted to restore the lost meanings of terms such as *proletarius,* which Ennius as well as the law of the Twelve Tables had employed but which in the course of time and other legislation had become obsolete.[17] For this reason, he explained, the Twelve Tables seemed obscure to modern readers: "For long lapse of time has rendered old words and customs obsolete, and it is in the light of those words and customs that the sense of the laws is to be understood."[18]

Aulus Gellius was deeply read in the early chronicles of Greece and Rome before the Punic wars, and he had a good sense of what distinguished the genre of history, though he sets this down, characteristically, in the words of another author. Sempronius Asellio distinguished between annals, for which correct dating was enough (and the smaller scale record called "diary"), and true history, in which "one should also show with what purpose and for what reasons things were done."[19] Moreover, this distinction was a political and a philosophical one, for as Sempronius went on to observe, "annals cannot in any way make men more eager to defend their country, or more reluctant to do wrong." Elsewhere, Gellius puzzled over the question of the priority of moral and political obligations, but he had no doubt that such wisdom was to be found in the sort of reading that made up the *Attic Nights*, although he did not offer a final solution. The same went for questions of law, in which history showed a decrease in the severity of early lawgivers like Draco, in contrast to the Roman fathers.[20]

The Roman historiographical canon as we know it begins most directly with Livy, the founder of histories (*historiae conditor*), as Cicero called him, but there was an extensive Greek prelude and Latin prehistory to his foundational work. The work of Timaeus in the early third century, universal in scope, touched on Italian affairs, while the various historical studies of national traditions — Hellenica, Persica, Egyptica, and especially Sicilica — served as possible models for pre-Livian historical writing on which Livy himself drew; and then of course Polybius featured the Roman success story in his survey of universal history. As Virgil worked in the shadow of the Homeric poems, so Livy worked under the influence of a vast historical literature, much of which is lost, preserved only in fragments taken for the most part from citations in historical works which the vagaries of literary and paleographical fortune have permitted to survive.

The acknowledged father of Roman history is the third century B.C. senator Fabius Pictor, who (like Livy) wrote a history from the founding of the city, though his *archeologia* (like that of Thucydides) was mainly a prelude to contemporary events and in any case survives only in fragments. Fabius — "most ancient of writers," according to Livy — was a member of the illustrious *gens Fabii*, which claimed a pedigree going back to the time of Romulus, and no doubt he drew on these family traditions.[21] He apparently wrote in a spirit of national propaganda, or at least bias, for which he was criticized a generation later by Polybius. Yet Fabius decided to write in Greek and, following Herodotean and Thucydidean precedent, turned, in his own way, from poetic fancy and mere pious ancestor worship to attitudes of historical curiosity and criticism. "If you and I read and occasionally write history," Momigliano has declared, "we owe this habit to a Roman who decided to write history in the Greek manner between circa 215 and 200 B.C."[22]

The first Latin historian of consequence — the true Herodotus of Roman historiographical tradition — was Marcus Porcius Cato the Elder, who was a soldier, statesman, and eventually censor as well as author of the *Origines,* which also traced the history of the city, for the first time in Latin, from its founding. Notoriously, Cato was an archconservative, champion of the old ways, agrarian habits, and military virtues that underlay Rome's rise to power in the Punic wars. Writing a generation after Fabius Pictor, he begins the tradition of antiquities and pursues a Herodotean interest in geography, customs, and national culture. In his antiquarian efforts Cato went beyond conventional sources; although he had little respect for the pontifical annals, he made use, for example, of the traditional banquet songs in praise of famous men — those *carmina* on which B. G. Niebuhr was to base his own attempts at antiquarian reconstruction.[23] Cato included speeches, including some of his own, in his narrative. But his horizons were broad, he admitted Hellenic influence on early Roman history, and he contributed to the project of comparative chronology by trying to correlate the Olympiadic dating of Greek history (from 776) with conventional Roman counting from the Founding of the City (753).

The most important of pre-Livian authors were the first century B.C. historians Julius Caesar and Gaius Sallustius Crispus, who raised Latin history — in the military and political mode of Thucydides — to a high literary art.[24] Both devoted themselves to contemporary history. Writing dramatically and somewhat self-promotingly (though from a third-person standpoint) on the civil and Gallic wars, Caesar identified the glorious imperial mission of Rome with his own career, fortune, and fate. Just after the murder of Caesar (44 B.C.) and the execution of Cicero (43), Sallust wrote, even more self-servingly than Caesar, first a stirring account of the conspiracy of Cataline against the Roman state twenty years earlier, next a narrative of the war with Jugurtha, and finally, on a larger scale, his unfinished Roman *Histories* (78–60 B.C.), only fragments of which survive.

Sallust took a high view of his historiographical calling: "Writing history is a difficult job: in the first place because what you put down has to correspond exactly to the facts; and secondly because if you permit yourself to criticize any wrongdoing, most of your readers will think that you are malevolent, or even envious."[25] Though linked to traditions of rhetoric and moral philosophy, this formula insists on the correlation between words and deeds (*dicta* and *facta*) and anticipates, as the statement of Lucian does, the premises of the self-styled scientific history of Ranke and his school.

Whether voluntarily or not, Sallust retired from politics and offered an unfavorable contrast between corrupt public life in his age and the impartial writing of history (*memoria rerum gestarum*). He lamented the disorder of his

age: "For harmony makes small states great, while discord destroys the greatest empires."[26] More generally, and playing upon the old *res-verba* and *vita
activa–vita contemplativa* topoi, Sallust contrasted the life of the mind with
the life of action, the divine with the animal aspects of human nature, and the
memorable qualities of the Greeks with those of the Romans.[27] Founded by
the Trojans, Rome, according to Sallust, had fought usurping enemies in defense of herself and her "constitution founded upon law" (*imperium legiti-
mum*); then the Roman fathers had made a second founding by replacing the
kings, who held first title to sovereignty (*nomen imperi*), with a republic. In all
this energetic action, however, the Romans failed to make a suitable record of
their achievements, whereas the less glorious deeds of the Athenians were
made immortal by the genius of their writers. It was to remedy this neglect that
Sallust quit politics to take up his pen. It may also be remarked that, Sallust's
vivid style and incisive judgments left an unequaled imprint on medieval
historiography — Thucydides and Tacitus being largely unknown before the
sixteenth century.[28]

The Roman poet Lucretius, a somewhat older contemporary of Sallust,
was also repelled by the political strife and moral decay of the Caesarean-
Ciceronian age, and he responded even more bitterly, if indirectly. For Lucretius, who introduced the philosophy of Epicurus to the Latin world, "the
nature of things" consisted in nothing more than "atoms and the void," and
he carried this reductionist mode of thought into his analysis of the human
sphere. Piety begins, famously, with the "fear of god," and Lucretius wanted to
eradicate this fear — and with it myth, superstition, and the sort of piety based
on credulity and self-abasement — on all levels of experience. He was also
interested in the question of human origins, at least in an abstract and conjectural way, and again he would have nothing to do with the unnatural and the
supernatural.

Concerning human history, too, Lucretius's vision was a purely naturalistic
one. The races of mortal men (there were no immortals) emerged from a state
of nature to protect themselves with "huts and skins and fire," which furnished
a hearth for the family and its natural agenda of procreation.[29] Next came
social intercourse with neighbors and the rude beginnings of speech, which,
replacing gestures, likewise had natural origins. For nature was ever the
teacher of humankind in its progress toward civility, the building of states, and
the pursuit of wealth, followed by the excesses of feuding and warring. "It
would come then in the end to the dregs of uttermost disorder," Lucretius
wrote, "each man seeking for himself empire and sovereignty."[30] Next, laws
were framed, religions established, and all the arts and sciences of civilization
devised, until, Lucretius concludes, the "nature of [social] things reached their

highest point of development."[31] This general theory of history, which clashed with both classical myth and Judeo-Christian providentialism, was to have an extraordinary fortune in modern secularist thought after Poggio's discovery of a manuscript of the *De rerum natura* in the early fifteenth century. Among others, Vico and Gibbon invoked Lucretius's vision of prehistory.[32]

On the very day of Lucretius's death, so the story goes, the poet Virgil assumed the toga of manhood; and Virgil was not without appreciation of the philosophical poet — associating him perhaps with his famous aphorism, "Fortunate is he who understands the nature of things."[33] Virgil, too, had a vision of history, though a more local and particular one, poetically playing Livy to Lucretius's universal historian. Compared with the Greeks, the Romans had been culturally deprived in their literary heritage, lacking not only a Herodotus and a Thucydides (at least until Sallust) but also a Homer. Virgil more than made up for this deficiency; he did so, however, not at the beginning but rather at a very late stage of national tradition. His poetry was not naive but sentimental (in Schiller's famous formula), and what he offered was not a primal source of myth and cultural ethos but only a sophisticated and ironic summing up of the story of Roman origins, in pious contrast to the crude and materialistic tale told by Lucretius. Nonetheless, Virgil, no less than Livy, provided an expression of national pedigree and tradition and of the fabulous aspects of history which prosaic scholars felt, and still feel, obliged to report, if not to believe.

For Virgil, writing in a prophetic as well as historical mode, Rome had a mission and a spiritual continuity that extended from Aeneas to Augustus and beyond. Invoking his own muse (Calliope, not Clio), Virgil sang of the prophecy of Juno, protector of the Trojans and the new nation — "a people, kings of broad realms and proud in war" — which would spring from Trojan blood.[34] Virgil's poem follows the adventures of Aeneas, but on another level it tells the story related in more prosaic terms by Polybius, Livy, and others, which fulfilled Juno's unprecedented gift to the Romans, limited in neither time nor space: "For these," she declares, "I set neither bounds nor periods of empire; dominion without end I have bestowed."[35] Thus was born, in its first form, *Roma aeterna*, sustained by equally eternal virtues, beginning with that piety which Lucretius had despised. Yet (in another famous formula) with unlimited power came responsibility: "Remember, O Romans, you keep universal rule over nations in these ways: by maintaining peace by means of law, by doing justice to the lowly, by bringing down the haughty."[36] Thus Rome was destined to excel in peace as well as war, as her immortal laws, which outlasted the empire, would demonstrate. In another incarnation this formula suggested (for example, to Valla, Machiavelli, and Vico) a model of historical explanation for the whole life of a civilization. All this offered further opportunities for the muses of poetry and history as well as museless philosophy, whose devotees also speculated about this tradition and about questions of origins in general.

Livy

The double visage of Janus, employed to suggest the contrasting perspectives of Herodotus and Thucydides, figures also in the opening pages of Livy's great history of Rome. The second king, Numa Pompilius, founded the temple devoted to Janus, porter of heaven and (also Numa's doing) namesake of the first month of the year. Numa did this "as an index of peace and war, that when open it might signify that the nation was in arms, that when closed all the peoples round about were pacified."[37] Only "twice since Numa it had been closed," Livy added: once at the end of the First Punic War and again after the battle of Actium (31 B.C.), when Octavian, Augustus to be, "brought about peace on land and sea."

For the historian Livy, too, the door of the temple was mainly open, and his work was dominated by military action, though he also treated matters of political and institutional history. Toga and sword — arms and the man, the fighters and the founders — these were the twin themes of Livy's vast narrative, and to this extent he belongs in the historiographical train of Thucydides rather than of Herodotus. Not for Livy were digressions about customs and culture, nor indeed speculations about underlying social or economic factors. His was l'histoire événementielle, full of people and dramatic action, and of course moral judgments thereon. Livy acknowledged larger forces, but these, too, were moral in character, especially the qualities and virtues which became abstract agents accounting for Roman successes on land and sea, in peace and war, at home and abroad, for Livy's present and for posterity.

Born in Padua (the ancient Patavium), Titus Livius had a good education in philosophy and especially rhetoric, which he may have practiced professionally, and came to Rome, where he was at work on his history by about 27 B.C. That was just about the time that Octavian took the title of "Augustus" and perhaps two years after Virgil had begun his *Aeneid,* poetic sibling to Livy's prosaic creation,[38] which Livy likewise began with the conceit of entreating the god for the success of his extraordinary labors, based on vast reading in both archival sources (the *annales maximi, senatusconsulti,* etc.) and secondary works by Cato, Fabius Pictor, and of course the Greeks, especially Polybius.[39] Livy's lifework — *Ab Urbe condita* (From the Founding of the City) — covered four and a half centuries of Roman history in 142 books, from one storied founder (King Romulus) to another (Augustus Caesar).[40] Of these, despite Renaissance rumors of "lost decades" still to be found, only a quarter have survived (Books I–X and XXI–XLV), not counting fragments and abridgments.

Unlike Herodotus, Livy was no traveler; unlike Thucydides, he was without military or political experience. He was a professional researcher and writer, and an incredibly prolific one at that. Like Herodotus, he was interested in origins, but he did not concern himself seriously with foreign customs and cultural matters, except for Roman myths. Although, like Thucydides, he focused on political and military history, he did not try to penetrate to social and economic causes or conditions, his gaze being fixed on individuals and on moral and political questions, especially those individual virtues and republican values which underlay Rome's rise to greatness. Hatred of kingship, respect for the law, piety, concord, and military discipline — these were the enduring conservative qualities, abounding in early ages, which Livy chronicled, celebrated, and found consolation in, and whose decline, in his own time, he deplored.

Livy began with the earliest origins of this "city, founded for eternity," as well as the traditions that had preserved the facts and legends of those obscure but wholesome times — hypostatized and idealized as "antiquity" — in which things human and divine were mixed.[41] Livy distinguished between fables of poetic provenance and true history based on monuments and, concerning the former, left it to the reader to judge. He believed in prodigies and portents, and while Rome was made by men, he acknowledged that the Fates must have been present at its birth. He had no doubt about the Trojan origins of Rome, but some traditions were too remote to trace ("Obscura est historia romana"). Whether the initial confrontation between Aeneas and King Latinus brought war or peace, for example, the twofold tradition (*duplex fama*) did not permit Livy to conclude.

Like Herodotus, then, Livy professed good intentions with respect to the truth, sometimes affirming the reality of an action (*est*), sometimes his belief therein (*credo*), sometimes only the rumor or report of its happening (*dicitur, traditur, fama est*).[42] In any case he aimed to tell colorful, meaningful, and useful stories; and so he did, though they were often inaccurate or confused in chronology. Much of the fortune of Livy's own text is the story of errors found and deplored by critics. Macaulay, with his high regard for Thucydides and no doubt speaking for many readers, thought him indifferent to truth, caring only for picturesque effect and "the honor of his country."[43]

Livy was concerned not only with "arms and the man" (of the moment) but also with morals and the men (of many ages), following in this the social vision of Ennius, for whom "the Roman state rests on its ancient customs and its men."[44] As Cicero wrote (citing Cato), Rome had a different provenance than the states of Greece: "Our nation was established, on the other hand, not by the genius of one man but of many, not in one lifetime but over many centuries and ages."[45] Yet of these social traditions there were founders, (*conditores*), and Livy's focus was above all on the masculine agents of foundation — the fathers who had created Rome, the great families making up the people, and the senate ruling the republic. *Paterpatria, paterfamilias, patres conscripti* were the epithets given to the virtuous warriors, property holders, and statesmen forming the heart and soul of the Roman state, whose fame, fortune, and accomplishments Livy traced from their mythical and moral beginning to their historical and political consummation and incipient decline.[46]

Livy assigned to Romulus the formation of many parts of the structure of the Roman state, including religion and the rules of law, although these were no doubt later and less calculated products. However, Livy was not prepared to doubt either the creative role of Romulus or his divine origin, both of which underlay his "wisdom in founding the city and in strengthening it by warlike and peaceful measures."[47] He showed a similar reverence for Numa Pompilius, whom the Romans chose as their next king and who gave the city, "founded by force of arms, a new foundation in laws, statutes, and observances," and (as mentioned earlier) established the temple of Janus to mark the twofold basis of the Roman state.[48] Like Romulus, Numa attended to religious matters, especially auguries and rites to propitiate the dead; but Livy refused to credit the anachronistic story that Numa had derived his wisdom from the teachings of Pythagoras, who lived much later and in any case spoke a different tongue.

The first stage of Roman history was the period of the kings, ending with Tarquinius the Proud, who was excellent in war but unjust and deceitful in peace. Following Fabius Pictor, who was the earliest source, Livy tells of Tarquin's accomplishments, including the building of the temple to Jupiter on the Capitoline, the Circus, and the Cloaca Maxima, and the establishing of colonies, but also his domestic crimes, most notably the debauching of Lucretia, chaste wife of Brutus, who committed suicide. In revenge for this offense, Brutus, Tarquin's brother-in-law, led a movement against the king and finally managed to send him into exile. So ended the monarchy in Rome as well as the first book of Livy's work, which turns its attention, in the next book, to the republic and the "new liberty" of the Roman people.

In the new age, which represented still another founding, the Romans swore never again to suffer a king. Under Brutus's leadership the annual magistracies were formed and the "conscript fathers," who had been decimated by Tarquin, were increased to the number of 300 in order to strengthen the senate and to insure the loyalty of the plebs. Livy then carries forward, in annalistic fashion (following the Roman calendrical system), the story of the Roman Republic, its heroes and villains, its military victories and party strife, its political advances and social conflicts, and the plagues and portents accompanying these events as well as the moral and political qualities which sustained and drove the Roman people throughout its history. Livy continues his stories in Book III, indicating, in connection with a possible revolt by the Latin town of Antium (459 B.C.), his concern for accuracy: "However, I should not venture to state this as a fact, as there is no mention of it in the older chroniclers."[49]

But Livy is more indulgent in his treatment of legend and tradition. Thus, describing the conflict between the senate and tribunes and appointment of the decemvirs, he describes the legendary commission sent to Athens in 451 to consult Solon about the laws of the Twelve (for Livy, only ten) Tables, "which still today remain the fountainhead of public and private law, running clear under the immense and complicated superstructure of modern legislation."[50] In Book IV he tells the story of Furius Camillus, brutal conqueror of Veii and four-time dictator, and makes him into another founder of Rome.[51] Camillus is given several dramatic speeches, one exhorting the Romans to resist the terrible Gallic invasion (390) and not desert their eternal city. And so they did — with the help of their destiny, the octogenarian Camillus, and the Capitoline geese.

The first pentad of Livy's history was devoted to what the Greeks called archaeology, "covering matters which were obscure both because of their great antiquity, like objects perceived in the far distance, and because in those days there were few written records, the only reliable means of preserving the memory of past events."[52] Moreover, the few records that were kept, such as the pontifical annals, had been destroyed by fire. Starting with Book VI (containing another preface for the second pentad), true history replaced prehistory, and monuments were built which still stood in Livy's day. Coming to the war with Carthage (Book XXI), he could finally claim to excel his Greek predecessors, since this conflict, more than the Persian or even Peloponnesian wars, was truly "the most memorable of all that were ever waged." Yet Livy continued to rely on these same predecessors and to tell his stories with an eye rather more to literary effect than to historical accuracy as he pursued the moral and political themes which preoccupied him in the age of a monarchy restored.

Livy's history is usually read as a chain of portraits and stories, but in his case, as in those of Herodotus, Thucydides, and others, formalist scholars have seen larger structures. In particular Livy's text seems to display a cyclical pattern, with recurring founders and crises.[53] This is in part the result of his didactic motive, which finds in the great figures of the past—the *conditores* and *maiores* and other possessors of ancient *nobilitas*—paradigms of behavior and moral as well as political authority, and which likewise links the past with the present and gives continuity to Roman history from origins to maturity, from the founding of the city to its claims to "empire without end" (*imperium sine fine*, in Virgil's phrase) in Livy's own time. Whatever Livy's weaknesses as a historian, whatever his ideological excesses and credulity, the destiny of his work was to offer, to readers of many different ages, tastes, and cultures, the archetype of a national history.

Livy's work also survived in the popular summary made in the second century A.D. by Lucius Annaeus Florus, who was even more enthusiastic in his praise of Roman imperial success through the interplay between *virtus* and *fortuna*. What Florus added to Livy was the imaginative periodization of Roman history based on the analogy between the state and individual life, according to which the childhood (*infantia*) lasted from the period of the kings to the beginning of the republic, followed by adolescence (*adulescentia*), mature manhood (*iuventus imperii et quasi robusta maturitas*) down to the time of Caesar Augustus, and finally old age (*senectus*) in Florus's own time. This conceit was later followed by other historians, such as Claude de Seyssel in the sixteenth century, who applied it to the French monarchy. In general, Florus declared, so extensive was Roman history "that those who read of their exploits are learning the history, not only of a single people, but of the human race."[54] This might be taken as a motto for many Eurocentric writers in the Western historiographical canon.

Tacitus and Ammianus Marcellinus

Livy was followed in this project by other Latin historians, of whom, in the opinion of Macaulay and Taine as well as Ronald Syme, Tacitus was by far the greatest.[55] Tacitus had a successful political career, which took him through the regular chain of offices from quaestor to consul, and the military experience of (as many scholars think) commanding a legion. He was also adept at oratory, but for him this was an art more appropriate for republican government than for the constricted politics of imperial Rome. After his dialogue on oratory and a laudatory biography of his father-in-law, Cnaeus Julius Agricola, he turned to the more private and perhaps more honest art of history, in which he could write without passion or partiality (*sine ira et studio*). "The consular orator," as Syme puts it, "was hankering after history," and even there he strove to avoid rhetorical excess: "In short, Sallust rather than

Livy."[56] Tacitus's two masterpieces are the *Histories,* which covered the years of his own youth down to the death of Domitian, and the *Annals,* which was a richly detailed account of Roman history from A.D. 14 to 68 (of eighteen books, or three hexads, only Books I–IV and XI–XVI and some fragments remain).

The theme of all of Tacitus's writings was Rome in decline after a glorious past founded on republican virtues and Catonian discipline. This attitude of "Silver Age cynicism" Tacitus shared with contemporaries like Suetonius and especially Lucan, whose *Pharsalia* was a radical lamentation in poetical form of Roman vices and decadence and the "fall of liberty."[57] In Tacitus's *Dialogue on Oratory,* written under the repressive rule of Domitian, this theme is expressed as a contrast between the modern orator, who studies the theory of rhetoric and declaims to no purpose, and the ancient, who, "like a soldier equipped at all points going to the battle-field, enters the forum equipped with every learned accomplishment."[58] According to the "modernist" Messala, the decline of oratory comes "not from dearth of men, but from the indolence of the young, the carelessness of parents, the ignorance, and neglect of old discipline. The evils which first began in Rome soon spread through Italy, and are now diffusing themselves into the provinces."[59] The result of this first moral and then political decline was popular unrest and conflict and finally (the inference is) the current predicament of liberty lost and tyranny ascendant. This was enough to send any honest man into the quieter fields of historiography. "Tacitus's heart, therefore, was with the Republic," as Michael Grant concludes, "but his head was on the side of the imperial present."[60]

Another early work of Tacitus, the *Germania,* pursues the contrast through the old Herodotean genre of ethnographic description. Here Tacitus finds some of the lost virtues of Rome in the customs of the Germans, as yet uncontaminated by other races and uncorrupted by the modern vices of adultery, moneylending, pacifism, and political tyranny. By contrast with the Romans, the Germans took pride in their belligerence and democratic customs — "They choose their kings by birth, their generals for merit."[61] Perhaps they drank too much, and since they had no cities, they might be lacking in social niceties, but "with their virtue protected they live uncorrupted by the allurements of public shows or the stimulant of feastings."[62] The force of Germanic virtue was further demonstrated by the successes of the storied Arminius, defier of Roman authority, whom Tacitus recognized as "the deliverer of Germany."[63] Like his contrast of ancient and modern, Tacitus's portrait of barbarian virtue — idealized and perhaps obsolete as it was — served well to highlight the decadent condition of Roman society in the second century.

Tacitus's historical writings evoked this decadence in more detail. The period covered in his *History,* though not lacking in some examples of virtue, was "rich in disasters, frightful in its wars, torn by civil strife, and even in peace full of horrors."[64] Indeed it was Tacitus's avowed purpose, writing in a Thucydidean mode, to address large questions concerned "not only with the vicissitudes of events, which are often matters of chance, but also with their relations and their causes."[65] Following good classical precedent, Tacitus also noted the portents and prodigies signaling the evil fortune which, reinforced by an unbridled "passion for power," was descending upon imperial Rome.[66] Nor did the influence of eastern religions, such as the nation founded by Moses — "prone to superstition, but hating all religious rites" — then flourishing in Judaea, promise to offset this decline.[67] In this case Tacitus's brief ethnographic sketch was merely a prelude to the Roman suppression of the revolt of the Jews.

In the *Annals,* Tacitus works on a larger canvas. "Rome at the beginning was ruled by kings," he begins — a pregnant phrase which Vico, one of his greatest admirers, would raise to the level of anthropological principle covering all peoples. In a few curt sentences Tacitus summarizes the ups and downs of Roman fortunes to the time of Augustus, which returned violently to the original form of government but not to the foundational virtues on which Roman greatness was built: "Thus," Tacitus characterizes the Augustan achievement, "the State had been revolutionized, and there was not a vestige left of the old sound morality."[68] In a speech to the senate, Augustus's successor, Tiberius, illustrated Tacitus's argument by contrasting the self-control of the ancient Romans with the present condition, in which "the people of Rome is daily at the mercy of uncertain waves and storms."[69] "How ready these men are to be slaves," Tacitus reports Tiberius as exclaiming in Greek. The emperor's solution to these problems was to take over the "substance" of power, leaving only its "shadow" to the senate, so that the Romans were a "people plunged into slavery."[70]

The *History* is a sparkling and "sententious" narrative of deeds and words, but the deeds are often depressing, or horrible, and the words are often empty.[71] "No other writer," according to Syme, "reveals so sharply the double-face of Roman rule."[72] Portraits of good and bad men and women and their efforts, high or criminal minded, are set down in incomparable Tacitean style, but the plot of his story continues to be the downward drift of Rome, characteristically leaving open "the question whether it is fate and unchangeable necessity or chance which governs the revolutions of human affairs."[73] Compared with earlier times, when public affairs were studied and managed by wise men, this modern period of despotism offered little except the wisdom of history writing, which was not only second-hand but also disheartening, con-

cerned as it was with "the merciless biddings of a tyrant, incessant prose-
cutions, faithless friendships, the ruin of innocence," and other topics of a
"wearisome monotony."[74] "Tacitus's real aim," Momigliano concluded, "was
to unmask the imperial rule, in so far as it was government by debasement,
hypocrisy, and cruelty."[75]

Behind this particular Roman trajectory Tacitus also saw a larger human
pattern that shaped history, and this is what Machiavelli, Vico, and others
admired in him. In the beginning humanity lived in a state of innocence and
equality, without shame and guilt but also without constraint. Because of
ambition and violence, however, this state of nature was replaced by despotism and later the rule of law and protection of liberty (referring in particular
to the Twelve Tables), but then societies moved into another cycle of violence,
as social conflict and sedition erupted, and "custom or law there was none."[76]
The reaction was the establishment of further laws, whose proliferation was a
measure of the corruption of the state (*plurimae leges, pessima respublica*),
and this brought the cycle back to despotic rule. In many ways Tacitus's narrative simply filled in these general ethico-political patterns, to which so many
other historians had testified.

Yet the mission of the historian had not changed. It was still commemoration, instruction, and truth telling, or reality facing. In obvious contrast to
Livy, Tacitus professed to tell "no story to excite wonder; I do but relate what I
have heard and what our fathers recorded" (making use, that is, of the archives
of the senate).[77] Beyond that, he explained, "My purpose is not to relate at
length every motion, but only such as were conspicuous for excellence or
notorious for infamy. This I regard as history's highest function, to let no
unworthy action be uncommemorated, and to hold out the reprobation of
posterity as a terror to evil words and deeds."[78] Tacitus also included, besides
the mandatory speeches, some digressions, for example, on spectacles and the
theater under Nero and on the development of the alphabet from Egyptian
hieroglyphs, along with the old legends of Cadmus and the unsuccessful innovations of Claudius. For the most part, however, Tacitus followed, in a Sal-
lustian style honed into a sharper analytical instrument, not the byways of
Herodotean cultural history but rather the Thucydidean model of mainly
contemporary politico-military or (in the Polybian term) "pragmatic," history,
which is the ingredient of modern "Tacitism" fashioned by his Renaissance
admirers.[79]

Tacitus's most direct follower was the "former soldier and a Greek" from
Syrian Antioch, Ammianus Marcellinus, who lived under Christian rule but
who wrote, in Latin and in Rome, from a pagan standpoint.[80] Ammianus's
history covered the period from the accession of the western Emperor Nerva

(A.D. 96) to the death of the eastern Emperor Valens (378). (In contrast to Livy's work, of which only the early sections survive, it is the last eighteen of thirty-one books that are extant, that is, those for which Ammianus was a participant and observer.) At the point when history became contemporary, Ammianus became more selective, "partly to escape the dangers which often attend on truth, and partly to avoid carping criticism of my work by those who feel injured by the omission of insignificant detail."[81] For him, as for Tacitus, "The task of history is to deal with prominent events, not to delve into trivial minutiae," although in fact he was often distracted by the sort of ethnographical digressions which had been characteristic of Herodotean historiography.

In general, Ammianus assumed, history required chronological order and both first- and secondhand evidence. "Using my best efforts to find out the truth," he writes, "I have set out, in the order in which they occurred, events which I was able to observe myself or discover by thorough questioning of contemporaries who took part in them."[82] The underlying and sometimes visible theme of his work, like that of Tacitus, is the decline of Rome, arising from both a weakening of the discipline and the intrusion of "barbarians." Even in Rome, "a city destined to endure as long as the human race survives," what was most conspicuous was "riots and taverns and similar sordid subjects," including sorcery, adultery, and "the worst of all disasters," famine, as well as the frivolous and sometimes brutal life-style of the Romans, who hated learning but liked to read their Juvenal.[83] Such disorder was only magnified by the persecutions and trials for magic and treason, especially under the savage Emperor Valentinian.

The empire itself fared better than its capital, especially under the rule of the Emperor Julian, whom Ammianus much admired, though not uncritically, and who was arguably "the historical inspiration behind" this historian.[84] Julian respected the old Roman virtues, lived a life of remarkable self-discipline, and, like Julius Caesar himself, combined laborious authorship with adventurous generalship. Ammianus, whose account of Julian's career and personality was followed approvingly by Gibbon, described the emperor's military successes both in the East, where he penetrated as far as Assyria, and in the West, where he crossed the Rhine and fought the Franks as well as the Gauls. Ammianus, who was not above reporting omens and portents, did not ascribe such success only to military virtue, for he also believed, as a moderate pagan, in a general sort of divine influence. Thus Julian's victory over the barbarians at Strasbourg came about because, Ammianus wrote, "the favour of a beneficent providence was on our side."[85]

Like Herodotus and the Tacitus of the *Germania*, Ammianus possessed an inquiring mind that went beyond Roman concerns, the horizons of the *urbs aeterna* (in Ammianus's phrase), to various foreign cultures — Egyptians, Persians, Gauls, and Franks, to name few of the contacts produced by imperial expansion. Ammianus was discriminating in his judgments about these cultural traditions, entertaining prejudice against the Germanic tribes but admiring the Persians and acknowledging Egypt's priority as a source of occult knowledge. For Ammianus, the Christians, too, were an alien form of life, but he admired the fortitude of their martyrs and supported the old Roman policy of toleration for all religious sects that did not pose a threat to government.

History and Rhetoric

From the very beginning, history, bound to writing, came into alliance with rhetoric. Herodotus designed his work to be delivered before an audience, but the principles of effective oratory carried over into literate culture, too. Herodotus, Thucydides, and all their successors also made liberal use of speeches in the effort to give meaning and value to their explanatory narrative. It was this focus on policy, motives, and deliberation that, for Werner Jaeger, made Thucydides a "political philosopher" and, for Lucian, made Thucydides a historiographical model, illustrating both the gift of political understanding and the intellectual achievement of literary power.[86] Latin historians, of course, followed suit in their reliance on rhetoric to transmute the raw materials of history and memory into a readable narrative, or meaningful analysis, and in this way to give utility as well as pleasure to readers.

The style wars between pretentious, bombastic eloquence and restrained, succinct diction — Asianism versus Atticism, in the Hellenistic period — intruded also into historical writing, with Sallust and especially Tacitus representing the standards of conciseness in contrast to the more opulent and colorful style of Livy and to some degree Ammianus Marcellinus, not to mention Cicero.[87] Yet for all their professions of truth, none of these historians were "objective" in a modern sense; all were eager to celebrate the moral virtues which had made Rome great and to decry the decline which was threatening its eternal claims; and so all were judgmental in their own ways, and not least Tacitus, whose "sententious" inferences belied the terse restraint of his narrative. These literary strategies, indulgences, and discipline were essential both to the composition and to the reception of the works of the classical historians, and this is what makes the *ars rhetorica* fundamental to the *ars historica,* in the sense of the practice as well as the theory of history.

Cicero was a philosopher of eclectic range, whose highest praise was reserved for the art of rhetoric and the role of the orator. In his dialogue *On Oratory,* in which Caesar himself put in an appearance, rhetoric was represented as requiring, more than religion or law, the most encyclopedic combination of learning and skills, so that "the complete history of the past [*omnis antiquitas*] and a store of precedents must be retained in the memory."[88] If the orator needed a knowledge of history for his craft, he was also the best prepared for writing history, which Cicero famously defined in this context as "the witness of time, the light of truth, the life of memory, the mistress of life, the messenger of antiquity."[89] Elsewhere he offered the formula "history concerns deeds remote from the memory of our age."[90] These commonplaces have been endlessly repeated over the centuries and have become inseparable from the concealed premises and larger claims made by historians for their craft.

Of course the foundation of historical writing — its "first law" (*prima lex historiae*), endlessly repeated by later historical writers — was "that an author must not dare to tell anything but the truth," Cicero stated. "And its second that he must make bold to tell the whole truth."[91] The standard of truth was also what distinguished history from its sister art, poetry, whose stress was rather on the pleasure that it gave — although admittedly Herodotus filled his historical work with fables.[92] For history, there must be no sign of partiality or malice. At the beginning, for the Greeks and Latin authors like Fabius Pictor and Cato, this sufficed. "For history began as a mere compilation of annals," which in Rome were set down by the priests in the *Annales Maximi,* and the first historians hardly surpassed such simple and unreflective chronicles.

In the course of time, however, eloquence was joined to this rudimentary effort "to preserve the general traditions," as illustrated first by Herodotus, "father of history" as Cicero calls him elsewhere, and then by Thucydides, who, though he was not public speaker, "easily surpassed everyone else in dexterity of composition."[93] In this mature stage of historiography chronological arrangement and geographical context were also needed, as was consideration of the causes and consequences of actions, as well as portrayal of the actors — all this accomplished in a smooth narrative which avoided the sharpness of judicial rhetoric and which was to be learned from the study of rhetoric. Unfortunately — the old lament recurs — the national past of Rome, unlike that of the Greeks, was deficient in histories, especially those concerning the early ages; and Cicero had one of his interlocutors inquire why he, Cicero, the most prolific of Latin authors, did not try his hand at this genre of writing. An interesting idea, Cicero agreed, but he explained that his other works were all tossed off in the "leftovers" of time, whereas the enterprise of history was a different sort of rhetorical labor, requiring unbroken concentration. In any case his preference would be to write not of these neglected early ages but rather of his own time, so that, like Thucydides, he might write of events in which he himself, and friends like Pompey, took part.

Another famous Roman public figure, rhetorician, and scholar who was tempted by the calling of Clio was Pliny the Younger, friend of Tacitus and Suetonius and nephew of the famous author of the *Natural History*. Like Cicero, Pliny also carried on a wide correspondence, and in one of his letters he reflected on the possibility of taking up the writing of history.[94] He admitted to one private motive, which was to follow the example of his uncle (whose lost history was praised by Quintilian), as well as a desire for "spreading the fame of others along with one's own." Unlike poetry and oratory, he remarked, history had an interest apart from its stylistic qualities, having "its attraction for anyone who can enjoy small talk and anecdote." Properly understood, however, it was oratory that traded in the trivial and history in "profound truths and the glory of great deeds," so as to be worthy of Thucydides' vision of a "lasting possession" for writing rather than a "prize essay" for speaking; and for this reason, and because of so many other commitments, Pliny declined to answer this high calling, in which (he wrote in another letter) Tacitus was gaining immortality.[95]

The perfect orator depicted by Cicero was the subject of the great treatise "on the education of the orator" written in the following century by Quintilian, who came from Spain to Rome to follow a career as practicing lawyer, teacher, and founder of the first public school of rhetoric in Rome. In his *De institutione oratoria*, written in his last years, Quintilian summed up the Greek model of education, formed some three centuries earlier, as it had developed in Rome. As a result of this pedagogical vision, the man of words, the orator, and (in his company) the writer approached equality with the man of deeds, the warrior, and the politician — the ideal being a combination of the two. Quintilian also wrote a critique on "the causes of the corruption of rhetoric," which has been lost but which probably treated the technical lapses from classical standards concomitant with political decline.

History had a major role in Quintilian's system of thought, overlapping with rhetoric and contrasting with other arts in a curriculum designed to produce the perfect orator. In an often-cited passage, Quintilian distinguished three forms of narrative: fiction (*fabula*), which is remote from the truth, as in tragedies and poems; realism (*argumentum*), not true but verisimilitudinous, as in comedy; and "thirdly there is the historical narrative, which is an exposition of actual fact" (*historiam, in qua est gestae rei expositio*).[96] On the most basic level both history and rhetoric were essential for correct speech. "Language is based on reason, antiquity, authority, and usage," Quintilian taught, so that reason derives from analogy and etymology (the root, or natural meaning, of a term), antiquity from its own sanctioned and sanctified quality, and authority from orators and historians, usage being limited to contemporary language.[97] Orators can also learn much about the persuasive power of speech by reading the orations devised by historians.[98] According to the Greeks, moreover, the two major departments of literary education were "the art of speaking correctly and the interpretation of authors; the former they call *methodice,* the latter *historice.*"[99] History was therefore tied to the reading of texts and contrasted, for example, with the theoretical methods of an art such as geometry.[100]

As Lucian and others had argued long before, history was distinguished from other sorts of writing — the fictitious narrative of tragedies and the realism, or verisimilitude, of comedies — by being "an exposition of actual fact [*gestae rei expositio*], including the causes of such phenomena as war, rebellion, or pestilence."[101] In contrast to rhetoric, history should be fluid and continuous, not pausing for effects as oratory does.[102] In contrast to poetry, Quintilian added, the force of historical writing was in proportion to its truth, not that history was free from fabulous elements, and indeed in some ways it resembled a "prose poem."[103] This affinity was also seen in the "poetic license" of Greek history and the doubts of historians like Livy about the facts surrounding the founding of Rome; but here the rhetorical devices of *anaskeue* and *kataskeue* — the "topos of critical rejection," in the phrase of Frank Borchart — could be applied in order to refute or to confirm such stories. "Livy for instance," as Quintilian remarked, "is frequently in doubt as to what actually occurred and historians often disagree."[104] It is interesting that the practice of historical criticism and exposure of myth, usually associated with philology and pure scholarship, should have its nominal source in these tropes of ancient rhetoric.

On the writing of history itself, Quintilian expressed opinions about the quality of earlier works, but almost entirely on the basis of style. "Thucydides is compact in texture, ever ready to press forward: Herodotus is pleasant, lucid and diffuse," he wrote. "The former excels in vigour, speeches and the expression of the stronger passions; the latter in charm, conversations and the delineation of the gentler emotions."[105] Quintilian also commented on Theopompus and other lesser lights of Greek historiography. As for the Latins, he continued, he "would not hesitate to match Sallust against Thucydides, nor would Herodotus resent Titus Livius being placed on the same level as himself." Perhaps the greatest of all, Quintilian concluded, was an unnamed contemporary whom posterity would surely celebrate — not Tacitus, who was too young, but probably Fabius Rusticus, who was one of Tacitus's sources, characterized as a new Livy and "the most eloquent of modern historians."[106] (Whatever became of Fabius Rusticus?)

The influence of rhetoric on history, theory as well as practice, reinforced literary values and judgments. In the imperial period, truth remained a formal requirement and the object of commonplace affirmations, but effective communication to a sophisticated readership was the dominant consideration. To this extent the idea of history in late antiquity was not unlike current attitudes emerging in the wake of the "linguistic turn" and the "new rhetoric" of the 1960s, and to that extent the devotees of Clio have strayed in some ways from the original vision and aspirations of Herodotus and Thucydides. But, of course, such literary inclinations and concerns with "discourse" were enduring, or recurrent, features of the Western historiographical canon.

The End of Paganism

Paganism had its own traditions of myth and historiography, and Christianity, with its rise to legitimacy under Constantine, set out to correct and purge the first and to exploit and appropriate the second. According to Christian revisionism, Constantine became the fulfillment of Roman history as well as of the divine plan of Scriptures, and with a new providential goal in place, ecclesiastical affairs became central in historical narrative. The spiritual ideology of the church was henceforth available to the empire, which eventually proclaimed itself to be "holy" as well as "Roman." For Eusebius the achievement of Constantine was not merely a foundation but also a "reformation" of empire and church, which was carried out in imitation of Christ himself.[107]

Paganism, however, which was disestablished but not destroyed by Constantine, did not give up its glorious past without a struggle. The pagan party in Rome staged a comeback with the support of the Emperor Julian, who reopened the temples and tried to revive pagan traditions. Julian's was a lost cause, of course, and he was himself assigned by later historians to the role of "apostate." Yet paganism still informed the religion of the people and still attracted a political following, as the affair of the Altar of Victory illustrated. This altar, which symbolized the glorious Roman past, had been brought from Tarentum to the Roman senate house and decorated (says Gibbon) by the spoils of Egypt. After Constantine, it had been taken down, later restored by Julian, and in 375 removed again by Gratian, perhaps with the encouragement of Ambrose; and a decade later there was a heated debate over the question — and by implication the underlying view of Roman history.

In 384 Senator Symmachus spoke on behalf of restoration and the sacred heritage of the *patria*, "the gods of our fathers, the native gods of Rome," which had for so long presided over the fate of the republic and empire. The response on behalf of the Christians, made by Ambrose, who scorned "the ancient days of chaos" and marveled at "how the world has developed since then, with the gradual invention of the arts and the advances of human history."[108] " 'Tis no disgrace to pass on to better things," Ambrose concluded. This was, as E. K. Rand characterized it, "a plea for progress to match that of Symmachus for tradition." Conservatives always suspect novelty, "but for all that the world moves," declared Ambrose (and here Rand does not blush to insert parenthetically, as a paraphrase, the legendary words of Galileo, "eppur si muove").

Twenty years later Prudentius, in his poem *Contra Symmachum,* reinforced Ambrose's line of argument, and indeed that of Eusebius.[109] Pagan gods led Rome to victory but also to defeat, wrote Prudentius, while the one, true "God, wishing to bring into partnership peoples of different speech and realms of discordant manners, determined that all the civilised world should be harnessed to one ruling power," and so bring a higher world harmony. What pagan Rome did through violence and superstition, the reformed Christian Rome would do through peace and the unity of spirit. Prudentius does indeed seem to speak in the utopian accents of a modern idea of progress — that, say, of Abbé de Saint-Pierre, whose universalist "plan for a perpetual peace," despite its rationalist base, likewise depended on the leadership of the powers that be in alliance with higher ideals. In general, as Jacob Burckhardt argued, the Christianization of the empire was accompanied by the "daimonization of paganism," which had the profoundest effects on historical interpretation.[110]

Yet paganism lived on in a secular way in the religious practices of the people and also in ancient philosophy, which indeed infiltrated Christian theology. Neoplatonism and various forms of syncretism preserved the pagan past; and it was these residues of "Hellenism" that became the target of Justinian's decree of 525, closing offices and schools to pagans and the "contamination" they carried. This decree, wrote J. B. Bury, "sounded the doom of the Athenian schools, which had enjoyed a continuous tradition since the days of Plato and Aristotle."[111] And as Christianity was imposed as the official religion of the state, so the patterns of historical thought and writing became captive to the same ideological and moral commitment.

The Second Rome

Historical writing was continued by the other self-designated Romans, those of the Eastern Empire, which was to persist for over a thousand years after the deposition of the last of the Western emperors, the inappropriately and ironically named Romulus ("Augustulus") — the last Byzantine emperor was, like the first one, sadly, named "Constantine."[112] Byzantine historiography is a complex accumulation, cutting its own channels, which followed and extended those of classical antiquity, but turning also to ecclesiastical history and continuing the Eusebian genre of world chronicle for a millennium and more.[113]

The best known of Ammianus Marcellinus's successors in the East was Procopius, whose works ranged from the polemic of his *Secret History* (Arcana) to his narrative history of the wars of Justinian against the "barbarians" — the Persians, Vandals, and Goths — and the efforts to reconquer Italy and Africa, largely ignoring matters of religion and jurisprudence. Like Herodotus and Thucydides, Procopius was a witness to many of the actions he described; and he followed these classical models, especially Thucydides, in style as well as subject and justification, in order that "time might not overwhelm" the great deeds undertaken in those "times of crisis" and that posterity, finding itself in similar circumstances, might derive benefit from his account.[114] In sharp contrast, shifting from the public to the private sphere, the *Secret History*, which Gibbon called a "satire," was a free-wheeling exposure, from the standpoint of a courtier, of the mismanagement and scandals of the empire under the diabolical Justinian, who was "a moral pervert," and his disgraceful consent, the lustful exhibitionist and former prostitute, Theodora.[115]

Also in the mainstream of Byzantine historiography was Michael Psellus (1018–78), who, though a Christian, wrote his *Chronographia* in a classical style for an elite audience, in contrast to the more popular Christian universal chronicles derived from Eusebius. Psellus, who had a career in the university and in imperial administration, was a herald of an intellectual revival. The previous generation "produced few men of erudition," he complained, and lacked understanding of the "hidden meaning" of Aristotelian doctrines and Platonic allegories, concerning themselves instead with "such mysteries as the Immaculate conception, the Virgin Birth, and metaphysical problems."[116]

Byzantine scholars revered the classical past and, unlike their Western counterparts, continued to appreciate pagan poetry as well as history. In the seventh century Theophylact Simocatta prefaced his history of the Emperor Maurice with an allegorical dialogue between "Queen" Philosophy and her daughter, "History," who had been resurrected and was ready to "stir the lyre of history" under the guidance of philosophy.[117] In his view, poets, who created myths and were reputed to be theologians and prophets, were most admirable, but history also had an important role, which was to be "the common teacher of all men [because] it shows which course to follow and which to avoid as profitless."[118]

The preservation of classical ideals may also be seen in the work of Anna Comnena, whose ornate *Alexiad,* continuing the work of her husband, concerns the life of her father, Emperor Alexius Comnenus (1081–1118), and the events of the First Crusade, of which she was a witness. Time is the destroyer of all temporal things, she wrote, and "the science of History is a great bulwark against this stream of Time."[119] Anna was learned in all the disciplines of antiquity, especially rhetoric and philosophy, with whose help she hoped, in her historical narrative, to avoid both criticism and praise and to please all parties and posterity by rescuing the deeds of Alexius in the time of the First Crusade and at a low point of the declining Eastern Empire. The long tradition of Eastern historiography kept in touch with classical theory and practice and was on the whole superior to the production of Western acholars; but for reasons at once geographical, political, religious, and linguistic, it preserved few ties with its Latin counterpart.

Carrying on Byzantine historical writing from Anna Comnena and her continuators was Niketas Choniates (1155–1215/16), who came from a noble family and had a career in imperial administration. Niketas's work covers the Third Crusade (led first by Frederick Barbarossa) and the Fourth Crusade, leading to the disastrous conquest of Constantinople in 1204 by the "barbarian" Latin crusaders, which sent him into exile. For Niketas, history was "the book of the living" whose purpose was "raising up those long dead" for "the common benefit of mankind," though he lamented his charge as "keeper of such evils" as befell his state and his family.[120] In his ornate and heavily illusive prose Niketas also reported omens, portents, dreams, and prophecies that signaled the misfortunes which he chronicled. "O City, City, eye of all cities!" he cries, invoking Jeremiah and other scriptural verses (as well as classical texts) worthy of the Byzantine tragedy.[121] Gibbon contrasted the historical accounts of the Marshal of Champagne Villehardouin and the Byzantine Senator Niketas on the terrible events of 1204. The crusaders rejoiced in their triumph and, loving gold but hating relics, seized the greatest booty won "since the world was created," while "the Greeks for ever wept over the ruins of their country."[122]

The last historians of the Byzantine Empire lived with the memory of the Latin conquest and the fear of the Turkish one to come. Commenting on the incursions of these new "barbarians" in his day, the fourteenth-century historian Nicephorus Gregoras held them responsible for "terrible events which are worthy of description in the *Iliad* itself."[123] Thus Byzantine historians clung to their ancient Greek traditions, including the literary heritage of Herodotus and Thucydides and the poetic presence of Homer. So Laonikos Chalkokondylas (as Gibbon reported) "most absurdly supposes that Constantinople was sacked by the Asiatics in revenge for the ancient calamities of Troy."[124] By contrast, another Byzantine chronicler, Michael Kritovoulos, turned his sympathies to the Muslims and celebrated the triumphs of Sultan Mehmed II by comparing them to those of Alexander the Great, preserving Greek memory in another antiquarian allusion.

One firsthand witness to this final tragedy of 1453 was George Sphrantzes, a courtier and ambassador under the Palaeologi and later a monk, who wished that he had never been born to see the events of his life. George's *Chronicon minus,* together with the expanded version made a century later by Makarios Melissenos (*Chronicon maius*), gives an account of the fall of empire in the year of creation 6962, according to the Byzantine system of dating. This chronicle quotes the last discourse of the last Byzantine emperor, which Gibbon called "the funeral oration of the Roman empire," but adding that "it smells so grossly of the sermon and the convent" that it was probably the work not of Constantine Palaeologus but of the chronicler.[125] "Our empire was founded by Flavius Constantinus and ended with Constantine Palaeologus," the chronicler concluded. "With our unfortunate city as its capital, the empire of the Romans lasted for 1,143 years, ten months, and four days."[126]

The last significant historian of the Byzantine Empire was Doukas, whose *Historia Turco-Byzantina* opened with a brief chronology from Adam to the first fall of the city in 6712 (A.D. 1204) and then down to the mid-fourteenth-century incursions of the Franks, Genoese, and Turks.[127] In the spirit of Herodotus, Doukas offered descriptions of Turkish customs and religion; but he remained faithful to classical style and even values, invoking fortune (*Tyche*) as the reason (along with the sinfulness of the Byzantines) for the misfortunes of the Roman Empire, repeating the jeremiad of Niketas, "O City, City, head of all cities!" "O body politic! O citizenry! O army! . . ." Yet like Chalkokondyles, Doukas looked forward to a Greek revival when the conquering Turks, he expected, would suffer defeat.

The last centuries of the Byzantine Empire and the Crusades reopened the horizons of Western Europe; although this did not bring the Greeks and Latins closer together in a political or religious way, there was an intellectual reconvergence between Greeks and Latins begun a century before the fall of Constantinople, including the heritage of Greek literature, philosophy, and the theory and practice of history cultivated during the Palaeologan revival. For historiography what this meant to the West was renewed contact with the major authors in the form first of manuscripts brought back by Latin as well as Greek scholars from the early fifteenth century and then of translations (Thucydides and part of Herodotus by Valla, Polybius by Perotti, Diodorus Siculus by Poggio, Strabo by Guarino, and so on) and soon thereafter printed editions.[128] In this Greek phase of the Italian Renaissance, the classical Greek idea of history, with attendant attitudes and assumptions, rejoined the mainstream of Western historiography.

What is extraordinary about the Byzantine tradition of historiography is its continuity with Greek antiquity despite the ups and downs of the history of the Eastern Empire over some dozen centuries.[129] The imperial story begun by Procopius was continued, with a few breaks, from the seventh to the fifteenth centuries. Many of these chronicles are derivative to an extreme, preserving archaic style and presumptions beyond the range of Western counterparts; but some were also (in Thucydidean fashion) based on firsthand knowledge of the events they described and so are significant as source materials, if not as models of historiographical art. Of course this tradition was preserved in the contentious context of Christian theology, and indeed the religious orientation of Byzantine views of the past is evident from the extraordinary popularity of hagiography, which is perhaps the largest single genre of the literature of the Eastern Empire. In general the historiography of the "second Rome" may be peripheral to the Western canon under consideration here, but it does form a bridge between classical antiquity and those Christian conceptions of the human condition which would so profoundly reshape Western visions of the human past.

4

The Education of the Human Race

The education of the human race has advanced like that of an individual.
— Augustine

In his enduringly influential conception of human history, St. Augustine of Hippo combined classical culture with the new dispensation fashioned by Christianity out of its transmutation, or subversion, of Judaism, and he represented this new doctrine as the result of a Platonic enlightenment. History was indeed the "mistress of life" (*magistra vitae*), as Cicero had taught, but in a very special sense: "The education of the human race, represented by the people of God, has advanced, like that of an individual, through certain epochs, or, as it were, ages, so that it might gradually rise from earthly to heavenly things, and from the visible to the invisible."[1] In this conceit, anticipating by more than a millennium and a half the famous secularized formula of Gottfried Lessing, the Judeo-Christian view of history also displays two faces, though in a different way than the Herodoto-Thucydidean pairing — one looking backward to origins, perhaps a golden age of innocence, the other forward to a transcendent and, finally, eschatological goal.[2] For Christians and Jews alike history was not merely deeds done, and recorded, according to human ambitions and designs limited only by incalculable fortune and inscrutable fate; beyond this it was a progression of actions, an ordeal carried on within a providential plan. The task of the historian was to find the higher spiritual meaning which lay behind the letter of the human record and which constituted the education of the human race.

Jewish Archaeology

The story begins with the Holy Scriptures of the nation of Israel and the constructions put on them by centuries of interpreters, beginning in the prehistorical period of biblical canon formation; and of course this opened a very different perspective from those of Herodotus and Thucydides. From an Augustinian point of view the Old Testament dominated the Judeo-Christian tradition much as the Homeric poems dominated Greek tradition, serving at once as theology, philosophy, history, and science — the primordial textbook of the people whose culture it expressed. In both cases older elements may be detected behind traditional Homeric and Mosaic authorship, echoes of Near Eastern religions and creation myths, Babylonian or Persian; but in both cases, too, it is the received and canonized text of historical times that must be taken as the bearer of meaning for later ages, including the speculative interpretations and archaeological reconstructions of modern scholarship.

In Hebrew Scriptures, history, reinforced by chronicle and genealogy, was intermingled with law, poetry, and prophecy; but all of these were attached to an overriding theme, the delivery of the people of Israel out of Egyptian bondage, and an original event, the Exodus, which bound them not to nature but to history and which turned them not, through wonder and curiosity, to the future but rather, through memory and tradition, to the past. Thus, as Herbert Butterfield put it, "Israel attached itself to the God of History rather than the God of Nature."[3] One result was that the Jewish view of history came to involve both projection into the future, through prophecy, and what Millar Burrows has termed "retrojection" into the past, according to which ideas and meanings emerging in a later period were imposed on accounts of the past, for example, Israelite disillusionment with kingship being anachronistically expressed by Samuel, the mythical founder of monarchy, as a warning to the people.[4]

Historicism has been defined by Friedrich Meinecke as a combination of the principles of individuality and development, and on this most abstract level the story of Israel seems to be a prototype of this concept.[5] What defined the Jews' idea of history was a sense of the uniqueness of their nation, tied to their destiny as God's chosen people, and of its development, whose "very key," Butterfield concluded, "seems to have been the power of its historical memory." The promise, the covenant, the judgment, the national mission — these were the ideas, he added, which sustained the Jewish sense of history. In contrast to modern historicism, however, the changing patterns of Jewish national experiences were expressed not in the Dantean form of comedy that underlay the Christian view of providential history but in the mode of tragedy, in which the local god of Israel was universalized and the plan of national development spiritualized, though in a downward trajectory.

For the Western tradition of historical writing, especially the Augustinian vision, the Bible provided not only the larger chronological and cosmological framework, the foundational Adamic genealogies, and basis for moral judgments but also one of the central themes of political history. This theme was the passing of empire from one nation to another, and of course it was done providentially, since "the Most High ruleth in the kingdom of men, and giveth to whomsoever he will."[6] This was the assertion of the prophet (and probably legendary figure) Daniel, writing in the early second century B.C. but retrojected back to the time of the Babylonian captivity, whose interpretation of the dream of the Babylonian King Nebuchadnezzar described the pattern of the succession of empires determined by God.[7] The king's vision — a monster with a head of gold, breast of silver, belly and thighs of brass, and feet of iron and clay, an image based on metals in decreasing order of value — was replicated by Daniel's own vision of four beasts emerging from a river. What these mystical images signified, according to Daniel, was a succession of four kingdoms and their rulers, beginning with Babylon, all of them subject to God's kingdom, which is everlasting.

This was the text on which the (originally Greek) theory of four monarchies was based as well as what came to be called the "translation of empire" (*translatio imperii*). What were these empires — "the big four" in the words of Frank Manuel — which came successively to claim world dominion?[8] Those of the Babylonians, the Medes, the Persians, and the Macedonians were the first response, and indeed these identifications were quite in keeping with Herodotus, Polybius, and the Greek historiographical tradition. According to later revelations, Rome took the place of the fourth beast, and in Christian tradition Babylon was conventionally dropped from the series. But eschatological fashions change, and still later the Turkish, Napoleonic, and Soviet empires came along to lay claim to the apocalyptic title of fourth monarchy.[9] In any case the rationale and legitimation of this plotting of universal history remained fundamentally providential and moral, since (according to another biblical text later associated with the Book of Daniel) "God transfers kingdoms from one people to another because of injustice, injuries, blasphemies, and other evils."[10]

The Herodotus or Livy — or perhaps only the Dionysius of Halicarnassus — of Jewish history was the priest of royal descent, Josephus ben Matthias, who came to Rome as a prisoner in the time of Nero and the great fire, after an unsuccessful rebellion in Judea in which he played a rather discreditable role. An exile like Polybius, Josephus turned to writing history in the time of Vespasian, having gained his freedom, Roman citizenship, and the family name of

Flavius. An anti-Zionist, he wrote in Greek, beginning with his account *The Jewish War* and followed — after lapsing into silence, like Tacitus, during the oppressive reign of Domitian — by his *Against Apion* and *Jewish Antiquities* (or *Jewish Archaeology*), to which was appended his autobiography.[11] This apologetic survey of the travails of Israel, drawing on a much richer written and oral tradition than its classical counterparts, followed or paraphrased Holy Scriptures and its later interpretations, including pagan sources such as Berosus and Manetho. It was intended to survey "our entire ancient history [*archeologia*] and political constitution" from natural as well as national beginnings — from Creation and the origins of the Jews (*archai Ioudaioi*) — down to his own lamentable times, the last part of his narrative being carried on by other scholars associated with him.[12]

Josephus's perspective on the recent past was a sort of inversion of that of Livy, with whom he agreed — alluding to the commonplace thesis of the succession of empires — that "evident it is that fortune has on all hands gone over to [the Romans]; and that God, when he had gone round the nations with this dominion, is now settled in Italy."[13] His experience in the Jewish rebellion, which gave him a claim to be a "pragmatic" historian after the fashion of Thucydides and Polybius, also made a defeatist of Josephus, convinced as he was that war was always disastrous for the Jews. Josephus professed to be as devoted to the truth as he was to his nation; although celebrating the venerable past of Israel, he also spent much polemical energy defending himself against contemporary Jewish accusers and attacking earlier historians who had failed in their respect for one or another of his ideals.

Josephus took a broader view of human history, incorporating natural history as well: while Livy began *ab urbe,* Josephus began *ab orbe condita.* In the *Jewish Archaeology* the centerpiece was the founder and lawgiver Moses, who was also a historian and a philosopher — the Homer and Plato as well as the Herodotus of Israel — and who, after his account of Creation, "begins to interpret nature" (*physiologein,* to physiologize) before proceeding to the subject of Adamic anthropology, the emergence of man from earth (as etymology showed), and the mixed fortunes of the progeny of the first parents.[14] After seven generations, Josephus continued, the children "abandoned the customs of the fathers for a life of depravity"; and as "angels" (*angeloi*), they consorted with women and produced offspring who, like the giants of Greek mythology, lived a life of violence and wickedness. Following the Mosaic account, Josephus attends to questions of genealogy, including the incredible (but not mythical) life spans of the ancients, the Flood (known also, he remarked, by pagan tradition) and its aftermath, the return of the sons of Noah to the plain, the building of the Tower of Babel, the subsequent dispersion, and especially the complexities of early chronology.

The story of Babel was confirmed, Josephus remarks, by the Sibylline oracle of the Romans, which declared that "the gods sent winds against it and overturned the tower and gave to every man a peculiar language, whence it comes that the city was called Babylon."[15] "From that hour, therefore," Josephus continued, "they were dispersed through their diversity of languages and founded colonies everywhere, each group occupying the country that they lit upon and to which God led them, so that every continent was peopled by them . . . , while some crossed the sea on shipboard and settled in the islands."[16] Such was the true beginning of world history, although this story had been obscured by later migrations, with original Hebrew names being replaced by Greek ones. After their rise to power, these short-memoried pagans "appropriated even the glories of the past, embellishing the nations with names which they could understand and imposing on them forms of government, as though they were descended from themselves." And here Josephus offered his own eponymous etymologies (equally mythical) to replace those of the Greek cultural overlay.

The establishing of laws, whatever the historical circumstances of their appearance, is a holy act, and Josephus reports the scriptural account in the same spirit that Livy approaches the sacred myths of Roman tradition, without either affirming or denying.[17] All peoples have a mythology surrounding an original lawgiver, and in this respect Moses (philosopher, though he was, in Josephus's view) and his divinely inspired commandments represent a cultural counterpart to classical legislators like Solon, Romulus, and the Roman decemvirs. The history of Israel, even more than that of Rome, is the history of this seminal legislative ideal, its loss and attempted restorations. For the Jewish nation the ideal was associated not only with monotheism but also with an impulse to universalism, expressed historiographically in attempts, such as that of Josephus, to subsume the histories of other nations into the biblical account and chronology.

Josephus continued his arguments on a more polemical and methodological level in his work *Against Apion,* which (while targeting one minor critic of the Jews) is a wide-ranging essay on historiography employed at once to defend his *Jewish Antiquities* from criticism and to assert the superior veracity and depth of his own Jewish perspective on antiquity. What Josephus insisted on was the "extreme antiquity" and racial "purity" of his nation, and for this purpose he set out to discredit Greek writers on the grounds of myopia, credulity, and bad faith.[18] Misfortunes had obliterated the Greek memory of the past, and as a result they were prone to take credit for the accomplishments of earlier peoples, including the Egyptians and Babylonians, not to speak of the Jews. The Greeks had learned the alphabet from the Phoenicians, belatedly at that; and the poems of Homer, written after the Trojan War, had been transmitted orally. Beginning with Pythagoras, Greek wise men had appropriated their ideas from the Egyptians and Babylonians, and indeed "that great man [Pythagoras]" introduced many points of Jewish laws into his philosophy.[19]

According to Josephus, the Greeks were not only conceited but also wrong "to think themselves the sole possessors of a knowledge of antiquity" and the only accurate reporters of its history. From Hellanicus to Herodotus, each of their historians had to correct the lapses of his predecessor, and Herodotus and even Thucydides had been charged with errors; nor did either of them include Rome in his field of vision.[20] "In the Greek world," Joseph sneered, "everything will be found to be modern, and dating, so to speak, from yesterday or the day before." What caused this parochialism and this disrespect for the past? For Josephus the reasons were, first, the failure to keep written records and, second, the subordination of truth to literary ambition: "In short, their invariable method is the very reverse of the historical."[21]

The case that Josephus argued was threefold. First, he wanted to demonstrate the antiquity of the nation of Israel beyond that of even the Egyptians and Babylonians, with the attendant assumption that antiquity was equivalent to superiority and God's special favor. Second, he declared his allegiance to truth, which in turn was identified with the world process as understood from his Jewish perspective and in repudiation of classical tradition. Third, he privileged the creation and preservation of written records as symbolized by and embodied in the Holy Scriptures of Israel. In combination these theses constituted the foundation of a unique and universal vision of history as a providential story encompassing both future and past. This was the foundation of Augustine's conception of history as the education of the human race, which has informed the faithful and the faithless for centuries ever since.

New Beginning

Hebrew Scriptures were present at the birth of Christianity, as was the memory of a pagan past, but these represented idolatrous or incomplete heritages that were to be cast off or fulfilled in the name of a new dispensation and, eventually, a new foundation and starting point for chronology. This "new song," as Clement of Alexandria called it, was the Word celebrated by St. John, which would replace the mythical, idolatrous, orgiastic, and fundamentally atheistic poetry of paganism.[22] Through monotheism, the story of

Judaism turned national history into universal history, and this was given a political base by the establishment of the world empire of the Romans a generation before the birth of Christ. The early Christians had to confront and somehow to cope with these problematic heritages, and to begin with they chose the easy path of a complete break and claims to novelty — a "new law" (*kainos nomos*), in the words of Barnabas, to replace the old Jewish one, which was mired in material concerns. "Let us be spiritual" (*pneumatikos*), taught Barnabas, and turn, as Paul had done, to the "way of light" against the "way of darkness."[23]

The first Christians were pioneers. "Thus," as Jürgen Becker writes, "Peter was the first witness of Easter (Luke 24.34; 1 Cor. 15.5), Stephen was the first martyr of Christendom (Acts 6–7), and Epaenetus became known as the first baptized person in Asia (Rom. 16.5). Paul was added to these as the former persecutor and present preacher of the faith."[24] After his conversion Paul became a "new man," critical of the burdensome law and the deadening letter, that is, of history as it had been viewed before the coming of Christ. What concerned him was his universal mission to the gentile nations, which was to make known the "unknown god," of whom (as a Greek inscription suggested to him) even the pagans had heard (Acts 17.28). Time, too, would be measured according to a different scale, as the dating of the Incarnation and Easter became as crucial as Creation itself, and came to replace the Olympiadic system devised by Eratosthenes in the third century B.C. or the traditional date of the founding of Rome.

It is useful to note that the term, and perhaps the concept, *history* in a Herodotean sense is not used in the Bible, and *philosophy* only once, pejoratively at that, but that the term *truth* appears over a hundred times in both the Old and the New Testament (Hebrew *emeth*, and so on; Greek *Aletheia*; Latin *veritas*) and *wisdom* (Hebrew *chokmah*; Greek *sophia*; Latin *sapientia*) over two hundred times. Classical tradition, embodied in the Ciceronian first law of history, conceived of truth as conformity to fact and proper meaning, which occasionally corresponds to biblical usage, as when Daniel was asked about the truth, that is, the meaning, of Nebuchadnezzar's dream and of the Fourth Beast in particular.[25] But most often *truth* is the word and law of God, which must be obeyed on the grounds of authority. So it was also in the New Testament, especially in the preachings of Paul, where the truth resides in Christ and, in contrast to human "fables," "traditions," and "philosophy," would set men free.[26] Such was the conception of truth, too, of the early Christian writers of history.

By the second century Christian authors began to come more directly to terms with the ancient culture and its conceptions of history and philosophy.

Justin Martyr, pagan born, studied Pythagorean, Platonic, Aristotelian, and Stoic philosophy before turning to the "safe and profitable" word of Christ, for which he did not hesitate to accept martyrdom in 165. "He is the first ecclesiastical writer," says Johannes Quasten, "who attempts to build a bridge between Christianity and pagan philosophy."[27] This bridge is defined by the Logos, which is Christ himself, but is also present to some extent in great men like Socrates and Heraclitus, who, mistakenly regarded as atheists, "were able to see the truth darkly."[28] Their philosophy was founded on still earlier wisdom. In his *Exhortation to the Greeks* Justin, invoking the "archaeological" studies of Diodorus Siculus and Josephus, urges his readers to reject Homer for the true antiquity of Moses, whose history "is by far more ancient than any histories of the pagans" and who, with the prophets, foretold the truth of Christianity.[29] For Justin's pupil, the Syrian Tatian, almost everything of value in the culture of the Greeks came from this more ancient source, "for which of your institutions have not been derived from the Barbarians?"[30]

Continuing Tatian's line of argument, Clement of Alexandria built an even stronger bridge between paganism and Christianity, representing Greek philosophy as a preparation for Christian truth while criticizing it as plagiarized from antecedent "barbarian" wisdom. "Non-Greeks invented not only philosophy," wrote Clement, "but practically every form of technical skill."[31] Compared with the barbarians — Egyptians, Babylonians, and especially Jews — the Greeks were not only (as Plato had suggested) "children" but even "thieves" (Clement's severe way of indicating intellectual influence). In particular they "stole" ideas from the Jews, so that, for example, "the philosopher Plato gained from the teachings of Moses material on his legislation." Indeed, what else was he, in the famous phrase of Numenius, but "Moses speaking Greek?"[32]

What bound Christianity to its Jewish and classical antecedents was the doctrinal truth which was at least partially shared. Like Tatian and indeed Seneca, Clement did not think that truth was the exclusive property of any school or nation. "When I speak of philosophy, I do not mean Stoic, Platonic, Epicurean or Aristotelian," he wrote. "I apply the term philosophy to all that is rightly said in each of these schools."[33] Without the light of the Gospel, however, "Human traditions [are] intellectual nonsense"; and Clement opposed the many forms of error of the ancients against the unified truth of Christianity, citing Paul's famous warning: "Beware lest any man spoil you through philosophy and vain deceit, after the tradition of men, after the rudiments of the world, and not after Christ."[34] This advice also applied to the interpretations of history that had been handed down in this fashion. Nevertheless, Clement was himself interested in one of the central problems of human tradition, that of chronology, a field of study pioneered by Eratosthenes in the third century B.C., which Clement included in his own comparative historical calculations of the period of the law designed to fix the date of the Savior's birth.[35]

Human chronology was but a pale reflection of God's timetable, but the great system of correspondences which mystical theologians saw linking heaven and earth made it possible to ascend, at least in thought, from one sphere to another. According to Origen, writing in the third century, it was Paul who taught "that it is possible for us to mount up from things we see on earth to the things that belong to heaven," and thus rise from human culture to nature and ultimately to the Creator of nature. Origen also found correspondences between temporal revolutions — the alternations of seasons and succession of years — and the unseen changes of incorporeal things and "eternal years" celebrated by the Psalmist.[36]

Origen, regarded by Jerome as "the greatest teacher of the Church after the apostles," saw chronological succession as grounded in spiritual continuity, such that the same spirit — the Holy Spirit — that informed Moses and the prophets also inspired the apostles.[37] For Origen, "The teaching of the church, handed down in unbroken succession from the apostles, is still preserved and continues to exist in the churches up to the present day."[38] If human history was a record of incidental actions, Christian history the expression of a higher truth, the Logos, that abided from Creation to the Last Things and was discerned by Plato and other ancient wise men. The "other world" referred to by Christ was not merely those "imaginary forms which the Greeks call 'ideas,'" although Origen, a pupil of Ammonius Saccus, founder of the Neoplatonic school, did believe in a form of ancient wisdom.[39] This *prisca sapientia* was not, however, the profane wisdom of the pagan Celsus, who attributed it to the Egyptians and other barbarians (not including the Jews);[40] rather it was closer to the vision of the Pythagorean philosopher Numenius, "who by studying several doctrines made from many sources a synthesis of those which seemed to him to be true."[41] Eclectic philosophy did not replace the Word, but it did offer glimpses of Christian truth and so provided a spiritual foundation for human history, and the history of philosophy in particular.

What Christians took as signs of antiquity, however, critics interpreted as unoriginality or plagiarism. "As to their doctrine," wrote the second-century Platonic philosopher Celsus, "it was originally barbarian, and while even barbarians are capable of discovering truth, it happens to be the case that Greeks are best equipped to judge the merit of what passes for truth these days."[42] In his day, Celsus complained, Christian myths were better known than the doctrines of the philosophers, yet they were all derivative of the Egyptians,

Assyrians, Indians, and Persians as well as those "runaway slaves," the Jews. Celsus rejected the narrow partisanship of both Jews and Christians, their absurd fables about their human leaders, and their misguided attempt to universalize their fables, and he offered instruction in the truth according to Greek philosophy. This was the work which provoked Origen to an impassioned and detailed response.

The Latin Fathers were more critical than the Greeks in their views of a largely unenlightened antiquity. Tertullian, an African convert from paganism (probably to be identified with the Roman jurisconsult cited in Justinian's *Digest*), attacked Greek philosophy as a faithless sophistry that had produced not the unity of Christian truth but a great diversity of "sects," which in the Greek language was to say "heresies," to several modern forms of which he devoted treatises. Athens had nothing to do with Jerusalem, nor the academy with the church, and the consequence was that ancient history had to be written mainly as the study of human error, except for the prophetic visions of the Old Testament. Moses was older than the Trojan War, older even than Saturn, and his writings were the source of pagan law and learning.[43] If it were not too much trouble, Tertullian added, this could be shown by the histories of the barbarian nations, including that of Josephus. What was significant, however, was the spread of the new revelation, which henceforth would be the central theme of history. Christianity would somehow prevail — "The blood of the martyrs is the seed of the church" being the famous motto given by Tertullian to this process.[44]

The story of early Christianity — beyond basic problems of organization, networking, missionary activities, and simple survival — centers on the question of how to make sense of the past, even if it meant imposing meaning. Of course Christians could rely on Hebrew Scriptures for the larger framework, but they had somehow to accommodate classical traditions as well. How could they reconcile the unity of their truth with the innumerable parties, sects, and syncretisms of late classical culture? The general formula for this was that of Eusebius, according to which the whole process of history was a "preparation for the Gospel," and it was in these terms that the Christian vision of history was formed by scholars, theologians, and preachers of the Word. It was in these terms, too, that the faces of Herodotus and Thucydides and their epigones made fitful appearances.

In the early fifth century, Jerome explained the relationship between the Christian present and the pagan past in utilitarian but at the same time evangelical terms. "You ask me . . . why it is that sometimes in my writings I quote examples from secular literature and thus defile the whiteness of the church with the foulness of heathenism," he responded to one hyper-Ciceronian correspondent. The reason was that prophets and apostles alike often drew on the writings of the ancient pagans, which are "full of erudition and philosophy." The clinching argument was from Paul, who "when he is arguing with the Athenians upon the Areopagus . . . calls Aratus as a witness, citing from him the words 'For we are also his offspring.' "[45]

Eusebius

Eusebius was the Christian Herodotus (without the darker side of his reputation as "father of lies"), the "father of ecclesiastical history"; and many events and persons of the early centuries of the Christian era are known only through his monumental *History of the Church*. Born in Palestine about 260, he died as bishop of Caesarea about 340, thus spanning the transition from the pagan to the Christian empire. A student of the martyr Pamphilius and a favorite of Constantine's, he was a political churchman who also admired the controversial Origen and who, while wavering in his own doctrinal commitment, remained orthodox. Eusebius was an extraordinarily prolific author, who wrote, among other things, a hero-worshiping biography of Constantine, idealized as "imitator and representative on earth of the Divine Word himself," a life of Pamphilius (now lost), and his authoritative work on church history and chronology.

Eusebius wrote during the triumph of the Christian cause, which inspired historical reflections not only on the miraculous progress of the Word but also on the vicissitudes of the Roman Empire, under whose jurisdiction true religion had suffered, survived, and finally received legitimacy. One major theme was the great line of martyrs who had testified to the faith, and the obverse was the parallel tradition of martyr-making persecutors. The negative theme was taken up by Eusebius's contemporary Lactantius, whose *Deaths of the Persecutors,* contemporary with Constantine's conversion and the "crushing" of Christianity's foes through God's wrath, traces the history of imperial tyrants and official persecution from the crucifixion of Christ under Tiberius Caesar down to the time when Christian faith had effaced the false glories of pagan Rome.[46]

Eusebius, whose project was the positive side of the story, claimed absolute originality for his *History of the Church,* which was intended to be a history of the words, deeds, and sufferings of Christians from the Year of Our Lord down to the martyrs of the author's own day. His premise was summed up in the words of the second-century bishop of Sardis, Melito, who addressed both Jews and Christians in his works. In his "petition to Antoninus" this "Janus-like figure" (as W. H. C. Frend calls him) declares:[47] "Our way of thought first sprung up in a foreign land, but it flowered among your own peoples in the glorious reign of your ancestor Augustus, and became to your empire especially a portent of good, for from then on, the power of Rome grew great and splendid. . . . Together, at the same critical moment, as if from a single divine will, two beneficial shoots were produced for mankind: the empire of the Romans and the teaching of true worship."[48] Such was the providential plotting of the epic story to which Eusebius dedicated his historiographical work.

The Eusebian first premise was the antiquity of the divine origins of Christianity, deriving as it did from the Word proclaimed by St. John, which was "the Light that existed before the world, the intellectual and essential Wisdom that was before time itself."[49] It was impossible for this light to be seen fully by the human race in its fallen state, but through the Jewish race chosen by God "savage and cruel brutality turned to mildness" and the seeds of true religion were sown, to bear fruit only in the reign of Augustus with the coming of God's son, which had been forecast by Moses and other prophets. The Christians were, to be sure, a "new people," Eusebius declared, but their way of life and thought were ancient, and their religion was most ancient of all.

The narrative of Eusebius was based on the writings of Josephus and the early Fathers, with some allusion to classical sources like Diodorus of Sicily's *Universal History,* but especially on the "inspired record" of Scriptures.[50] It surveyed, chronologically and with a scrupulous regard for precise dating, martyrdoms, the lines of emperors and bishops, the various heresies, famines, plagues, and wars, and the teachings of authors such as Justin, Origen, and Irenaeus, including stories and anecdotes; and it culminated in the destruction of the enemies of true religion and the "peace and recovery" achieved by Constantine, the greatest of all rulers, according to the prophets. Eusebius was, as it were, the original Whig historian, and no less self-servingly selective in his account. His purpose was to describe not all the misfortunes which he knew about or had witnessed but "only enough to justify the divine judgment," he wrote, and "only those things by which first we ourselves, then later generations, may benefit."[51]

Questions of continuity obsessed Eusebius: "Are we Greeks or Barbarians," he wondered, "or intermediaries between the two?" Like the Hebrew Scriptures, the fables of the Egyptians, transmitted to and transformed by the Greeks, formed a sort of historical continuum which, Eusebius assumed, Christians should not ignore.[52] But of more direct concern to Eusebius's *History* were problems of legitimate succession, and the model for this was the succession of teachers in the Greek philosophical schools, which preserved teachings over the generations, from master to disciple.[53] Eusebius recognized successions of prophets and emperors as well as the wise men of antiquity, but it was apostolic and episcopal successions which more concerned him. He accepted Origen's principle of the spiritual continuity of the church. Yet his account, like Diogenes Laertius's *Lives of the Philosophers,* was historical and not mystical, relying on "human traditions" and not the passage of correct doctrine. Nor did he accept the exclusive, doubly apostolic position of Rome; for in his account he also included Jerusalem, Alexandria, Antioch, and local successions such as his own see of Caesarea. This perspective further expanded the universal scope of Eusebius's work.

Other themes figured in Eusebius's *History,* drawn from oral and written tradition. He celebrated the persecutions and martyrdoms of the reign of Diocletian, stories of those "eager to imitate Christ," for purposes of instruction as well as memorial; and he denounced, in the abusive language rejected by the classical notion of history (Lucian, for example), the "abomination" of heresy which disfigured ecclesiastical tradition. He wrote of the fate of the Jews, who came to grief for what he called their "plots" against Christ. He commented on the scriptural canon, following much the same line as Origen, accepting the four Gospels but rejecting the book of the Apocalypse. He also reported miracles, especially the great political miracle of Constantine, and he reflected on theology and the providential basis of Christian history for the religious posterity to which his book was addressed.

Despite his deep faith in, or blind partisanship for, Constantinian Christianity, Eusebius was committed to fixing an accurate chronology for the scriptural canon and the successions which he retraced and also for the events whose meaning was emerging in the light of the Christian Word. This was the purpose of his *Chronological Canons* (a lost work employed in many early medieval Bibles), which attempted to synchronize pagan and Judeo-Christian history through a wide range of sources, including the anti-Christian chronology of Porphyry, by aligning the Olympiadic system with regnal lists (*fila regnorum*), historians' calculations, biblical genealogy beginning with Abraham, and historical information in the so-called *spatium historicum* between the columns.[54]

Eusebius's main predecessor was Julius Africanus, whose *Chronographiae* (now lost beyond reconstruction) had carried on, in Christian terms, the work of Eratosthenes and other post-Herodotean Greek chronographers; his many successors included Jerome, who continued the chronology to 378, and Prosper of Aquitaine, who continued Jerome to 455 — predicting that the spiritual kingdom of Christ would surpass the material empire of the Romans.[55] The "turning point" of 476 — that is, the conventional date for the end of the Western Empire defined by the deposition of "Romulus Augustulus" — was apparently determined first by Justinian's chancellor Marcellinus in the sixth century.[56]

Precise dating within this tradition began with the Olympiadic list, according to Africanus, and on this basis a general system of calibration could be constructed: "Taking one Hebrew event of the same time as another event included in the history of the Greeks, bearing both in mind, I shall by a process of selection and juxtaposition make clear what event, Greek, Persian, or other, was synchronous with the Hebrew event and so perhaps achieve my purpose."[57] This was exactly the procedure followed by Eusebius, who thus, filling the "historical space" of his compilation and listing his authorities, joined comparative chronography with universal history — legendary as well as sacred and civil history.

Formal and stylistic considerations were no longer of major importance in Eusebius's conception of history. His project was neither Herodotean inquiry nor Thucydidean analysis. While his scope was universal and his concerns in a sense pragmatic, he celebrated a very different sort of triumphal progress than did Polybius; and he had a conception of truth that was worlds apart from his pagan predecessors and sources — his linear conception amounting to a rejection of the cyclical views of classical authors. Eusebius was the proud champion of a higher cause, which was expressed within a framework so plainly revealed in Holy Scriptures that there seemed little for a historian to accomplish except to fix the sequence and parallelism of events and to collect the words that testified to the providential plan — the "grand design of God" — which the "inspired record" had laid down and which survived in a variety of secular forms, including the modern idea of secular progress.

Eusebius's ecclesiastical history was continued by three Byzantine scholars — Socrates "Scholasticus," Sozomen (covering the same ground), and Theodoret of Cyrrhus — all of whom aimed to celebrate the achievement of Constantine and his successors and to defend the church from charges of heresy. Each of them declared his intention of supplementing the authoritative work of Eusebius; Theodoret compared his efforts with the painter's art, except that words were more permanent than pigments.[58] These Byzantine continuators of Eusebius, especially the "lawyer-historian" Sozomen, attended to secular as well as sacred matters and did so on the basis of serious archival research.[59] Socrates proposed to remedy the failings of Eusebius by detailing the debates over the fundamental dogma of the Trinity, though at the same time to relieve the tedium of theological debate by attending to political history. But in this new mixture of secular and ecclesiastical history, which was pioneered by Eusebius and carried on by Socrates' own successors, Socrates professed an allegiance to truth greater than that of classical historians, who regarded themselves "at liberty to amplify or curtail matters of fact."[60] Like the best of the ancients, Socrates wrote, "I shall in like manner obey the laws of history, which demand a simple and faithful narration, unobscured by a veil of any kind." So the spirit, or at least the rhetoric, of Cicero prevailed in Christian historiography. Through the efforts of Cassiodorus, this trinity of Byzantine histories was translated by Epiphanius and made available to the West under the name *Historia Tripartita*.[61]

After Eusebius the chronological tradition in the East persisted to the end of the Byzantine Empire, and indeed to the Greek revolution of 1821.[62] In general it followed the Bible story, with an admixture of myth detached from its Greek origins: Hebrew was the language of Adamic naming, but Chaldean letters also antedated the Flood, after which Jewish and Chaldean history merged, confused by accounts of gentile gods. Abraham was himself a Chaldean and brought knowledge of letters, astronomy, and the true God to the Jews. Moses was not only the greatest of prophets before John the Baptist but also the first historian, like Solomon a master of learning that was only later exploited by the Greeks. After Solomon, Jewish history was a story of decline, and the Incarnation, coinciding with Roman world dominion, marked a new stage climaxed by the work of Constantine.

In the West, universal chronicles continued to appear in all parts of Europe between the third and twelfth centuries—fourteen in German territories, eleven in French, seven in Italian.[63] Bound to Biblical authority, they followed the conventional periodization by generations and reigns from Adam to Christ and "ages of the world." These world chronicles have left an indelible imprint on Western historical consciousness both in the science of chronology and in the structure of histories and chronological tables of Western civilization down to the present.

Augustine

From the fourth century, *Romanitas* and *Christianitas* became synonymous: "We desire that all peoples who fall beneath the sway of our imperial clemency should profess the faith which we believe to have been communicated by the Apostle Peter to the Romans and maintained in its traditional form to the present day."[64] So, two generations after Constantine, declared the Emperor Theodosius in the famous edict *Cunctos populos* (380); those outside this theologico-political dispensation were not only heretics and outlaws but also "madmen." So two currents of history, sacred and profane, were officially joined and henceforth could be traced along a single narrative line; so, too, the themes of conventional Livian history and of scriptural tradition could be interwoven into a single providential story.[65] At just this same time the twenty-six-year-old Augustine was still in Africa, writing in a pagan mode; but within three years he had gone to Rome, and within seven years he would be baptized into the Catholic church.

The Janus image, associated with Herodotus and Thucydides, also applies
to Augustine; for this greatest of Latin fathers looked back to a pagan past and
a rhetorical training which stood him in good stead in his polemical battles
while he also looked forward, from a Christian perspective, to the brightening
future of the religion of Christ, Paul, Constantine, and now Theodosius,
which he took as his own.[66] He escaped the errors of Manichaean, but not
dualistic, patterns of thought in the effort to reconcile classicism and orthodoxy. Through his education he inherited the Greco-Roman *paideia,* with his
personal renewal and baptism he accepted the sacred tradition of the church,
and out of the conflation of the two experiences, he fashioned his dualistic
conception of history.[67] In this crypto-Manichaean idea Augustine brought
together the spiritualism of Platonic philosophy and that of the prophets and,
moreover, found a way of expressing his vision of the city of man and the city
of God.

The City of God, like the masterpieces of Thucydides, Machiavelli, Sleidan,
and many others, was the product of a crisis, a "great calamity," which Augustine described in his *Retractationes.* When the city was overthrown by the
Goths, led by their Arian chief, Alaric, "the worshippers of many false gods,
whom we call by a name in general use, pagans, tried to attribute [the disaster]
to the Christian religion, and . . . to blaspheme the true God more sharply and
more bitterly than usual."[68] Augustine was provoked by this atrocity, too, and
"fired with zeal" to set the record straight. The upshot was an antipagan
polemic and also a magisterial and archetypal philosophy of history, in whose
intellectual shadow modern metahistorical speculators still argue.

Augustine was a man obsessed with time: not only God's absolute time but
also personal, human, and relative time—time passing, in experience and
language, from a bygone age that no longer existed to a future not yet born.[69]
A child of paganism in a "postpagan" world, as Peter Brown terms it, Augustine ended as a Father of the Christian church, and he was eager to seek out
the causes and circumstances of his conversion and progress from classical
knowledge to true wisdom—that "science of things divine and human" explored by Cicero and Varro, but in the postclassical light of the Incarnation.
The human measure of time comes in the awareness of time passing, but the
longer periods of times past and future are beyond this awareness since they
are not present, and in that sense do not in fact exist.

This line of introspection led Augustine to the mysteries of history and
prophecy, which transcend experience and for which only Scripture can offer
meaningful answers. This is especially true of questions of origins, and so
Augustine rejected the conventions of classical historiography—preferring to
"omit the conjectures of men who know not what they say, when they speak of

the nature and origin of the human race."[70] Above all he wanted to reject the fables about the pagan gods — both the "mythical" and the "civil" theology identified by Varro — and the notion that the greatness of Rome derived from such perverted sources. Roman historians such as Sallust had themselves testified to the vices and corruption of the Roman Republic (undeservedly so called, Augustine thought) and Empire, "which, though it be mistress of the nations, is itself ruled by its lust of rule" (*dominandi libido*).[71] It was the one true God, not the Roman idols of Virtue, Victory, Faith, and Felicity — as Augustine argued and as history taught — that produced the success of the Roman state.[72] And it was belief in this God that made wisdom possible: not understand in order that you might believe, but believe that you may understand.[73]

This famous formula applied also to history. Augustine's conversion drew him away from the sectarian search for wisdom to the stable truth of the Gospel and gave him a grand perspective on both the classical and the Judeo-Christian past, which he saw as morally similar and chronologically parallel. In the great work of his old age, *The City of God against the Pagans*, Augustine captured his vision in the image of the two cities, the city of man (*civitas terrena*) and the city of God (*civitas Dei*), Babylon and Jerusalem, Jerusalem (in another sense) and Heaven, and perhaps "eternal Rome" in its pagan and Christian incarnations. These in turn symbolized a number of dualities of human life — body and soul, real and ideal, the material and the spiritual, uncertainty and certainty, evil and good, human (or natural) law and divine grace, sin and saintliness, bondage and freedom, and violence (or war) and peace. Human experience was thus divided according to criteria that were at once anthropological, metaphysical, epistemological, theological, philosophical, moral, social, and political. Human society was the individual writ large, and so human history was homologous to individual development and should be judged in much the same dualistic terms.[74]

According to Augustine, humankind lives within three concentric circles — the household, the city, and the world at large.[75] Moving from the inner circle of family into the social world is essential, but it is accompanied by dangers and miseries, including (says Augustine) marriage and children, not to speak of oppression and (in his immediate experience) torture. The third circle is made more hazardous by the diversity of languages ("by which the intercourse of men is prevented") and the incidence of violence and wars. Universal peace and justice remained only ideals; the historical reality was incessant conflict and discord.

Justice was the law of the city of God, but the city of man lived according to different rules. Human society was born in violence and fratricide — Cain and Abel, Romulus and Remus — and preserved this condition both externally, through wars and persecutions, and internally, through class and religious divisions. Israel was divided against itself, as history showed, and so was Rome; and this was the record that writers of history had tried to explain. Unfortunately, Augustine believed, their efforts had been largely in vain, since they did not understand the fundamental principle, the beginning and end of history, that is, the one true God according to trinitarian interpretation. As Creator, God was the first mover of history; as incarnate Son, he joined divine and human history; and as the Holy Spirit, he gave mystical continuity and meaning to the historical process which pagan authors, misled by fables and pride, had misunderstood.

Rightly understood, history — together with its temporal twin, prophecy — was indeed "the grand design of God," but within this overarching framework Augustine recognized more conventional human patterns, of which two were destined to inform historical interpretations for centuries. One was the idea of the four monarchies, derived from Daniel, especially as interpreted by Augustine's colleague Jerome. These successive kingdoms were normally taken to be the Assyrians, Persians, Macedonians, and Romans; but Augustine reminded his readers that it was the kingdom of Antichrist that was prophesied to be the last of these states before the last judgment. In general, Augustine wrote, and according to the judgment of God, who is the source of such dominion, there were two kingdoms "grown far more famous than the rest, first that of the Assyrians, then that of the Romans," the one arising in the East and the other in the West, the other states being mere appendages of these.[76]

The second, more fundamental pattern was that of the "ages of man," which Augustine outlined briefly on the last page of his work.[77] In antiquity there was dispute about the number of these ages, the historian Florus, for example (second century A.D.), assigning four ages to Roman history, and Seneca five, while the convention of Hippocratic medicine and Ptolemaic astrology made it seven. This was also the choice of Augustine — seven corresponding to the days of the week, the last of which referred to decline and death. Augustine also projected the physiological divisions onto biblical history, the first five ages extending from Adam to the birth of Christ, the sixth passing in Augustine's time, and the seventh featuring the Sabbath to come, the end of human time and history, and "the kingdom without end. . . . Amen."

Orosius

Augustine's young colleague Orosius took up where he left off — or rather filled in what Augustine had left empty, which was the story of humanity under the four empires and divided up according to the six historical ages.

Orosius was a Spanish priest who came to Africa when Augustine was beginning work on his *City of God*. After traveling to Palestine to see Jerome and attend a council in Jerusalem, he wrote his *Seven Books of History against the Pagans*, a work requested by and dedicated to the old bishop and published in 417, almost a decade before the last books of *The City of God* were completed. It was a rather superficial and very partisan survey of universal history, carrying his derivative story "from the beginning of man's sin" down to that date. Orosius's work, like Augustine's, aimed at correcting the errors of the *pagani,* or *gentiles,* as well as collecting damaging stories about these "enemies," such as the fire set by Nero (a rumor doubted by Tacitus but confirmed by Suetonius) "as a spectacle for his pleasure."[78]

Orosius begins his narrative with a survey of the geography of the world according to the threefold division established by "our ancestors," and then takes up the fortunes of humanity, mainly under Roman rule, with many a judgmental and sermonizing aside. He followed a strictly chronological order, calculated piously "from the founding of the city" even for the years after the birth of Christ. While he naturally preferred the scriptural account of Moses, he did not hesitate to make extensive use of the *Histories* of Tacitus and especially the abridgment of Trogus Pompeius by Justin, who (though evidently no Christian) had testified to the wisdom of this leader of the Jews. Orosius mixed myths in with historical narrative, citing Virgil's *Aeneid,* for example, as authentic history as well as a source of timeless wisdom, although he also omitted many disgraceful stories derived from pagan sources.

According to Orosius's sources, the Kingdom of Babylon came to an end at the same time that "the seeds of the future Rome were sown" by the legendary Procas, great-grandfather of the bloody founder, Romulus; and Babylon, having passed its power on to the Medes, was finally overthrown by Cyrus just as Rome — founded 414 years after the destruction of Troy, won its liberation from the Tarquinian kings.[79] This was the beginning of God's universal plan leading from the empire of the Babylonians to that of the Romans, which, despite its blood-stained origins and savage early history, was sanctified by the coming of Christ. Greedier for power and more "insatiable for blood" than Romulus was the Macedonian Alexander, "that whirlpool of evils and most horrible hurricane sweeping the east."[80] These and other so-called great men inspired Orosius to periodic jeremiads on the pitiable human condition produced by paganism. "O wicked soul of man and heart always inhuman," he cried. "Did I not fill my eyes with tears as I reviewed these events to prove the recurring in cycles of the misfortunes of all ages."[81]

The result of chronological order was, Orosius confessed, "an inextricable wicker-work of confused history," whose disorder increased "the more I kept to the order of events."[82] Yet in this maze of actions there was a plan, for "God is the one ruler of all ages, kingdoms, and places."[83] Orosius repeatedly compared the misfortunes of ancient times with those of the present — such as the persecutions by the Egyptians and those by the Romans, and the sack of Rome by the Gauls and the Goths almost eight centuries later — and he criticized recent historians for their lack of perspective on the afflictions of antiquity. More generally, he discerned alternating periods of good and evil, to which he assigned moral and religious praise or blame, relying on the researches of pagan historians. However, his was not a triumphalist history, as contrasted to his pagan precursors; for "whereas they unfold wars, we unfold the miseries of wars."[84]

The governing will of God was finally made manifest in the incarnation, mission, and martyrdom of his Son in the period of Augustus, when the temple of Janus was again closed to mark the establishment of imperial peace.[85] Imperial peace did not end the horrors of pagan rule; and in one of his many efforts at sensationalism Orosius retold the story of Nero's fire, set for his own pleasure, which burned in the Eternal City for six days and nights. Nero himself rejoiced over the flames ("it is said") and declaimed the *Iliad* in the costume of an actor of tragedy.[86] "Moreover," Orosius added, "he was so aroused with cruel madness that he killed the greater part of the senate, and almost annihilated the equestrian order."

The coming of the Word revealed the falseness of the pagan gods and the true raison d'être of the Roman Empire, which was fulfilled by the conversion to Christianity three centuries later and then by the Christianizing legislation of Theodosius. Orosius praised the imperial acts suppressing pagan sacrifices, quoting ironically the words placed by Virgil in the mouth of Aeneas on the destruction of Troy, that "all the gods went forth, abandoning sanctuaries and altars, by whom this Empire had stood firm" — thus preparing the way for the true word of God.[87] Following Augustine, Orosius also retold the story of the Gothic King Radagaisus, "worshipper of demons," who was overcome, providentially, by the Christian army from Rome without a single drop of blood being shed — a pious exaggeration which gained Gibbon's "silent contempt."[88]

In this way Orosius accomplished the charge laid on him by Augustine, recounting "the struggles of the world and the judgments of God" during a period of 5,618 years, "separating Christian times . . . from the former confusion of belief"; and he filled in some detail and marginal judgments in Augustine's grand vision of history as the education of the human race — a vision that would be recapitulated later by Bishop Otto of Freising after seven centuries of postclassical experience and the emergence of a very different Rome. In general Orosius's subsequent influence was extraordinary, providing along with Sallust (as Beryl Smalley argued), "the twin keys to medieval historiography" — Orosius supplying the framework and Sallust the ways of treating style and the moral substance of history.[89]

Spirit and Letter

For Augustine, history had both a literary and an ontological signification, expressed in *res* as well as *verba*. He repeated the conventional Ciceronian views about the value of history in a human sense, but his perspective was much richer, joined as it was to his spirituality.[90] "Although the past institutions of men are related in historical narrative, history itself is not to be counted among human institutions," he wrote. "For events which have already occurred and cannot be undone are to be considered as part of world order, whose founder and ruler is God." Thus "history itself" was not a matter of words but, no less than nature itself, a creation of God.

This was history in its higher, its true, divine, and spiritual form. Yet — the Augustinian dualism persisting in this area, too — the term continued also to have a lower, human, carnal, and literal meaning, and indeed Augustine himself admired historical scholarship (*historica diligentia*). This practical sense of the term *history* referred to classical prose narrative and to the literal interpretation of texts. In the first case, history, that is, secular history, is a written form of human memory, and perhaps even more fallible, though to be distinguished from fable and useful as a store of examples. In the second case, history represents a level of reading that corresponds to human language in its grammatical sense (*secundam historiam*) as opposed to a spiritual or prophetic reading (*secundum prophetiam*).

The writing of history and textual exegesis represent separate realms, but they overlap in important ways. From its nominal Herodotean beginnings history depended not only on eyewitness (*opsis*) and hearsay (*akoe*) but also — and for ancient history almost exclusively — on written reports (*graphai*, "scriptures"), and this leads directly to questions of interpretation and hermeneutics. Here historians drew on two rival, but sometimes intersecting, traditions of learning and criticism, that is, biblical and Homeric. Christian scholars such as Origen and especially Jerome, poised so precariously between Cicero and Christ (to judge from his famous dream), derived their methods from both classical philology and Hebrew midrash, technical practices, which indeed had intermingled in some ways — for instance, in the work of Philo Judaeus — and this eclectic exegetical heritage was of fundamental importance for understanding secular history.

Both traditions made distinctions between literal and figurative modes of interpretation that established the poles of controversy over texts, canons, and, in many cases, doctrines. Were Homer and Moses the authors of the texts transmitted under their names? Were the actions reported factual — "historical" — or did they represent another level of meaning, whether true or false? Both Homer and Moses, theologians and perhaps prophets as well as historians, could claim some form of divine inspirations, but both were also vulnerable to hostile criticism. Homer was the archpoet of that tribe of literary liars banned from the republic by Plato, whose opinion many Christian authors applauded; for the gentiles Moses was the founder of an obsolete legislation which had been supplanted by a new law. These foundational texts and the commentary appearing in their wake have defined a field immensely rich in learning, debate, and theory; and included in their intellectual offspring are the practice and theory of literary and historical criticism and modern hermeneutics.

The problem of interpretation, secular and scriptural, is basically that of finding sense in, or giving sense to, written texts — especially with regard to gaps, difficulties, or contradictions — and, beyond that, interpreting in the sense of translating.[91] In the case of Christian Scriptures there was the additional task of harmonizing not only the four Gospels but also the New and Old Testaments. Historical, or strictly literal, interpretation, such as emphasized by exegetes of the school of Antioch, was often inadequate to the task, and recourse was made to the allegorizing and symbolizing devices of Alexandrine scholars, including Philo. This was the path taken especially by the Gnostics and scholars sympathetic to spiritualizing attitudes, such as Origen and Clement of Alexandria, for whom the Mosaic law in a literal sense, though it undoubtedly prefigured the Gospels, was no longer valid for Christians. Origen quotes Paul's interpretation of the Jews' crossing of the Red Sea as symbolic of Christian baptism.[92] For him, as for Paul, the letter of the old law was the way of death, and only the spirit offered life. History represented human traditions, in short, and only the revealed Word offered truth.

It was Origen — "father of allegorical interpretation in the Christian Church," as M. L. W. Laistner called him[93] — who gave systematic form to the multiple modes of interpretation and levels of understanding: the historical, corresponding to the body; the moral, corresponding to the soul; and the mystical, corresponding to the spirit. Paralleling these modes of interpretation — "somatic," "psychic," and "pneumatic," respectively — is what Origen calls "the threefold wisdom": the wisdom of the world, in effect, unenlightened individual judgment; second, the wisdom of the rulers of the world, equally unenlightened, such as "the secret and hidden philosophy of the Egyptians and the astrology of the Chaldaeans and Indians"; and finally God's wisdom, which has to do with heavenly things.[94] These two triads represent both a ladder of learning and a hierarchy of theological values, with history occupying at once the lowest and the most fundamental level.

History, the first aspect of Origen's hermeneutical trinity, is for those "who reject the labour of thinking and seek after the outward and literal meaning of the law . . . , disciples of the mere letter," who desire only "pleasure and bodily luxury."[95] The second aspect is moral prescription, as in the unreflective law, which, though imperfect, is edifying and instructive. Only the third is spiritual and has "a shadow of the good things to come," which is to say, salvation. It was obvious to Origen that "in most instances the truth of the historical record can and ought to be preserved," and moreover that the sacred body of Scriptures is preserved in human language. Yet it had been composed by the Holy Spirit and was ideally to be understood in such terms, to the extent indeed that some passages are only symbolic and have no historical value. Often, however, spiritual meanings are concealed "within ordinary language under cover of some historical record." Origen conjectured that "to those who know how to examine writings of this sort, certain unspeakable mysteries are revealed," so that history seems "a kind of outward covering and veil for spiritual meanings . . . , woven by the art of wisdom." Here speaks a philosopher of history, anticipating the speculations of Augustine, Joachim of Fiore, Vico, Hegel, and others seekers for spiritual meanings in history and illustrating the remark of Philippe Ariès that the Middle Ages "had an existential sense of the past."[96]

The Latin Fathers were somewhat more conservative, perhaps more fundamentalist, than those of the East and were concerned more with the literal sense of Scriptures — Tertullian, for example, warning against allegory as the way of heresy. Yet they, too, prized the spirit above the letter of the text in the sense that it was the higher truth behind the human words which constituted their interpretive target. Augustine did not really distinguish between history and prophecy except for temporal direction, while Jerome preferred a "spirit for spirit" to a "word for word" translation of the Old Testament into Latin, whether from the Greek version or from the Hebrew original (*Hebraica veritas*). Not that he claimed the inspiration to speak for the author of Scripture, that is, the Holy Spirit, but he did not want philology to obscure the spiritual meaning.

The story of biblical exegesis (*lectio divina*) in the Middle Ages is long and complicated, but the patristic framework was retained, and it was institutionalized in monastic and cathedral schools before emerging in the universities as a discipline, or auxiliary discipline, of theology. The Origenic theory of three- or fourfold interpretation was preserved and extended, with history retaining its inferior, but still foundational, position. Boethius spoke of the historical mode (*modus historialis*), which, in contrast to allegory, "did nothing but describe actions."[97] According to Peter Lombard, "The historical sense is easier, the moral sweeter, the mystical sharper; the historical for us beginners, the moral for the advanced, the mystical for the perfect."[98] The work of the Victorine school (named after the Augustinian abbey of St. Victor) shifted emphasis back from allegorical license to history and the literal dimension of meaning; Hugh of St. Victor, for example, emphasized the study of history and geography for the continuing challenge of the "divine reading." Again and again the Victorines insisted that students learn to walk before attempting to fly, that is, to seek the truth of the letter and *sensus historicum* before trying to ascend directly to allegory and things of the spirit.[99] This would be the message, too, of Renaissance scholars such as Valla and Erasmus, who, while seeking to retrieve a classical sense of history, built on these patristic and scholastic exegetical foundations.

Renaissance scholars were increasingly concerned with the historical dimensions of humanity and the historical mode of textual interpretation, and so the stock of historical studies rose in the early modern period. Yet the unscholarly and piously speculative habits of early Christian, especially Augustinian, interpretations persisted on the level of universal history, linking the medieval theology of history with the modern philosophy of history. As Collingwood wrote, "We have gone so far back to the medieval view of history that we think of nations and civilizations as rising in obedience to a law that has little to do with the purposes of the human beings that compose them, and we are perhaps not altogether ill-disposed to theories which teach that large-scale historical changes are due to some sort of dialectic working objectively and shaping the historical process by a necessity that does not depend on the human will."[100] Collingwood was thinking of such theoretical schemes as those of Vico, Hegel, Comte, Marx, Spengler, and Toynbee (and indeed Collingwood himself), who have taken their place in another canon, which is that of "philosophical history."[101] Through leaps of faith or conjecture, these metahistorians lifted themselves above the horizons and beyond the aims of Herodoto-Thucydidean history to carry on the Augustinian project of comprehending history as not merely a process of human inquiry but also the answers to that inquiry in the form of the education of the human race.

5

History in the Medieval Mirror

The knowledge of past events . . . forms a main distinction between brutes and rational creatures.
— Henry of Huntingdon

In the mid–thirteenth century the Dominican scholar Vincent of Beauvais produced an enormous encyclopedia, a *Speculum universale* (Universal mirror), of which the last part, compiled mainly by associates, was a "Historical Mirror" (*Speculum historiale*).[1] This historical summa, which combined both old and new — "old as to subject and authority, new as to compilation and arrangement" — represented the state of scholarship in the age of Thomas Aquinas. It is arranged "following not only the succession of holy scriptures but also the order of secular history" (*secularium hystoriarum ordinem*) and, invoking the formulas of Cicero and Quintilian, promises the usual benefits of truth and utility. This conflation of opposites, of sacred and profane history set in a context of classical and Christian values, reflected the structure and substance of medieval views of the recent and the remote past, which was held in place largely unaltered for more than a millennium — from the time of Augustine to that of the Augustinian monk Martin Luther, when many new horizons opened up to transform Augustine's conception of the human race and its education. No wonder historians, when they take a long perspective, continue to speak of a "middle time" separating modernity from antiquity. All of these terms represent, to be sure, idealizations or stereotypes detached from the immediate realities of historical experience, and yet they remain in general accord with the larger contours of history reflected in the medieval mirror of conventional learning.

What Is History?

Like Holy Scripture itself, Western historiography established a more or less orthodox canon of authors, following the revisions made in universal history by patristic interpretations of the relations between paganism and Christianity. Cassiodorus Senator, himself a historian as well as founder of a monastery, wrote a work divided, like Varro's, between studies divine and human, in which history figured significantly. Among essential "divine and human letters" he recommended especially the following: that "second Livy," Josephus, part of whose work (since Jerome could not undertake the job) he had translated; Eusebius, his chronicle as well as history, and certain Byzantine successors such as Theodoret; Orosius, who was also "on hand, if you desire to read him"; Jerome and his lives of famous men; and the authors of other "venerable" texts testifying to the faith and illuminating, however fitfully, ecclesiastical as well as secular history.[2]

Such Christian continuity is also evident in the succession of universal chronicles leading from Eusebius (with Julius Africanus and a few other antecedents) in the fourth century to Otto of Freising in the twelfth, and indeed much further, to Johann Cario (sixteenth century), Bishop Bossuet (seventeenth), Herder (eighteenth), Leopold von Ranke (nineteenth), H. G. Wells (twentieth), and various bibliographies, universal histories, and derivative handbooks and diagrams of universal chronology of our own times, all of which work within "the grand design of God," or at least in its secular shadow.[3]

Medieval authors did have a recognizable idea of history, though it had more to do with rhetoric and the liberal arts than with higher forms of knowledge such as philosophy and theology, this last, of course, being the primary guide and control for all the other disciplines. In fact history did not appear among the seven liberal arts except as an auxiliary (*appendentia artium,* in the phrase of Hugh of St. Victor)[4] or a genre related to the study of grammar, which, according to John of Salisbury's philosophical defense of the liberal arts, represented the first step on the ladder of learning, since — not unlike history — "it introduces wisdom through ears and eyes by its facilitation of verbal intercourse."[5]

In general, *history* was defined in commonplace terms stressing truth, utility, and, secondarily, aesthetic or literary value, but all of these classical qualities were reinterpreted in the context of Christian faith, piety, doctrine, and the different attitudes toward what was "worth remembering" (*digna memoria*). Many authors followed Quintilian's threefold categorization, sometimes modified, as in Martianus Capella's fourfold scheme, which included "history, fable, fiction, and the statement of law or business," the last referring to Quintilian's *historia*, while, Martianus adds, "history is, for example, Livy's."[6]

With grammar, history was located in the lowest place in the intellectual hierarchy of Christian doctrine, which prized the spiritual above all human traditions: "There are some which have neither beginning nor end, and these are named eternal; there are others which have a beginning but are terminated by no end, and these are called perpetual; and there are yet others which have both beginning and end, and these are temporal."[7] So Hugh of St. Victor explained the three "manners" of things and the subordinate position of the art of history to the sciences of philosophy and theology, which treated the eternal.

This invidious distinction was in part the reason for that neglect of historical writing which saddened Peter the Venerable in the twelfth century: "It was an ancient custom, not only with the first fathers of the Christian faith, but even with the gentiles, to consign to writing every undertaking, good or evil; but our contemporaries . . . allow to die out the memory of everything that is happening in their times and which could be so useful to those who might come after them."[8] Much of what happened in the previous four or five hundred years had been lost; and if this "sterile silence" continued, this monastic scholar asked, how could the works of God be known?

> In fact our times are so different from former times that, while we are perfectly informed about everything that happened five hundred or a thousand years ago, we know nothing about later events. . . . [By contrast] the ancient historians . . . took from far distant nations and from foreign tongues whatever these peoples and languages had to offer that was worthy of interest and that could benefit humanity. The Egyptians ardently embraced the language and learning of the Greeks; the Greeks those of the Latins; the Latins, those of the Greeks, the Hebrews and many other peoples . . .

Only the study of history—which in fact was undergoing a certain revival at this time—could restore this knowledge, at once mundane and spiritual, of the larger world of God's creation.[9]

To judge from rhetorical and poetical pronouncements, medieval authors regarded history as a major force in the drive toward a truth that was divine as well as human. For some of them poetry was the natural enemy of other history and truth: "Beware the muse, beware falsehood," warned Godfrey of Viterbo in his poetic rendering of the deeds of Frederick Barbarossa (relying on Otto of Freising): "I sing a true chronicle, not fable."[10] In any case, according to one of the saints' lives, the function of history was not just to memorialize the past; it was to restore it "as if present to the eyes."[11] The opposite of death, history could make mortals live again after a thousand years — "longer than deeds liveth the word" — although in the case of saints the life portrayed was highly conventional and idealized.[12]

History was frequently associated with the faculty of a sight; for example, the standard entry in the encyclopedic *Etymologies* of Isidore of Seville represents the Greek word *historia* as meaning "to see" or "to know," and indeed modern etymologists also associate the term with vision or knowledge.[13] His notion is that of Thucydides, who wanted to base his writing on "autopsy," firsthand experience, with hearsay a less desirable source of information. According to Isidore, Herodotus was the first historian of the Greeks only, for Moses was the first historian in "our" Judeo-Christian tradition (*apud nos*). Isidore recognized the continuity of history, especially through the succession of rulers and through the human memory carried by ancient monuments. At the same time he distinguished history from diaries, calendars, and annals and limited it to "those times when we see," so that Sallust was a historian and Livy and Eusebius annalists, who treat "those years of which our age is ignorant." Isidore was, in his own way, very much a "presentist," arguing that the value of history (which, following Quintilian, he distinguished from fable and argument) lay in its instruction for contemporary learning.

In the writing of history, a fundamental distinction was drawn between natural or chronological order (*ordo naturalis, ordo temporum*) and artificial or logical order (*ordo artificialis*).[14] The first followed the style of annalists and historiographers (*sub stilo historiographo*), attending, for example, to regnal years; the second was associated with rhetorical or philosophical questions; and both of course, written for men and not God, were distinct from the eternal realm of things divine. This distinction locates problems, conceptual as well as literary, that have always troubled historians, that is, reconciling linear narrative with deep analysis. In medieval terms this meant harmonizing the *what* and the *why* of human actions so as to associate history with philosophy, whose aim was knowledge through causal explanation (*scientia per causas*).

Historians have always been creatures of the medium of writing and the world of books, which the fourteenth-century bibliophile Richard de Bury praised to the skies. Of this earthly passion, he wrote: "In books I find the dead as if they were alive . . . , [for] all the glory of the world would be buried in oblivion, unless God had provided mortals with the remedy of books. O Books who alone are liberal and free, who give to all."[15] In books all things may be found, so that the only task of moderns is to summarize and "condense" what happened and was said before. "Being dead," Richard wrote, "they cease not to reach, who write books of sacred learning."[16] Such was the scholarly license and charge which defined the historian's craft.

Bernard Guenée has described the semantic field in which medieval writers of history operated and found authorial identity.[17] Various writerly terms defined their activity: not only *chronicus* and *historicus* but also *chronographus* and *historiographus* (or *historiologus* — Hugues de Fleury). Their common business was to write down (*scribere, describere*), to excerpt, to compile, to compose (*componere, dictare, texere, contexere, retexere,* and so on), and other operations, but they did so under different warrants. A distinction was made in the medieval period between an author and mere copyists or compilers ("*auctor necnon scriptor,*" in the phrase of one medieval manuscript). These terminological distinctions, employed between the extremes of invention and plagiarism, became, by the early modern period, ways of giving definition to historiography not only as a craft but also as a calling and a profession.

Modern historians have been proud to claim for themselves a discriminating "sense of history," but medieval scholars were not entirely innocent of this faculty. They appreciated, for example, the changes wrought by Christian belief in the law (whose pagan colorings were apparent in the *Corpus Iuris* of Justinian taught in the universities) and even in philosophical truth; and on a more concrete and technical level they recognized the problem of anachronism, especially in connection with that popular medieval genre, forgery, and the technique of determining documentary authenticity (*discrimen veri et falsi*) on the basis of style and other aspects of grammatical criticism. This dimension of historical consciousness was most striking in the traditions of civil and canon law and theology, but it is evident also in the work of John of Salisbury and other historians.[18] This sense of historical change also appeared in the awareness by Christian scholars of the disparity between ideals and human instability and mutability. For legal judgments, wrote one eleventh-century author, "One must take into account geography, the quality of the times, the weakness of men, and other unavoidable realities which often change rules."[19] In general, laws had always to be interpreted in terms of place, time, and person (*locus, tempus, persona*), and such attitudes informed the writings of historians and chroniclers as well.

There has been much discussion about the loss of historical memory in the Middle Ages, and indeed there was a resurgence of myth not only in poetry but also in the efforts of historians to establish legitimacy through ancient pedigrees, biblical and classical. In this way, the conventional idea of history was modernized, or rather medievalized, to give it relevance to the world of Western Christendom being shaped by the "barbarian" peoples of the north, whose transforming presence made authors like Augustine, Jerome, and Orosius believe that an old world was passing and a new and better one was being born — and that eternal Rome itself, which Jerome saw "falling" before his eyes, was assuming a new form that Caesar and Cicero would never have recognized.[20]

Barbarian History

Barbarism was a term bestowed by classical authors on all peoples outside the bright circles of Greek and Roman culture, referring especially to the Egyptians, Assyrians, Persians, Jews, and other nations of the Near East. Older than the Greeks, these nations had their own forms of wisdom, but as Diogenes Laertius argued, none of these deserved to be ranked with Greek philosophy (of which he was the authoritative historian).[21] This was also the view taken by Celsus, who consigned Christian extensions of Jewish religion to the level of barbarian superstition.[22] By Augustine's day, however, the invidious sense of the word had shifted and was applied by Christians, in the process of gaining mastery over the Roman Empire, to the Germanic nations still living, for the most part, outside the Christian faith, or else (like Alaric, the ravager of Rome in 410) professing the heresy of Arianism. These were peoples who, lacking letters, were without history in the Herodotean or Judeo-Christian sense, though of course they had their own mythical traditions, but it would not be long before they took their own first steps toward the stage of culture marked by the writing of history.

Between the time of Ammianus Marcellinus (late fourth century) and Jordanes (mid–sixth century) historical inquiry was, if not dormant, then conspicuously derivative. Christian chronicles followed Eusebius and Jerome, although those of Prosper of Aquitaine and Sulpicius Severus (whom Gibbon much admired) had some original elements.[23] Historiography was dependent still on the vision of Roman history formed by Livy, and indeed Polybius, though to be sure it was given Christian coloring, and its "universal" form was modified through interaction with biblical cosmology and genealogy. But just as the Western Empire itself was undermined and overthrown by peoples from the North and East, so mainstream Western historiography was transformed by the particular experiences and fortunes of barbarian tribes entering Roman territories with their own sense of identity and tradition, mythical if not historical.

The "barbarians" had already received a good press from Roman authors like Tacitus, who contrasted their purity and virtues with the corrupt civilization of the imperial period, and Christian authors followed a similar line of interpretation. Salvian, a younger contemporary of Augustine and Orosius, denied that the Romans, Christians included, were in any way superior to the Goths and Vandals. The former were unjust and neglectful toward the poor, while "the Franks . . . are ignorant of this wrong; the Huns are immune to it; there is nothing of the sort among the Vandals, nothing among the Goths." "What hope . . . can there be for the Roman state," he asked, "when barbarians are more chaste and pure than the Romans?" Classical civilization was indeed falling, but not because of the barbarians, for "it is our vicious lives alone that have conquered us."[24]

The age of Salvian and Augustine was also the age of the complex and confusing barbarian migrations — whether "invasions" or "wanderings" — in and around the territory of the crumbling empire. The Visigoths came into the Balkans in the later fourth century and, after defeating the Emperor Valens in 378, passed through Italy (sacking Rome in 410) on their way to Spain; the Vandals were in Gaul by 406, en route to Africa (Augustine died during their siege of Hippo in 430); the Burgundians settled in the Rhone Valley in 443, to be conquered in the next century by the Franks; the Huns reached the height of power under Attila in Gaul in the mid–fifth century, settling after their defeat on the lower Danube; the Ostrogoths, split off from the Visigoths in the late fourth century, came to Italy in 489, to be conquered a generation later by Justinian; the Lombards, Anglo-Saxons, and other northern tribes began arriving later in the sixth century. All these nomadic movements, interactions with the Romans and Greeks, and European settlements were the subject of a new wave of historiographic efforts, which followed simple chronicle forms and, if loosely and inelegantly, classical precedents but which introduced new themes into historical narrative.

The epic story of the Goths was the subject of a number of historical treatments, beginning with the post-Eusebian chronicle tradition and the apologetic history of Orosius. Following this tradition, Isidore of Seville celebrated, in a most conventional way, the splendors of the Spanish geographical situation and the "very ancient" heritage of the Gothic invaders, the etymology of whose name was either from "Magog" (son of Japhet) or, as Jerome had preferred, the "Getae."[25] However, the meaning of their name was *tectum,* or "strength," added Isidore, "and rightly so, for there was never a people on earth that exhausted the Roman empire to such an extent." Orosius had speculated that if — "which God forbid!" — the Goths should, like the Romans, succeed in their efforts, they would be transformed from "cruel enemies" into "great kings"; and so indeed it turned out.[26] Although infected with the heresy of Arianism, the Goths were represented by Isidore and later historians in light of the military triumphs (despite setbacks) of these great kings, who were feared by Alexander, Caesar, and finally "all the peoples of Europe" (except perhaps the Huns), although they had shown unusual mercy in sacking Rome.[27] Through God's favor, Isidore concluded, the kingdom of the Goths had by then lasted 256 years, while that of the Vandals (crushed in 525) lasted only 113 years and that of the Suevi, transferred to the Goths, 177 years.[28] The question, whose answer was perhaps to be found in the Book of Revelation, was how long such divine favor would last.

The First Historians of Europe

Between the sixth and the ninth centuries there were four major historians who devoted themselves to aspects of the European past which had been located outside the Roman perspective adopted by universal history. These authors were all national historians with fairly local horizons and were separated in time and space, but in retrospect they form a historiographical quartet that sheds light on what still seem the darkest ages of Western history. Jordanes (ca. 500–554) told the story of the Goths from a Byzantino-Roman perspective; Gregory of Tours (538/39–94) wrote of the Franks from the standpoint of a highly placed churchman; Bede (672/73–735) chronicled, from Northumbria, the affairs of Britain and the English church; and Paul the Deacon (720/30–99) was the historian of the Lombards, late arrivals on the European scene.

Jordanes was also author of a hasty abridgment of the history written by his older contemporary Cassiodorus, who also encouraged translations from the Greek, including Josephus. Cassiodorus (480–575) would himself deserve recognition as the first "national historian" in the West, from what can be surmised about his lost history, which treated the "origins, dwelling places, and way of life" of the Goths. According to Cassiodorus's own testimony, "he made 'the Origin of the Goths' a part of Roman history, collecting as it were into one wreath all the growth of flowers scattered over the expanse of many books."[29] However, the vagaries of textual fortune require that this honor go instead to what Walter Goffart calls the "Byzantine travesty" of Jordanes.[30] Whether a "pale, servile shadow" of Cassiodorus or (as Goffart concludes) an independent-minded and creative borrower, Jordanes had a larger design, not inferior to that of his contemporary Procopius but with more attention to religious matters, which was to compose Roman and Christian history in the age of Justinian and only secondarily to write about his fellow Goths.

Referring to Tacitus, Strabo, Ptolemy, and other classical sources, as well as to Christian historians like Orosius, Jordanes provided a conventional geographical framework for his story of great deeds and heroic noble lines that made obscure Gothic traditions part of Roman history and gave them an equally glorious ancestry, which he was proud to claim as his own. According to Jordanes, the Goths originated in Scandanavia, that "hive of races or womb of nations"; moved south, first by ship and then on foot, toward the boundary between Europe and Asia; subdued the Vandals; after five reigns came to Scythia and later Dacia, Thrace, and Moesia (probably Jordanes's place of birth); and came finally to be divided into western and eastern — that is, Visigothic and Ostrogothic — branches.[31] The Goths first confronted the Persians, who were afraid to do battle with them; then the Greeks, and indeed overran Greece and Macedonia after Alexander's death; and finally the Romans, beginning with Caesar, who subdued almost the whole world "and yet was unable to prevail against the Goths."[32] Thereafter the history of the Goths merges with that of Rome, as allies as well as enemies, and Jordanes gives a more detailed account of the interactions between and conflations of barbarism and civilization. For Walter Goffart (drawing on the formulas of Hayden White), the shape of Jordanes's imperial history was that of tragedy, the fall of Rome finding its analogy in that of Adam and Eve, while recent history was a love story featuring the convergence between the Goths and the Christian empire, and a "happy ending" in his own age.[33]

Like the Greeks and Romans, the Goths had their heroic poetry; and Jordanes referred to the ancient songs, sung to the accompaniment of the cithara, which celebrated heroes not inferior to those of (classical) antiquity and told stories of the Amazons and other tribes in contact with the Goths. He also recited the ancient genealogies of his people, which he begged his reader to hear "without repining; for I speak truly."[34] The Goths were best known for their military prowess — "Mars has always been worshipped by the Goths," he remarked — but at the same time they were, he judged, "wiser than other barbarians and . . . nearly like the Greeks," and by the first century B.C. they had themselves reached a civilized state through the teachings of their counselor Dicineus.[35] In fact, since the Goths had no written laws before the sixth century, Jordanes may be exaggerating here, and indeed he has been impugned by later scholars for his carelessness and inaccuracies (if not, as Mommsen charged, fraud). Yet Jordanes made the usual professions of truth and accuracy expected of historians, denying that (as he put it) "I have added aught besides what I have read or learned by inquiry."[36]

A more careful and comprehensive "barbarian" historian was Gregory, Bishop of Tours, who devoted much of his churchly career to the compilation of an ecclesiastical history which focused on the Frankish monarchy of the sixth century and which gave its author recognition by a Renaissance

successor, Claude de Fauchet, as "the father of French history."[37] Gregory
wrote in times both good and bad, with rulers fighting each other, churches
attacked by heretics, and letters in decline in Gaul, and yet saints and some
rulers had championed the cause of trinitarian Christianity. In this moral and
religious confusion Gregory set about the lonely task of keeping alive the
memory of the barbarian past for generations yet unborn and holding up
examples, such as Clovis and his wife Clotilde, of ideal Christian rulership.

If Gregory's narrative seems less coherent than required by historiographical standards, ancient or modern, this may be because his practice was based
on the organization of images rather than concepts, as Giselle de Nie has
argued at length.[38] He respected historical truth but gave priority to Christian
belief and indeed opened his work not with commonplaces about the value of
history but with his personal credo, adhering to the doctrine established by the
Nicene Fathers. This set the tone for his summary, written in a proudly un-
polished and unrhetorical style, of biblical and Roman history, the deeds of
saints and martyrs, the coming of the barbarians, the origin of the Franks, and
their Christian fortunes from the time of Clovis down to his own day. Gregory
wrote within the limited horizons of the field of activity and reputation of St.
Martin of Tours and on behalf of the episcopal power to which he succeeded;
but he also paid homage, or lip service, to the universal tradition of Eusebius
and Jerome, and later Orosius, by projecting his story back to the Adamic
beginning of history.[39] But his summary of biblical history was perfunctory,
and he quickly settled into the small Gallic world of his personal experience,
six of his ten books being devoted to contemporary history (*gesta praesentia*).

Gregory's chronological focus narrowed rapidly. At the end of the early
books he totaled up the years covered — Book I, 5,596 years from Creation to
the death of St. Martin of Tours; II, 112 years to the death of Clovis; III, 37 to
the death of Theudebert; and IV, 29 to the death of Sigebert. His geographical
outlook was likewise progressively narrowed. After recounting the death of
Our Lord, Gregory surveyed the persecutions of the emperors from Trajan to
Diocletian and consequent martyrdoms and then turned to affairs in Gaul:
the conversion of the whole city of Lyon by St. Polycarp, followed by more
persecutions and unnumbered and unnamed martyrs, and the mission of seven
(named) bishops to convert Gaul, culminating in the miraculous career of
Gregory's revered predecessor, St. Martin. "So far Jerome [covered]," Gregory
wrote when he came to the bloody reign of Valens, acknowledging the derivative character of his narrative — "from this point onwards the priest Orosius
took up the task of writing."[40] The grand total of years covered by Gregory
was 6,063, although his own figure was 5,792, given perhaps to keep his own

age within the time allotted to human history calculated by analogy with the week of Creation — one millennium for each day.[41]

Gregory had little information about the origins of the Franks except that they were led by long-haired warriors, and he cites the remarkable work of the fifth-century historian (and biographer of St. Martin) Sulpicius Alexander concerning their early conflicts with the Romans. The historians Gregory knew never gave the names of Frankish kings but told of the passage of this nation from Pannonia across the Rhine through Thuringia, stopping short of the lands controlled by the Goths and the Burgundians.[42] The Frankish people were idolaters until Clovis, son of Chilperic, was converted to Christianity with the urging of his wife and the divine proof shown by his victory over the Alamanni in the fifteenth year of his reign — all of which, along with Clovis's words, are given in colorful detail in Gregory's account. The reason for Frankish success, for example, over the heretical (Arian) Goths, according to Gregory, was their defense of Nicene orthodoxy: "Clovis, who believed in the trinity, crushed the heretics with divine help and enlarged his dominion to include all Gaul; but Alaric, who refused to accept the Trinity, was therefore deprived of his kingship, his subjects and, what is more important, the life hereafter."[43] The Holy Trinity, whose form Gregory thought could be seen even in the Old Testament, presided thenceforth over the uneven fortunes of the Frankish (posterity would say "French") monarchy.

Much of Gregory's narrative was occupied with sensational accounts of crimes, atrocities, murders, and tortures. Yet at the same time he wrote piously but unphilosophically about a world featuring daily miracles under the governance of God, emphasizing events both bad and good — the "slaughter of peoples" and the "downfall of worthless men." He offered models such as Clovis, but not uncritically, and he collected terrible tales of the malice of women rulers, such as Queens Brunhild and Fredegund. He was a master of anecdotal history, but he was above all a moralist writing (as Goffart argues, again applying the categories of White) in an ironic and even satirical mode. He insisted several times on his plain style (*rusticus loquens*); yet to Goffart it seems that Gregory's work — "a collection of short stories" — does have a detectable literary design, which was to present a gallery of figures, case studies, including atrocities and miracles together with personal moral judgments.[44] Gregory also aspired to literary immortality; for at the end of his *Histories,* besides listing his various works, he had enough authorial pride to order that his successors in the cathedral of Tours "never permit these books to be destroyed, or rewritten or otherwise altered. . . . You may rewrite them in verse if you wish to . . . but keep them intact."[45] Such, however, was not to be

Gregory's medieval fate, for his *Histories* were known for a long time through a severely edited version by Aimon, who shifted the main focus from ecclesiastical affairs to the fortunes of the Frankish monarchs; and it is through this version that Gregory's work took its place as primum in genere of national "French" historiography.

Of medieval English historiography the masterwork is Bede's *Historia ecclesiastica*, finished in 731.[46] The "Venerable Bede" was a great classical scholar, a diligent martyrologist, biblical exegete, and historian, who repeated the ancient formula about the Ciceronian law of history (*vera lex historiae*) and the good examples to imitate and evil ones to avoid. In his preface Bede gave an account of the extraordinary pains he took to gather information from a wide range of sources, oral as well as written and archival. This care and solicitude was a reflection both of his own piety and of the reliability of history — that "faith of history" (*fides historiae*), a formula that would be taken up again in the early modern period.[47]

In this connection, too, Bede developed a profound and critical interest in Christian chronology, of which he gave a revised version in his *De ratione temporum;* and indeed his *Historia ecclesiastica* was a linear descendant of the work of Eusebius and Jerome. Like Nennius, Bede begins with a brief geographical sketch of Britain and Ireland and then turns to the beginnings of the Roman occupation under Caesar, the departure of the Romans, and the progress of Christianity in Britain, especially with the coming of Augustine (Austin) in the sixth century. The *History* transcends its Northumbrian setting and stands out in sharp contrast to other early chroniclers such as Nennius not only in literary and scholarly quality and in its favorable view of the English people emerging from a deplorable pagan past. As Goffart comments, "The H. E. is predominantly a gallery of heroes," and he sees its "unity" as more dramatic than that found in Jordanes and Gregory of Tours.

It was also the contribution of Bede to lay down the manner of reckoning chronology for Western historiography down to the present. Having carried his story to his own generation, Bede remarked on the appearance of two comets in 729 and the invasion of Gaul by the Saracens (alluding to the battle of Tours in 732). He celebrated the "catholic peace" in his own day, especially in his own Northumbrian land, which was threatened only by the "national hatred" held by the Britons for the English. Bede concludes his story as follows: "This, then, is the present state of all Britain, nearly two hundred and eighty-five years after the coming of the English to Britain, but seven hundred and fifty-one years since our Lord's Incarnation. May the world rejoice under his eternal rule, and Britain glory in his Faith. Let the countless isles be glad, and sing praises to the honour of his holiness!"[48] So like Jordanes, Gregory, and Paul, the Venerable Bede placed the story of his people in the center of universal Christian history, setting the tone for many successors for centuries to come.

The fourth major historian of barbarian Europe was Paul the Deacon, whose *History of the Lombards* was composed about a half-century after Bede's *History* and was regarded by Gibbon as more lively and faithful than any of the others. After becoming a monk, Paul traveled from Monte Cassino to France and resided for a time at the court of Charlemagne, who had conquered the Kingdom of Italy in 774. Like Jordanes, Paul began his historical writing with a Roman history, which, although based on Eutropius, began earlier, that is, not with Aeneas but with Janus, who according to some was the first ruler of Italy. With what Goffart calls its "recognizably Orosian coloring," this book was a popular survey of the history of the empire and the barbarian invasions down to the death of the Ostrogothic leader Totila in 552. The *History of the Lombards,* composed after Paul's return to Italy, is in effect a continuation of the earlier work but on a more local scale.[49]

Paul's major work opens with a conventional geographical survey, embellished with ethnographic commonplaces about the qualities of the climate of Germany, "teeming" with various "fierce and barbarous nations," and then he settles into a narrative based on an anonymous work, "The [Scandanavian] Origin of the Nation of the Lombards." But no more than Jordanes, Gregory, or Bede is Paul a copyist or simple recorder of *res gestae*; and he, too, shows a heavy interpretive hand in his account of Lombard traditions, especially (remarks Goffart) in his employment of "a well-known Old Testament pattern of action: the Chosen People prosper; they lapse into the worship of false gods and are punished; and Providence mercifully raises up a hero to save them."[50] King Grimoald I is the Christian yet cunning hero, and his deeds include the repulse of a Byzantine invasion and suppression of an internal revolt. Paul succeeds admirably in placing his people and their struggles in a Christian setting, although he stops short (whether by design or not) of the Carolingian conquest and the grand narrative of Western imperial history, which overwhelms the busy subplots of barbarian history as the barbarians themselves had overwhelmed the ancient empire and confused its unitary history.

National Traditions

The chroniclers and historians of medieval Europe all worked in the shadows cast by this quartet of "barbarian" authors — the earlier ones eclipsed by their work and later ones borrowing from and adding to their foundational efforts. Before Bede the earliest barbarian chronicler of England was the sixth-century author Gildas "the Wise" (*Sapiens*), contemporary of King Arthur, who (tradition had it) is the first. Gildas's *Ruin of Britain,* first discovered and published by the humanist historian Polydore Vergil, is a historical jeremiad like Salvian's *Governance of God.* Writing in a "vile style," but claiming to know writers such as Tacitus, Gildas did not celebrate the victories of a brave people like the Romans but lamented the troubles of "an indolent and slothful race" in the last period of Roman occupation, treating British religion, persecutions, martyrs, heresies, tyrants, political divisions, and devastations. Gildas reported it as a well-known fact (though it is doubted by modern scholars) that Britain had been converted to Christianity as early as the reign of Tiberius. Once the Romans left, the barbarian Scots and Picts emerged, "like worms . . . come forth from their holes," to bring further havoc.[51] Yet neither the remnants of Roman civilization nor the subsequent ordeals, which Gildas likened to those of Israel, seemed to improve the character of his countrymen; for (he remarked sarcastically) they remained "impotent in repelling foreign fores, but bold and invincible in raising civil war." In his own day, he concluded, the foreign wars were over, but the cities lay desolate and civil troubles continued.

The next substantial text in the British chronicle tradition is the *History of the Britons,* written in the eighth century by Nennius. Apparently Nennius did not have a particularly high sense of calling, for he remarked, with refreshing candor, that he "had rather . . . be the historian of the Britons than nobody." His book, full of errors and fabrications, was derived, he wrote, "partly from the traditions of our ancestors, partly from the writings and monuments of the ancient inhabitants of Britain, partly from the annals of the Romans, and the chronicles of the sacred fathers, Isidore, [Jerome], Prosper, Eusebius, and from the histories of the Scots and Saxons."[52] Nennius's aim was, like that of Jordanes, Gregory of Tours, and so many others, to fit the story of his people into universal chronology based on the correlation of biblical and Greco-Roman history, genealogy, and mythology, beginning with the Trojans. For Nennius the British themselves were of Roman extraction, being descended from the consul Brutus, conqueror of Spain and Britain, whose pedigree could be traced all the way back to Aeneas and thence to Noah.

After Bede almost all the major English chroniclers — Eadmer, Matthew Paris, William of Newburgh, Roger of Hoveden (a Northumbrian like Bede), Henry of Huntingdon, and others — invoked his work; and other authors (such as Ordericus and John of Salisbury) added other sources to the expanding bibliography of English historiography, including Orosius, Isidore, Paul the Deacon, Sigebert, and Hugh of St. Victor.[53] In English historical tradition Bede's book had one serious rival, the *Anglo-Saxon Chronicle,* which may have been commissioned by King Alfred and which, hardly less influential than Bede, introduced a secular and a vernacular tone into the writing of history. This annalistic narrative mixed brief notices of births, deaths, marriages, successions, and notable natural phenomena with increasingly longer accounts of political and ecclesiastical affairs. Compiled by a number of hands, it offered a continuous record of a Nordic people from their arrival in England down to the accession of Henry II, whom "everybody loved . . . because he maintained strict justice and made peace."[54] Because of its account of cultural as well as political matters, this chronicle became, like Bede's *History,* a revered monument in a national tradition.

In the twelfth century the early vernacular tradition, which closed with the last entries of the *Anglo-Saxon Chronicle* in 1154, was already being superseded by the new Anglo-Norman school of historiography, beginning with Eadmer and especially William of Malmesbury (d. 1142), who claimed to be the first English historian to write in Latin since Bede.[55] Among William's major successors were Henry of Huntingdon (d. 1155), William of Newburgh (d. ca. 1198), and Roger of Hoveden (d. 1201), a clerk in the service of Henry II and Bede's last successor as a Northumbrian chronicler, taking up his annalistic account after Bede's last sentence.[56] In sharp contrast to these prosaic historians was the popular work of Geoffrey of Monmouth, *History of the Kings of Britain,* which reintroduced a poetic and mythological element into national historiography in the form of the Trojan and Arthurian legends and which was denounced by conventional historians for its violations of the canons of historical truth.

In the French tradition Gregory of Tours's work was continued by the so-called *Chronicle of Fredegar* (whoever was the author, or were the authors, of this seventh- and eighth-century compilation), which itself accumulated continuations, both original and derivative.[57] *Fredegar* was based acknowledgedly on Eusebius-Jerome, Isidore, and other Christian world chronicles, as well as on Gregory himself, before narrowing, like Gregory, to local Frankish horizons. The chronicle — written in a vulgar form of Latin and invoking the topos of a "world grown old" (*mundus iam seniscit*) — was self-consciously remote from classical antiquity. It was also the first extant text which (borrowing from the romance of Dares on the Trojan War) ascribed a Trojan origin to the Franks, imaginatively reconstructing a parallel genealogy through Adam and Christ on one side and the Trojan heroes and Roman emperors on the other.[58] This fabricated hybrid of a pagan-Christian pedigree became a commonplace of European historiographical practice as a way of enhancing the antiquity and prestige of barbarian rulership. *Fredegar* was also associated with more modern legends, notably that of the Solomon-like "good king"

Dagobert, the first French monarch connected specially with the church of Saint-Denis, which had been the object of his endowments and which then became the center of a national historiography.[59]

The major historian of the transition from the Carolingian to the Capetian dynasties in France was Richer, whose *Histories* (late tenth century) included not only conventional political narrative but also cultural and intellectual history. Richer described the achievements of Gerbert of Aurillac, who introduced the liberal arts, and especially logic, to Gaul, both music and astronomy to Italy, and established the principal divisions of philosophy. In the same terms that Ruotger used in his life of Archbishop Bruno of Cologne in the time of Otto I, Richer represented the achievement of Gerbert as a process of enlightenment, which contrasted to the darkness of earlier generations and which then spread to the rest of the Christian world.[60] Just as political successes were attributed to particular rulers and heroes, so too were such intellectual revivals conventionally represented as the product of the teachings of gifted individuals and doctrinal father figures.

The French tradition, like the English, could also boast an official vernacular record: *Les Grandes Chroniques de France* (beginning in the early twelfth century) were attributed to a certain "Primat" and were based on the eleventh-century history of Aimon of Fleury, who himself exploited Gregory of Tours's *History of the Franks* and other later texts. Alluding to Vincent of Beauvais's representation of history as a mirror of life and referring to the chronicles of Saint-Denis to authenticate his story, Primat denied any intention of lying; yet like Geoffrey of Monmouth and following the lead of Fredegar, he embraced the poetic accounts of Trojan origins.[61] The result is a curious mixture of fable and authentic history serving to celebrate both the "lofty lineages" associated with Priam and his equally legendary offspring, including Brutus, Turcus, Francio, and King Pharamond. Then, having established this ancient heritage, Primat indulged in analogous etymological speculations as an introduction to the familiar story of the Merovingian and Carolingian Franks preserved in chronicle tradition, especially the founding figure of Clovis, who not only gave warrant to the "most Christian" kingship of France but also, prophetically and (for modern scholars) mythologically, "began national history" in a political and territorial sense.[62] For Gabrielle Spiegel (alluding to the work of Pierre Nora on "places of memory") the work of Primat "represents a significant moment not only in the history of medieval France, but in the unfolding of French historical consciousness."[63] The chronicles thus formed a canon which linked not only memory and history but also medieval myth and modern ideology.

In the *Grands Chroniques* women appeared in the background as supporting players and also in the foreground as protagonists. The work carried on Gregory of Tours's atrocity stories about the terrible Merovingian queens, Brunhild and Fredegund, who were worse, if anything, than the husbands whom they ruled and corrupted: "Through malice, pride, and arrogance Fredegund committed crimes and atrocities fearlessly, as is true of such women."[64] Among other things she drove her husband, King Chilperic, mad and then had her lover murder him. These and other stories—despite the defense of female rulership by Christine de Pisan—were drawn on by later historians to reject the idea of rulers who were female or ruled after the fashion of women (*muliebriter*) and to justify the "Salic law," which from the fifteenth century was, whether through error or calculation, identified with the private law of the Salian Franks.

The accession and imperial coronation of Charlemagne in 800, which restored ancient ideas of world empire to the West (rivaling the claims of Byzantine emperors), provided a universal base for writing the history of Europe and the quasi-mythological reconstruction of the histories of the "French" and "German" nations. Unlike King Arthur, Charles the Great, king of the Franks and Roman emperor, was a historical figure, and a historical presence for later French and German history; but like Arthur, he also became a locus of legends, which made him a larger-than-life hero and mythical founder of many institutions, including the University of Paris; and these legends were enhanced and elaborated in the heroic poetry produced by Charlemagne's military ventures.[65] The worshipful historical portrait of Charlemagne by Einhard was supplemented by the anecdotal and almost hagiographic chronicle of Notker the Stammerer, whose allusion to the Book of Daniel identified Charlemagne with the "head of gold" Daniel attributed to King Nebuchadnezzar.[66] More generally, Charlemagne was associated with the theme of translation of empire (*translatio imperii*) and concomitant translation of studies (*translatio studii*), which received support from the royal and imperial patronage of learning underlying the cultural myth of a Carolingian renaissance and which became part of the official narrative of French and German history.[67]

In the German (imperial) part of Charlemagne's heritage, as elsewhere, historical writing took the form variously of local, monastic, episcopal, and city chronicles, and biographical works, although recognizably "national history" was late in appearing.[68] One popular historian of note was Widukind of Corvey, whose tenth-century study of Saxon history, like Jordanes on the Goths earlier, made use of folklore and ancient songs and speculatively derived the Saxons from either the Vikings or the soldiers of Alexander the Great. Widukind glorified the German emperors after the fashion of ancient heroes and as the successors of the Roman Caesars, likewise defending the

imperial heritage from "barbarians" like the Magyars.[69] His work was continued by the chronicle of Bishop Thietmar of Merseburg, who likewise employed poetic sources in his account of Italian and German affairs under the
last of the Saxon emperors.[70]

There were other significant contributions to what in retrospect could be
seen as a "German" historiographical tradition. The episcopal chronicle of
Adam of Bremen, writing a century after Widukind, brought the Northmen,
Danes, and Slavs into the context of European history.[71] The best historian of
the Salian dynasty was Lambert of Hersfeld, whose *Annals* exhibited Livian
influence and extended its vision back to creation. It also shared the partisanship of other political writings during this incendiary period of the Investiti-
ture Controversy between papacy and empire in the eleventh century, which
was distorting in effect but which also reflects what Walter Ullmann called a
"causal" historiography.[72] The best of the world chronicles was probably the
eleventh-century compilation of Ekkehard of Aura, which was especially good
on the Investiture Controversy.[73] The earliest vernacular contribution to
world history (*Weltgeschichte*) was the *Saxon Chronicle* (first published by
Leibniz), which drew on Orosius as well as the Daniel prophecy and which
had Thuringian, Bavarian, and other continuations.[74] Another even more
popular vernacular work was the rhymed *Kaiserchronik,* though it is perhaps
closer to myth than to history.[75]

The most impressive contribution to imperial history was Otto of Freising's
chronicle — a primary illustration of and testimony to the "renaissance of the
twelfth century" perceived by Charles Homer Haskins — which covered the
immediate background and first years of the reign of Frederick I of Hohenstaufen, who also happened to be Otto's nephew.[76] In 1152, just 1,800 years
after the founding of Rome, Frederick was elected emperor; and Otto's quasi-
official work carried out the primary task of a historian, which in his view was
"to extol the famous deeds of famous men in order to incite the hearts of
mankind to virtue, but to veil in silence the dark deeds of the base or, if they
are drawn into the light, by the telling to place them on record to terrify the
minds of those same mortals."[77] Otto's chronicle, which begins with a sketch
of the background and the problems of Frederick's grandfather and father,
self-consciously avoids any pretension "to loftier — that is, to philosophical —
heights," and settles into a narrative of military and political accomplishments, especially the violent suppression of the rebellions of barbarians such
as the Saxons and Lombards.

Ancient Roman history was much on the mind of Otto as well as that of his
imperial relative and patron; and he reported the actions of the rebellious
Arnold of Brescia — "precursor of Zuinglius" Gibbon called him because of
his period as a teacher in Zurich. Arnold "set forth the examples of the ancient

Romans, who . . . made the whole world their own" and, opposing papal rule, "advocated that the Capitol should be rebuilt, the senatorial dignity restored, and the equestrian order reinstituted."[78] But it was imperial and not republican Rome that was the object of Otto's veneration, the ancient Roman *imperatores* being the ancestors of the elected Hohenstaufen emperors, who would overcome "the turbulence of the past" and preside over "an unprecedented brightness of peace dawn[ing] again."[79] When the ambassadors of the city of Rome praised their glorious imperial past, including senate, consulate, equestrian order, and army, Frederick responded in anger that this glory was in no way "past," for it lived again in his own state: "All these things are to be found with us. All these have descended to us, together with the empire. With us are your consuls, . . . your senate, your soldiery."[80] The emperors Charlemagne and Otto were the equals of the Caesars, Frederick argued, and so was he, the "lawful possessor" of this ancient heritage, which was made even more glorious in its Christian incarnation.

Paralleling the imperial tradition was that of the Roman pontiffs, who claimed an even grander heritage, their apostolic succession leading back not merely to falsely divinized pagan rulers but to St. Peter himself, whose commission came directly from Christ. Papal history was thus the human core of sacred history, and this was given historiographical form in the *Book of Popes*, a sequential collective biography of all the popes, synchronized with imperial history, based on earlier episcopal lists, assembled in the sixth or seventh century and carried on with increasing detail down to the twelfth century by official papal biographers. The earlier sections, which were enhanced by later forgeries, are a bare listing of popes, with a few of their accomplishments, especially ordinations, buildings, decrees, and later gifts. What gave special sanctity to this priestly tradition was the "crown of martyrdom," which was bestowed on twenty of the first thirty popes down to the age of Constantine.[81] After Augustine this tradition was cited by theologians as well as historians. In the Renaissance, papal historiography, or rather biographical history, was continued by Poggio Bracciolini, Platina (Bartolomeo Sacchi), and others.

Another contribution to papal history was that of John of Salisbury, who rehearsed the canon of ecclesiastical history, including not only the familiar names of Eusebius, Jerome, Orosius, Isidore, Bede, Hugh of St. Victor, and Sigebert of Gembloux, but also the earlier precedents of Luke and the Old Testament Book of Chronicles. On this tradition John built his own *Pontifical History*, which described events of the mid–twelfth century. In the spirit of Hugh, as well as of Cicero, John declared as his purpose to write both for posterity and for contemporaries and, in particular, "to relate noteworthy matters, so that the invisible things of God may be clearly seen by things that are done, and men by examples of reward and punishment be made more

zealous in the fear of God and pursuit of justice."[82] On good classical precedent John also promised to report nothing more than he had seen or learned
on good authority.

Medieval Spain, too, had a very rich chronicle tradition, traceable back to
Isidore of Seville and Orosius. From the time of Alfonso III of Leon there were
official chronicles, which were the basis of a tradition that, though centered on
Leon and especially Castile, was national in tone, praising the "excellence of
Spain," in the words of Bishop Lucas of Tuy's *Chronicon mundi*.[83] Examples
of this include Rodrigo Jiménez's thirteenth-century Latin history of Spain,
translated into Spanish, and the seminal works of the reign of Alfonso el Sabio
of Castile, the *Primera crónica general de España* and the *Estoria de España*,
which adapted classical myths, including that of Trojan origins, to the biblical
story. In the later Middle Ages Spanish accounts of the Reconquista and especially the discoveries of the New World would be major factors in the expansion and transformation — in both time and space — of the old framework of
universal history.

In general the national historiographical traditions of Europe emerged from
the histories of the barbarian nations, or *gentes* (in the terminology of the
Roman law that accommodated foreign customs through the *ius gentium*).
However, the process by which the "nations" of late medieval and modern
Europe issued from the barbarian groupings has always been a matter of
serious debate. How Franks and Gauls became "French," Anglo-Saxons and
Normans became "English," Iberians and Visigoths became "Spanish," and
Teutons, Allemans, Saxons, and (again) Franks became "German" involved
complex processes of Christianization, dynastic state building, and vernacular
linguistic and cultural formations; but in fact the emergence of national traditions was due in large part to the retrospective labors of scholars — the legal
fictions of jurists, the ideological constructs of publicists, the sentiments of
poets, and especially the mythologizing of historians, usually with the Roman
model in mind. As Carlrichard Brühl has written, "It is a great historical
falsehood to pretend that one is dealing with 'French' or 'German' history
when in fact one should speak of Gallic, Frankish, or Germanic history."[84] The
contentious and chauvinistic ways in which nationality was projected back
into medieval times is a striking example of modern "work on myth," and it is
ironic that this has been a project carried on by the most learned and "scientific" of historians working in the service of political interests.[85]

Shapes of Medieval Time

The chronicle was a popular genre of recording and writing for centuries
between the time of Eusebius and the Renaissance.[86] Not only universal

chronicles continuing or modeled on Eusebius-Jerome but also local, monastic, and national chronicles more or less self-consciously attached to the genre have survived in manuscript and printed form in large numbers, and their variety and richness cannot be captured in a brief summary. A. D. von den Brincken has provided a valuable overview of sixty universal chronicles from the third down to the twelfth century, indicating their scope, train of influence, and reliance on the theme of the six ages and four monarchies which gave temporal and geographic definition to the "world."[87] In England the followers of Bede and in France those of Gregory of Tours in particular constructed a tradition of historical writing that persisted into modern times; and as a result, while few of them have achieved high literary status, they have nevertheless served both as models and as sources of information for modern historians, who in their turn have become, in a somewhat critical way, part of this historiographical tradition.

On the lowest level the chronicle was little more than a random diary reflecting the narrowest of interests. As one prescription reads, "In this book there should be at all times a blank sheet on which you can note with a pencil such matters as the decease of a well known man or anything memorable about the affairs of state if you should chance to hear of it. And at the end of the year you should write out briefly in the body of the book itself, what you consider to be reliable and worth preserving for the knowledge of posterity."[88] Easter tables — compiled to determine holy days more accurately — also commonly furnished a framework for such jottings.

On a higher level and on the basis of different "modes of perception," William Brandt distinguishes between clerical and aristocratic chronicles, though he also recognizes modes that are mixed.[89] Clerical chronicles, at least down to the time of William of Malmesbury, offered only disconnected and undiscriminating records of human, natural, and divine phenomena — memorable actions, natural disasters, portents, and miracles — without a sense of causality or continuity but only a "principle of interest" (equivalent, perhaps, to the modern historian's taking refuge in the suggestion that an event, whatever its significance, is at least "interesting").[90] By contrast aristocratic chronicles (such as Froissart's) displayed some sense of relevance, which, though narrow and class bound, featured moral and political judgments, concerning for example honor, glory, or treachery, and they gave a privileged position to human will. Yet they, too, were tied to a largely unreflective chronological arrangement which left larger patterns to religious or social convention.

In general the medieval view of history, in contrast with that of antiquity, was both more ordered and more diverse.[91] It found order in the providential plan which came to overlay the "universal history" imputed to the fortunes of the Roman state and, no less significant, to project the historical process into the future. Yet it also tended toward randomness, not having any sense of relevance other than the "grand design of God," which was often inscrutable in detail. Within such a panoramic vision, time was not a function of narrative succession but rather a measure of distance from sacred events, and especially the central phenomenon of the Incarnation, from which, after Bede, human happenings were dated. The chronicle itself was linked to the Easter tables, and indeed one of its forms was that of random recordings in the margins and other entries reflecting the presence of a universal time scale which located events both natural and human. For historical genres such as diaries and annals, recorded day to day and year after year, chronological order was "natural"; but beyond exemplarist moralizing, the chronicle form, too, avoided secular meanings in favor of chronological distribution. It was as if particular human events, such as the lives of saints, could find no other narrative context than the temporal chain of creation measured by linear calendar time.

Not that the ideal of a rich and contextualized historiography was forgotten, only that the chronicle form seemed to be more appropriate for the old ideals of truth and accuracy, which authors continued to profess behind a facade, or topos, of postclassical humility. A remarkable expression of this sense of difference between chronicle and history can be found in the *Chronicle* of Gervase of Canterbury (who died about 1210), and it is worth quoting at length:

> The historian and the chronicler have one and the same intention and use the same materials, but their modes of treatment are different and so is their style of writing. Both have the same object in mind because both eagerly pursue truth. The style of treatment is different because the historian marches along with a copious and eloquent diction, while the chronicler steps simply and briefly. . . . It belongs to the historian to strive for truth, to charm his hearers or readers by his sweet and elegant language, to inform them of the true facts about the actions, character and life of the hero whom he is describing, and to include nothing else but what seems in reason to be appropriate to history. The chronicler reckons up the years of the Incarnation of Our Lord and the months and kalends that compose the years and what takes place in those same years and months . . . [including] events, portents and miracles.[92]

The chronicler had no such purpose but merely followed the random events of the Years of Our Lord — although Gervase admitted that some chroniclers had higher aspirations and that these two genres had become mixed by his time. Sometimes, he added disapprovingly, these genres were blurred, so that some authors, "writing chronicles or annals, go beyond their proper limits, for they delight to make broad their phylacteries and enlarge the borders of their garments. Setting out to compile a chronicle, they march along in the manner of a historian, and try to weigh with swelling words what they ought to have said shortly and in unpretentious language after the manner of ordinary writing."[93]

Although some critics might regard the simple chronicle as inferior to more elegant historical narrative, scientific-minded historians like Bishop Stubbs (the editor of Gervase's work) took a different view to the extent that they regarded chronicles as closer to the aim of truth telling. As Stubbs argued, "The chronicle thus retains its value forever as a record of facts; the history loses its importance as soon as the principles which it was written to illustrate, or which have guided its composition, become obsolete."[94] Stubbs, of course, recognized the failings of the chronicle, since it contains, he continued, "no relations of the manners and customs of common life, things which to those who live amongst them are scarcely matters of consciousness, and which are only curious when they have ceased to be spontaneous; such details belong properly to the department of the foreign traveller, or to the historian of the next age." Did Stubbs forget the Herodotean tradition of historical writing, or was Herodotus merely one of those "foreign travellers" unqualified for the charge of historian?

In practice, however, Stubbs's contrast is surely overdrawn. For one thing the blurring of genres became more pronounced in the later Middle Ages; for another the chroniclers, too, attempted to find human meanings in their compositions. Classically inspired notions of history and even narrative practices invaded the chronicle traditions in England and Europe. As chronicles grew from disconnected one-line entries to connected prose, expanded from local to "national" horizons, moved from sacred to secular topics, from ancient to modern events, so they also took increasingly elaborate attitudes toward the office of the chronicler/historian and the status and value of his productions.

Elaborations of the theory of history are more conspicuous than of the practice, since they can be followed conveniently in the conventionalized statements, advertisements, or disclaimers which authors prefaced to their works for purposes of dedication and justification.[95] Here it is that the art and conventions of rhetoric reappear — the thin end of the wedge, as it were, of Ciceronian-Livian historical thinking — and further enrichments of historical writing derived from classical sources. A large range and variety of topoi appear in these prefaces and testify to the growing status of history and calling of the "historiographer," especially in comparison to philosophy and its supporters. Some of these topoi continue to haunt the prefatory poses and indulgences of modern historians.

Medieval chroniclers and historians almost all preserve the habit of humility.[96] The humility topos appeared in the writer's sense of being not only a "barbarian" in relation to Latin letters (as displayed by Gregory, Einhard, and

William of Newburgh, and, for the vernacular, the chroniclers of Saint-Denis) but also inadequate for the claims of higher learning and theology: they might write ecclesiastical history, as did Bede and Ordericus Vitalis, but they would not reach for divine mysteries. They often portrayed the almost superhuman labors entailed by historiography, the obligations of patronage or specific commissions (such as noted by William of Newburgh and Ordericus), and strict adherence to truth, but they never invoked the higher inspirations of poetry, theology, or (except indirectly) philosophy. For monastic chroniclers the writing of history was regarded as just another form of day labor.

Yet the writing of history raised even the humblest monastic authors above local and quotidian perspectives. They had to consider a deep antiquity preserved in myth and religious tradition as well as in debatable historical memory, if only to conclude that they were unequal to the task of recovery. They had to envision a more limited future, if only, in human terms, to address a posterity which might learn from the lessons of the past and so to consider, in the words of Eadmer, "the good of future generations."[97] They also had to take a position with respect to their predecessors, whom they praised, exploited, plagiarized, and sometimes criticized. They might also indulge in metahistorical speculation, as in the case of Ranulf Higden, whose *Polychronicon* offered a variation on the old theme of microcosm and macrocosm within the conventional providential framework of history.[98] In these ways they were conscious of belonging to a literary genre and tradition.

An inevitable and ubiquitous Ciceronian commonplace — and indeed "law" — defining the historian's office was of course that requiring truth, and here the old Thucydidean criterion of *opsis* was often invoked. Either the historian was himself an eyewitness, or else he made use of the best authorities. Not reason and authority, as with philosophers, but firsthand perception and authority derived from a single human source was the guarantor of authentic history. One reason for avoiding remote antiquity was this dependence on easily accessible testimony, as with Richard of Devizes, who admitted that, "because I could not hope to unravel the whole story, I have undertaken only the latter part of it."[99] However secured, such truth was to be located in a tacit context of both religious truth and, frequently, political commitments, as in the *Chronicle* of Fulcher of Chartres, who portrayed the First Crusade of God's working through the glorious deeds of French soldiers and martyrs. "The deeds of God through the French" was the memorable phrase of Guibert of Nogent: Christian truth did not preclude extreme prejudice and partisanship.[100]

Crusading chronicles constitute a large literature produced under the spell of the crusading ideal and ideology. Founded on faith and filled with marvels, they were in part a form of propaganda; and their view was limited — beginning as a rule with the taking up of the cross, celebrating the deeds of princes and knights, lamenting the atrocities of the infidels, and ending still in medias res. To this extent they also signaled — religious fanaticism aside — a return to Thucydidean political and military narrative and concern for memorable *res gestae* relating to the project at hand, sometimes including quoted dialogues. Only the First Crusade was celebrated as a success, while the late ones, informed by crasser motives, provoked questions about the causes of failure. The mixture of religious and secular motives is well illustrated by Villehardouin's account of the Fourth Crusade and the conquest of Constantinople. Joinville's crusading narrative was joined to a hagiographical account of the sainted King Louis XI, relying on secondary sources as well as Joinville's own testimony, though he would vouch only for the latter.[101]

In general French chronicles were written in a literary space somewhere between literature and history, between poetry and prose, between Latin and vernacular, oral culture, between learned historiographical tradition and myth — as well as between "clergy" and "chivalry." The vernacular chronicle was an expression of royalist ideology, as Gabrielle Spiegel has argued, but also, for other writers, an exercise in nostalgia and a "quest for a lost world of aristocratic potency."[102] Royalist and antiroyalist authors alike exploited the rich legacy of European myth and classical history to promote or legitimize current agendas.

But Christian truth did occasionally require historical criticism, especially in an age of growing literacy (or at least of the authority of written texts), and orthodox chroniclers drew the line at poetic invention. They continued to accept the idea of Trojan origins, which suited the genealogical and ideological pretensions of the royal lines of European kings — the *Chronicles* of Saint-Denis repeating this story derived from the older French texts going back to Fredegar — but they resisted the wholesale importation of legends, as exemplified notably by Geoffrey of Monmouth's *History of the Kings of Britain.* Listening not to the rules of history but rather to the siren songs of poetry, Geoffrey rejected the narratives of Bede and Gildas, which described and deplored the faults of the Britons, in favor of the undocumented legends of Arthur and Merlin.[103] Geoffrey's work provoked reactions from more literal-minded authors such as William of Newburgh, who assailed "the laughable web of fiction" which Geoffrey wove about the ancient Britons. His motive, William concluded, "was either an uncontrollable passion for lying . . . or a desire to please the Britons, most of whom are still so barbaric, that they said to be still awaiting the future coming of Arthur."[104]

Even more important than truth, to judge from the attention given the topic, was the utility of history, which was again defended on the basis of Ciceronian formulas. Once again, too, the utility in question was specifically Christian, the lessons of postclassical history being intended, as Roger of Wendover put it, "for the faithful" and in order to escape the sort of "divine vengeance" described in the Old Testament. Within a Christian context, history preserved its exemplarist utility and the sort of wisdom offered by historical experience and perspective. What earlier historians wrote and left written, Ranulf Higden noted, were the marvels and wonders, the deeds of "oure forme fadres, of stalworthe wit, wise and worthy, and of dyverse manere men that were in old time."[105] "For as the pagan says, 'the lives of others are our teachers,'" John of Salisbury quoted, adding that "whoever knows nothing of the past hastens blindly into the future."[106]

For Henry of Huntingdon, "History therefore brings the past into view as though it were present, and allows judgement of the future by representing the past"; and he suggested an even more sophisticated — and classicizing — argument for the value of history, for "the knowledge of past events has further virtues, especially in that it forms a main distinction between brutes and rational creatures, for brutes, whether men or beasts, do not know . . . about their origins, their race and the events and happenings in their native lands."[107] Not only reason but also memory and imagination were part of the unique constitution of human nature. These are reflections which, rooted in classical notions of history, would be drawn out further by Renaissance humanists, who likewise, but more self-consciously, hoped to elevate the study of history to the level of philosophy or even higher.

The most comprehensive portrayals of the medieval conception of history remained the world chronicle, embodied in a long series emanating from, elaborating on, and continuing Eusebius-Jerome. Of these the culmination — the summa, as it were — was the *Historical Mirror* attributed to Vincent of Beauvais, which combined classical commonplaces about the value of history with a mystical reliance on the principle of the Trinity as the underlying structure of human experience in time, although learning and monastic institutions were also included.[108] This narrative combined sacred with secular history — the overarching biblical framework with the familiar materials of Roman history — and moral judgments with prophetic discussions of the Antichrist and the end of things. Like the universe itself, which was represented in the familiar form of the Great Chain of Being, human history had a clear and symmetrical structure, reflected as it was in the mirror of Christian theology.

The Theology of History

Writing chronicles and histories in the Middle Ages neither called for nor provoked much thought, since conceptualization and judgment were pre-established by classical convention and scriptural teaching. History certainly had human uses and meanings, but it was also bound by biblical perspective, premises, and precedents. The basic semantic shift of *history* from classical antiquity to the "world grown old" of Christian dispensation was from a narrative crafted by self-conscious and critical authors to a real history produced by the workings of nature and providence — from a literary form of man's making, limited to perception, hearsay, and scholarship within the horizons of human experience, to an ontological process of divine origin beyond human senses and comprehension. Thus medieval thinking about history was not a form of literary criticism but rather an aspect of theology. In effect the Western philosophy of history, as it emerged in religious context, was a matter not of exemplarist moral and political judgment but of pious speculation about the meaning of temporal experience according to a higher plan with a revealed beginning and a promised and predictable ending.

This had been the vision of Augustine and Orosius, and it was the vision of Augustine's more remote disciple, Otto of Freising, who was separated from his patristic source of inspiration by more than seven centuries. Like Augustine, Otto addressed himself to the grand theme of the education of the human race and, like him, took a Janus position between past and future, between chronicle and prophecy, which was one of the dualities expressed in Otto's masterwork, *The Two Cities*. In an Augustinian spirit, too, this work traced the "vicissitudes of history" and cast them in the form of tragedy, since the earthly city was sunk in sin.[109] Yet unlike Augustine, Otto celebrated the checkered Roman past of the empire and the deeds of his imperial patron, Frederick Barbarossa, who inherited and extended this glorious political heritage and was first to style it "holy." In fact the empire had from the beginning been sanctified by God, who "in the fullness of time," that is, in the last days of pagan unbelief, allowed the sacrifice of his Son so that humanity might gain passage from the earthly Babylon to the heavenly Jerusalem.

Otto had studied Aristotelian philosophy in Paris, and he realized that history was a lower form of study, treating, as it does, not generalities but such composite and unstable particularities as man.[110] So he designed his work "not after the manner of a disputant, but in the fashion of one telling a story."[111] Like grammar, however, history was an essential preparation for higher wisdom, since it was through visible things, as Origen had taught, that one rose to the invisible — another form of the pilgrimage from the city of man to the city of God.[112] Despite his tragic outlook, Otto believed that after creation the course of history "gradually grew and made progress" through human association and the establishment of laws and also "through the agency and the wisdom of the teachings of the philosophers."[113]

The vehicle of this progress was the immortal empire which, though founded in sin, had—only God knows why—"expanded from a poor and lowly estate to such heights and to a great sovereignty under the primacy of one man."[114] Invoking the authority of Tacitus and Varro as well as Eusebius, Augustine, Orosius, and Jordanes and recalling Daniel's prophecy, Otto rehearsed the theme of the four monarchies and translation of empire (translatio imperii)— as well as the parallel translation of wisdom (translatio studii)—as "earthly power passed from Babylon to the Medes, from them to the Persians, afterward to the Greeks, finally to the Romans, and under the Roman name was transferred to the Franks," and thence to the Hohenstaufen of Otto's own time.[115] The periodization marked by the eight books of Otto's work combined classical and Christian turning points, the first stage extending from Creation to the rise of Rome, second to the death of Caesar and the birth of Christ, third to Constantine (founder of the Christian empire), fourth to Odovacar's deposition of the last Western emperor (476), fifth to Charlemagne (Frankish ruler with Trojan pedigree, who revived this empire), sixth to the accession of Henry IV (1056), and seventh to Emperor Conrad, first of the Hohenstaufen dynasty and uncle of Frederick—the eighth age being that of Antichrist and the end of the universal tragedy chronicled by *The Two Cities*.[116]

The theme of the earthly and the heavenly city suggested one other duality, which again took tragic form, and this was the opposition between papal and imperial Rome.[117] The perennial conflict between church and state had reached a climax in the previous century; indeed Otto began his chronicle of Frederick with the deposition of Pope Gregory VII by Emperor Henry IV, and later he described, with rich documentary evidence, the clash between Frederick himself and Pope Adrian IV.[118] The quarrels stirred up by the Investiture Controversy produced a mass of polemical and historical writing about the authority and legal heritages of papacy and empire, but Otto declined to take a position on the incendiary question of the Two Swords, of church and state.

Having surveyed and imposed intellectual form on the past from his dual perspective of prelate and imperial champion, Otto turns in his last book to the future, which he interprets in terms of the Trinity. Just as the heavenly city displays three parts (past, present, and future; Old Testament, New Testament, and Prophecy), so the earthly city moved through three stages: "Of these the first was before the time of grace, the second was and is during the time of grace, the third will be after this present life."[119] So the tragedy of the city of man will be transformed into the "gloriously perfect and blessed condition" of the divine comedy and finally to be beholden in the city of God.

For historians the present has always given shape to the past, but in the theology of history, as represented by Otto of Freising, the future was no less significant—with biblical prophecy and the Book of Revelation furnishing the key to the mysteries of time. In the twelfth century mystical thinkers such as Rupert of Deutz and Anselm of Havelberg interpreted history as "a progressive illumination of the trinity," and Joachim of Fiore employed the trinitarian conceit to express the various spiritual meanings of human experience in time.[120]

Born a generation later than Otto, Joachim was the product of a richer mixture of cultural influences (Greek, Jewish, and Islamic, as well as Christian), but he also began with the notion of a fundamental contrast between two cities, the old Jerusalem of human wickedness and the New Jerusalem of spiritual perfection. Joachim also had a more elaborate historical periodization, identifying the sixth with the Years of Our Lord, and reserving the seventh, the Sabbath, for the spiritual future; and he worked within a broader framework, referring the trinitarian principle to the three sons of Noah, especially Shem and Japhet, whose progeny gave threefold form to the genealogical and national processes of world history.

But for Joachim the primary manifestation of the Trinity was in the threefold progression of ages, the age of the Father corresponding to the law, the Old Testament, and secular knowledge (*scientia*); the age of the Son to grace, the New Testament, and wisdom (*sapientia*); and the age of the Holy Spirit to complete grace, prophetic revelation, and perfect understanding (*plenitudo intellectus*).[121] The last age, aspiring to the spiritual ideals of monasticism, seemed to many to be fulfilled by St. Francis; and the historicized theology of Joachim lived on not only in the ideas of the spiritual Franciscans (as indicated in the chronicle of Salimbene) but also in those of other history- and prophecy-minded mystics who, over several centuries, founded their hopes, dreams, and revolutionary plans on Joachimist, or Joachimoid, ideals of purity and spirituality.[122]

A century later another application of the trinitarian conceit was linked to the theory of the translation of empire, which was a common topic among defenders both of the empire and of the papacy. One example of the latter is Alexander of Roes, whose treatise *Translatio imperii* (ca. 1281) described the tripartite division and cultural heritage of Christendom which emerged in the wake of the Carolingian Empire. According to this theory — one of the many legalistic legends surrounding Charlemagne — the European world was partitioned among the Germans, who retained the empire, in elective form; the French, [*Francigenae*], who received the hereditary monarchy of the Franks; and the Italians, who possessed the Roman church. According to this Carolingian judgment, the Germans held supreme political authority; the French monopolized learning, or studies (*studii*), centering on the university (*Studium*) of Paris (which, according to another legend, was founded by Charlemagne);

and the Italians were granted the priesthood and its divine leadership. Thus, Alexander wrote, "By these three, namely, *Sacerdotium, Imperium, Studium,* as by the virtues, namely the vital, natural, and spiritual, the Holy Catholic Church is spiritually vitalized, augmented, and ruled. By these three, as by foundation, walls, and roof, the Church is materially made perfect."[123] Through this wise separation of faculties, Alexander concluded, the Christian flock would be safe from the incursions of Antichrist, and history could run its course.

Defenders of French tradition made the best of this divided heritage to celebrate the monopoly of learning which was vouchsafed the French monarchy. In the poetic rendering of Chrétien de Troyes,

> Our book tells of a Greek alliance
> Of chivalry, law, and human science.
> Then chivalry passed on to Rome,
> While science now finds in France its home.[124]

The medieval conception of history ranged widely in its interests between the sacred and the secular, kings and popes, saints and sinners, and displayed a sharp sense of class. The one element that seemed to be missing, except perhaps in genres of courtly poetry and perhaps hagiography, was that of gender; but here, too, a voice arose to defend the interests and the worth of that human being who was not "made in God's image." In her *Book of the City of Ladies,* written in the early fifteenth century, Christine de Pisan defended both the virtue and the historical significance of women, giving, for example, "examples of several great women rulers who have lived in past times."[125] The first woman chosen by Christine from the French chronicle tradition, Fredegunde, was hardly a model of womanly rectitude, but she rivaled her male counterparts in political aptitude and military boldness; and there were other women of all classes who exceeded men in religious worthiness. Christine's way of holding a mirror up to history promised to make history more fully human and so, according to the professed ideals of Christian historiography, to render it truly universal.

Medieval interests in the past, whether utilitarian, nostalgic, pious, superstitious, or merely curious, are richer and more diverse than can be captured in the categories and conventions established by Herodotus and Thucydides and their progeny, who preserved the vocabulary if not always the standards of *historia* and its offshoots. A full appraisal would require a scope as panoramic, and an appetite as omnivorous, as those of G. G. Coulton, who pursued the curious and the quotidian — "the real Middle Ages" and "Medieval Life as a Whole" were his terms — in many volumes of translations and summaries drawn from six languages. While preferring illustrations of popular culture, Coulton also included examples of medieval craving for historical knowledge, such as Ralph Higden's confession: "I take it not upon me to affirm forsooth all that I write here, but such as I have seen and y-read in divers books, I gather and write without envy, and [make] common with other men."[126] And Higden went on to a detailed listing of the sources of his eclectic gathering from Josephus and Eusebius to Gildas, Bede, and William of Malmesbury.[127]

In any case the time is long past when a "sense of history" can be denied to the Middle Ages. From Bede to Otto of Freising many medieval scholars, historians, and chroniclers, possessed an awareness of historical change and cultural relativity — in terms of persons, places, and times — and a fascination with chronology and an appreciation of deep antiquity, within the framework, of course, of the Judeo-Christian creation story. They preserved many old myths (and created some new ones) but did so on behalf of a cultural tradition which honored, in their own terms, the stories told by predecessors. Yet they respected historical sources and developed ways of judging their validity, which is to say, their authority, authenticity, and truth value. If history is, as Johann Huizinga wrote, "the intellectual form in which a civilization renders account to itself of its past," the medieval mirror, retrospectively viewed and reconstructed, reflects vividly the efforts of Christian — European — historians to make sense of the traditions, good and bad, which gave it meaning.[128]

6

Renaissance Retrospection

What is all history but the praise of Rome?
— Petrarch

The Middle Ages, which was itself a terminological creation of Renaissance humanism, had a strong sense of the past, as the work of Dante, torn between pagan and Christian Rome (and wanting to enjoy the best of both worlds), abundantly illustrates. Scholars in the Middle Ages also had an appreciation of classical historiography, including the rhetorical forms and values on which this rested. Yet this historical sense was selective and subordinated to deep religious commitments and inhibitions which frustrated both a discriminating perspective on the ancient world and a clear perception of the differences that separated a remote "antiquity" from a present age that was conceived not so much as "modern" as a world darkening or "grown old," with a bright future reserved for things spiritual and posthumous. In general, chronological awareness was tied to a rigorous concern for the Year of Our Lord, and geography to small circles of local experience, natural as well as human; and historical knowledge was limited to rumors of farther-off happenings and relevance to the myopic concerns of monastery, cathedral, court, and, eventually, city. To humanists like Petrarch, however, this was not history; it was an expression of the "dregs of time," a sad "middle age" (*medium aevum*) in which, he lamented, "genius, virtue, and glory now have gone, leaving chance and sloth to rule."[1] And yet, Petrarch believed, "once there was, and

130

yet will be, a more fortunate age" (*felicium aevum*), and to this dream of revival he devoted his own life's energies.

Petrarch and the Past

"What is all history but the praise of Rome?" Petrarch asked, with humanist hyperbole.[2] While he registered the usual Christian reservations about the enticements of a pagan past, he preserved this retrospectively patriotic vision through most of his writings. In his epic poem celebrating the achievements of Scipio, *Africa,* for which he received the laurel crown from the Roman Senate, Petrarch placed a prophecy about his historical role in the mouth of the Roman soldier-scholar-poet Ennius. Of Petrarch, Ennius remarked, Rome had not

>   . . . seen his peer
> over the span of ten full centuries. . . .
>   Zealous in study, he
> will sing the glories of man of old
> and trace from their first origins the sons
> of Romulus.[3]

Africa was Petrarch's nostalgic celebration of antiquity and vision of posterity, which

> when the dark clouds are lifted, may enjoy
> once more the radiance the ancients knew.[4]

Petrarch's poetic ambition was also expressed in his sonnets, in which he aspired to be Homer for his lady, Laura, although toward the end of his life, he shifted from conceits of love to topoi of old age and religious regret:

> I go lamenting my past history
> That I spent in the love of mortal things.[5]

Petrarch, too, was Janus faced, and in more than one way. He found alter egos in both Cicero and Augustine, being attracted, alternately, to the life active and the life contemplative.[6] In a posture that was at once ancient and modern, he took both origins, and goals, both a remote antiquity and an idealized future, into his conception of history. Like Augustine, but in a secular mode, he included beginnings and endings in his view of the human condition. For Petrarch, however, there was no longer simply a midpoint between old and new fixed by the Incarnation but rather two turning points — one marked by the end of classical culture and the appearance of barbarism, which coincided with the coming of Christianity, and the other marked by Petrarch's own vision of a revival of eloquence and all the learning associated with this, including the study of history in the broadest sense. Petrarch certainly retained many medieval traits in his outlook, sharing, as he did, the anxieties of Augustine and Jerome about the dangers of an immoderate fondness for secular learning. Yet no one can read him and not be struck by the originality of his posture, which seems even more striking by the ways in which he attempted to recover and to employ ancient modes of expression while situating himself, his ambitions, and his fate in a historical process that was at once tragic and joyful, destructive and creative.

Much of Petrarch's work indeed concerned history in one way or another, beginning with the ancient genre "On famous men" (*de viris illustribus*), to which Jerome had also contributed and which was the classical counterpart of the "lives of the saints" (*vitae sanctorum*). In his contribution to this tradition Petrarch did not claim to be original but only, following the rhetorical lead of Cicero, to collect "the praise of the illustrious men who flourished with outstanding glory and whose memory — which I found scattered far and wide and scattered in sundry volumes — has been handed to us through the skill of many learned men."[7] Unlike his poetic efforts, these studies, echoing Cicero's law of history, would not invent new things but would selectively "retell history," not to "transcribe their words but to . . . describe the events themselves." The goal of this retelling, of course, was the collection of *exempla* for moral and political instruction.[8]

Petrarch cultivated a prejudice against the previous centuries of "barbarism," which he usually associated with northern Europe. He deplored the stories about Charlemagne, "whom they [in this case the citizens of Ghent] dare to equate with Pompey and Alexander by giving him the surname of 'the Great.' "[9] Petrarch recounted a story of the mad lust of Charlemagne and how, guilt ridden after the woman's death and the terrible sight of her cadaver, he became dependent on the bishop of Aix and even transferred his capital to this marshy area, where he spent the remainder of his life. "This tradition continues and will continue," Petrarch concluded, "as long as the reins of the Roman empire are in Teutonic hands." And like Machiavelli a century and a half later, he lamented the descent of the barbarians into the defenseless Italy of his own day.

In his thoughts, however, Petrarch lived and sometimes wrote in the very midst of history. In 1351 he bought a copy of Livy's history, which he annotated with celebratory and critical comments; he put the book to good use in his *Africa*, and it was later studied by Lorenzo Valla.[10] Petrarch had a sense not only of perspective but also of anachronism, which he employed in a pioneering piece of historical criticism, responding to an inquiry of Emperor Charles IV about a grant, allegedly from Caesar himself, exempting Austria from imperial jurisdiction. As a close student of Caesar (the subject of the longest biography in the *De viris illustribus*) and owner of several of Caesar's personal letters, Petrarch was able to demonstrate, on historical grounds, that the document was a much later and very clumsy forgery. "I omit the question of style . . . ," Petrarch concluded, "which from beginning to end is both barbarous and modern [and is] a childish attempt to imitate the style of the ancients."[11] In general this question of style led Petrarch, inadvertently or not, to a sensitivity to neologisms, anachronisms, and other signs of linguistic change essential to the development of historical criticism, which was realized more fully by Valla and other philologists.

Petrarch had material and monumental as well as documentary links with the national past, and here again he displayed his originality, offering in a letter to Giovanni Colonna (who was author of another *De viris illustribus* collection) what has been called "the first antiquarian document of humanism."[12] "This is the Janiculum . . . , that is Monte Sacro, on which the angered plebians withdrew from the rulers," he wrote in this little cicerone: "Here Caesar triumphed, here he perished. In this temple Augustus viewed the prostrate kings and the whole world at his feet. . . . This is the temple of Peace, which was rightly destroyed at the arrival of the King of Peace. . . . Here Christ appeared to his fleeing vicar; here Peter was crucified; there Paul was beheaded. . . ."[13] Romans were sadly ignorant of this past, yet "who can doubt that Rome would rise again instantly if she began to know herself?"[14]

Although devoted to an idealized classical *patria* — glorified most famously in his sonnet "*Italia mia*" — Petrarch recognized that Rome could be identified with Babylon; yet his final belief was that Golden Rome (*Aurea Roma*), as he called her, is both the head of the world (*caput mundi*) and the city of God. There was one problem, which Petrarch expressed in an old commonplace inserted in his *Africa*: "Rome, unlike Greece, where such are found in numbers, produced few chroniclers. For us, to act is better than to write."[15] Yet there were exceptions, including Caesar, Cicero, and other noble Romans (not to speak of Petrarch himself) who stepped aside from matters of sword and toga to take up their pens, and this would insure the *fama* of the Eternal and "once Golden" City. "Whatever misfortune strikes the city of Rome," Petrarch predicted, "her name will live as long as any memory of Greek or Latin letters survives."[16]

In Cola di Rienzo, Petrarch imagined that he had found a modern incarnation of the Roman ideal and the sovereignty (*majestas*) of the Roman people, which was witnessed by the ancient *lex regia*, which Rienzi himself had deciphered and incorporated into his republican program.[17] For Petrarch, who was at the time full of Livy and the writing of his *Africa,* Rienzi seemed at first to be a combination of classical rhetoric and divine inspiration—the "third Brutus" destined to recall Rome to its past glories—and his resumption of the ancient title of tribune represented the culmination of a campaign of national restoration. Petrarch was soon disillusioned with Rienzi and his mad and finally disastrous plans to restore the Roman Republic, but disenchantment with the human symbol of Roman history did not turn Petrarch away from his retrospective and antiquarian idealism.

Petrarch's sense of history was not primarily that of a scholar; rather it was that of a poet, whose fascination with the ancients was associated with his quest for models to imitate and, in his ironic fashion, to debate, and betimes to surpass.[18] So Petrarch's imagination looked back not to "once upon a time" but to specific cultural moments in the past (*in illo tempore*), with specific qualities, moral or literary, to be understood and imitated, though in the fashion of a poet, not an "ape." The relationship of moderns to ancients was that of sons to fathers, and this allowed for criticism as well as emulation. There can always be something new under the sun. What complicated matters was that Petrarch has multiple fathers, or chosen precursors, and this compounded his ironic and dialogical inclinations.

At all times Petrarch's sense of history, and of time, turned above all on his ego—that is, on his sense of distance from, yet identification with, selected ancients, his desire for fame and a sympathetic posterity, and, again like Augustine, his ironic self-criticism and self-review. All these sentiments— nostalgia, ambition, self-preoccupation—were reinforced by his intense sense of authorship and the pressures of scribal culture. As Descartes found identity in cogitation, so Petrarch finds it in writing. "I write," he repeats (or rather has Joy repeat) in his dialogue "On the Fame of Writers"; "I write books"; "I have written much and am still writing"; and, despite the warning of Reason, "I write nevertheless, yearning for fame."[19] Writing also carries an author beyond his own consciousness to that of his readers: "Thus writing entails a double labor: first to consider to whom you have undertaken to write, and then what his state of mind will be when he undertakes to read what you propose to write."[20]

The greatest test of this requirement was posterity itself, and to this imagined audience (for which Dante had also written) Petrarch addressed his most stirring and narcissistic yearning for fame. In this painfully self-conscious essay Petrarch reviews his background, education, experiences, travels, places of residence, and career, especially his laureation and friendship with the greats of his day, down to 1351. He went to law school, but while revering the texts of the legal tradition for the light they shed on Roman antiquity, he was repelled by the scholastic method of teaching at Montpellier and Bologna, from which his father's death liberated him. On the other hand he admitted to a special fascination with the study of history:

> I have dwelt single-mindedly on learning about antiquity, among other things because this [present] age has always displeased me, so that, unless love for my dear ones pulled the other way, I always wished to have been born in any other age whatever, and to forget this one, seeming always to graft myself in my mind onto other ages. I have therefore been charmed by the historians, though I was no less offended by their disagreements; and, when in doubt, I followed the version toward which either the verisimilitude of the content or the authority of the writers pulled me.[21]

Like Miniver Cheevy, Petrarch was "born too late," and called it fate — except that Petrarch shook his head and, instead of drinking, kept on writing.

The most extraordinary expression of Petrarch's sense of identity with the past appears in the imaginary correspondence which he carried on with his ancient friends Homer, Virgil, Cicero, Quintilian, Seneca, Varro, and Livy — to whom he sent regards to the other historians who came before and after and who had been outshone by Livy. In part these exchanges were inspired by nostalgia — "I should wish," he complained to Livy, "either that I had been born in thine age or thou in ours"[22] — and in part by the wish to understand and perhaps, in a Christian context, to imitate the values of a better age. How many questions would he put to Virgil if he could! How sorry he was that so much of Varro's and Cicero's work had not survived! How excited he was to discover in 1345 a manuscript of Cicero's letters to Atticus! With Cicero, inspired by hearing, as it were, Marcus Tullius's own voice, he had an imaginary correspondence over the relative value of the active and the contemplative life, praising him for combining the two and yet expressing regret that he had not spent less time in "wasteful strife" in a declining republic and more in writing for posterity. "Farewell, forever," Petrarch concluded, with his usual dramatic attitude toward time and death.[23] It is said that he died, as if sleeping, with his face in a book — as usual, looking forward, backward, and no doubt inward.[24]

From the Old to the New Historiography

Petrarch's role in the renaissance of letters was described in glowing terms by Leonardo Bruni, his disciple and chancellor of the Florentine Republic in the early fifteenth century:

Francesco Petrarch was the first with a talent sufficient to recognize and call back to light the antique elegance of the lost and extinguished style. Admittedly, it was not perfect in him, yet it was he by himself who saw and opened the way to its perfection, for he rediscovered the works of Cicero, savored and understood them; he adapted himself as much as he could and as much as he knew how to that most elegant and perfect eloquence. Surely he did enough just in showing the way to those who followed it after him.[25]

Here is a classic statement of the mythical and foundational position which Petrarch claimed and was granted in the Florentine humanist tradition and which was so central to modern historical thought and writing. For the study of history Petrarch was indeed *il Primo,* and the legend continued to grow. "We are indebted to Petrarch for the intellectual culture of our century," Rudolf Agricola wrote: "All ages owe him a debt of gratitude — antiquity for having rescued its treasures from oblivion, and modern times for having with their own strength founded and revived culture, which he has left as a precious legacy to future ages."[26]

Yet if Petrarch in a sense created history, he was marginal to the writing of it in Italy, which had its own chronicle tradition, or rather traditions; for the centers of significant historical writing were not retreats like Petrarch's Vaucluse but rather the busy Italian communes, beginning as early as the eleventh century in Venice and Milan and the twelfth century in Genoa and Florence.[27] There are countless chronicles, repetitive and overlapping, most of them still in manuscript, reflecting the emergence of a new, or renewed, civic spirit and the need of cities to preserve records for commercial and administrative as well as political and ideological purposes. As early as the eleventh century, one civic-minded chronicler of Pisa wrote,

> I am going to write the history of the famous Pisans,
> and revere the memory of the ancient Romans:
> For Pisa only carries on the admirable glory
> which Rome once achieved by vanquishing Carthage.[28]

Although local in focus and information, these works were fashioned within the old framework of the Eusebian universal chronicle, with the attendant accumulation of classical fables. According to this mélange of myths, European culture appeared as the product of two dispersals — that of Noah's sons after the Flood and that of the Trojan heroes after the fall of their city. As in the national traditions of northern Europe, the Italian cities all associated themselves with this conventional prehistory and genealogy, agreed upon in all but minor details, which had generally to do with their own pretensions to be oldest and best.

In Florence the first major city chronicle, though written in the vernacular, was in most ways full-fledged historiography. Giovanni Villani produced a comprehensive survey of the story of Florence from mythical foundation to the crisis of his own day, in which financial ruin was capped by the appearance of plague, which indeed carried off Giovanni himself, leaving his brother Matteo to continue his chronicle. Under the spell of Dante's *Commedia* (and also, probably, fictitiously), Villani set the inspiration for his work in the jubilee year 1300, which found him in Rome. "And I," he wrote, "finding myself on that blessed pilgrimage in the holy city of Rome, beholding the great and ancient things therein, and reading the stories and great doings of the Romans, written by Virgil, and by Sallust, and by Lucan and Titus Livius, and Valerius, and Paulus Orosius, and other masters of history . . . , myself to preserve memorials and give examples to those which should come after took up their style and design, although as a disciple I was not worthy of such a work."[29] Like Dante and Petrarch, Villani wrote for posterity, though his theme was only one particular earthly city which had enjoyed good fortune and great renown, which was to say God's special favor — and he wrote not with solicitude for salvation or the ideal of world government but only so "that in the future men of knowledge may be able to increase the prosperity of Florence."

Writing as a prominent citizen and member of the municipal government, Villani set out to glorify his Florentine *patria*, but he displayed an impressive acquaintance with classical literature (Sallust, Lucian, Livy, Valerius Max-imus, Orosius, and others), and he aspired to a larger view. He situated his history, with due attention to the natural environment, within the conventional and providential framework of the world chronicle, rehearsing the story of the postdiluvian peopling of Europe, including not only Japhet but also Janus, who "did many things in Italy"; Atlas, founder of the city of Fiesole; Antenor and Priam, descendants of the Trojans, who built Venice and Padua, as well as Pharamond, first king of the French; Aeneas, Latinus, and the seven kings of Rome. Villani repeated the legends of the Cataline-inspired rebellion of Fiesole and its destruction; the subsequent founding of Florence, "city of flowers," by Caesar; the coming and the martyring of Christians; and the de-struction of Florence by Totila and its supposed rebuilding by Charlemagne.[30]

Villani was a believing, not to say credulous, historian, devoted to "Holy Mother Church" and her earthly expression, which was the Guelf Party (the "black," as opposed to Dante's exiled "white," Guelfs), and to the honor and superiority of Florence. In repeating these fabulous episodes in Tuscan tradi-tion, he was exploiting earlier compilations concerning "the origin of the city" as well as earlier world chronicles, but in the later sections of his chronicle he was much more down-to-earth and practical minded.[31] He retold the story, too, of the European origins of the Guelf-Ghibelline division, which entered Florence in the form of a family feud, and of later conflicts that divided the Guelfs and sent many, including Dante, into exile. Conscientious chronicler that he was, he regularly noted the effects of natural disasters; but he also attended to the commercial and cultural progress of the Florentine people, as illustrated by architectural triumphs, the coinage of the florin (which became a standard of exchange), and the career of his contemporary Dante, who, even in exile and despite political excesses, brought honor to his city.

After Villani the Florentine chronicle tradition continued well into the sixteenth century.[32] The dramatic story of the emergent Guelf and Ghibelline parties that rent Florence was retold by his contemporary Dino Compagni, whose work, resting on firsthand observation as well as hearsay, was meant to teach his fellow citizens the penalties of "arrogance, wickedness, and struggles for office" and the civil strife produced by these vices.[33] Among other fourteenth-century chroniclers, Goro Dati was notable for his defense of Florentine liberty (which had become the polemical motto of the Guelf party) against its Milanese rival, led by Giangaleazzo Visconti, a theme that was a secular version of the providentialism of earlier writers. For Dati, whose chronicle covered the years 1380–1405, the Florentines, besides being allies of the Roman church, were "born and descended from those Romans [enemies of Caesar] who, under the rule of liberty, acquired the lordship of the world and brought Rome more peace, tranquillity and honour than it ever had."[34] It was in the light of such republican values that Dati set his interpretation of Florentine history.

The political turn taken by late fourteenth-century Florentine chronicles was paralleled by a similar change within the humanist tradition, including Bruni and his elder colleague Coluccio Salutati. Petrarch had idealized Cicero as an author more than a man of action, but his successors shifted emphasis from the charms of a "life of solitude" to the demands of civic commitment, and their view of history shifted accordingly. For Bruni, Cicero represented the ideal combination of the *vita activa* and the *vita contemplativa*, so that "when he was active in the republic that was mistress of the world, he wrote more than the philosophers living in leisure and devoted to study; on the other hand, when he was mostly occupied in study and in the writing of books, he got more business done than those who are involved in no literary endeavor."[35] Taken together, the Florentine poets Dante and Petrarch, exiles both, achieved this goal — Dante in heroic political striving, though his poetry was unadorned by true Latin eloquence, and the self-indulgent Petrarch in restoring Ciceronian style, if not substance.

The study of history should involve just this balance between the practical and the theoretical, the political and the literary, recalling the old conceit of Mars allied with Minerva, except that Bruni's civic ideal celebrated the arts of peace as well as war. This is apparent in Bruni's treatment both of Roman antiquity and of the previous century of Florentine civilization. Latin language and literature reached a peak at the time of Cicero, along with republican liberty, but with the coming of imperial tyranny both letters and liberty went into decline, hastened by the invasions of the barbarians. Petrarch marked the second coming of Latin letters, and his accomplishments, too, had a political dimension; for after the conquest of the Lombards by Charlemagne, Italy began to recover its lost liberty, and "the Tuscan cities and others began to recuperate" and turn to learning.[36] Such were the social and political conditions — the material base, as it were — which made possible the literary efforts of Dante and then the pioneering achievements of Petrarch. This was the basis on which Bruni himself, two generations later, tried to build a political program in a time both of political crisis and of literary refinement, including a knowledge of Greek philosophy.

Bruni's major contribution to the canon of Western historiography was his more or less official *History of the Florentine People,* on which he worked from 1416 until his death in 1444. This book covered the same ground as Villani's chronicle but did so in humanist style and with the benefit of a century of scholarship and criticism. Writing in Latin rather than the vernacular, Bruni also went beyond Villani's naive chronicling by his fidelity to Ciceronian notions of history as an explanatory form of knowledge and a source of valuable moral and political lessons. "History," he wrote in his preface, "involves at the same time a long continuous narrative, causal explanation of each particular event, and appropriately placed judgments on certain issues."[37]

Following the lead of Livy as well as the Florentine chronicle tradition, Bruni began with the origin of the city — for "it is a fit and seemly thing to be familiar with the origins and progress of one's own nation, and with the deeds in peace and war of great kings and free peoples" — and carried it through the centuries of darkness down to his own age.[38] He broke with precedent by focusing on the "known history of this city" and rejecting the fables of Trojan foundations, the destruction by Totila, and subsequent Carolingian restoration. (This insistence on documentary sources, reflecting practical legal and administrative attitudes, would also be one of the premises of the nineteenth-century "science" of history, whose practitioners would survey and judge their Renaissance predecessors in the light of this principle.)[39] According to Bruni, Florence had been an Etruscan settlement and later a military colony under Sulla; and he followed the rise of Florence from these anti-Roman beginnings, through imperial decline, the darker period after the fall of the empire in 476, and the later reemergence of Tuscan cities (Pisa, Perugia, and Siena, as well as Florence), down to the modern period of republican grandeur, Guelf ideology, humanist culture, and a critical view of history.

The new humanist view of history, restoring and updating the ancient model practiced by Livy and Tacitus and theorized by Cicero and Quintilian, was expressed most clearly in the work of Bruni's younger friend Lorenzo Valla. Archgrammarian, radical rhetorician, and reformer of dialectic, Valla was a champion of the *studia humanitatis* and in this connection a promoter of historical studies. Like Petrarch, but more systematic, Valla turned his hand to historical criticism. He continued Petrarch's commentary on Livy's history on the very same manuscript; he gathered a number of annotations on the New Testament which would later inspire and be continued by Erasmus in his biblical studies; and most famously he exposed the famous donation of Constantine as a forgery. Deploying legal, grammatical, rhetorical, geographical, and chronological arguments, Valla ridiculed the author of this supposed imperial concession and denounced the Italian and universal claims of the papacy based on this crude fabrication, which was "unknown equally to [Pope] Silvester and to Constantine."[40]

Nevertheless, Valla was a tireless champion of the Roman tradition, papal as well as imperial, and the culture which it had preserved across the doctrinal caesura between paganism and Christianity. In his immensely popular *Elegancies of the Latin Language* Valla repeated the old motif of the four world monarchies, but with a twist, since it was the posthumous linguistic victories of the last of these empires that he celebrated. The triumphs of *Latinitas* outshone all the military glory of ancient Rome: "For this language introduced those nations and all peoples to all the arts which are called liberal; it taught the best laws, prepared the way for all wisdom; and finally, made it possible for them no longer to be called barbarians."[41] The posthumous victory of Roman civilization was such, Valla concluded, that "wherever the Roman tongue holds sway, there is the Roman Empire." And there too, he might have added, was the humanist and rhetorical conception of history.

The Brunian, or neo-Livian, model of historiography was imitated by Bruni's imitators not only in Florence — for example, by Poggio Bracciolini, Bartolomeo della Scala, and, in a vernacular mode, Machiavelli and Guicciardini — but throughout Italy and Europe.[42] Benedetto Accolti, one of Bruni's successors as Florentine chancellor, carried on the classicist tradition and the attendant interpretation of the darkness and literary silence following the fall of the Roman Empire. The reason for this was that the intruding barbarians "changed the entire pattern of life," after which "learned men saw that there would be no reward forthcoming, and so they preferred to be silent rather than record the deeds of that time for posterity." The other possibility was that "learned men wanted to devote their labour to the deeds of the saints and the defense of their religion rather than to this kind of history [and] history was rendered almost mute so that the memory of the most eminent men has been obliterated, from the end of barbarian rule up to the present time."[43]

Bruni's greatest successor was Flavio Biondo, who combined in his work, to a remarkable degree, erudition and narrative.[44] His *Italia illustrata* (1448–53) was a geographical and historical survey, based on travel and observation, of the fourteen regions of the peninsula, while his *Roma instaurata* and *Roma triumphans* were pioneering investigations of the topography, institutions, and antiquities, Christian and classical, of the city. Most important was his seminal *History from the Decline of the Roman Empire,* whose theme is the gradual replacement of the declining pagan *respublica* by the emergent *orbis christianus* of the Caesars, succeeded by an imperial Christ, through a "middle age," which was at least partially illuminated by the civilizing mission of the Roman church, down to a miserable and schismatic "present time"; and his system of dating shifts accordingly from the empire to the "Year of our Lord." In this book, which affected Ciceronian style and employed archaeological and epigraphic as well as literary sources, Biondo provided a standard, though of course Romanist, interpretation of postclassical and medieval European history that was exploited by many later scholars in their own national terms.

The new historiography penetrated to many other parts of Europe and was represented by a large number of Latinate contributions to national histories in Europe, eastern as well as western: Bernardo Giustiniani and Marcantonio Coccio (Sabellico) for Venice; Bernardino Corio and Lodrisio Crivelli for Milan; Pandolfo Collenuccio for Naples; Robert Gaguin and Paolo Emilio for France; Polydore Vergil for England; George Buchanan for Scotland; Conrad Celtis, Jacob Wimpheling, Johannes Aventinus, and Beatus Rhenanus for Germany; Juan Margarit, Lucio Marineo, and Juan de Mariana for Spain; Antonio Bonfinio for Hungary; Filippo Buonacorsi for Poland; and Albert Krantz for Scandanavia and Russia.[45] Thus the most diverse heritages of Europe found a common denominator in Latinate narrative, so that Christian and barbarian experience was reduced to classical forms and language, giving further coherence to Western historiographical tradition while adapting it to modern needs.

Political History in France

Despite the encyclopedic impulse of humanism, it was Thucydides' gaze that dominated mainstream history in the Renaissance. Not that he was yet a literary presence, but political and military history in a Thucydidean spirit was the preoccupation of most chroniclers and historians, vernacular as well as Latin, local and city based as well as national. Chronicle literature flourished in Italy, France, and Spain, and city chronicles in Germany, Switzerland, and northern and eastern Europe (England, with the ending of the St. Albans school in the early fifteenth century seems to have suffered a relative decline, except for the London chronicles). The preoccupation of most writers was memorable and newsworthy deeds — war, conquest, and destruction, to a lesser extent government and institutions. This was particularly the case with the chroniclers of the Crusades and the Hundred Years' War, who combined some knowledge of classical historical writing with noble, chivalric, or royalist (but in any case military) ideals.

In the early fifteenth century Enguerrand de Monstrelet, "descended from a noble family" in Picardy, invoked Sallust on behalf of his lofty project, which was taking up where Froissart had left off (in 1400) and "handing down to posterity the grand and magnanimous feats of arms, and the inestimable subtleties of war."[46] Admitting, in a medieval commonplace, the great disparity between his ability and the royal majesty and great deeds of his narrative, Monstrelet dedicated himself to reporting truthfully and impartially his experiences, seeking out the best testimonies, describing the various turns of fortune, and determining the causes of the divisions and discords in the France and Burgundy of his day. Monstrelet's chronicle, which ends in 1467, was continued by others down to 1516.

Georges Chastellain has been called "the French Thucydides"; and although he may not deserve this hyperbolic judgment of Joseph Calmette's, he was indeed an honest and sometimes perceptive witness, from a Burgundian standpoint, of the political dramas of the mid–fifteenth century. He also took pride in his historiographical calling (*condition de l'hystoriographe*), which was honored with an official appointment in 1455. Some men worked with their hands, some ruled, and others prayed, he observed: "Should we not believe that there are also others destined by nature to observe and understand the variable things of this world?" Chastellain proposed to give a "literal" account of the conflicts between France and Burgundy, especially the "war of the public good"; but he also offered in effect verbal and political "mirrors of the prince" based on Plutarchian parallels between two Valois kings, Charles VII and Louis XI, and the last two Burgundian dukes, Phillip the Good and Charles the Bold.[47]

Philippe de Commynes, too, has been likened to Thucydides. His *Memoirs* both overlaps with the work of Chastellain in subject matter, especially the conflict between Louis XI and Charles the Bold, and resembles it in outlook, offering not only realistic politico-military narrative but also advice for princely consumption.[48] Commynes claimed to perceive larger patterns in the fortunes of states, which were dependent in the final analysis on the will of God. In the opposition of various states or dynasties — France versus England, England versus Scotland, Spain versus Portugal, Aragon versus Anjou — he saw a divine balance, within which princes and other powerful men could maneuver but which they could never master. People who worked for a living had their share of misery, and more than their share of taxes; but the highborn suffered even more, though they were often the cause of trouble, while the poor people could only bear it with patience. In any case it was the former who attracted Commynes's attention.

Commynes wrote his accounts in French to memorialize the character and achievements of his late master, Louis XI, and to supply materials for a more finished Latin account by Angelo Catone, Archbishop of Vienne; but his plan grew into a panoramic and analytical narrative, embellished with words of moral wisdom and statecraft. A man of vast experience, strong opinions, and uncertain loyalties, Commynes knew many European rulers, and he was as concerned with character and royal grandeur as he was with the historical process. Individual virtue was important, although "great knowledge makes wicked men worse and good men better," and accepting good counsel from men like himself was even more important to political success. Inexperience combined with the failure to listen to such counsel (not to mention an inadequate supply of money) accounted for the failure of the Italian venture of the young King Charles VIII in 1494, a crucial and seminal event which produced the political framework for modern Europe and which was the subject of the last two books of Commynes's work as well as a focus of curiosity and speculation for generations of European political and historical writers.

As Commynes's experience and writing overlapped with that of Chastellain, so too, in its last stages, it overlapped with another keen political analyst and promoter of historical studies. Like Chastellain and Commynes, Claude de Seyssel, bastard son of a noble Savoyard family, had extensive political experience in the service of the French monarchy; but unlike them he also had a degree in civil law (from the University of Turin in 1486), inclinations toward humanist learning, and an ecclesiastical vocation which elevated him, at the end of his life, to the dignity of archbishop of Turin. Seyssel's diplomatic career partly coincided with the reign of Louis XII and with the first stages of the Italian wars, which had been analyzed by Commynes and which would be formative in the thought and writing of Machiavelli and Guicciardini, whose Italianate views of the "new politics" of that age he indeed shared. More than any of these contemporaries, however, even Machiavelli, Seyssel associated his political vision, forged in the school of hard experience (and, because of Seyssel's Savoyard background, likewise Italianate in inspiration and vocabulary), with the vicarious wisdom of classical history, which reinforced the Thucydidean spirit of French historical thought. He was a devotee of *la lictera-ture,* of which, he added, "history is the most profitable" part because it permitted the analysis of political change.[49]

Like Machiavelli, Seyssel saw ancient history as vital for the construction of a modern "political science," which later received expression in his *Monarchy of France.*[50] This book, which described the sources of the "force" and "grandeur" of France, represented a sort of political testament for the young King Francis I that in many ways paralleled Machiavelli's almost exactly contemporaneous *Prince.* However, while the younger Florentine political analyst and author looked to Latin history for inspiration, Seyssel was more interested in Greek precedents. In 1504, in the company of the great Hellenist Janus Lascaris, Seyssel visited the royal library in Blois; the upshot was a collaboration producing a series of pioneering translations of mainly Greek historiographical classics, including Xenophon's *Anabasis,* Justin's abridgment of Trogus Pompeius, Diodorus Siculus (including extracts from Plutarch), Appian, Eusebius, and finally, relying on Valla's Latin version, Thucydides himself.[51]

Seyssel honored Herodotus as well as Thucydides, citing him in particular for the famous and seminal passage in the third book of his history on the three forms of government, which offered support for Seyssel's own opinion that, while monarchy had shown itself historically to be most civilized (*politique*) and stable, a mixture of the three forms was preferable to democracy, aristocracy, or monarchy. Not accidentally, this was the case with "the French empire as a whole," which "partakes of all three forms of political government."[52] Seyssel pursued this argument more comprehensively and with modern examples in his *Monarchy of France,* in which the uniquely French system of "religion, justice, and the polity [*police*]" seemed to fulfill the ancient ideal. It also furnished a richer context for Thucydidean narrative than Machiavelli's tendency to see politics without law, or at least without the institutional "bridles" of Seyssel.

Perhaps the most conspicuous sign of the success of the Greeks and Romans was the way in which their language came to prevail, and one of Seyssel's aims—like that of his contemporaries in Spain, Italy, England, and even Germany—was to bring the vernacular and so *la nation françoise* up to the literary and imperial standards of the ancients. In this way Seyssel was a seminal figure in the tradition of vernacular humanism, which culminated in the works of poets and prose writers who were devoted to (in the phrase of

Joachim Du Bellay, opposing the claims of Italian) the "defense and illustration of the French language."[53] Even in Italy, French was no longer regarded as a barbarian tongue; and Seyssel's efforts, concentrating especially on histories, "which are the true pastimes of great princes . . . because they contain lessons and examples," would further promote this process of cultural change that, along with unique French laws, institutions, and social structure, underlay the "grandeur" of the "grand monarchy of France" (which was the title of the printed versions of Seyssel's book).[54]

Seyssel also contributed to the national tradition of historiography, his biography of King Louis XII taking up in effect where Commynes's memoirs left off, though much more eulogistically. According to Seyssel, Louis XII deserved comparison not only with Charlemagne but also with Trajan for his work as re-founder — "father of his country" in the contemporary phrase (*pater patriae, père du peuple*) — of the "grand monarchy" which Seyssel served and celebrated for much of his life. His book offered royalist propaganda and also a review of national tradition, adapting Florus's notion of four ages to French history — infancy covering the period from the legendary Pharamond to the first Christian king, Clovis; youth down to the end of the Merovingian line; maturity under the Carolingian dynasty; and old age under the Capetian dynasty.[55] So an ancient theory of history was modernized. As Louis Le Roy wrote later in the century, "As in persons there are by nature four ages in monarchies . . . , their beginning being comparable to infancy, early growth to adolescence, maturity to manhood, and decline to old age, dissolution, and death. The four ages of the [Roman Empire] have been distinguished by Seneca, Lactantius, and Florus; those of the kingdom of France by Seyssel in his panegyric of Louis XII; and those of England by Polydore Vergil."[56] And for France the royal historian Bernard Du Haillan worked out this conceit in greater detail, together with the Seysselian notion of the "mixed" form of government developed in France.

In the sixteenth century the tradition of national historiography, stemming from the authoritative chronicles of St. Denis, entered a stage that was at once official and humanist in style, beginning especially with the pioneering work of Robert Gaguin. Humanist, university figure, and head of the Order of Mathurins, Gaguin inquired into the origins of the Franks, making use of mostly historical sources, including the modern works of (among others) Flavio Biondo, Sabellico, and Christine de Pisan.[57] Prizing eloquence, devoted to national tradition, and following closely the narrative of the chronicles of St. Denis, Gaguin was nevertheless devoted to truth (*praeter hystoriae fidei reverentiam* was his phrase) and criticized the linking of the *Franci* with the Trojan myth of "Francion." He also rejected the story of Charlemagne's voyage to Jerusalem, though he continued to accept his associations with the University of Paris.

Gaguin's book, published at the beginning of the sixteenth century, was for some reason overshadowed by that of Paolo Emilio, who was one of the first of the *historiographes du roi*.[58] "Paul-Emile" ranged beyond political narrative, for he was also a student of French antiquities — his philological, ethnographic, and topographical investigations being collected in his unpublished *Gallica antiquitas* of 1487. Little use of these researches is apparent in his much praised official history of the "deeds of the French," which, though written at the same time as Gaguin's work, did not begin to appear until 1516. Better founded than Gaguin's work, it employed a wider range of sources, drawing in particular on Flavio Biondo and other non-French chroniclers and historians; and it was imitated, continued, and translated for generations. Paolo Emilio's work was praised for its style by contemporaries and for its critical attitudes by later scholars. For example, he rejected the Trojan and Carolingian legends, his rule being the bookish demand for textual evidence for assertions of fact.[59]

Perhaps the most significant figure in this national tradition, in retrospect at least, was the royal secretary and archivist Jean Du Tillet, who not only made a critical analysis of French origins (discarding the old Trojan myths in favor of a Germanic progeny) but also assembled a comprehensive inventory of the legislative, ecclesiastical, and diplomatic records of the monarchy. Although born out of the practical and polemical need for titles and precedents to sanction policies and political claims, Du Tillet's work was also the first "collection des documents pour servir à l'histoire de France." It was linked through this genre to the great collections of the seventeenth and eighteenth centuries and the scientific history of the nineteenth, when Du Tillet's project was taken up anew in the wake of antihistorical revolutionary devastation. Indeed there was a great revival of interest in the works of these forerunners in the nineteenth century, most notably (and ironically) Augustin Thierry, who associated them genealogically with his own "new history."[60]

Machiavelli and Guicciardini

Machiavelli took very much the same view of the value of history as did Commynes and Seyssel and on the basis of similar experience in diplomacy and war: properly understood, it was the key to successful statecraft and warfare for a ruler and his counsellors. "As to exercise for the mind," Machiavelli wrote, "the prince ought to read history and study the actions of eminent men, see how they acted in warfare, examine the causes of their victories and defeats in order to imitate the former and avoid the latter."[61] This, the simplest and most brutal version of Machiavelli's celebration of the art of history, was the message of his *Prince,* and it was repeated in similar forms in both his *Discourses on Livy* and *Florentine Histories.* For Machiavelli, as for Thucydides, the study of history was not a mere antiquarian activity; it was the key to political science and to making rational and prudent policy.

This was the impulse underlying his efforts, in the *Discourses,* to open a "new route" to the science of government and concomitant art of war.[62] Virtually every other field of learning, including law, medicine, and all the arts, had been revived by scholars on the basis of the imitation of ancient wisdom, so why should politics not benefit from the study of history and "the comparison between ancient and modern events," with particular reference to Roman experience and virtue and the Roman model of government as reflected in the writings of Livy? Drawing on the first ten "decades" of Livy, then, Machiavelli sought answers to questions about human nature, class structure, political faction, the role of religion, republican liberty, and the sources of political power. In Ciceronian terms history was, for Machiavelli, not merely "the light of truth" but "mistress of life" and even, beyond Cicero, a principal counselor of state.

In some ways Machiavelli wrote in a Thucydidean mode. Yet like most of his contemporaries, he thought more highly of the Roman than the Greek historians — and indeed, among European readers, popular Latin authors like Sallust, Caesar, Suetonius, Tacitus, Florus, and even the anecdotalist Valerius Maximus were far more popular than Herodotus, Thucydides, Polybius, and others.[63] Before 1500, for example, eighty-nine printed editions of Sallust had appeared, twenty-nine of Valerius, twenty-three of Livy, and sixteen each of Caesar and Suetonius, but only two each of Herodotus and Polybius and none at all of Thucydides were available. In any case Machiavelli, in marked contrast to Bruni, who preferred the precedents suggested by the Greek polis, chose the national model of the Roman republic, and Rome's historian Livy, to follow for his own theoretical and exemplarist insights.

Beyond the particular examples to be derived from Roman history, Machiavelli also speculated about larger patterns of change, including the idea of the translation of empire, with the wheel of fortune transferring power to each of the four world monarchies.[64] He also drew upon the cyclical conception of Polybius (*anacyclosis*), also based on the conception of the three forms of government, and associated it both with the wheel of fortune and with a general theory of human evolution.[65] Emerging from a state of nature in which they lived like beasts, men chose a single ruler, began to distinguish right from wrong and so to institute laws and punishments; but then — also "naturally" — corruption set in and, to the accompaniment of disorder and conspiracies, monarchy became tyranny. It is important to note that there was also a generational driving force behind this mechanical pattern, according to which sons forgot the virtues and problems of their fathers, or reacted to their vices, thus providing a social context for political revolution. According to the second phase of the Polybio-Machiavellian cyclical theory, aristocracy arose in opposition to this misrule but similarly degenerated into its evil form, oligarchy. The third turn of the cycle began with democratic revolt, followed by another stage of decline, and finally by the emergence of a single virtuous leader and the return to monarchy. "Such," concluded Machiavelli, "is the circle which all republics are destined to run through."[66]

Machiavelli stated the deterministic views implied by his "new route" more bluntly later in the *Discourses:* "Whoever considers the past and the present will readily observe that all cities and all peoples are and ever have been animated by the same desires and the same passions; so that it is easy, by diligent study of the past, to foresee what is likely to happen in the future in any republic, and to apply those remedies that were used by the ancients, or, not finding any that were employed by them, to devise new ones from the similarity of the events."[67] Yet, elsewhere, Machiavelli took a subtler and more nuanced view of the possibilities and limits of political and military mimesis, and the implied determinism, recognizing as he did that virtue was ever accompanied by fortune and doubting that political analysis could always extend into the future. As he once confided to a friend, "But the reason why different ways of working are sometimes equally effective and equally damaging I do not know, but I should much like to know."[68] The reason, he conjectured, was that men received from nature different dispositions and imaginations, and that sometimes the actions of a man were "out of harmony with his times and with the type of its affairs" — which was to say that a man sometimes had good and sometimes bad fortune. Machiavelli was well acquainted with political failure, being himself a striking example of it, as indeed was the government which he served; and his turn to historiography was taken in the enforced retirement — and pessimistic state of mind — attendant on his disgrace and fall from power and favor after the overthrow of the Florentine republic in 1512.

Machiavelli's more specifically historical work took a similar view of the significance of history, except that, unlike the *Discourses* and the *Prince,* his *Florentine Histories* presented analyses that were more autopsy than prescription. What the history of Florence seemed to offer, in contrast to that of Rome, was examples to be avoided, not imitated. The basic reasons for this were the unseemly secular power wielded by the papacy and the ruin of the Florentine nobility, which produced party divisions (not unlike the worst periods of Roman history) and which left Florence dependent on foreign mercenaries — these "barbarians" who, compelled by demographic pressure, periodically intruded upon Italy, most decisively after 1494, though Machiavelli prudently ended his strenuously argued account with the death of Lorenzo de' Medici in 1492.

In his survey of the Florentine past Machiavelli relied on both chronicle and humanist traditions — Villani and Bruni — but subjected the record to strong interpretations in the light of his political premises and purposes. He honored the work of his predecessors in the Florentine chancery, Bruni and Poggio, but deplored the neglect of internal history at the expense of foreign wars, and he proposed to remedy this fault. He began with the first barbarian invasions, admitting that more was at stake than mere politics and suggesting a largely concealed cultural dimension to his view of historical change. These invasions had caused more fundamental change than the usual civil discord, "for not only did the government and princes vary, but the laws, the customs, the mode of life, the religion, the language, the dress, the names."[69] It was in the wake of these postimperial conditions that the Roman papacy emerged as a political force, and the later alliance between the popes and the Carolingian Empire reinforced this unfortunate transformation of a spiritual foundation into a secular monarchy. "So henceforth," Machiavelli wrote, "all the wars of the barbarians in Italy were for the most part caused by the pontiffs, and all the barbarians who invaded it were most often called in by them."[70] From the twelfth century, the interplay of the Guelf and Ghibelline — papal and imperial — parties continued to shape the destiny of Italy.

For Machiavelli the origins of Florence were to be sought not in the deeds of legendary heroes but in economic convenience and the founding of markets.[71] Through commercial activity and the growing power of the noble families Florence pursued its fortunes and its freedom; but unfortunately Florence, like Italy as a whole, was a community divided against itself. As Commynes did, but more reflectively, Machiavelli drew large political lessons from his narrative. "Usually provinces go most of the time, in the changes they make, from order to disorder and then pass again from disorder to order, for worldly things are not allowed by nature to stand still."[72] The most elemental causes of disorder in a state were private feuds, such as that between the Cerchi and Donati families (described by Villani, Campagni, and other chroniclers), which converged with the conflict of Guelfs and Ghibellines. Reinforcing this was class conflict, especially the hostility of the populace toward the nobility;

for whereas Rome had resolved its social differences through a law, Machiavelli observed, the Florentines fought among themselves and sent into exile the losing party — the "white" Guelfs, including the fathers of both Dante and Petrarch — which represented the military class, and so the old-fashioned virtues, of Florence.[73]

This was the beginning of Florentine decline and loss of freedom. There was some measure of restoration under the rule of the Medici (1434–92), the family for whom Machiavelli was writing his history, and an extended period of peace and prosperity, but in the long run Machiavelli's sad task was only to "show how in the end the way was opened anew for the barbarians and how Italy put itself again in slavery to them."[74] So Machiavelli provided the background, from an Italian standpoint at least, for understanding the causes of the invasions by the French and Spanish "barbarians," leading to the crisis of European political relations and the Italian wars, which in turn led to the calamity that overwhelmed Italy as a whole and Florence in particular. Like Orosius, but in a mood of secular pessimism, Machiavelli often began or ended individual books of the *Florentine Histories* with general reflections about the nature of the historical process. His book furnished materials to illustrate the principles of statecraft and warfare which he had accumulated in a lifetime's experience in the service of a doomed republic. Florence had fought for survival in a new world of power politics dominated by the national "barbarian" monarchies, which made city states like Florence obsolete, as well as the independence and "liberties" they had intermittently enjoyed. After the death of Lorenzo de' Medici, who had managed to keep a balance among the Italian states for over a generation, the "bad seeds" of partisan conflict, Machiavelli concluded, have "ruined and are still ruining Italy."[75]

Machiavelli's younger colleague and friend Francesco Guicciardini shared some of the same experiences (though in higher reaches of Florentine society and political service) and attitudes, including fascination with the crisis of 1494, ideas about history, and (living until 1540, while Machiavelli died in 1527) an even gloomier view of the prospects of Florence and Italy. He wrote a youthful *History of Florence* from the beginning of the Great Schism in the church (1378) down to the early stages of the Italian wars (the siege of Pisa in 1509). For Guicciardini the turning point came with the invasion of 1494, when the rules of the game of politics seemed to be redrawn. In his words, "States toppled and the methods of governing them changed. The art of war changed too. . . . The French invasion, like a sudden storm, turned everything topsy turvy. The unity of Italy was shattered, and gone were the care and consideration that each state used to give to common affairs . . . , [so that] states were maintained, ruined, given, and taken away not by plans drawn up in a study . . . but in the field, by force of arms."[76] It was this transformation that inspired Guicciardini, Machiavelli, and others to ask fundamental questions about political change and to produce what J. H. Hexter called the "vision of politics on the eve of the Reformation."[77]

This turning point served Guicciardini as the starting point for his historiographical masterwork. His pioneering *History of Italy* offered a comprehensive explanation of the Italian "calamity," which had been heralded by various prodigies and portents. Like Machiavelli, and for similar dramatic contrast, Guicciardini celebrated the "happy state" of Italy under Lorenzo de' Medici. With Tacitean subtlety and cynicism and in much greater detail than Commynes or any other historian, Guicciardini analyzed, in a critical fashion and with sour psychological acumen and occasional use of archival sources, the complex diplomatic preparations, deceptions, and maneuvering underlying the French invasion; the Spanish reactions; the characters of Charles VIII, Ferdinand of Aragon, Ludovico Sforza, and other major players; and the complex and brutal interactions of the great powers over the next generation.

Like Machiavelli and Tacitus, too, Guicciardini joined his historical analyses to general political reflections and principles, set down in his *Ricordi*. He agreed with Machiavelli that "past events shed light on the future. For the world has always been the same, and everything that is and will be, once was; and the same things recur, but with different names and colors. And for that reason, not everyone recognized them — only those who are wise, and observe and consider them diligently."[78] Yet if he celebrated the value of direct experience and the vicarious one offered by history, he had less confidence in the possibility of predicting the future on the basis of past happenings because of pessimism growing out of bitter experience, an awareness of the variability of human temperaments and the role of accidents, and an appreciation of the power of fortune over human affairs. The winners always receive praise, he noted, while the losers are discredited no matter what; and Guicciardini, even more than Machiavelli, felt that his wisdom was that of a unappreciated loser.[79]

While this may not be an attitude useful for a maker of policy, it suits the purposes of an analytical and reflective writer of the "wind-tossed sea" of history.[80] Both Guicciardini and Machiavelli wrote in a Thucydidean mode — inspired by political crisis and failure and impelled to seek out the causes of — and perhaps even remedies for — their predicament. Political realism and moral cynicism were by-products of the flood of historical literature produced by the invasion of 1494 and its calamitous aftermath. Chivalry and crusading fervor were dead, greed and duplicity were the order of the day, and it was Sallust who provided the literary model for historians of war like Bernardo

Rucellai and Alessandro Benedetti.[81] According to the latter, who was a Venetian eyewitness, "Charles VIII, king of the French, was seized in the twenty-fourth year of his life with a desire for power, and to lend credence to the affair he feigned religious motives and let it be known everywhere that he was preparing a war against the Turks."[82] Charles, splendid though his promenade through Italy undoubtedly was, drew not only on false claims but also on prophetic traditions about recovery of the Holy Land, and used all the machinery of publicity to justify his enterprise. Such views informed much of the historiography of the beginning of the Italian wars even before Machiavelli gave his name to this age of the new and unscrupulous politics.

Here are all the ingredients of the Thucydidean (and Tacitean) vision of history, which well suited the power politics of the age of Machiavelli and which survived even the revival of religious enthusiasm during the Reformation. *Machiavellianism* and *Tacitism* designated secular ways of understanding human behavior that seemed impious — and political in a pejorative sense — to many contemporaries and yet not inappropriate to the dynastic conflicts of the sixteenth century. But the highest representative of the art of history in this mode was surely Thucydides. As Thomas Hobbes wrote a century later in the introduction to his translation, "For the principal and proper work of history being to instruct and to enable men, by knowledge of actions past, to bear themselves prudently in the present and providently in the future: there is not extant any other (merely human) that doth more naturally and fully perform it than this of my author."[83] Thucydides suited the tastes of devotees of both the new politics in the sixteenth century and the new science in the seventeenth, as he would the tastes of many modern professional historians.

Cultural History

If Thucydides presided at least symbolically over the political histories of the Renaissance, especially in Italy and France, Herodotus also became a presence in the sense that his view of the office of the historian attracted not a few authors. The conventional view was that history had to do with political and military actions — "things done," res gestae — but under the impulse of humanism scholars began to open their eyes to many other humanly created things, which came to include all the arts and sciences of humanist learning. When Polydore Vergil wrote about the human inventors of things (*De rerum inventoribus,* first published in 1499), he included the whole humanist "encyclopedia," ranging from letters (*litteratura*) to laws, from myth to philosophy and religion, from tribal organization to the state, from agriculture to modern science, from technology to commerce. In the work of scholars like Vergil,

Juan Luis Vives, and Guillaume Budé, history was employed as a way of organizing and understanding, ante litteram, human culture in the broadest sense.

One point of entry of such concerns was what Eric Cochrane called the "lateral discipline" of biography, which was extended beyond its ancient and medieval precedents. Many humanist biographies and collections of illustrious men turned increasingly from princes and popes to men of letters and the arts. The Florentine bookseller Vespasiano da Bisticci classified his biographies (which were not known for another two centuries)[84] according to callings in the church, politics, and the arts; and Paolo Giovio, in both his history and his biographies, showed an eye for matters of cultural history, extending to the fine arts and even cuisine.[85] It was Giovio who encouraged Giorgio Vasari to compile a collection of biographies devoted specially to the lives of painters, sculptors, and architects, each of these types of artists serving the larger goals of "design" — representing in effect the *primum in genere* of the genre of art history.

It is important here to keep in mind one of the primary conditions of early modern historical consciousness and writing, which is the culture of print and all of the restrictions and potential this medium brought. For authors, typography, by the sixteenth century, brought together original texts, translations, commentaries, and reference works pertaining to all previous times — "gather[ing] into one focus," as Daniel Heinsius wrote, "the immeasurably great vastness of ages and generations."[86] For readers, printing brought a cluttered wealth of information, but also an unprecedented exposure to alien and remote cultures, an exposure that was intensified by the accounts, images, and interpretations being imported from the New World. Moreover, printing itself became the object of study by historians, whose hyperbolic judgments raised the new German art of typography to the level, if not of a miracle, as some religious enthusiasts suggested, at least to that of a transforming force inferior only to the invention of writing — and of course to the spiritual Word embodied in sacred history.

One of the major targets and vehicles for the expansion of historical thought and writing in the Renaissance was civil law, which represented a direct link with ancient culture. The philological and the historical study of law — following the leads of the grammarian Aulus Gellius and the jurist Pomponius — were revived in the Renaissance. The first modern history of law was Aymar du Rivail's *Historia iuris civilis* (1515), which built on the work of Pomponius and Livy and also, in a historicized form, the Aristotelian-Polybian division of governmental species — monarchy represented by the regal laws, aristocracy by the *senatusconsulta,* and democracy by the *plebiscita.* Du Rivail's work was continued by other scholars, including Valentinus Foster's similarly titled book published just a half-century later, and expanded on by scholarly investigations of the early sources of Roman law, beginning with the Twelve Tables, which would be an important impetus to antiquarianism and to historical reflections about origins, most notably those of Vico. The study of legal history was extended, too, into areas of canon law (Du Rivail also published the brief *History of Pontifical Law* in 1515) and feudal law; and all of these lines of inquiry were carried on by vernacular scholars such as Etienne Pasquier in France and William Lambarde in England, whose work extended the study of comparative jurisprudence and the complex institutional heritage and legal culture of the European states defined by the "law of nations" (jus gentium).[87]

In a broader and richer perspective Marsilio Ficino, Pico della Mirandola, and other modern scholars began to investigate a whole sequence of barbarian cultures, including not only the Jews but also Babylonians, Indians, Persians, Egyptians, Celts, and later Chinese and Amerindians. According to Vergil and Vives, the Hebrew prophets, the Egyptian priests, the Persian Magi, and the Celtic Druids were all engaged in essentially the same project, which was the pursuit of true wisdom (*vera sapientia*); and it was the task of modern scholars to trace the development of this wisdom, or "perennial philosophy," as Augustino Steuco called it, from its mythical beginning through a "succession of doctrine" (*successio doctrinae*) to its fulfillment in Christian philosophy.[88]

Perhaps the most striking contribution to cultural and literary historiography in the Renaissance is the work of the Swiss scholar Christophe Milieu entitled *Writing the History of the Universe of Things* (1551). Though usually classified with the Renaissance *artes historicae*, the book is really much more than a contribution to literary theory. "History," declared Milieu, "is the eternal treasury of the human race."[89] More than that, he argued, it was history, or historical reason (*historica ratio*), rather than reason or philosophy that provided the best way to organize the "universe of things." "The use of history," Milieu remarked, "is spread through every branch of learning."[90] What is more, nature itself displayed a historical shape: "From its beginnings [*à suis primordiis progressa*] the history of nature follows this pattern: infancy, childhood, adolescence, youth, manhood, old age, and decrepitude."[91]

In this pioneering book Milieu, inspired by a tour to the Greek East, offers the broadest possible framework for the interpretation of universal history within the Christian worldview (as modified by Renaissance discoveries and scholarship), and it follows a carefully constructed design with original as well as traditional features and terminology. In his symmetrical plan Milieu distinguishes, within the universe of things, three connected levels, or "grades," of existence accessible to human cognition and interpretation: "The first level is

Nature and its history. . . . The second level is Prudence and its history . . . , and the history of Government is joined to that of Prudence. The third level is wisdom and its history . . . , and the history of literature is joined to that of wisdom."[92] Such, for Milieu, were the three stages of the "course of things" — five, including those of government and literature — which is also to say, the "progresses" of cultural history.[93]

Each of these five spheres of human experience is analyzed by Milieu through a "narration" (*narratio*) of its history; and the resulting formulas — *historia naturae, historia prudentiae, historia principatus, historia sapientiae,* and *historia litteraturae* — from the five books of Milieu's treatise. The books are lined by "excurses," "transitions," or "progressions" that produce a sort of historical and intellectual hierarchy followed by Milieu's narratives not only down the Great Chain of Being, the ladder of God's creation, but also, through human cognition and representation, back up the artificial ladder of human re-Creation, culminating in the culture of writing and print, which is the foundation of civil society. "To wisdom is joined, as in a partnership," he wrote, "the history of literature, by which we pass from the times of brilliant and learned men to the state of civil society."[94] The high point of this passage was the "revival of letters" (*literarum renouatio*) that was crowned by the work of Erasmus and Budé and that gave the impulse for Milieu's own striking historical vision.[95]

An equally broad view of history was taken by Louis Le Roy, disciple and first biographer of Budé and professor of Greek at the Collège Royal and translator of both Plato and Aristotle. Like Milieu, Le Roy took on the whole universe of things. His *Vicissitude or Variety of Things in the Universe* (1575) celebrated both the positive and negative aspects of mutability and change, both the acquiring and forgetting of knowledge, both the lighting and the extinguishing of what he called the "torch" of learning, and the "revolutions" in studies as well as in political organization. Praising the "new inventions" of the latest "heroic age" beginning in the fifteenth century — especially printing, the compass, and gunpowder, that trinity of modernizing devices made famous by Bacon — Le Roy defended the Moderns against the Ancients, though he granted that some of the novelties, especially in warfare and religion, were destructive and inferior to the technology of print.[96]

Le Roy's discourse was not intended unambiguously to praise history as a comedy in the Dantean sense; for it was really to show "the vicissitude in all human affairs, arms, letters, languages, arts, states, laws, and customs, and how they do not cease to rise and fall, growing better or worse alternately." Yet he clearly felt optimistic about his own age, believing that reason was also present in modern vernacular languages and that the Moderns had to follow their own lines of inquiry and thought. "The road," he concluded, "is open" (*Le chemin est ouvert*). In the light of Le Roy's enthusiastic statements of the advancement of learning since the fifteenth century, J. B. Bury was not altogether wrong in listing him among the prophets of the idea of progress, which has provided the master narrative of modern history, in its cultural if not its political dimensions.[97]

The New World

Louis Le Roy noted another novelty that promised to have an even greater impact on European history: "The enterprise was begun by Cristoforo Colombo the Genoese, and by Amerigo Vespucci the Florentine, a person of excellent understanding and fine judgment who deserves no less praise than the famous Hercules; then it was continued by the Castilians, rivals for the same honor and eager for gain, who by great courage and incomparable endurance have continued to make other discoveries."[98] More-interested parties made even strong claims, arguing that the discovery of the New World was not only novel but unique. As the greatest of the Spanish humanist historians, Juan de Mariana, wrote at the end of the sixteenth century, "The most memorable, honorable, and advantageous enterprise that ever succeeded in Spain was the discovery of the western Indies, which are with reason called the 'new world,' a marvelous event which after so many centuries has been reserved for this age."[99]

The facts were simple enough, but not so the meaning of these facts, which verged indeed on the marvelous, although they had to be assimilated to human dimensions. There had been anticipations of a New World in the West by poets like Dante, Petrarch, and Pulci; but from the first news of the Columbian expedition, beginning with the admiral's own letter of 1493, the historians took over from the poets, though with no less sense of the marvelous. The basic question was how the new hemisphere, with its two new continents, new peoples, and unknown history, fitted into the old story of the three continents, four monarchies, and six ages of the world? How could historians do justice to what the historian Francesco López de Gómara called "the greatest event since the creation of the world" — excepting, for Christian peoples, the Incarnation?[100]

To begin with, they could only adapt old categories and methods to these new experiences. What Le Roy did was to incorporate this event into his account of the "vicissitude of things" and to embellish it with the old rhetoric of novelty, which represented the discoveries as just another example of the triumph of the Moderns over the Ancients. In the 1520s Peter Martyr, the

Columbus of New World historiography, had admitted to a "joyous mental excitement" and told Pope Clement VII that "the vastness of the subject I am treating requires Ciceronian inspiration."[101] What he and other contemporaries did, with the help of classical style and precedent, was to tell the story as a continuation of the European drive for empire. In Western historiography the discovery — *inventio, la descubrimiento, la découverte, die Entdeckung* — of the New World was directly assimilated to, and indeed made the cynosure of, the epic story of the Spanish monarchies. This earthshaking and earth-encircling event crowned a millennium-long tradition of imperial claims and mythology enhanced by the glorious *Reconquista* and recent victory over Granada, which Columbus himself had witnessed; and it became a matter of intense national pride, involving the territorial pretensions of states and claims to priority in the "discovery" of a hemisphere and the shaping of modern global history.[102]

The resources of Western historiography were barely up to the task of describing a wholly "new" world. Spanish historical writing at the turn of the sixteenth century was a mixture of the old and the new — medieval chronicles and universal histories competing with humanist narratives, historical criticism with entrenched myths, the new art of printing easily accommodating both.[103] Spanish celebrators of the art of history such as Juan Luis Vives, Sebastián Fox-Morcillo, and Luis Cabrera de Córdoba continued the humanist quest for an authentic and complete history (*legítima y perfecta historia*).[104] Yet older medieval assumptions, values, and expectations persisted, as did the old genre of universal history. "It is well to learn the course of history from the beginning of the world or of a people continuously right through their course to the latest times," wrote Vives, invoking the names of Paulus Orosius and Paulus Diaconus as well as Bruni and Biondo.[105]

Like the "Holy Roman Empire of the German nation," Spain had a long and honored imperial tradition, traceable back to the time when, according to the old proverb, "Spain gave many emperors to Rome."[106] The idea of a unified kingdom of Spain underlying the several crowns of Castile, Leon, Navarre, and so on was reflected in both historical and legal sources, especially from the time of Alfonso el Sabio. *La Prima Crónica general de España* commissioned by Alfonso expressed the "moral unity of Spain"; and from the thirteenth century what José Antonio Maravall calls the "rich Alfonsine tradition" of historiography was further enriched by the incorporation of a Visigothic mythology and by the claim, shared by other European monarchs, that the king of Castile was "emperor in his kingdom."[107] Long before the joint reign of Ferdinand and Isabella, then, there were notions of union and aspirations to empire, enhanced both by the crusading impulse against Islam leading to the Reconquista and by the drive to exploration leading to the Neuva Conquista of the Columbian age.

Historians of the New World took up and adapted these old themes. Years after the voyage of Magellan had opened even grander vistas, Oviedo continued to represent the "empire" of Charles V as a descendant of the Roman *imperium*. Tommaso Campanella's vision of a Spanish empire still had associations with the old Translation theory, and Mariana, too, preserved this theme, derived from the tradition of vernacular chronicles dominating Spanish historiography since the thirteenth century.[108] By the fifteenth century, however, the notion of empire was acquiring more mundane and "Machiavellian" connotations. For reasons both old and new, then, the idea of imperial dominion was radically redefined, and it acted powerfully to reshape interpretations of Spanish, European, and universal history.

This conflation of the old and the new is well illustrated in the history of the Indies written by Bartolomé de las Casas in his declining years. Las Casas defined history in the famous Ciceronian formula and emphasized the importance of eyewitness testimony over the secondhand fabrications of armchair historians.[109] This old argument — taken from Thucydides, illustrated by Isidore of Seville's etymology (deriving *historia* from the term meaning "to see"), and confirmed by canon law rules for documentary authenticity — was reinforced by Las Casas's personal experiences in New Spain (1502–66). Yet this elderly Dominican friar also set the story of the Conquista within the framework of the Augustinian and Orosian vision of history — that is, as both "the true education of the human race" and an account of "the desires and punishments of sinful men." Though a proud Spaniard, Las Casas wrote in the spirit not only of national expansion but also of Christian universalism — of the "living God" (here citing the apostles Barnabas and Paul) "who in times past suffered all nations to walk in their own ways."

In one fundamental respect the humanist vision of history was transformed by the first encounters with the New World, and this was a new appreciation for the creative power of nature. This is illustrated by a locus classicus of the old humanist perspective. Francesco Petrarch's account of his ascent of Mount Ventoux. Recovering from his awe at the grandeur of the mountain scenery, Petrarch was possessed by another thought, which turned him, as he put it, "from the contemplation of space to that of time" and then, in his Augustinian way, to various retrospective and introspective explorations. In a sense, what the Columbian moment of discovery signified for humanist historians was just such a turn back from the contemplation of time to that of space and the opening up of new horizons. For the discovery of a new hemisphere fantas-

tically expanded the old universal history, which had been confined to a Eurocentric notion of the four world monarchies and the translation of empire. The
conventional "theater" of human history was enlarged beyond recognition by
the outpourings of sixteenth-century travel literature. The *mundus novus* of
Vespucci and the *Orbis novum* of Martyr made the fabled Antipodes into a
reality that was illustrated not only by spectacular maps and globes but also by
writings of geographers, topographers, chorographers, and by those whom
Bodin called "universal geographistorians."[110]

How could the new members of the world of nations be understood and
characterized by practitioners of the old historiography? At first, only in the
ethnographically impoverished, but mythologically rich, categories and language of European tradition. In his first report Columbus represented the
natives as "virtuous savages," and as Howard Mumford Jones remarked, the
"myth-making process began at once."[111] The image of the "good savage" was
countered by that of the bad barbarian — Las Casas pictured them as virtuous
cultivators of "natural reason," while Martyr accused the Indians of behaving
like "Scythians," or superstitious pagans.[112]

Of course both ideal types could find support in classical tradition, and, for
example, there were repeated efforts to interpret the behavior of the Amerindians in terms of ancient conceptions of barbarism, employing especially Tacitus's descriptions of the customs of the ancient Germans. Moral judgments
aside, however, these conventions broke down under careful examination,
and it has been through the ancient topos of novelty that the history of the
Americas has been written for five centuries. The ancients were palpably ignorant about much of the natural and the social world; and — as every historian
of the New World found it necessary to demonstrate at length — Augustine
and the other Christian Fathers were wrong on the question of the Antipodes.[113] So in the vast literature of discovery, judgments of novelty and alterity have tended to prevail among both admirers and critics of the inhabitants of the New World.

The story of the New World was taken up by Protestants as well as Catholics, and with very much the same sense of a mission that was, as the Huguenot
Jean de Léry put it, "holy and truly heroic."[114] Underneath this conventional
awe Léry displayed a curiosity and a range of human sentiment — "between
disapproval and delight," writes his translator — which opened his eyes to
behavior rivaling the prodigies reported by Pliny and other ancients. In fact
Léry was more horrified by the actions of the turncoat (as he believed) Vil-
legagnon, who allegedly had several Huguenots drowned "because of their
adherence to the Gospel," and his account was inserted in his friend Jean
Crespin's martyrology.[115] Léry had himself barely escaped such martyrdom

in France during the massacres of St. Bartholomew, and he had suffered terribly in its aftermath, but none of this measured up to his experiences in the New World. Eschewing the "painted lie of fine language," Léry hoped his unadorned narrative would do justice both to the truth and to the fantastic character of his experiences.

This trajectory of imperial advance has remained central to the story of the discoveries, and it has been reinforced by that sustaining myth of modern historiography, which is the modern belief in progress. The idea of progress again illustrates the curious collaboration of medieval and modern ideas, being in effect the offspring of the marriage between two offshoots of Western Platonism — the Augustinian conception of history as a pilgrimage toward enlightenment and Renaissance ideals of limitless human learning. The topos of the superiority of Moderns over Ancients, publicized by humanist rhetoric and documented by reports of new inventions and discoveries, produced a secular eschatology of progress, perfectibility, and emergent modernity. Humanist scholars like Christophe Milieu, Louis Le Roy, and Pierre Droit de Gaillard celebrated this theme in terms of geographical and scholarly explorations a generation before Bacon took it up.[116]

The ideology of progress originally found its legitimacy in a theory of providential history, even as it found its confirmation in new factors of political expansion and material gain — the Renaissance version of modernization theory. Here again medieval notions joined humanist rhetoric in expressing a modern, or modernized, myth, such as the idea of the providential succession of empires. In the age of Columbus the last of the four world monarchies seemed to have devolved finally on the German nation. Yet for at least two centuries the national monarchs of France and Spain had laid claim to imperial status, and in the sixteenth century the arguments of their jurists were reinforced by the fact that many parts of the Western world, especially the kingdoms of France and Spain, had never been under the rule of the Roman Empire.

In any case the new imperial idea (transferred from the Austrian line of the Habsburgs) was seized upon and elaborated by all the historians of New Spain. "Amidst the storms and troubles of Italy," wrote Peter Martyr, "Spain was every day stretching her wings over a wider sweep of empire, and extending the glory of her name to the far Antipodes."[117] And as Gómara put it at the end of his history of the Indies, "Never before has a king or nation occupied and subjected so much in so short a time as ours, nor has deserved what they have done by preaching the holy gospel and converting idolaters, for which our Spaniards are deserving of praise in all parts of the world."[118] A new theory of four monarchies was proclaimed poetically by Lope de Vega, who instructed King Philip III about the extent of his *Invicta monarchia:*

> You hold four crowns,
> ... in Africa and Europe,
> in Asia and, triumphantly, in America.[119]

In many ways the New World was assimilated to the legal and historio-graphical categories of Europe and subject to its judgments, and it is in this sense that "America" was not so much discovered as "invented." *Inventio,* a commonplace figuring centrally not only in humanist rhetoric and scholastic logic but also in ancient and modern myth, suggested founding as well as finding; and indeed, in his famous little encyclopedia *On the Inventors of Things,* Polydore Vergil honored both the founders of arts and sciences and the navigators and merchants who came in their wake—among whom he proposed to nominate Columbus as one of the greatest.[120]

Yet the ambiguity is appropriate, for at first this was not "America" either in name or conception; it was an "imaginary space" (as Anthony Pagden and others have remarked) to be filled in by European "prejudices" and "fore-structures," which ranged from medieval lore to Aristotelian philosophy and Roman law. Even the dim outlines of the new continents would not be apparent until after many years of exploration; and the character of the natives would demand centuries of study and the creation of disciplines hardly imagined by Renaissance scholars, including the new sciences of ethnography and anthropology as well as conventional history, which all cooperated in "inventing" America and reshaping "universal" into a truly global history.

7

Reformation Traditions

History [is] continuous from the beginning of the world, whence arise the principles and sources of true religion.
—Philipp Melanchthon

"Upon thorough reflection," declared Martin Luther in 1538, "one finds that almost all laws, art, good counsel, warning, threatening, terrifying, comforting, strengthening, instruction, prudence, wisdom, discretion, and all virtues well up out of the narratives and histories as from a living fountain."[1] This would seem to be little more than a curiously enthusiastic variation on the humanist praises repeated so often in the genre of the *ars historica,* as in Pierre Droit de Gaillard's declaration that "all disciplines take their sources and the basis of their principles from history, as from an overflowing fountain."[2] The difference was Luther's pious addition, which affirms that "histories are nothing else than a demonstration, recollection, and sign of divine action and judgment, how [God] upholds, rules, obstructs, prospers, punishes, and honors the world, and especially men, each according to his just desert, evil or good." Joining human virtue and divine grace, this statement is not only eclectic; it is paradoxical and even contradictory, for it displays the divided mind of Protestantism about the ecclesiastical past. Again the opposition is between spirit and letter; for spiritually, history might be understood as the life and progress of God's Word on earth, but in more literal terms it stood for those vile "human traditions" which, for Luther, had spawned all the troubles of Christendom at the turn of the sixteenth century.

7

Christian Tradition

Luther's statement highlights the polemical role which history occupied during the Reformation and religious wars; and Luther himself, in his preface to Robert Barnes's *Lives of the Roman Pontiffs,* expressed gratification at this turn to what Barnes called the "faith of histories."[3] In its premises, if not in its applications, Protestant as well as Catholic historiography remained in its medieval channels. In Luther's time European history in its universal form continued to be situated between the poles of sacred and secular, sacerdotal and lay, church and state—the "two cities"—and of course each of these ideological poles laid claim to its own ancient tradition. In the most obvious terms the opposition and interplay were between imperial and papal Rome, which seemed to have achieved harmony with the conversion of Constantine in the fourth century but which had in fact, almost continuously thereafter, carried on disputes and even open warfare over power, principle, and precedence. The Gelasian conceit of the "two swords" symbolized the transcendent pretensions of two universal monarchies—and shaped and unsettled European historiography, torn as it was between two conflicting sources of authority, on a high level of generality.[4]

Church and state were also dual in their intellectual and cultural heritages. Imperial tradition rested on the ancient ideas of the translation of empire, the supreme sovereignty derived ultimately from the Roman people, and the expression of this sovereignty found in the imperial legislation extending from Justinian down to his legal successor, the Habsburg Emperor Charles V. Papal tradition rested on divine foundations, on Scripture, and on legislation expressed in the decrees of the councils, writings of the Fathers, and papal decretals over an even greater span of time. Both legal traditions also accumulated a vast overlay of gloss, commentary, interpretation, and systematic jurisprudence which exalted the respective positions of pope and emperor—each "lord of the world" in a sense—often at the other's expense. Both traditions also attracted the services of historians, who constructed appropriate narratives to justify and to enhance the papalist and imperialist ideologies which had emerged in mature form from the eleventh and twelfth centuries.

Imperial tradition had its problems and its critics, but papal tradition was at once more elevated in its provenance and more vulnerable in its human incarnation. A classic account from the imperialist side was that of Dante, who—in terms historical, philosophical, and legal—celebrated the antiquity and legitimacy of the Roman Empire from its brutal, pagan beginnings down to his own time and who then proceeded to demolish the rival claims of the bishop of

Rome. Among his and the empire's enemies Dante listed the pope, his greedier followers, and especially the canon lawyers — "Decretalists" — who rested their case not on right but on later "tradition." Dante accepted Holy Scripture and the early Fathers of the church such as Augustine, but he was suspicious of those "traditions called 'Decretals,'" which needed to be authorized by Scriptures. "Those who rely solely on the traditions, therefore," Dante concluded, "must be thrown out of the arena."[5]

These were essentially the grounds not only for critics of the papal monarchy and curialism but also for the Protestant rewriting of history in the wake of Luther's own assault first on canon law and then on papal supremacy. Of course Luther took a much harder line than Dante had done, for him the "traditions" preserved in the canon law being the entry point "from which all misfortune has come into all the world."[6] This was the reason for Luther's burning of the books of canon law in the courtyard of the University of Wittenberg in December 1520 — itself a "traditional" act ("It is an ancient traditional practice to burn poisonous evil books": Acts 19.19) — thus symbolically annihilating the "human traditions" of the Roman church, which was contemporaneously burning Luther's own writings. There could hardly be a more glaring illustration of two conceptions of tradition at war with each other — and two views of ecclesiastical history which impelled research as well as directed interpretation.

There were of course other traditions that gave shape to the practice and theory of history, including that of the ecumenical council, which was the principal rival to the pope for leadership in the church. Originally, ecumenical councils had been called and controlled by emperors, and this was the case again in the wake of the Great Schism which divided Europe from 1378 to 1417. "Conciliarism" became the last, best hope to reunite Christendom after more than a generation of misrule by two, and in the end three, rival popes, and moreover to reform the church after the mounting abuses produced by the schism and the deplorable Babylonian Captivity (1305–78) which preceded it. The conciliarist remedy called upon an alternative tradition in the church's past, which had its roots deep in canon law, and produced an alternative perspective on its history.[7] What had been a theory became, in the ecclesiastical predicament of the late fourteenth century, the fulfillment of a potential historical development.

At that time a German master at the University of Paris, Henry of Langenstein, saw the evil results of the schism that was destroying the mystical body of the church: "The devil has raised himself up; the malice of succeeding generations has rendered the straight paths of the fathers crooked; and the decrees of the Church have been violated."[8] According to Henry, "the record of past events" revealed the solution to this dilemma in the form of "a way of peace, a way oft trodden by our fathers before us," namely, the calling of a council, which would at once heal the schism and begin a reformation of the church without the help of papal leadership.[9] Henry was joined by others in this call, which not only upset the principle of papal sovereignty but also opened up a new — or rather, for its advocates, restored an old — perspective on Christian history.

When the Council of Constance finally began meeting in 1415, the controlling force was in the hands of neither the pope nor indeed the hierarchy of the church but rather (as at the Council of Lyons in 1274) of the secular rulers — the four and later five "nations" controlling the voting on constitutional and reform issues. The upshot was the splitting off of a number of other traditions, that is, the national churches, which sought and attained new legitimacy in the course of the schism and the concordats produced by conciliar negotiations. The Gallican, Hispanic, German, and English churches all gained, or reaffirmed, some of their privileges, which they proceeded to legitimize by tracing back to the "primitive church." Once again the result was the opening of alternative perspectives on the European past and an impetus to historical inquiry, interpretation, mythmaking, and even forgery, which not only challenged papal ecclesiology but also revised the prevailing Romanist orientation of mainstream historiography.

This was especially the case with Gallicanism, which traced its "ancient liberties" back to the primitive church.[10] By the conciliar period Gallican tradition was already established, with authors such as John of Paris arguing for the historical — and therefore political — priority over the papacy.[11] At the beginning of the fourteenth century the French apologist Pierre Dubois, under cover of a manifesto for a crusade, not only criticized the presumptions and corruption of the Roman pontiff but even recommended calling a council to reform these abuses and the subjection of the papacy to the kingdom of France (heralding the Babylonian Captivity of the church in the fourteenth century).[12] This was political polemic, and its historical revisionism was only implicit. The golden age of Gallican historical scholarship was the sixteenth century, when French historians and antiquaries began collecting the documentation of their national tradition and, reinforcing it with notions of sovereignty and precedence borrowed from both civil and canon law, incorporated it into their official historiography.[13]

The English national church was also rooted in history, although the major expressions of independence from Rome did not come until the break under Henry VIII. The key statement is that of (presumably) Thomas Cromwell in the preamble to the Act in Restraint of Appeals to Rome (1533), which invokes "sundry old authentic histories and chronicles" to justify England's imperial status and, on the basis of this appropriated legacy, priority to the Roman papacy. In separating from the papacy, the Reformation parliament drew on English statutory precedents going back to the Babylonian Captivity as well as on imperialist and Gallican propaganda (Marsilius of Padua and Jean Lemaire de Belges were translated on behalf of the Henrician Reformation), and this also shaped the English tradition of historiography. The argument, parallel to the French, that the Anglican church was quite as ancient as the Roman was taken up also by Protestant and Puritan authors. "In witnes whereof," wrote John Foxe, "we have the old actes and histories of auncient tyme to give testimonie with us . . . , to declare the same form, usage, and institution of this our Church reformed now, not to be the begynnyng of any new Churche of our owne, but to be the renewyng of the old auncient Church of Christ."[14]

A similar story can be told about the Spanish monarchy, which likewise glorified itself through legal precedent and myth as well as official historiography.[15] In Spain the national church took shape in the context of the centuries-long Reconquista, in which the "Catholic kings" (the title granted by Pope Alexander VI in 1494) were the chief defenders of Christianity against the Muslim infidels. It was in reward for this epic service that popes granted the Spanish monarchies, especially those of Castile, Leon, and Aragon, special privileges and immunities from interference by Rome. The Spanish Inquisition, too, was an instrument of royal authority and as such a bulwark of the national church and a theme of Spanish national historiography. Spanish history became truly universal and "imperial" in another sense with the discovery of the New World, which threw all of the older European traditions, religious and political, into confusion. (When Adam delved and Eve span, where was then the Indian?)

Each one of these national traditions had its own conception of autonomy and reform, locating political and moral ideals in a period of primitive simplicity and virtue; but, with the emergence of Luther, ideas of "reformation" and Christian tradition became deeply divisive and, with the intersection of theological and political controversies, even explosive. All Protestant parties sought a usable ecclesiastical past purged of the human expressions of church organization centering on canon law, the hierarchy, and other expressions of papal supremacy. Radicals, or fundamentalists, looked fondly on the earliest period of the primitive church and the "imitation of Christ," even to martyrdom; Luther and Melanchthon accepted the Constantinian church and the early Fathers at least to Augustine; and Gallicans and Anglicans sought to impose a national slant on church history. In this predicament history, caught up in storms of confessional and national controversies, showed many different faces — still protesting the ancient ideals of truth and wisdom even while being conscripted into a plurality of causes. No wonder Henry Cornelius Agrippa warned of the "great damage" that the modern study of history was bringing.[16]

Johann Sleidan and the Reformation

From the standpoint of the history of history, the Protestant Reformation represented a massive project of revisionism, which proposed, first implicitly and then explicitly, to rewrite universal history so that it would convict the Roman hierarchy and justify the "true religion" which Luther and his colleagues were preaching. If Luther was both the Augustine and the Jerome of the reformed religion, the Strasbourgeois Johann Sleidan, with a humanist education, law degree, and diplomatic experience, became its Livy and its Eusebius. At any rate he was its official historiographer, having been hired and paid by the German princes of the Schmalkaldic League to tell the story of Luther's words and deeds and the program and efforts of the Protestant party, which gave its support to the new confessional movement.[17]

Sleidan had a twofold career in several senses. His circle of acquaintances included Luther, Melanchthon, Bucer, Johann Sturm, and Calvin, but he spent much of his time on diplomatic missions in the service of the brothers Jean and Guillaume Du Bellay and other secular company. Committed to the reformed religion, he was especially concerned with the political ties between the German, French, and English supporters of the movement. Following closely the progress of Protestant doctrine, he also had a deep interest in political history, as illustrated by his Latin translations of the works of Froissart, Commynes, and Seyssel. This bifocal approach carried over also into his commissioned history, his *De statu religionis et reipublicae Carolo V Caesare* (1555). "In the history of religion," Sleidan wrote in his preface, "I would not omit what concerned the civil government because they are interwoven with the other, especially in our times, so that it is not possible to separate them."[18]

Agreeing with Thucydides about the value of firsthand knowledge, Sleidan also prized the vicarious experience offered by history. For one example of such experience Sleidan had chosen Froissart because "he lived in a time that was indeed much troubled" and because, following the French court, "he could speak of events with authority and set them down truthfully in his book." Like Seyssel and Machiavelli, Sleidan took a political and "pragmatic" view of history. "In order to manage such affairs as war, peace, treatises, alliances, marriages, the means of increasing one's territories, the loyalty of a people, parties and other business of as kingdom," he wrote, "It seems to me that there is no more useful knowledge than the study of history."[19] This neo-Polybian *historia pragmatica* was, according to an eighteenth-century scholar, one enduring "fruit of the Reformation."[20]

This was also the motive behind his translations in 1548 of two later French authors, which were dedicated to the young Edward VI of England, the hope of international Protestantism. "I only ask that you become familiar with these two books of Commynes and Seyssel, one historical and the other political, both from another time," Sleidan wrote. "You will not be displeased by the work, and I know of no other books written in French that will do more to improve judgment."[21] He commended Seyssel in particular for his contributions to what he called "political and social science" (in the *Monarchy of France*). Although ignorant of true religion (having died in 1519 before receiving the message of Luther), Seyssel had not only accumulated the best of ancient and modern insights but had also "accommodated them to recent conditions and explained their utility." Commynes was an equally able and honest observer, writing in times of trouble; and although he drew lessons from his experience, "in no way did he praise those of his own country or race, even kings who had raised him to high honor, unless it was true . . . , [and] everywhere he presented the facts in themselves."[22] This was Sleidan's own ideal, and eventually he got in almost as much trouble for his pains as Commynes had.

From 1539 Sleidan had also been working on his own masterwork, which he first conceived as a "history of the restored religion" (*historia restauratae religionis, histori der ernewter religion*) but which later included the political dimension as well.[23] For this first effort, Sleidan was diligent in collecting manuscript and archival as well as published materials and was almost fanatical in preserving an impartial stance — as befitted a moderate Protestant residing in Strasbourg and poised between German, French, and English parties. Published in 1555, the book offered a comprehensive survey of European history from All Saints' Eve 1517 to February 1555, that is, from Luther's appearance on the public scene to the retirement of his great nemesis, Charles V; and it was extended in later editions, from Sleidan's own notes, down to September 1556, when the author died.

Despite Sleidan's fondness for Thucydidean political narrative, his design and commission led him far beyond the territory explored by the likes of Commynes, Machiavelli, and Guicciardini. They all lived in times of crisis, but Sleidan was a witness to "such a change in religion as is not to be parallelled since the apostles . . . [and followed by] a great commotion in the civil state, as is usual."[24] As Christ was born under Augustus and sanctified his empire, so too Luther emerged in the time of Augustus's successor Charles V. In what was in effect the first treatment of "the rise of modern Europe," Sleidan had to attend not only to questions of policy and interest but also to ideological factors and, in the fashion of Herodotus, to several levels of social history. Beginning with the inflammatory Ninety-Five Theses posted by Luther, Sleidan had to investigate the movers and shakers and also the moved and the shaken — conversions, the preaching of the Gospel, religious dissent, political resistance among less visible classes of society, and the persecutions of heresy and the tradition of martyrs. His last major topic was the Diet of Augsburg of 1555, which put an end to the first phase of the Reformation.

Reactions to Sleidan's work were extreme, ranging from the adulation of friends, Calvinists as well as Lutherans, to the denunciation of enemies, not only Catholics but some Protestants such as the Hohenzollern Margrave of Kulmbach-Bayreuth, who (so the story goes) inspired a book recounting the "1,000 lies of Sleidan."[25] Not that there was anything surprising in such attacks: Commynes was still being attacked ten years after his death for revealing the secrets of royal counsel which he had heard. Nevertheless, Sleidan was repelled by such charges, and in order to defend himself and to affirm his devotion to the Ciceronian laws of history, he composed a brief apology for his history (though withholding publication during his lifetime), which made public his historiographical confession of faith and which constituted his own contribution to the art of history.[26] Though professing the Gospel, he carefully avoided all "exasperating language and simply delivered everything as it came to pass."[27] "What disturbs me most," he wrote to a friend attending the Diet of Augsburg, "is the suggestion that truth in lacking in my work, for I am the enemy of all falsehood and do not boast when I affirm that I would rather die than say, still less write, anything without proof."[28]

The larger background against which Sleidan cast his narrative was the story of "the first four great empires of the world," of which, through the translation of empire, Sleidan's own sovereign, Charles V, was the beneficiary. This master narrative — heralded by the prophet Daniel and carried forward by Orosius, Otto of Freising, and (in Sleidan's own day) Johann Cario and Philipp Melanchthon — was rehearsed again by Sleidan in his *Four World Monarchies.*[29] For Sleidan the Janus motif once again seems appropriate — torn as he was, in a sense, between church and state, and looking back to the old myth of universal empire and forward to the triumph of the evangelical faith in the last age of this decrepit empire.

Confessional History

In the sixteenth century, religious history became in many ways pluralized, politicized, and polemicized, subverting the master narrative of Christian universal history.[30] Yet rival interpretations provoked not only confusion and discord among parties but also massive investigation into the sources of medieval and early Christian history. The impetus for this came in large part from controversies inspired by Luther and other promoters of the reformed religion (so-called, the Catholics added). Not only the humanist study of the Bible and patristic literature led by Erasmus but also Christian antiquities and the sources of lay and church history were explored and published primarily in the interests of one or another religious order, confession, party, institution, or state. Celebrations of the art of history became even more urgent, the laws of history were even more frequently invoked, official historiographers became more common, university courses were initiated, and works of reference were published; but history became ever more immersed in public controversy.[31] These were the conditions in which the modern study of history made its appearance and achieved scientific and professional status.[32]

Reformation (and Counter-Reformation) views of history — another incarnation of Janus — were formulated within the chronological and geographical framework of Scriptures and the scheme of universal history elaborated by medieval chronicles. Of this genre, indeed, the *Chronicon* of Johann Carion, adapted by Melanchthon to Lutheran purposes, was a late example. "Without history," Melanchthon repeated from Cicero and many others, "one remains forever a child" — referring to "continuous history from the beginning of the world, whence came the principles and sources of true religion."[33]

The larger patterns of history according to Protestant views were noted by Bucer and formulated more elaborately by Melanchthon in his oration "Luther and the Ages of the Church." Here the story was one of doctrinal expansion from the founding of the church, then medieval degeneration, and finally restoration. The first three ages were those of the primitive church, of Origen, and of Augustine; then came the ages of monasticism and of the new "barbarism" of scholastic doctors such as Thomas and Scotus, in which a "very small remnant" of pure doctrine was preserved; and lastly that of the reformation — the *ecclesia repurgata* — of Luther.[34] Not accidentally, this trinitarian periodization was homologous to the threefold humanist scheme of a bright antiquity, a dark middle age, and a rebirth of "new learning" (a term was usually reserved for evangelical religion).

Protestant theologians saw history in moral rather than political terms. For Melanchthon, as for historians and jurists, history was distinguished from nature because it was a product of human will; but unlike secular scholars he took this to mean the story not of "words and deeds" but of sin and its fruits, which is to say, vices. It is true that laws — civil and pontifical laws, at least — were also a product of history, but they were also reprehensible in a spiritual sense; for as Melanchthon showed by various examples, "there has been no tradition, pious though it be in appearance, which has not wrought great evil for Christianity."[35] According to Zwingli's successor, Heinrich Bullinger, this was also true of the "succession of doctors and pastors," which were nothing without the continuing presence, "from age to age from the very first," of the spiritual word.[36]

Despite theological differences, Lutherans and Calvinists shared much the same view of history, accepting the ideas of a "succession of doctrine" from the early church, however tenuously preserved by marginal and even heretical carriers, and of a degeneration of the modern church through the accumulation of human tradition. Bullinger devoted a whole book to "the origins of errors."[37] Jean Calvin described the process of earthly corruption in his *Institutes of Christian Religion,* judging it as a loss of rights by the community, the usurpation of authority by the papacy, and attendant fraudulent claims such as the false Donation of Constantine.[38] This forgery had been repudiated by Valla and, even more vigorously, by Luther, who had regarded it as typical of the Romanist methods of forging its claims and, he inferred, tradition more generally.

Protestantism had to approach the problem of finding a tradition, of constructing its history, in a different fashion. One way was the Melanchthonian strategy of tracing a spiritual tradition of "pure religion" that preserved the ideals of the ancient church: what Melanchthon sought was doctrinal continuity, and with the help of the early Fathers this is just what he found.[39] Melanchthon's opponent, the ultra-Lutheran Flacius Illyricus, compiled his vast *Catalogue of the Witnesses of Truth* (1556) to celebrate the tenuous tradition of pious champions of pure Christian faith, victims of impious persecution, and opponents of the doctrines of the "papists." *Historia est fundamentum doctrinae* was the motto of Flacius. "From all authors and histories," he declared, "it is evident that our church . . . is truly ancient and takes its origin from the time of Christ and the apostles."[40] Like the translation of empire (a theme on which Flacius also wrote a treatise), there was a holy succession of Christians preserving the continuity of the true church. Flacius accumulated some four hundred names of the precursors of Luther, beginning with the prophets, patriarchs, apostles, and mystics and including imperialists such as Dante, the reformers of the Conciliarist period, humanists such as Petrarch, Valla, and Pico, and even men of little faith but much politics such as Machiavelli, to the extent that he was a critic of papal usurpation.

In Greek the word for witness was *martyr,* and this leads us to the most effective sort of confessional historiography. As evangelical Christians were urged to the imitation of Christ, the "captain of martyrs," so too second-generation Protestant authors imitated the recorders of the victimized witnesses whose persecutions are immortalized in the form of Christian martyrology — the *de viris* [and *mulieribus*] *illustribus* as well as the *vitae sanctorum* of proto-Protestant tradition. In the sixteenth century there was a sort of international *équipe* of Protestant martyrologists, centering especially on Geneva, Strasbourg, and Zurich, including, at least marginally, Sleidan and Flacius but more prominently Jean Crespin, Theodore Beza (the *History of the Protestant Churches* was often ascribed to him), John Foxe, and Heinrich Pantaleone, who exchanged information and source materials in what amounted to a collective effort of historical research and propaganda.[41]

The central theme of this genre was, in Crespin's words, "the conformity of the modern history of the martyrs with that of antiquity." The purpose of Crespin's *History of the Martyrs* (first edition, 1554) was both to give "profit" to his brothers and to demonstrate the justice of his Huguenot cause to the "poor ignorant ones" outside it.[42] For Crespin the story of the martyrs was truly universal, as it included "all conditions, ages, sexes, and nations." Martyrology performed many of the functions of conventional historiography, offering consolation, constituting a treasury of examples for imitation and a kind of moral and anagogical mirror for Christians, and preserving for posterity the words and deeds of exemplary men and women of faith. Moreover, the sufferings of the faithful represented a major source of continuity with the primitive church, being, as it were, the carnal counterpart of the progress of grace on earth. ("The blood of the martyrs," in the famous phrase of Tertullian, "is the seed of the church.")[43]

Even more influential was the work of John Foxe, who was one of the Marian exiles from England when he began publishing his *Acts and Monuments* in 1557. Foxe had the same purposes in mind as Crespin, and in the course of a lifetime of research he gathered a rich harvest of materials about the medieval religious movements underlying the English Reformation and the Puritan movement. Like Crespin and Flacius, Foxe invoked the classical justifications of historical writing — truth, utility, and so on — but at the same time, like them, he wanted his "tragical history" to prove the antiquity and historical legitimacy of evangelical religion in contrast to the diabolical and idolatrous novelties of popery, including monasticism and the canon law.[44] In such polemical tones Foxe, showing the "fruit and utility to be taken of this history," carried on the historiographical revisionism associated with the reformed confessions.

History was vital to the religious controversies of the Reformation, being the cornerstone of legitimacy and confessional correctness, and this became even more obvious with the growing interest in the more remote phases of the history of the church. In the Lutheran camp this was initiated especially by the

Magdeburg Centuries, assembled by a team headed by Flacius Illyricus and published from 1559.[45] This survey of the ecclesiastical past reached only the thirteenth century and was far from being critical in any modern sense — accepting, in its desire to discredit papal tradition, legends such as that of "Pope Joan" and the identification of the pope with Antichrist — but it does illustrate the remarkable antiquarian turn taken by Christian scholarship in the later sixteenth century.[46]

Responding to Protestant revisionism, Catholic apologists also turned to a review of history to defend their traditions. Cesare Baronio, who lectured for many years on ecclesiastical history at Rome, also produced an edition of the Catholic martyrology, which counteracted the works of Crespin, Foxe, and company, but much more significant was his multivolume response to the Magdeburg "centuriators." Baronio's chosen form was not history but annals, because for him the historian deals with contemporary narrative, while the annalist "entrusts to memory most of all what his age does not know" and does so in a manner — chronological and not topical — that is better suited to the "almost religious sanction" required by truth.[47] His *Annales Ecclesiastici,* which began appearing in 1588, was based on no less massive research than the centuriators and, what is more, access to the Vatican archives. The work reached the end of the twelfth century in its ponderous and clumsy effort to defend and amplify papal tradition and primacy. Baronio's work was in its turn answered by the great Calvinist scholar Isaac Casaubon; and so the debate over tradition continued, over many generations, in ever more detailed and pedantic fashion.

Another defender of the church was the ex-Huguenot and friend of Etienne Pasquier and Montaigne, Florimond de Raemond, who, unlike Pasquier, was little interested in institutional and cultural questions and preferred to tie his historical work to personalities.[48] He turned against his former co-religionists to attack Luther as the chief perpetrator of the "tragic" schism of his age and Sleidan, the "Lutheran Livy," who wrote so falsely about the Reformation.[49] He also assailed Calvin (as well as Sacramentarians and Anabaptists) as Luther's offspring, and Geneva as the center of present-day heresy. Raemond published books against the myths, kept alive by Protestant scholars, of Pope Joan and of the papacy as the Antichrist before taking up his major project, which was a comprehensive history of the over two hundred heresies of the sixteenth century arising under the pretext of a politicized "liberty of conscience."

The greatest historian of the Counter-Reformation was, by common consent, Paolo Sarpi. No Protestant (as far as told from his protective "mask"), Father Paul was nonetheless a bitter critic of the Roman church, who began his researches while his native Venice was under papal interdict and while he himself, as theologian and canon lawyer to the *Serenissima,* was an excommunicant. He was an admirer of the Reformation in general and the work of that "very accurate writer" Johann Sleidan in particular. Sarpi's *History of the Council of Trent,* published pseudonymously in London in 1619, was both an erudite narrative of the modern turning point of Catholic tradition and a polemic against ultramontanist excesses, especially the papal "monarchy," the Jesuits, and the dogmatic intransigence keeping Christendom divided. The council "was planned by the princes to reform the Church," Sarpi remarked, "but it has brought about the greatest corruption of the Church since the name of 'Christian' was first heard."[50] Praised by Protestants, the book provoked Romanist responses, most notably by the Jesuit Sforza Pallavicino, who offered an almost line-by-line attack against Sarpi as Casaubon had done against Baronio. Modern ecclesiastical and, to a large extent, secular history was forged in the crucible of such polemic, in which history fulfilled the function both of the "mistress of life" and of a weapon of ideological warfare. Yet despite this pandemonium of traditions, bedlam of interpretations, and riot of disputes, history remained boastfully a servant of truth.

National Tradition: Germany

In the sixteenth century, truth took both national and confessional forms, as the European states, in imitation of ancient Rome, generated their own secular cults and ideology and as their historiographers began the task of inventing traditions to suit modern needs and hopes. Classical tradition remained not only a source of inspiration and ideas but also a discouraging obstacle to the ambitions of nations which could not claim a classical pedigree except through questionable myths. To humanists like Petrarch, Valla, and Aeneas Sylvius Piccolomini (Pope Pius II), "barbarism" and an ignorance of classical languages seemed to be a barrier to rationality and to civility; and Machiavelli, too, had wanted Italy liberated from the still-invading "barbarians," meaning all the other European nations.[51] By the time of Luther's call to the "German nation," however, a backlash to invidious Romanism had set in. In reaction to classicist calumnies, German scholars like Hartmann Schedel, Johannes Trithemius, Jacob Wimpheling, and Heinrich Bebel rejected the charges of Italians and began a counterattack through the celebration of Germanic traditions, protonationalist literature like Biondo's *Italia illustrata* being rivaled by the *Germania illustrata* of Conrad Celtis — like Petrarch, a poet laureate — and his colleagues.[52]

Invoking the old topos applied to the early Romans, Bebel lamented the neglect of the ancient glories of Germany. In fact, "Germany can hold its own not only with attainments considered excellent in our own day but also with the greatest of the feats of antiquity," Bebel argued, and further, "Germany contains within herself all the excellent and praiseworthy things claimed by other peoples."[53] Wimpheling's *Epitome* was written to fill just this gap, in order that his readers "might discover the antiquities of Germany, read the biographies of the emperors, learn to know their merits, intelligence, campaigns, victories, inventions, nobility, fidelity, courage, constancy and love of truth of the Germans, and in order to encourage posterity . . . to try every day to add still greater achievements, thus augmenting Germany by new merits."[54] This was part of a rising chorus of tributes retrospectively bestowed on Germanic culture, with special emphasis on the revolutionary German invention of the printing press, which made it possible to restore the attainments of the Ancients and to carry on those of the Moderns. So the faces of Herodotus and Thucydides as well as the more popular authors of the Latin tradition reappeared, and in the descendants of the ancient barbarians their writings found a new posterity to enlighten and to entertain.

The locus classicus of the modern praise of barbarism was the *Germania* of Tacitus, which had been rediscovered in the early fifteenth century, which was exploited thereafter by generations of historians, and which was the vehicle of a huge accumulation of commentary and interpretation.[55] The most comprehensive of these commentaries was that of Andreas Althamer, for whom "our Tacitus" was the first and best author devoting himself to "to illustrate, to dignify, and to celebrate Germany."[56] What Tacitus offered to his modern Germanist disciples — through eyewitness testimony as well as knowledge of the poetic sources — was an "original image of Germany" and its original manners. The Germanic virtues noted by Tacitus — *pudicitia, liberalitas, integritas, fides, libertas, constantia, fortitudo, ingenium, nobilitas,* and so on — were incorporated into historical works by Wimpheling, Albert Krantz, and especially Erasmus's younger friend Beatus Rhenanus (who had also published a commentary on Tacitus) in order to give substance to a cultural tradition traceable back to prehistory and perhaps even to nature. "The German people have always lived in total liberty" (*summa libertas*), declared Beatus.[57] And what was no less a point of national pride, they were racially pure — "indigenous" and "unmixed." In this neobarbarian tradition there was arguably even a sort of solicitude toward women that has been termed "Germanic feminism."[58]

The old theme of Ancients versus Moderns was given a national and even racialist edge by the *Kulturkampf* waged by German humanists. Lorenzo Valla had famously praised the posthumous victories of Roman civilization and language, declaring — according to a fabricated literary genealogy — that "ours [the Romans] is Italy, ours Gaul, ours Spain, Germany . . . , and many other lands; for wherever the Roman tongue holds sway, there is the Roman Empire."[59] Yet the "Roman" Empire was itself now German; and the Bavarian historian Aventinus answered Valla with a sort of inverted paraphrase, arguing that, on the contrary, "Ours [the Germans] are the victories of the Goths, Vandals and Franks; ours the glory attached to the kingdoms that these peoples founded in the most illustrious provinces of the Romans, in Italy, and in the queen of cities, Rome herself."[60] Needless to say, the "Luther affair," which had a large national dimension, intensified such ideological quarrels.

Essential to the Germanist ideology was the myth of empire and its translation, which had been celebrated by jurists and historians of the empire for generations, not only by credulous medieval chroniclers and popular authors like Sebastian Brandt but also by humanists like Wimpheling, for whom the translation was actually the restoration of empire to its true possessors.[61] Protestants too, joining their theological complaints to the secular discontents expressed in *gravamina* and anticlerical sermons, took up the theme, provoking conflicts with their Catholic opponents, notable examples being Flacius's derivative essay on the translation of empire and the response of the Jesuit scholar Roberto Bellarmino.[62] Contending for the old imperial myth, Germanists and Romanists also struggled for control over cultural tradition and the universal historical narrative which preserved it.

A fundamental critique of the imperialist tradition and the fiction of the translation of empire was launched in the following century by the Lutheran philosopher Samuel Pufendorf, for whom history was a sideline to his enormously influential works on natural law. In his *Constitution of the German Empire* (1667), Pufendorf undermined the sentimental or ideological appeals of modern Germans to tribal or Carolingian roots.[63] The title of "Holy Roman Emperor" signified no connection with the ancient Romans but only a deplorable alliance, or even subjection to the Roman papacy, reflecting a "yearning in the hearts" of Germans for Italy, and representing a sort of political version of the perennial *italienische Reise*. The Protestant princes opposed this obsession with Italy, and so did Pufendorf, who saw the political scene in seventeenth-century Europe in terms of the sovereignty and interests of states and history as subordinate to philosophy and natural law.

The "conjunction of history and jurisprudence" had been proclaimed by Baudouin a century before, but for him the alliance was based on the analogy between a legal continuity founded on positive (civil and canon) law and a historical integrity founded on the Polybian concept of organic unity.[64] With Bodin this conception was retained to some extent, with universal law and universal history meeting in the law of nations (*jus gentium*), meaning the particular legal traditions, modern as well as ancient, beyond the pale of Roman law: "In history lies the better part of universal law" was Bodin's maxim.[65] By the time of Pufendorf, however, although historical erudition continued to be prized, the study of history had a very limited practical or conceptual value and, for "jusnaturalists" like Pufendorf, Grotius, Leibniz, and Hobbes, was subordinated to the higher sciences of law and politics. In the later Enlightenment history had to find another conceptual grounding and another relationship to philosophy, out of which emerged modern historicism and the refurbished erudition of the several historical schools of the nineteenth century.

National Tradition: France

"Frenchmen," wrote the humanist scholar and vernacular jurist Louis Le Caron, "You have enough examples in your own histories without inquiring into those of Greece and Rome."[66] This vulgar modernism may be taken as the motto both of "vernacular humanism" in France and of the modern tradition of national historiography. Like German humanists and reformers, French authors in the sixteenth century — Gallicans as well as adherents of the "so-called reformed religion" — wanted to declare their independence of Roman tradition, to contribute to what Le Caron's poetic colleague Joachim Du Bellay called the "defense and illustration" of the French language, including French culture more generally, and to construct a national history in keeping both with these ideological goals and with the classical "laws" of history.[67]

Despite the caution of scholars like Gaguin and Paolo Emilio, the mythological tradition was still very much alive in the sixteenth century — Trojan origins, the legendary Francus and Pharamond, and all. These popular stories, implanted in chronicles and histories ever since Fredegar, were continued by Nicolas Gilles, Symphorien Champier, Jean Bouchet, Sleidan's patron Guillaume Du Bellay, and many others well into the seventeenth century. They were also reinforced by dubious and discredited modern scholarship, most notably the work of Giovanni Nanni (Ennius) of Viterbo, who in 1498 published a fraudulent collection of allegedly ancient authors, including the Chaldean Berosus, whose account of humanity after the Flood (supposedly the predecessor of the history by the Egyptian Manetho) mentioned Francus as Hector's son. The fabrications of "Berosus Babylonicus" were accepted by Jean Lemaire de Belges, Gilles Corrozet, Guillaume Postel, and Robert Ceneau, and other French Celtophiles, though it did not take critical scholars such as Beatus Rhenanus long to reject these "incredible genealogies."[68]

The most outrageous mythical constructions gave way to historical criticism under the influence of two forces. One was the new science of philology cultivated by scholars like Valla, Poliziano, Erasmus, Budé, and Beatus Rhenanus, who were increasingly sensitive to the niceties of stylistic imitation, anachronism, and forgery; and the other was the old science of law, which likewise demanded textual rigor and solid proof—and whose practitioners were also, though on rather different grounds, aware of problems of conventional (or official) style, anachronism, and forgery.[69] Under the scrutiny of such disciplines, theories of Trojan origins and eponymous founders gave way to demonstrable historical fact and matters of textual proof. Most important of all was the exploitation of the royal archives, most notably by the official *greffier* Jean Du Tillet, whose commission to reform the archives furnished the material for his massive publications in French history.[70]

Medievalist scholarship was not only becoming more critical but it was also acquiring a more substantial base as a result of the accumulation of editions of medieval authors, succeeding and accompanying the flood of classical historiographical texts of previous generations.[71] In France in the early part of the century Josse Badius published editions of Eusebius, Gregory of Tours, Paul the Deacon, Luitprand, Aimon, Geoffrey of Monmouth, and others, and at the end of the century Pasquier's and Fauchet's friend Pierre Pithou published—besides his own valuable historical, legal, and critical works—an ambitious collection that included Paul the Deacon, Salvian, Otto of Freising, and (following on the editions of Bishop Jean du Tillet, brother to the archivist of the same name) various Carolingian capitularies and documents illustrative of the Gallican church. In giving substance to medievalist scholarship, of course, Pithou was also, like Pasquier, reinforcing the ideological—and especially Germanic—traditions of the French monarchy.[72]

There was much discussion in the later sixteenth century about the overall shape of French history, beginning with Louis Le Roy's abortive "Considerations," written in 1568 for Catherine de Médicis. Two years later he published a "project or design of the kingdom of France," which (bearing the imprint of Seyssel's work and terminology) proposed to survey in ten topical and historical and books the monarchy of France and which was followed by another fragment, "Les Monarchiques," adopting the four-age theory of Seyssel to give structure to French history.[73] In fact (whatever the motive for the discourse), Le Roy was so fascinated with humanist learning in general—he published his translation of Aristotle's *Politics* also in 1568—and so distracted by the turmoil of the religious wars and a world apparently in decline that he was never able to pursue his ambitious plan for a narrative history of France. Instead, he was deflected into a wider-ranging, comparative, but still historical study of the "vicissitude of things in the universe" more generally, in which he could combine his worries about political instability with his hopes for intellectual progress.[74]

Contemporaneously, a less accomplished scholar, Bernard du Haillan, who indeed had a commission as royal historiographer, dedicated a similar plan, *Promise and Design for the History of France,* to King Charles IX and his brother, the future Henry III. This labor would require much expenditure of physical and spiritual energy, not to speak of material support, for the necessary research in "titles, charters, memoirs, registers, and other monuments needed for the building of such a work."[75] The result of sticking to written evidence, he added, would be to cast doubt on the "monstrous fables" disseminated by the poets, including Ronsard's *Franciade.* "I have said with an unusual boldness many things which no one before me has dared to say," he continued, rejecting "the coming of Pharamond to France, the institution of the Salic Law attributed to him, the creation of the Peers of France by Charlemagne," and so on.[76]

The third revisionist scheme was a "Design for the New History of the French," which appeared as an appendix to the *History of Histories, with the Idea of Complete History* and was published by Lancelot Voisin de la Popelinière in 1599.[77] Seeking a *modelle du vray historiographe,* La Popelinière invoked not only the commonplaces of humanist historical theory but also the whole historiographical tradition in France from Gaguin, Paolo Emilio, and Seyssel (to whom he misattributed the treatise on the Salic Law often published with the *Monarchy of France*) to Du Tillet, Nicholas Vignier, and Du Haillan, whose 1,200 ecus per year suggested the liberality of the monarchy for such intellectual labor. La Popelinière proposed to improve on his predecessors by concentrating on the neglected phases of Gallic history (*Gaule ancienne, romain, germaine,* and *françoise*) before coming to the fifth age, which was that of France proper. His own effort would be superior in both critical understanding and breadth, proposing as he did to include accounts (as Seyssel had done, but without historical background) of all the political, legal, religious, and social factors which had generated the "force" of the French monarchy in the course of its history.

None of these later sixteenth-century historians accepted the royalist myths of Trojan origins and alleged Carolingian creations, but new mythical constructs had arisen to replace the old ones. In particular, a Germanist paradigm, based especially on Tacitus's *Germania* and barbarian historians like Jordanes, was formed by historians seeking the true "origins of the French" (that is, the Franks). "Those who have written that the French are of true German origin," wrote Du Tillet, "have done them more honor than those who have regarded them as coming from the Trojans, since honor is due only to virtue."[78] But, citing modern scholars such as Beatus Rhenanus as well as ancient authorities (Tacitus, Ammianus Marcellinus, Gregory of Tours, and Jordanes), Du Tillet argued that this derivation was also historically the case, supporting his arguments by linguistic points, such as the famous etymology of "Frank" and "free" (*francus, id est liberus*), and this position was accepted by most French historians in the later sixteenth century. Feudalism, too, was Germanic in origin (again linguistic arguments were decisive), as in spirit were the "liberties" of the Gallican tradition.

The Germanist thesis, founded and elaborated by Lutheran scholars, was promoted by French Protestants, who also found in it useful ammunition in their struggle against Romanism and the Catholic party in France. The classic statement appears in the notorious *Franco-Gallia,* published in 1573, in the wake of the massacres of St. Bartholomew, by the Calvinist agent and jurist François Hotman. Arguing for his beleaguered Huguenot "cause," Hotman offered an extraordinarily well-researched and heavily argued reading of French history as the product of pristine Germano-Celtic traditions originally free — like the primitive church celebrated by his patron Calvin — from the taint of "Roman tyranny" in religious as well as institutional terms. Hotman combined massive scholarship and disputatious style in pursuit of what he once called "French truth."[79]

The new Germanist orthodoxy was received into the tradition of the official historiographers of that period, descendants of "Paule-Emile," of whom the most able was perhaps Bernard Girard du Haillan, whose *State and Success of Affairs of France* appeared in 1570, the year of Du Tillet's death, but years before his appointment as *historiographe du roi.* Du Haillan gave credit to such predecessors and contemporaries as Gaguin, Paolo Emilio, Seyssel, Bodin, Le Roy, Belleforest, De Serres, Fauchet, Vignier, Pasquier, La Pope-linière, and of course Du Tillet (whose work he employed in the second edition of his *State and Success*), who are some of the major figures in the mainstream of early modern French historical thought and writing.[80] Du Haillan had reflected on French history in classical terms (especially the topos of the "fortune and virtue" of France) and with regard to its larger patterns ("the promise and design of the history of France"), and he followed Seyssel not only in his notion of the "three bridles" of the French monarchy (religion, justice, and polity) but also in the four-stage idea of French history derived from Florus, that is, infancy and adolescence under the Merovingians, maturity under the Carolingians, and decline under the Capetians.[81]

Of this line, the most distinguished scholar was probably Etienne Pasquier, whose *Researches of France* began appearing in 1560 and continued for over half a century, illuminating, in monographic form, many aspects of French antiquities and history.[82] Although he had a training in law, Pasquier, like

Petrarch and many a humanist after him, was attracted to a literary career, hoping to join, and later writing historical accounts of, the tradition of French poetry of the medieval past and the "Pléiade" of his own day. Pasquier wrote on the history not only of literature but also of language, proverbs, law, institutions, the universities, and many other aspects of French culture, popular and elite. Eschewing bare political narrative, Pasquier spent his scholarly life in quest of the "spirit" of the French nation in its long historical emergence from its "Franco-Gallic" beginnings, yet approached his task with a critical attitude that permitted demolishing various myths, both Trojan origins and legends associated with Charlemagne, such as the foundation of the University of Paris.

Paralleling and overlapping the antiquarian labors of Pasquier were those of his colleague Claude Fauchet, who based his *Gallic Antiquities* on extensive preliminary reading in medieval and modern French historians. Fauchet honored history as the "mirror of life," which might, "by a circular revolution," permit judgment of "facts present and to come by those past."[83] Yet he was concerned more with the accuracy of the facts than with larger patterns; and while he criticized Monstrelet and Commynes for their inaccuracies, he rejected the learned Jean Lemaire de Belges as more poet than historian.[84] Like Pasquier, Fauchet had a legal training and a special interest in institutional history, including feudalism and the "Gallican liberties," which also gave definition to the monarchy.

In fact, historical scholarship in the sixteenth century was as productive and supportive of modern myths as it was critical and contemptuous of medieval ones. The effort to construct a continuous historical narrative depended in many ways on the legal fictions which tied the monarchy to a Frankish past through the notion of three successive dynasties ("races"), and "the memory and legends" of Charlemagne were part of the heritage that accompanied such fictions. The same went for the traditions of the Gallican church, which Du Tillet, Pithou, and Fauchet so carefully documented but less carefully suggested were traceable back to the time of the apostles.[85] The old assumptions about the value of antiquity as a sign of legitimacy were taken over without question into even the most critical historical scholarship.

With Pasquier and Pithou's colleague Nicolas Vignier, we return again to the genre of universal history. Drawing on the widest range of modern scholarship as well as ancient and medieval sources, Vignier also wrote on French origins and subscribed to the Germanist thesis; but his major work was his *Historical Library,* published in three massive volumes and founded on the Polybian organic premise — though without the enslavement to the Roman tradition — "that it is impossible to write a particular history because the affairs of this world (especially in political terms) are such that, like the human

body, each part is always dependent on the other."[86] Drawing on the work of
Scaliger, Vignier's work followed the Eusebian scheme of parallel columns
distributed to all the nations of the world, which were likewise traced back to
their origins; and it was devoted to giving universal history the soundest
chronological base in order to accommodate, to synchronize, and to integrate
all of the national histories of the ancient, medieval, and modern world.

The most famous of all French historians of this period, and one who also
worked on a global canvas, though limited to contemporary history, was
Jacques-Auguste de Thou, member of a great dynasty of French jurists. De
Thou's massive, multivolume, much-revised *History of His Times,* first published in 1604, covered more than sixty years of European history, almost all
of it dominated by civil and world war.[87] Dedicated to Henry IV and reverent
toward the grandeur of the French monarchy as well as the "public good," de
Thou nonetheless prided himself, like Sleidan, not only on conventional love
of truth (Cicero's first law) but also an unusual impartiality, similar perhaps to
that of the much-maligned *politiques* of the previous generation, that allowed
him to speak well even of Protestants, the king's former co-religionists — and
that attained for him a place on the papal *Index* in 1609. France had risen to
greatness under the law, de Thou concluded, and now that peace was finally
achieved, it was perhaps time to extend this rule of law to the rest of Europe. It
was in the light of this aspiration that de Thou's history, and other universal
histories as well, were written — even though much of the substance of his
narrative concerned death and destruction.

In the seventeenth century the French historiographical tradition hardened
into a royalist orthodoxy to match the Gallican doctrine of Louis XIV's monarchy, and practitioners were indeed, in Orest Ranum's phrase, "artisans of
glory" locked into monolithic ideology and commonplace notions of the role
of history.[88] Projects of erudition, historical criticism, source collections, and
the extension of the international network of scholars all continued at an
increasing pace, but with little consequence for the writing of history. The old
regime under the Bourbon kings was attracted more by the mirrors of Versailles than the mirror of history; and the monarch himself, who not only
identified himself with the State but, through his court historians, claimed
control over the national past. This provided the context for another turn to
traditional learning and antiquarian scholarship in the service of politics.

National Tradition: England

In broad outline, English historiography followed much the same course
as that of Germany and France, with Polydore Vergil occupying the position of
humanist founder in much the same way that Flavio Biondo did for the Italian

tradition, Beatus Rhenanus for the German, and Paolo Emilio and Robert Gaguin for the French. Like the Italians and the French (but not the Germans), English historians turned toward the vernacular in the generations after these founding figures — and, under the impetus of religious controversy, toward medievalist studies.

Polydore Vergil's *Anglica historia,* which began with a conventional geographical survey, was built on, and in many ways replaced, the English chronicle tradition, supplemented by foreign sources, including Flavio Biondo and Froissart, and achieved virtually official status.[89] A self-taught medievalist, Vergil discovered and published Gildas, and reckoned the chronicles of William of Malmesbury and Matthew Paris true histories as distinguished from mere monkish annals and the reprehensible "new history" of Geoffrey of Monmouth; but he put first trust in classical authors and, though he still believed in providential intervention, was undiplomatically critical toward the venerable legends of Brutus and King Arthur (namesake of Henry VIII's late brother), which had acquired new currency in the eclectic romance of Thomas Malory. In fact Vergil, as an Italian-born humanist, believed in the primacy of Rome and so was skeptical of national mythology; and like George Buchanan, national historian of Scotland, he tended to associate civilization with classical Latin, to the detriment of barbarian tongues.[90] Nevertheless Vergil's history was drawn on, as well as criticized, by later continuators of the "great chronicle tradition";[91] and the Tudor "cult of the British history" continued, thanks to the support of Arthurians like John Leland, John Bale, Raphael Holinshed, William Harrison, William Lambarde, and (for his own purposes) Edward Coke.[92] This embarrassing battle of the books, like the debates in France over Trojan origins, was not resolved until long after Vergil's death.

English historiography took a truly antiquarian turn with the career of John Leland, who claimed to be the Beatus Rhenanus of Britain, and indeed he was superior in knowledge to Vergil but not his equal as a writer.[93] Before he went mad, Leland had become "inflamed with a love" of exploring the English countryside and the riches of English libraries; and in the course of these Herodotean efforts he compiled a vast record of his researches, including a collection of the lives of British authors, similar to Trithemius's *Catalogue of Famous German Men* (1491) as well as Jerome's *De viris illustribus.* Interested in places as well as books, things as well as words, Leland was a choreographer and archaeologist as well as frustrated poet and "antiquarius." His work was continued by the Protestant Bale, who was, as it were, his posthumous collaborator, representing a link between him and the martyrologist John Foxe, whom he supplied with materials.[94] Bale was also associated with the Joachimite tradition and the not entirely discredited work of Ennius of Viterbo, still cited in support of the politically useful Trojan genealogies.

Polydore Vergil's Romanist prejudices did not survive the English Reformation, when English scholarship, like that of Lutheran Germany, turned against the classical heritage and looked to its own national past as a source of legitimacy and prestige. As English Protestants rejected the tyranny of the pope, so students of Anglo-Saxon liberty sought to throw off, retrospectively, the "Norman yoke" and attendant French attributes. One of the clearest statements of the "Germanist" slant of English history in the wake of the Reformation was by Richard Verstegan, who sought to satisfy English readers hoping "to hear of the woorthynesse of their ancestors." Searching for the "original of Nations" after the Flood and Tower of Babel, Verstegan devoted himself to showing "how the ancient noble Saxons, the true ancestors of Englishmen, were originally a people of Germanie: and how honorable it is for Englishmen to be descended from the Germans."[95] Following the Germans by a generation or more, this English turn toward its "barbarian" and "Gothic" past, taken also by distinguished scholars like John Selden and Henry Spelman, likewise employed the works of Tacitus, Jordanes, and other historians of Germany.

The founding figure of British historiography (after Vergil) was William Camden (1551–1623), who followed the path of political narrative, although, like Sleidan, he found it impossible to ignore ecclesiastical matters in that age of confessional confusion.[96] He had a good classical education and many contacts with continental scholars, and like Leland, in good Herodotean style, traveled extensively in the attempt to examine archives and monuments as well as to give a sound geographical basis to his history. Camden took as models not Thucydides and Livy, however, but Polybius and Tacitus. He professed the usual historical virtues, including truth and impartiality, which he did not see as opposed to his fervent patriotism and devotion to Queen Elizabeth. His aim was analytical, that is, to seek "causes" and what he referred to as "Why, How, and to What End" things had been done in history, although this did not break him of the old annalistic habit of noting occasional natural "prodigies." Yet Camden never lost his classicist inspiration; and it is interesting that at the end of his life, endowing a chair of history at Oxford, he directed that it be devoted to the reading of Florus.[97]

John Selden (1584–1654), a disciple of Camden, was an even more accomplished scholar, who was likewise fully abreast of continental scholarship, looking to the likes of Budé, Alciato, Hotman, and Cujas for scholarly example and to Bacon for theoretical guidance—though he was also familiar with the work of Bede, Eadmer, Einhard, Adam of Bremen, Matthew Paris, and other medieval authors, as well as the Magna Carta, embodying the "main freedom of the English commonwealth."[98] Selden's contributions took the form of monographs on legal and institutional history, such as his survey of "titles of honor" and his controversial history of tithes. In general it was from the legal tradition that, like Baudouin, Bodin, Pasquier, and others, he derived his respect for written authorities and distrust of later tradition, so that, for example, he rejected the poetic "fictions or impostures" of Trojan origins, which he likened to "Talmudic traditions."[99]

Like the Lutherans, Anglican scholars had to confront the problem of the church in a reformed condition, and they resolved it in much the same way, that is, by arguing in Eusebian style that the English church was "no new thing."[100] ("Neither is this any new thing," the Catholics answered, invoking the authority of Vincent of Lèrins, "but always usuall in the Church of God.")[101] On the Anglican side this was the thesis of Bishop John Jewel, and it was a thesis pursued in more secular ways from the Elizabethan period on. The most successful defense was that of Richard Hooker, whose *Laws of Ecclesiastical Polity* began to appear in 1593. While Hooker's aim was to ground the Anglican church in principles of natural law, what he did was to politicize it by grafting religion onto the legislative and parliamentary tradition of the English monarchy. In practical terms the Anglican Church, though it was essentially a divine foundation, was also an expression of human will and English experience; and as such it became part of the history of the English nation.[102]

In the wake of the Reformation, English authors were creating what Richard Helgerson has called a "rhetoric of nationhood," which found expression in many intellectual and cultural fields, including language, poetry, drama, law, religion, and travel literature as well as the writing of history itself.[103] Reconstructing the English past involved exploration, historical scholarship and criticism, and establishment of legal traditions and intellectual genealogies, but also new interpretations and myths, which always accompany the processes of state and church building. It may be going too far to call this a "historical revolution," but it surely marks a heightened consciousness, within the reading public and indeed within English society more generally, of the uses and forms of historiography.[104]

In the seventeenth century, English historiography required revision on two grounds, as the union with Scotland in 1604 and the Puritan Revolution at midcentury each opened up a different perspective on the past. The union prompted historians like John Clapham (1606), Edward Ayscu (1607), and especially John Speed (1611) to cast their national narratives as the history not of England but of Great Britain, and so to emphasize the imperial aspects and destiny of insular history. In this connection, too, the uniqueness of English laws, customs, and institutions became a central part of historical narrative, with particular emphasis on the mythology and tradition of common law, as expressed by John Fortescue in the fifteenth century and Edward Coke in the Stuart period. Like French scholars such as Du Haillan (who was indeed cited by Stuart historians), English historians drew on legal sources and methods in celebrating the excellence, antiquity, and continuity of English institutions and the English constitution. Coke, who preferred legal concepts based on the authority of common law rather than untrustworthy chroniclers and historians, regarded the institutional inheritance of England as "immemorable," but after the Great Revolution this was replaced by a more historical sort of myth, which was the idea of "Gothic" descent.[105]

Another British historian who drew inspiration from Du Haillan was Samuel Daniel, whose history of Britain was carried down to the time of Edward III. Daniel made use of Gildas but avoided discussion of mythic origins except to compare the state of Britain and other European nations to New World savages "in their first, and naturall free nakednesse."[106] At the same time he defended medieval times from charges of barbarism, referring to the Venerable Bede, Gervase of Tilbury, "and an infinite catalogue of excellent men" learned in all the sciences.[107] Daniel's *Collection* followed the reigns of English kings in more or less annalistic fashion, but it also emphasized the centrality of customs and laws in making the English community and what he called the "state."[108] Another aspect of English exceptionalism was the Parliament, which Daniel dated back to the early twelfth century, and he remarked on the Magna Carta of 1215, which he, like Coke, knew only from Matthew Paris's chronicle. In his rewriting of English history, Daniel also displayed a certain sense of relativism, or perspectivism, which allowed him to acknowledge that "we" deal with antiquity as posterity will deal with us.[109]

Another perspective opened up when, a century later, England followed France with its own civil war, and this experience, too, required rethinking and rewriting. Here the history of the Reformation converged with national tradition, and the narratives of John Foxe and English Protestants acquired new relevance. The focus of history shifted, too, from a remote and traditional past to a present predicament of political and religious factions, from the broad horizons of Herodotean history to the analytical focus of a Tacitus, or a Thucydides, whose work on the causes of war Hobbes translated in 1529.[110] Parliamentary history became presentist, as in the republican account by Thomas May (1647). Appalled by the destructiveness of Civil War, men also were reminded of the French experience a century earlier, as in Edward Chamberlayne's *The Late War Parallel'd* (1660).

Edward Hyde, Lord Clarendon, wrote as a royalist in exile under the pressures of civil war; and while he began with the pious topos of an angry Providence, his emphasis, based on firsthand knowledge of royal counsels, was on political rather than religious factors, following the model of Thucydidean narrative. Behind the hand of God, Clarendon saw the causes of violent change noted by so many classical historians — "the distempers and conjunctures of time, the ambition, pride, and folly of persons, and the sudden growth of wickedness."[111] Yet despite the break marked by the Puritan Revolution, Clarendon based his view of England on the traditional story of the growth and continuity of the national constitution, church, and state.

English historiography continued, or rather resumed, its antiquarian drive in the later seventeenth century, especially in areas of church history and the Reformation. Besides Thomas Fuller's *Church History of Britain* (1655), Gilbert Burnet's *History of the Reformation of the Church of England* (1679–1714), and John Strype's *Annals of the Reformation* (1700–1731), all sought to give a documentary guide to the historiographical battlefields of the preceding century; while the deeper recesses of medieval history were being explored by the extraordinary group of "worshipful men" studied by David Douglas.[112] William Dugdale, Thomas Hearne, George Hickes, and others, though deeply divided on political and ecclesiastical issues, carried on a common antiquarian enterprise and in Douglas's view deserve to be counted among the "architects of England." They and the "riot of learning" which they helped to stir up are also part of that European-wide antiquarian movement which figures so importantly, if obscurely, in the crisis of learning that prepared the ground for the Enlightenment of the eighteenth century and the historicism of the nineteenth.

In the wake of the Reformation and Counter-Reformation in England, France, Germany, Spain, and elsewhere, historiography took a national turn, compelled by many interests — political, religious, institutional — which sought legitimacy, encouragement, and a basis for policy in the historical records and monuments discovered, studied, published, and interpreted by state- and church-supported scholars and more popular writers. The motives and forces of partisanship are clear. Yet the rhetoric of historical impartiality, disinterested curiosity, and scientific aspirations remained; and even the most committed historians contributed, if only inadvertently, to the project of historical inquiry — to tell the truth, be humanly useful, and perhaps even be a way to wisdom. Clinging to these ideals — and at the same time vastly increasing the quantity, accessibility, and critical understanding of source materials — history reinforced its potential to become a true science.

8

The Science of History

Know thyself. . . . Now this knowledge depends on history both sacred and
profane, universal and particular.
— Pierre Droit de Gaillard

Renaissance humanism is defined in large part in terms of its idealization
of classical culture and its attempts, implicitly dependent on historical understanding, to imitate the ancient Romans and Greeks in moral, social, and
political as well as literary terms.[1] Humanism is defined, too, by its particular
attachment to the humanities (*studia humanitatis*), which meant the first two
members of the medieval trivium — grammar and rhetoric — together with
moral philosophy, poetry, and history. History was central to the humanist
agenda not only as an "art" in its own right but also because of its ties with the
other humanities. That is, "history" was (along with "method") one of the
parts of classical grammar,[2] and a "historical sense" (*sensus historicus*) meant
grammatical or literal, as distinguished from figurative, interpretation; it overlapped with rhetoric in its dedication to explanatory and persuasive narrative;
it could also, as *magistra vitae* and (in the famous phrase of Dionysius of
Halicarnassus) "philosophy teaching by example," be regarded as a branch of
moral philosophy; and it shared many features with poetry (except for being
devoted to literal and particular truth), including a common historical origin.
Thus history spanned much of the medieval and Renaissance encyclopedia of
learning and shared, or inspired, many of its intellectual transformations in
the early modern period.

The Art of History

Renaissance humanism attended to the theory as well as practice of historiography, though often not in any perceptible combination, and this appeared most clearly in a genre which also had its beginnings in antiquity, namely, the *ars historica* (analogous to the *artes rhetorica* and *poetica*). Ancient examples of this literary and critical tradition include Lucian's *How to Write History*, Dionysius of Halicarnassus's critique of Thucydides, and various prefaces to classical histories. The genre was continued in modern times in a series of "arts of history" written from the fifteenth century, first in Italy and then in the other European countries. The idea of history reflected in these essays was indeed commonplace, rehearsing endlessly the formulas of Aristotle, Cicero, Quintilian, and others; but they acquired new meaning in a modern literary context enriched — enchanted as it were by distance — by the rhetorics of self-consciousness, nostalgia, envy, imitation, cultural loss, and cultural origins and by the difficulties of translating words and thoughts across centuries, cultural boundaries, and religious interdictions.

The Renaissance idea of history was indeed a literal imitation and elaboration of what the ancients had professed. Within the program of humanist studies, history holds first place, wrote Bruni, for "knowledge of the past gives guidance to our counsels and our practical judgment, and the consequences of similar undertakings [in the past] will encourage or deter us according to our circumstances in the present."[3] "As the soul is to the body, so history is to other inheritances," wrote Pomponio Leto, "for it offers the best part of wisdom [and] an imitation of life."[4] Among all the so-called liberal studies, wrote Pier Paul Vergerio, "I accord the first place to History on grounds both of its attractiveness and of its utility, qualities which appeal equally to the scholar and to the statesman."[5] The aim of history, wrote Guarino da Verona, was "to gather many ages into one view."[6]

To these formulas Lorenzo Valla added a more theoretical endorsement, turning the tables on Aristotle by refuting his famous argument that poetry was more philosophical than history. "History is more robust than poetry because it is more truthful," wrote Valla in his *History of King Ferdinand of Aragon,* and "it is oriented not to abstraction but to concrete truth," not to mention philosophy teaching by example.[7] And, Valla added, "the discourse of historians exhibits more substance, more practical knowledge, more political wisdom . . . , more customs, and more learning of every sort than the precepts of any philosophers." And the inevitable classical formula, "Without history one remains always a child."

For humanists, grown to intellectual maturity with the acquisition of historical perspective, history was a way of understanding the world and giving structure to knowledge, and naturally enough they imposed historical form on the art of history itself. Thus Bartolommeo della Fonte, in his contribution to the art of history, rehearsed the genealogy of history from Herodotus to Thucydides.[8] Polydore Vergil likewise gave historical shape to the subject in his encyclopedic survey of the "first inventors of things." He accorded priority to Moses as the first historian, living (he believed) almost seven centuries before the first Olympiad — although here, as elsewhere, he showed formal respect for mythology by recognizing Cadmus only as the importer of letters to the Greeks but also as their first historian.[9] Annals and chronicles preceded history, according to Vergil, but only history reached "perfection" under the influence of rhetoric and the rule of the Ciceronian laws of truth and impartiality.

A more extended historical celebration of history in the context of the humanist educational agenda is that of Juan Luis Vives, who also begins with the legendary Cadmus as well as the Egyptians and the Jewish historians before Moses (especially Abraham, who received his information from the sons of Seth).[10] Indeed, Vives wrote, history began with the human race, and so universal history, as Polybius had taught, is the proper mode of writing. It was proper, too, to follow the account in Genesis, since other efforts, such as those of Berosus and Diodorus Siculus, are fictitious. In general Vives found Greek and Roman history obscure and full of fables, even in Herodotus, though he added that, like proverbs and maxims, the "erudite" sort of fables did possess value for moderns. He lamented, however, the care given to pagan history as contrasted with the neglect of the Christian apostles, martyrs, and saints (except for untrustworthy and idealized hagiography). Vives continued his detailed survey of historiography, classical, medieval, and modern, down to his own century, including works of erudition as Diogenes Laertius's lives and opinions of the philosophers, Vergil's *Inventors of Things*, and the accounts of the extraordinary discoveries in the New World.

Herodotus is called the father of history, Vives recalled, but to some he was also the father of lies, and this reminds us of the negative criticism that followed the art of history. In the time of Vergil and Vives this criticism was expressed most trenchantly in Henry Cornelius Agrippa of Nettesheim's *Vanity of the Arts and Sciences* (1520), a skeptical treatise that left no part of the humanist encyclopedia untouched, offering a sort of counter*laudatio* of the art of history in particular. History may inspire the imitation of virtue, Henry admitted, but the opposite also occurs, leading readers to admire "great and furious thieves and famous despoilers of the world," legendary and real, such as Hercules, Cyrus, Hannibal, Caesar, and many other men who had achieved fame and a posterity despite the inhuman aspects of their careers.

More fundamentally, Agrippa continued, "Historiographers disagree mightily among themselves and write such variable and different things about one event that it is impossible that a number of them should not be liars. They disagree about the beginning of the world, the universal flood, and the building of Rome. . . ."[11] Ignorance of origins is understandable and forgivable, but ancients and moderns alike — writers from Herodotus and Tacitus to Flavio Biondo and Paolo Emilio — also lie and argue about more recent events, whether through ignorance, malice, hatred, fear, or partisanship. So authors have told tall tales about "strange beginnings" and about legendary founders and kings; so, blinded by fame, they omit the crimes of the great subjects of their narratives, as for example (here Henry cites Flavio Biondo), Orosius neglecting to mention the great ruin wrought by the Goths when they descended on Italy. The study of history indeed brings singular "wisdom," but at the same time it brings "great damage"; for such are the fruits of political ambition, greed, and lust for military glory, not to speak of religious ideals and causes.

In the sixteenth century the Italian treatises on the art of history by such authors as Giovanni Pontano, Francesco Robortello, Francesco Patrizi, and Bartolommeo della Fonte, many of them collected in Johann Wolf's famous anthology, remained focused for the most part on formal and stylistic questions, beginning with the relationship between history and poetry.[12] They agreed that history originated in poetry and retained affinities with it, especially on the common ground of rhetoric; and under the influence of Cicero, Lucian, and other ancient predecessors, they inquired in those terms into the development of history from mythical origins to the stage of polished narrative, bound to truth and scientific causal explanation, according to the conventional formula "science is knowledge through causes" (*scire est per causas cognoscere*). Fonte in particular offered "a sketch of the origins of historical writing among the Greeks, how it flourished among the Romans, declined with ancient culture, revived in Petrarch, was sustained by the generosity of rulers" and — common complaint of humanists — "is now endangered again."[13]

The Italianate tradition flourished north of the Alps, too, and the Ciceronian liturgy was repeated by humanists throughout Europe. Marc-Antoine Muret ventured a small criticism of Cicero for his statement that "history is a thing done but removed from the memory of our age."[14] This is obviously not what Cicero meant to say, Muret remarked, since history was not a thing (*res*) but a narration thereof, and it was not necessarily remote from our memory, since things done in the present may also be the subject of historical narrative. Nor must history necessarily study causes, since this is rather the office of the philosopher, but if it does so, it is better called "philosophical history." For Muret, it was sufficient to declare that "history is a narration, full and continuous, of things done publicly."

Posing the scholastic questions of "what," "how many," and "whence" (etymology) and reviewing critically earlier opinions, ancient and modern, G. J. Vossius distinguished the art of history (*historices*) from history plain and simple in the same way that poetics was distinguished from poetry — theory from practice, or writing from witnessing or from the subject of writing.[15] *Historices* was indeed an art, not a science; it was not part of grammar, rhetoric, poetry, logic, or any other art but a form of knowledge designed to teach prudence through human examples rather than precepts, and its goals were utility and the determination of causes, not pleasure (while treating questions of form and style at some length). For Vossius, history began with "mythistory," and the Egyptians and Chaldeans were both antecedent to the Greeks in this early practice.[16] Except for its vast learning and despite its criticisms of the Platonist Patrizi and other authors of the arts of history, Vossius's treatise hardly departed from the conventions of this genre.

One of the most hyperbolic celebrations of history in the humanist style was that of Daniel Heinsius, who saw history as the only self-sufficient field, while politics, law, and other disciplines are useless when cut off from history. History is all the things that Cicero said it was and more, offering transcendent as well as practical wisdom: "That fretful animal, whom we call man . . . , would be free from the limits of time and space. Unhampered by the difficulties of travel, he would be present without danger at all wars and events, he would gather into one focus the immeasurably great vastness of ages and generations."[17] Taking all human creation as its province, "History renders man contemporary with the universe." And such accolades could be multiplied with reference to many essays, prefaces, inaugural lectures, encyclopedia entries, and larger treatises.

Despite such sentiments (and perhaps partly because of them) the art of history was, from the sixteenth century, a barren genre, divorced in large part from the practice of history, but keeping faith with the rhetorical conception of the form, content, and purpose of history. In the work of authors like Bartholomeus Keckermann, G. J. Vossius, Thomas Blundeville, and Degory Wheare the discussion of history, its nature, parts, and goals, had become almost liturgical in its repetitiveness.[18] Yet archaic and inert as it had become, the tradition continued well into the eighteenth century, whether in the form of empty rhetoric or erudite habit.[19] One of Bodin's many disciples, Lenglet du

Fresnoy, touted his "new method of history" in most traditional terms: "To study history is to study the motives, opinions and passions of men, to be able to discover their engines, their windings, and inventions, finally to know all the delusions they put upon our intellects, and the surprises they seize our souls with; in one word to know ones self by others."[20] Indeed some might argue that the genre has persisted down to the present day, at least for those who continue to ask "What is History?" and to seek a general "method" of history and ways to teach it to and justify it for modern students.

The Method of History

This rhetorical definition of history as an art, however, was insufficient for many sixteenth-century scholars, who aspired to a more systematic idea of history as a form of knowledge. One of the pioneers in the attempt to achieve this goal was Lelio Torelli, who was perhaps the first to associate history with the notion of "method" (*methodos*).[21] The analogy was perhaps suggested by Quintilian's division of grammar into "history" and "method" — words and syntax, as it were — but method had richer meanings in the early modern period, with many disciplines seeking one for knowledge, teaching, and re-membering. Of these disciplines one of the most prominent was the field of history, which until then had qualified only as an art, but which in the works of some French authors was aspiring to the level of method.

As history was assuming global form in the sixteenth century, through the expansion of the horizons of universal history, it was also attaining scientific status, at least in the eyes of some reflective authors. In that age history became, literally and conceptually, a science because it was organized according to a systematic method, oriented toward universals rather than particulars, and so raised above the arts. The distinction between history as art and as science corresponded roughly to that between writing and reading historical works. The classical essays included in Wolf's collection (Lucian of Samosata and Dionysius of Halicarnassus) and most of the modern Italians (Pontano, Patrizi, Robortello, Folieta, Viperano, and Riccobono as well as Fox-Morcillo) were inclined to problems of writing according to rhetorical conventions, while Jean Bodin, François Baudouin, and Simon Grynaeus were more concerned with the study and teaching — and, in this pedagogical sense, the method — of history for the philosophical, legal, political, and religious purposes to which it could be put.

The art of history in a Western sense, that is, in its associations with the art of writing, was two thousand years old when French scholars began to reflect on its method and meaning in the sixteenth century. The first of the French methods of history was Baudouin's *Institution of Universal History and Its Conjunction with Jurisprudence,* which was published in 1561 while the author was in contact with Johann Sleidan, Melanchthon, and the Magdeburg centuriators and involved in irenic ecclesiastical politics aimed at heading off the fast-approaching wars of religion. This work, fortified by a learned survey of the history of history, presented variations on the old Polybian themes of "universal," "integral," "perpetual," and "pragmatic" history, for which Baudouin also called on the testimony of Diodorus Siculus and Eusebius. The novelty was that for Baudouin the best expression and guarantee of the integrity and continuity of history was jurisprudence, ecclesiastical as well as civil, for like Sleidan he took secular and sacred affairs as the body and soul of history. "Historical studies must be placed on a solid foundation of law," he wrote, "and jurisprudence joined to history."[22] Like the law, moreover, history was a form of wisdom, which had been defined by Cicero and Augustine alike as "the knowledge of things divine and human."

The "universe of history" *(universitas historiae)* — universal in terms of times, places, and things, Baudouin repeated — was a theater in which man was not only "spectator" and "interpreter" but also "actor"; and this at once facilitated and complicated writing and understanding history.[23] Baudouin prized eyewitness testimony, but failing this, he turned to monuments, records, and especially legal instruments as the best testimony to the products of human will; and here was another link between history and the law. While Cicero had remarked that history should be the business of rhetoric *(munus oratoris),* Baudouin elaborated on this by arguing that the "office of historians" *(scriptorum historicorum officio)* should also be that of the jurisconsult, who was even more expert in judging human actions. Strategically located, as a human being, in the center of the chain of Creation (Baudouin began and ended his treatise with this statement) and trained, as a jurist, in the science of law, which was dedicated to understanding human causes (as natural philosophy was to natural causes), the "perfect" historian could attain not only knowledge of the past and wisdom in the present but also a sense of the future.

Five years later Bodin published his own more ambitious *Method for the Easy Comprehension of History,* which was also devoted to exploiting history for legal and political purposes — the sixth chapter, "The Type of Government in States," being a preliminary sketch for Bodin's *Republic,* which appeared a decade later. (Because of its weight and influence, Bodin's book merits separate discussion, standing as it does in the center of the genre not only in the sixteenth century but, at least indirectly, down to present-day handbooks of historical method.)

Following Bodin, Pierre Droit de Gaillard published an even wider-ranging "method," which pronounced history — since it was the source of all the arts and sciences — to be the primary means to that self-knowledge prescribed by the Greek oracle and the pre-Socratic philosophers.[24] Gaillard began his book with an extensive commentary on the Ciceronian commonplaces representing history as "the witness of time," "light of truth," "life of memory," and "mistress of life." He then went on to survey the providential transmission of this wisdom (*translatio studii*) from nation to nation, and finally to France, whose history (with reference to Seyssel, Budé, Le Roy, Du Tillet, Pasquier, and others) he represented according to prominent examples, chronologically arranged, with remarks on the modern convergence, through the influence of humanism, between history and other disciplines, especially law and theology. Like the programs of Le Roy, Du Haillan, and La Popelinière, Gaillard's work furnishes an agenda for a full cultural history of modern France.

Another prominent contributor to this Bodinian genre was the Huguenot historian, Lancelot Voisin de la Popelinière, whose *History of History, with the Idea of Perfect History* appeared in 1599.[25] Among modern historians La Popelinière had some kind words for Guicciardini, though not for the injudicious Machiavelli; but for the most part his critical survey consisted of bibliographical listings, large generalities, and small complaints. Bodin was only a "theoretical historian" (*historien contemplatif*), and none of the other arts and methods of history, including the superfluous discourse of Baudouin, offered a useful account of the idea of history. On the practical side the French, like the Romans and other ancient nations, possessed rich archives (as Baudouin had also noted), but these were still not really exploited by historians. More important, however, was the "encyclopedia" of human learning, which deserved a more prominent place in any modern history which aspired to "perfection."

The real originality of La Popelinière's work was in effect to historicize the discipline of history. "It is quite evident that the poets were the first historians," he declared.[26] Now, there was nothing new in this judgment, which had been made by Cicero and others; what was original in La Popelinière's argument was the devising of a stadial scheme, similar to that of Florus, to describe the trajectories of national historiographies. The four stages of Greek history were, first, "fabulous" history (from the Flood to the Trojan War), poetic (from Homer to the first Olympiad), prose (from that point to Herodotus), and elegant (and decadent) history from Herodotus to the end of the Greek Empire.[27] Similarly, the stages of Roman historiography were from the appearance of the Italian peoples on the peninsula to the first landing of the Greeks, from then to the time of Cato, then to the fourth century, and finally the period of decline.

Presumably the writing of history followed a similar pattern in other national traditions, but in any case La Popelinière's major purpose was to formulate a modern ideal of history in the light of this critical survey of ancient, medieval, and modern writers of history. Despite the modernist tone of his argument, however, it was the crushing burden of ancient rhetoric that gave substance to his celebration of the art of history — the value of history, the attributes of the ideal historian, the order and disposition of narrative, the requirements of causal analysis and critical judgment, the need for impartiality, and the priority (neglected by the ancients) of truth over beauty.

In the sixteenth-century quest for method, history was one of many fields to be subjected to restructuring in the mnemonic and pedagogical sense associated with Petrus Ramus. Bartholomeus Keckermann was one Ramist who wrote on the "nature and properties" of history in this topical mode, criticizing the lack of organization of Bodin and listing other methodizers in this tradition, including Robortello, Fox-Morcillo, Folieta, and Milieu. For Keckermann, history was to be defined as a mode of arrangement rather than subject matter, and so he recognized such fields as economic and political history.[28] History was a matter of particulars, and in this sense was "imperfect"; and only when joined to such areas could it achieve the general truths which constituted science. For Vossius and J. J. Beurer, history was a form not of literature but of knowledge, though it proceeded by narrative and not explanation.

These opinions illustrate the common sixteenth-century view of history, that it encompassed only particular facts, possibly invocable as examples but lacking the status of general truth. While rhetorical in origin, such conceptions were also in keeping with the new empirical science, according to which history, the memory or study of things, achieved scientific status only by the application of reason.[29] As in *natural history*, the term had no essential connection with time. *History* referred to sense data, according to Tommaso Campanella, and only in this way — "nothing in the intellect that was not previously in the senses," according to the old scholastic maxim — came into contact, though reason, with philosophy. Like the historical signification of a term (*sensus historicus*), *history* had no further meanings beyond the things described in its discourse.[30]

This was the normal usage of Francis Bacon, too, for whom history signified particularity and represented the empirical foundation on which reason constructed science: "Knowledges are pyramids, whereof history is the basis."[31] Leaving aside divinity, Bacon distinguished between natural and civil history, the latter being divided into sacred (ecclesiastical), civil (the species "which retains the name of the genus"), and literary. Civil history Bacon subdivided into "memorials" (source materials), "antiquities" (material and verbal remnants, including monuments and coins, proverbs and etymologies), and "perfect history," including chronicles, lives, and narrations. Of these the first excels in glory, the second in profit and examples (no doubt as Bacon's own history of Henry VII did), and the third in veracity. Writing for the benefit of James I, Bacon lamented the inadequacy of English histories in particular because of the failure to include the affairs of Scotland, which was part of the Stuarts' realm since the union. Bacon made other divisions, including the conventional distinction between particular and universal history.

Within civil history, Bacon found that what he called literary history was, unfortunately, wholly uncultivated. His remarks in this regard show that Bacon was himself no vulgar "Baconian," regarding history as the mere accumulation of facts or data, for the advancement of learning was a cooperative process over generations. The learning of the past had its role to play in later discoveries, and so Bacon called for "a just story of learning, containing the antiquities and originals of knowledges, and their sects; their inventions, their traditions; their diverse administrations and managings; their flourishings, their oppositions, decays, depressions, etc. . . . , with the causes and occasions of them, and all other events concerning learning, throughout the ages of the world."[32] Like the "perfect history" of Milieu, Baudouin, Bodin, Gaillard, and La Popelinière, Bacon's vision, too, would embrace all of the arts and sciences contained in the old literary tradition and informing modern civilization. For Bacon this was the first step in giving a positive turn to history and for his own methodological project, which he compared to that of Columbus.[33] Of course the earlier literary tradition might well reveal the efforts of pre-Columbian explorations, and Bacon also included "literary history" in his agenda.

Jean Bodin

The conceptual status of history had always been in question, and sixteenth-century scholars were inclined to make a virtue of necessity. As Valla has placed history above philosophy because of its human value, so Bodin and his followers praised it as the very foundation of the encyclopedia of arts and sciences. For Bodin, surpassing the hyperbole of the *artes historicae,* history was not only above the arts but also "above all sciences."[34] Gaillard's analogy was that of "an overflowing fountain," but Bodin himself preferred the image of a garden from which he picked the "flowers of history," which happens to be the title of a well-known medieval chronicle, for more universal and philosophical purposes; but the point was the same, which was not far removed from the dictum of Dionysius of Halicarnassus (philosophy teaching by example): history was a "treasury of examples" which provided materials for a philosophical understanding of the human world and a kind of self-knowledge. It is hardly going too far to regard these arguments as the grounds for the modern philosophy of history.

According to Bodin, long before either Bacon or Campanella, history was, precisely like the law, of three sorts — human, natural, and divine — "The first concerns man; the second nature; and the third, the Father of nature." Human history was whatever "flows from the will of mankind, which ever vacillates and has no objective."[35] In other ways, too, history resembled the law — one in that it described and judged the willful actions of men, another in that it covered the whole world of nations (the arena of the jus gentium of civil law), still another in that its practitioners ought to have an understanding of public affairs, and finally in that it required a method for correct understanding. From the jurists, too, historians took over the conception of documentary evidence not as merely illustrative or exemplary but as precedent and even as proof.

Bodin's major goal was what may be regarded as the codification of history, beginning with a comprehensive, classified list of histories (a bibliography of 282 items) and the proper order of reading them, and with the methodical structuring of the knowledge produced by such reading. For Bodin, as for Ramus and other adherents of the new rhetoric of the sixteenth century, method implied "invention," but in the sense not of strategies for discovery but rather of the dialectical organization of knowledge for ulterior purposes. Method was thus theoretical — mnemonic and pedagogical — and pursued with juridical and political purposes in mind; and to that extent history was an auxiliary field of study, so much so that Bodin's treatise seemed to La Popelinière to be less a method of history than a "method of law."[36]

In any case human history was the main target of Bodin's reflections, although natural history provided essential context for judging human behavior, and in his extensive discussion of the influence of climate Bodin commended Tacitus for his judgments of the ancient Germans in relation to environment.[37] Bodin ransacked other "geohistorians," from Strabo to Sebastian Munster, for such medico-astrological insights into the human nature underlying historical change. He agreed that education might change this nature, but he continued to believe that "the man who compares the modern historians with the ancients and the ancients with each other and adds physical considerations also, will make the most certain judgments about history."[38] In this context Bodin endorsed the sort of concern with customs and cultural matters characteristic of Herodotean historiography.

Much of Bodin's *Method* is taken up with appraisals of particular historians, ancient and modern, in terms of the qualities, however unattainable, of the ideal historian.[39] These qualities included natural gifts, industry, and especially (following the Thucydidean dictum) firsthand experience — civil, military, or both. Though holding no political office, Dionysius of Halicarnassus was preferable to Suetonius(!); but normally there was no substitute for experience and participation in the affairs to be described, as was the case, for example, with Thucydides, Sallust, and Caesar and, among moderns, Commines, Guicciardini, and Sleidan. If inhibited by fear, the need to flatter, or other contemporary pressure, however, some historians were well advised to turn to more remote subjects and to posterity for readers, as was the case with Polybius, Dionysius, Tacitus, and various modern historians such as Polydore Vergil, Paolo Emilio, and Beatus Rhenanus.

Bodin's primary concern was with truth and impartiality, and he had little patience with the rhetorical emphasis on pleasure, which was the cause of so much criticism of Herodotus, among others. Partisanship, whether paid (as in the case of Bruni) or not, was a basic fault; and as a remedy Bodin recommended consulting rival authors — on Louis XI, for example, not only Commynes but also Lemaire de Belges and Paolo Emilio (who had himself followed such practice). The judgments of historians were often to be trusted with regard to foreigners, as Tacitus on the Germans, Polybius on the Romans, and Ammianus Marcellinus on the Franks; and Bodin praised some historians for their impartiality even toward their own age — most notably, Thucydides, Sleidan, Du Bellay, and Guicciardini, whose work was filled with subtle judgments and sage opinions.

Beyond adherence to the truth and avoidance of partiality, political analysis in the style of Thucydides was essential to an understanding of history in terms of "the causes of things, the origins, the progresses, the inclinations, all the plans of everyone." Analysis might also go beneath the surface of words and actions, and Bodin praised the value of Sleidan and Machiavelli in revealing "the secrets of princes" beneath the surface of words and actions. But it was foolish to expect perfection in any of even the most highly recommended of historians, and the best policy was "to collect the remnants of other works just as gems in the mud, if better are lacking."[40]

Bodin was interested in history in terms not only of Thucydidean analysis but also of the universal interests of Herodotus (whom he indeed ranked among universal historians), and he addressed questions crucial to the critical understanding of history in a longer perspective, especially those having to do with inherited myths of universal history. One was a refutation of the old four monarchy thesis associated with Daniel, which was still being rehearsed by historians like Sleidan and Panvinio, not to speak of theologians like Luther and Melanchthon.[41] To Bodin this idea — the historiographical equivalent of the controversial legal claim of the emperor to be "lord of the world" (*dominus mundi*) — reflected the arrogant and parochial view of German supporters of the Habsburg empires, and it seemed especially ridiculous in view of the "French" background of Charlemagne as well as the multiplicity of national traditions and the imperial successes of, for example, the Britons and the Arabs. To understand this, one had only to look at a contemporary map, especially in the wake of recent discoveries in the other hemisphere.

Hardly more defensible was the idea of a golden age, which went against the testimonies of all the ancient historians, beginning with Thucydides, "the most truthful father of history," who had described the "barbarity and ferocity of men" before his time, and including Suetonius, Tacitus, and others.[42] On the contrary, Bodin inferred, mankind had improved from its natural condition, and in many ways modernity represented an improvement on antiquity. Thus Bodin provided arguments for the Moderns in their continuing quarrel with the Ancients. "Printing alone," he wrote, "can easily vie with all the discoveries of the ancients."

Another locus of myth was the question of the origins of peoples, for which Bodin urged the study of geography and language, especially etymology, in which he was himself a most adventurous speculator.[43] The ancients deserved indulgence, given their limitations, Bodin admitted, but not modern authors such as Polydore Vergil, Althamer, and other interpreters of Tacitus, who foolishly insisted on the indigenous character of the English and German nations. He was contemptuous of authors such as Althamer, Wimpheling, Peutinger, Sabellicus, Paolo Giovio, and (among the French) Robert Ceneau for their vain boasts of parity with the gods. For Bodin, following both Herodotus and Moses, the Chaldeans were the most ancient of all nations, and it was there, he believed, that historians ought to concentrate their search for origins. Bound up with the problem of prehistory, too, was the Eusebian question of universal chronology, and Bodin contributed to this endless debate with his own proposal for "a system of universal time," which remained the primary goal of European scholars.[44] In fact Bodin's younger contemporary Joseph Justus Scaliger was already at work on such a project, and likewise, of course, within the framework of scriptural chronology.[45]

Antiquity

"No question has exercised the writers of histories more than the origin of peoples," wrote Jean Bodin — the reason being the conjunction between human curiosity and human pride.[46] For many peoples, too, the question of national origins is associated, if not identified, with that of the origins of the world; and so myths of origins have a theological and philosophical as well as historical dimension. Here is another manifestation of the Janus-faced appearance of history: interested observers, often admirers of Thucydides, who look around at their predicament asking why and whereto and scholars who look back at their forebears asking who we are and where we came from. If the Herodoteans, in their inclination toward archaeolatry, often lapsed into philosophy, theology, mythology, and other forms of speculation, they also made their own contributions to historical method and meaning. This is part of a complex story that comes into focus, though it does not really begin, in the early modern period.

Like poetry and philosophy, history has from the beginning shown a drive toward questions of origins, which promise understanding from first principles — the difference being that history has a human dimension that associates beginnings with begettings, foundations with fatherhood. Yet ideally, history should be written not merely ab urbe condita but ab orbe, or ab ovo. Thucydides largely avoided this temptation on the grounds of a prudent regard for attainable truth, and early modern historians such as Pasquier agreed on the secondary grounds that straying from textual authority was unhistorical. Herodotus, however, faced the question of remoteness in time as well as space, which is to say myth and alterity; and so did Christian chroniclers, humanist antiquarians, and more speculative and credulous investigators of "utter antiquity."

The barbarian past of Europe was subjected to wide-ranging philosophical inquiry, as can be seen especially in the old notion of an ancient wisdom preceding Greek philosophy, which Thomas Burnet called *philosophia mythologica,* or *sapientia antiquo-barbarica.*[47] The idea of barbarian philosophy was ancient, having been suggested by Diogenes Laertius, who admitted that "there are some who say that the study of philosophy had its beginnings among the barbarians."[48] Diogenes himself rejected this view; but some "philobarbarians," ancient, medieval, and modern, including Pico, Vives, and Polydore Vergil, accepted the idea of a protophilosophical wisdom among the Egyptians, Jews, Chaldeans, Indians, and Persians. Such was the view defended in the first monograph on the subject, Otto von Heurne's *Antiquities of Barbaric Philosophy,* published in 1600, and by the pioneering scholars in the new field of the history of philosophy, Georg Horn, Thomas Stanley, and many others, including Giambattista Vico, whose "new science" sought to penetrate the mentality of the "first barbarism."[49] In this way philosophers, too, searching for the "original" of their discipline, inferred historical continuity between ancient barbarism and Christian and modern civilization.

For the Western historiographical canon the scriptural story of Creation was an inescapable premise, except for a few pre-Adamite radicals, though the variations on this providential theme were endlessly contradictory.[50] The story, told in many different historical contexts, began with the Flood, the Tower of Babel, and the dispersal led by the children of Noah, who numbered more than thirty during his 860 years and included his daughter Pandora as well as sons Prometheus, Zoroaster, Ham, Shem, and Japhet. The most popular version of the story in the sixteenth century was that confabulated by Annius of Viterbo and accepted by the credulous historians as an appendage to the theme of four world monarchies. "Not many years after the setting up of the monarchie of Babylon," wrote Richard Lynche, "*Noe* divided four particular kingdoms in Europe, *viz.*, the kingdome of Italie, Spain, Fraunce, and Almaigne."[51] Actually there were five: Janus, who gave his name to the Janiculum, was king of Italy, Gomerus of Gaul, Tubal of Spain, Samothes of France, and Tuisco ("Teutsch") of Germany. Other versions elaborated confusingly on this hybrid genealogy and extended it through Noah's grandsons, including the sons of Tuisco — eponymous founders in their own right — Suevus, Vandalus, Prutus (Prussia), and Hercules Alemannus (Bavaria).[52]

Within this jerry-built imaginative framework, which combined Trojan myths and biblical accounts (it would be another two centuries before the two could be placed in the same historical category), the epic story of Rome, descended from Troy and converging with scriptural history, was of course central.[53] Moreover, the present ruins of the Eternal City, enhanced by the memory of past glories, were a visible reminder of the link with antiquity, Christian as well as classical, and medieval views of Rome's history incorporated this mythological apparatus.[54] The twelfth-century *Mirabilia urbis romanae,* for example, began with the story of Noah and his sons, the "tower of confusion," his voyage to Italy, and the building, by Janus, of the city of Janiculum on the Palatine hill (site of St. John's church), which was later renamed after Romulus, descendant of the Trojans and builder of the city's walls, who was born 433 years after the fall of Troy.[55] The author of this medieval travel guide went on to describe the topography and monuments of the pagan city and also the Christian cemeteries and places of martyrdom.

In the sixteenth century historical criticism was already at work eliminating myths of origins, Trojan origins anyway, or rather diverting them into literary channels, so that historians like Pasquier were bound by their historiographical conscience to banish the Homeric and Virgilian offspring to the writings of poets like Ronsard. The history of Rome, too, came to be revised through the labors of scholars like Flavio Biondo and Carlo Sigonio, who began the task of separating the facts of Roman history from what was later denounced as the "literary tradition."[56] The rhetorical pronouncements of the artes historicae and poeticae had long since set barriers between history and literature, and now the ars critica was transcending these inhibitions and putting literary methods to use in the practice of historiography.

In the case of Rome there were other forces at work, too, and especially the rise of antiquities — antiquarianism — as a field of study separate from history proper.[57] *Antiquitas* (like its opposite, *novitas*) is an abstract noun giving vague expression to a temporal condition dependent on the vagaries of human memory. For Renaissance humanists it acquired a favorable connotation, so that Lorenzo Valla, for example, could celebrate the "authority of antiquity" above the authority of any particular person as the standard of literary, and perhaps moral and social, excellence. But in order to serve as a model, antiquity had to be studied in detail; and this was the basis of a number of technical fields, auxiliary to history and to philology, which opened countless windows and doors on the classical past.

The monuments, relics, and "marvels" of Rome were open to examination in the form of inscriptions, medals, coins, and sculptures, which inspired the passions not only of collectors but also of students of antiquities like Petrarch, Cola di Rienzo, Flavio Biondo, and Poggio Bracciolini. The new attitudes characteristic of the "new humanism" were obvious in Poggio's work *On the Variety of Fortune,* which lamented the destructive effects of time on human creations such as Roman monuments.[58] Poggio was an obsessive book hunter who was also an enthusiastic tourist and devotee of ruins: in Grottoferrata he reported on "a villa which must have been Cicero's or have belonged to someone like him," and to his friend Niccolò Niccoli he wrote of the Greek inscriptions he found in Ferentino, amazing the inhabitants by his ability to decipher them.[59] Biondo was even more systematic and professional in his contributions to epigraphy, archaeology, numismatics, and art history, and in the next century Guillaume Budé extended such archeological ventures in his *De asse,* which studied ancient Roman coinage. From the mid–sixteenth century fascination with coins and medals produced a rich literature, exemplified by the work of Enea Vico, which added "visual sources" to supplement textual evidence.[60] In portraits and sculptures, scholars sought authentic images that would supplement, or even endorse, written descriptions of princes, popes, and other agents of historical change. Here is was in effect "things not words," according to the classical topos, which brought scholars into contact with a revered antiquity.[61]

The tradition of Poggio and Biondo continued into the sixteenth century, especially in Rome, and came increasingly to include Christian as well as classical remains.[62] The genre goes back to Maffeo Vegio in the fifteenth century and includes Panvinio's work on the churches of Rome, but it was given new impetus by the discovery of the catacombs of Saints Priscilla and Cecilia in the last quarter of the sixteenth century.[63] So Counter-Reformation studies in *Roma subterranea* gave underground reinforcement to the classically inspired *Roma triumphans* of Biondo and the work of successors like Sigonio. So, too, Catholic scholars found new acquaintance with early Catholic martyrs to counterbalance those being celebrated in the Protestant martyrologies of Crespin and Foxe and the resurrection of proto-Lutheran antiquity by Flacius Illyricus.

Between mythology and antiquarianism there is a fine line which speculation crosses easily and which history is supposed to respect, although sometimes it overcomes this inhibition through etymology or some other half-reasoned device. Sixteenth-century scholarship pushed back the frontiers of "antiquities" through the study of the early medieval past of Europe: the "Celtic renaissance" in France, Anglo-Saxon studies in England, Tacitist commentary in Germany, and so on.[64] These lines of research were inspired by deep curiosity about cultural heritage, but none of course was ideologically — religiously, politically, or socially — impartial. The Elizabethan Society of Antiquaries, many of whose members were lawyers, was one early institutional expression of antiquarian research, until its suppression on political grounds.[65] For anxious rulers, the past was not only prologue; it was also, through its wide range of examples, potentially prediction or subversion.

The antiquarian movement of the later sixteenth century converged with the "new philosophy that cast all into doubt," in John Donne's phrase, and was soon, in retrospect, eclipsed by it, at least for those who associated history with the party of the ancients. The study of history and other aspects of the humanities was no less "science" than the natural philosophy of Bacon, Galileo, and Descartes, but skepticism created a large and growing breach between these disciplinary traditions. Galileo opposed historians, or "memory experts," to true philosophers; and still more radically, Descartes proposed to eradicate the past and memory as the primary source of error. The divergence between these intellectual traditions continued to widen: "Men who take pride in philosophy and reason customarily disdain antiquarian researches," Leibniz remarked to the skeptic Daniel Huet, "and antiquaries in their turn are contemptuous of what they call the dreams of philosophers."[66]

Leibniz himself was a fascinating example of a scholar who, trained in the tradition of encyclopedic humanism, was converted to the new philosophy, and indeed saw no essential conflict between the two. As official historiographer of the house of Hanover, Leibniz was a serious and pioneering érudit. For his ambitious "Opus Historicum," directed to German antiquities, he made the required *iter italicum* for the study of manuscripts, which was, he remarked, "not without great prejudice to my eyes"; and he came to appreciate history not only as a form of panegyric but also as a means of "proof."[67] He also wrote about the "history and origin" of the calculus, the first referring to ancient predecessors such as Archimedes and the second, naturally, to himself.[68] How this can be reconciled with his metaphysics has been debated, since his notions of preestablished harmony and the possibility of a universal language seem to be in conflict with a sense of history. Yet Leibniz's own syncretism probably allowed him to transcend any such contradiction, and his "law of continuity" places him among the forerunners of historicism.[69]

Scholars clinging to the humanist tradition hoped to salvage traditional learning, arguing that it was important to study error as well as truth in order to attain an understanding of the human condition. Within philosophy itself — the "eclectic philosophy" of the seventeenth century — history continued to be appreciated for what passed for scientific reasons, especially since history, no less than natural philosophy, had a method (though debates over the nature of this method continued) and since, however inadequate for the understanding of nature, it was essential for human self-knowledge. At least this was the case when history encountered criticism and began, like the new philosophy, to purge itself of error.

The Art of Criticism

Historical criticism reached a peak in the nineteenth century, but it had much deeper roots, going back to the philology of the Renaissance and even to what Eratosthenes called the "many-sided philologia" of the Alexandrine period.[70] This was the humanistic science carried on by Renaissance humanists. "Once an ornament," Budé wrote, "philology is now the means of revival and restoration"; and in this context he also praised the virtues and trustworthiness, or "faith," of history (fides historiae).[71] As a philologist, Budé aimed at the "restitution" (*restitutio*) of corrupted texts and also of letters and of antiquity as a whole. As his friend Erasmus also knew, this was a task for a historian, since it was essential to attend "not only to what is said, but also by whom it is said, with what words it is said, in what time, on what occasion, what precedes and what follows."[72]

Critic (in Latin, French, and English) had first a medical meaning (sixteenth century), then a literary one (seventeenth century), and then a philosophical one — cumulatively, not successively — and the last two usually had favorable connotations, except for the objects or victims of such criticism. In the later sixteenth century, the vocabulary of criticism was adopted by philologists like

Henri Estienne (who continued Budé's great work on Greek lexicography), Joseph Justus Scaliger, Isaac Casaubon, and Justus Lipsius, who were the founders of what Jean Jehasse calls "capital C criticism."[73] "Scaliger," remarked Jehasse, "thought himself authorized to *rethink* all of written tradition."[74] From that time no scholar wanted himself to be thought uncritical. For Vossius criticism was "part of philosophy"; for the office of textual critic was, through historical judgment (rhetorical *judicium* in a special sense), to gain true understanding of the ancient mind[75] (*Criticis est veram cognoscere veterem mentem*).

This was the line of argument pursued, too, by Giambattista Vico, who virtually identified philology and history: "Philology is the study of speech, and it treats words and their history, then shows their origin and progress, and so determines the ages of languages, thus revealing their properties, changes, and conventions. But since the ideas of things are represented by words, philology must first treat the history of things. Whence it appears that philologists study human governments, customs, laws, institutions, intellectual disciplines, and the mechanical arts."[76] It was in this sense that Vico identified philology with his New Science, to both of which criticism and history were essential: if eloquence was to be sought in topics (the *ars topica*), Vico wrote, truth was to be found in criticism (the ars critica).[77]

From the sixteenth century, then, *criticism* was a word to conjure with, although the term, often used ambiguously and, indeed, uncritically, has had an extraordinarily complex semantic history. According to Diderot's *Encyclopédie, critique* meant either "the restitution of ancient literature" or rational judgment on human creations. There was philological criticism, and there was philosophical criticism, one being a matter of learning and judgment and the other of logic and reason, and both, reinforced by skeptical attitudes, being put to use by historians. La Mothe le Vayer, Christian skeptic as well as *libertin érudit*, did not carry his destructive Pyrrhonism into the study of history. So he praised Herodotus, in the face of centuries of adverse but misdirected criticism of his tall tales, for his prudence both in refusing to credit stories for which he lacked personal knowledge and in respecting divinity; and he passed a similar judgment on Livy.[78] For La Mothe radical skepticism was a philosophical enterprise having little to do with history, except perhaps (like Hume a century later) to encourage a turn to historical studies, which were, after all, situated in the realm not of pure reason but rather of human will, opinion, and probability.

Skepticism and historical curiosity met in the work of Pierre Bayle, who was likewise dubious about the dreams of philosophers. Bayle's *Historical and Critical Dictionary,* first conceived in 1690, was the record of a lifelong search for historical truth, and even more for error, in literary tradition, from antiquity down to the quarrelsome present.[79] Through the smoke of religious controversy and the impediments of doubt, Bayle pursued truths small and large in entries on curious topics and earlier and often little-known authors who had added to, or subtracted from, faith and knowledge. As his Calvinist forebears sought a pure or purified religion in an old and corrupt tradition, so too Bayle, with a sublimated Calvinist rigor, sought to cleanse the tradition of secular learning from accumulated errors arising from ignorance, superstition, or faulty method.

For Bayle the proper method was fundamentally that of the humanist call for the rejection of tradition in favor of a return to the "sources rather than streams," in the words of Marsilio Ficino (*fontes potius quam rivulos*).[80] Both Pasquier and Selden had refused to speculate on the undocumented prehistorical past. Pasquier would trust only ancient authorities and so rejected Trojan and Carolingian legends alike; and similarly, Selden concluded that, since there was no textual evidence before Caesar, the stories of Brutus were no more credible than those of Francus, Hispanus, Italus, and the rest.[81] This was most directly a product of both humanist and juridical reliance on, or perhaps fetishism of, textual evidence; but it was also in keeping with history in a Thucydidean (rather than a Herodotean) mode, which preferred eyewitness testimony to secondhand information — and consequently accessible history to remote antiquity.

One of the major threats to — and indeed tests of — historical criticism was the old problem of forgery, which had troubled jurists no less than historians, and the legal distinction between true and false evidence (*discrimen veri ac falsi*) was often attended by more material consequences. The challenge faced by some Renaissance scholars was not only how to detect a forgery but — given the emphasis placed on imitation — how to create modern texts or artifacts as good as (that is, indistinguishable from) the "original." "Forgery and philology rose and fell together in the Renaissance as in Hellenistic Alexandria," Anthony Grafton says;[82] and, as usual, critics as well as forgers had confessional or ideological motives.[83] In the seventeenth century the art of uncovering forgeries became an essential part of historical criticism — culminating in the hypercriticism of nineteenth-century scholars.

Falsifications aside, some original sources are more original than others, and from the sixteenth century interest turned to archives and "authentick records" for insights into memorable words and deeds. Archives are an ancient institution which, in Europe, go back to the twelfth century and earlier, the Roman church in particular taking the lead in this and other state-building devices. Archival sources offer a marvelous example of the intersection of

political and antiquarian motives — providing both material for legal precedents and defense of claims and for the "defense and illustration" of governments. Papal registers were well tended at least from the time of Innocent III
and existed at least from the time of Bede.[84] From the fifteenth and sixteenth
centuries, officials, including members of the Budé family, Jean du Tillet, and
Pierre Dupuy in France and Thomas Wilson and Arthur Agarde in England,
were commissioned to bring order to the national archives of their states and
to publish materials for the mixed motives suggested above.[85] In the late seventeenth century Thomas Rymer, in the office of royal historiographer, had a
similar commission, though it was entirely for the purposes of publication in
his *Foedera*.[86] Ancient topoi featured in the rhetoric of historians about the
weakness of memory, destructive effects of time, and the power of writing to
counteract these factors were invoked in these quasi-antiquarian and para-
historiographical projects — on which, of course, neo-Thucydidean historians
were happy to draw as the next-best thing to personal knowledge and the most
reliable basis for historical science. In the nineteenth-century Ranke was still
preserving this faith while exaggerating his own originality.

Questions of historical truth still hinged most essentially on ecclesiastical
tradition, and all of the "great historical enterprises" inaugurated in the seventeenth century centered on this sacred battleground.[87] In the work of Jean
Mabillon, the old tradition of monastic history and hagiography converged
with modern historical method and criticism. A member of the Maurist con-
gregation and a circle of monastic érudits, Mabillon began his scholarly career
editing the work of St. Bernard and the acts of the Benedictine order before he
was drawn into controversy over the authenticity of the charters of the Benedictine Abbey of St. Denis, which had been attacked by Daniel Papebroch,
member of the arriviste Jesuit order, thus undermining both knowledge of
Christian antiquity and legal rights. Such was the reaction of Mabillon, who
devoted himself to clearing up these confusions and, in 1681, published his
foundational work on diplomatics. On the basis of both canonist and philological methods Mabillon's *De re diplomatica* set the rules for the dating and
criticism of medieval charters and documentary sources, though he warned
that experience and intuition were also essential for determining antiquity and
that probability — based not on metaphysical demonstrations but on "moral
certitude" — provided the standard of historical judgment.[88]

What kind of truth could history bring to an age in quest of certainty? In the
seventeenth-century debate over the "faith of history" some authors wanted to
preserve standards of absolute certainty, while others, including Christian
Thomasius and his follower F. W. Bierling, were content to regard history as a
form of probable knowledge, despite the Protestant prejudice against "proba-

bilism" associated with the ethical casuistry of the Jesuits.[89] In the early eighteenth century, C. A. Heumann published a study of this modern theme and ancient topos, the faith of history, comparing it to the analogous issue of legal credibility (*fides juridica*), which Thomasius had discussed.[90] In support of this Heumann quoted a remark by Bayle, recalling that "the compiling of errors is a very important part of history," for — citing the old proverb which was confirmed by history — "to err is human."

The "truth and certitude of history," as Lenglet du Fresnoy wrote, differed from that of mathematics, being "a matter entirely of human certitude, based on the testimony and report of wise and honest men."[91] This was just Heumann's point; for like Thomasius, he recognized a difference between logical and "historical demonstrations," between the truth guaranteed by reason and that offered by probability and authority — between "logic" and "philologic," in the coinage of Theophilus Gale.[92] This is another feature of historical criticism, and indirectly of hermeneutical understanding: even Protestants like Heumann could reject such fables as that of Pope Joan because it possessed neither probability nor textual authority.

Unlike research and writing, criticism is fundamentally dialogical, implying not only debate and rivalry but also an audience and competition for acceptance by that audience. The extensive scientific community, or rather several scientific and professional communities of the seventeenth century, made up a larger world of learning which since the fifteenth century had been called the "republic of letters." The *Respublica literarum* had its own mythology, being "of very ancient origin . . . and exist[ing] before the Flood," according to a seventeenth-century scholar.[93] In early modern times it was an arena for important scientific cooperation, according to the Baconian vision of advancing learning, but it was also a battlefield where many intellectual and ideological conflicts were waged. These "quarrels" were carried and intensified by the learned journals, such as Bayle's *Nouvelles de la République des Lettres,* Leclerc's *Bibliothèque universelle et historique,* and Leibniz's *Acta eruditorum,* which came to supplant, or to supplement, casual scholarly correspondence as a medium of exchange and debate, and such quarrels were of major significance for historical study and criticism.[94]

Of these public dialogues the longest standing was the "quarrel between the Ancients and the Moderns," which can be traced back to Tacitus and which in a sense is still going on.[95] This *querelle,* whose most famous phases were in late seventeenth-century France and England, lay at the heart of historical and literary criticism, posing as it did the fundamental question of the uses of history as well as the value of ancient culture. In its radical form, it was a conflict of methods — or, alternatively, of myths. One was an approach that would reject history, eradicate memory, avoid prejudice, and begin thinking afresh. "I will believe that my memory tells me lies," declared Descartes, "and that none of the things that it reported ever happened."[96] The other extreme inclined to a view of "nothing new under the sun." As Goethe asked,

> Who can conceive anything either foolish or wise,
> Which the ancient world has not already conceived?
> [Wer kann was dummes, wer was kluges denken,
> Das nicht die Vorwelt schon gedacht?][97]

Invoking standard works such as Vergil's *Inventors of Things,* Louis Dutens published a polemical book "which demonstrates how our most celebrated philosophers have taken their learning from the works of the Ancients."[98] The argument was endless, its tradition bottomless; for once upon a time the Ancients had themselves been Moderns. As Jonathan Swift pointed out, those whom we call the Ancients were positioned between the Moderns and the Most Ancients, so that "the moderns had only such knowledge of the learning of Chaldea and Egypt as was conveyed to them through the medium of Grecian and Roman writers."[99]

In the 1720s a debate most vital to the "faith of history" erupted at the Académie des Inscriptions et Belles-Lettres over the "certitude" or "incertitude" of the earliest stages of Roman history, with L.-J. Lévesque de Pouilly rejecting the authority of historians like Livy and Dionysius of Halicarnassus and the Abbé Claude Sallier trying in response to salvage classical historiography in the face of skeptical hypercriticism. At bottom, however, was the larger methodological question of the "foundations of history," and these were established by the statement of Freret rounding off this debate — all of the arguments collected in a volume on *"fondements de l'histoire,"* which included "critical essais on the fidelity of history."[100]

By the eighteenth century the notion of the "critical" was undergoing a profound semantic bifurcation, or ambiguity, arising from the confusions between accuracy and higher truths. "Philology once a handmaiden, now a queen," is the aphorism attached by Paul Hazard to his discussion of the work of Richard Simon, who wrote several books on the Bible entitled *Critical Histories,* referring to his radical textual exegesis that undermined the notion of Moses's authorship of the Old Testament and that insisted on a literary tradition underlying both Testaments and guaranteeing the letter of the text.[101] But it was primarily rational criticism that J. J. Brucker had in mind when he wrote his monumental *Critical History of Philosophy,* to which he applied an "eclectic method" that proposed, along the lines of Protestant theology but on the basis of enlightened reason, to sort out the valid elements of philosophical tradition from the accumulated errors of paganism, scholasticism, and other misguided sects.

In general, philosophical criticism took the high road of pure reason, and historical criticism the low road of positive and backward-looking learning. The first required only logic; the second demanded intuition as well as erudition. "The Critic is born, not made," declared the philologist P. A. Boeckh (*Criticis* [or *interpres*] *non fit, sed nascitur*).[102] The drama featured not truth versus error but the beginnings of the rivalry of what in the nineteenth century were called the philosophical school and the historical school — each advancing its causes, of course under the banner of "criticism."

Universal History

For humanists like Sabellico, Protestants like Melanchthon, and methodizers of history like Bodin, the larger field for their thinking about humanity remained universal history, though this construct had changed fundamentally over the centuries and was being challenged, at least indirectly, in the early modern period.[103] The genre of universal history was tied to a succession of master narratives, beginning with the Herodotean drama of East versus West; transformed by Polybius into the brutal epic of the rise of Rome; revised again by Eusebius, Augustine, and their followers into the sacred story of Christian triumph; supplemented or countered by the modern continuation of Romanism based on the translation of empire; and undermined by larger views of a world of nations transcending both church and empire. Moreover, the biblical framework continued to be troubled by memories of pagan notions of the emergence of humankind from a state of barbarity and nature, perhaps even before the Jewish creation story of Adam and Eve — a possibility that seemed more plausible after the discovery of the New World. Finally, the accounts of this natural process, given by Lucretius and other pagan authors recovered by humanist scholarship, opened the door to the evolutionary ideas of the eighteenth century.

Yet even in its modern forms the tradition of universal history had little to do with discussion of historical method and criticism, distracted as it was by interest in questions of ultimate origins, general patterns, and final goals that were inseparable from religious doctrines. Universal history transcended, or fell short of, the ideal of history as a science and encouraged philosophical, theological, or mythological speculations which were closer to Hesiod or Augustine than to Polybius or Bodin.[104] This continued through the philosophies and theologies of history of the eighteenth, nineteenth, and twentieth centuries — and they will surely persist into the next millennium.

There were more entertaining books than universal histories, and a sixteenth-century translator of Eusebius and his Byzantine continuators lamented the popularity of "vayne books in the vernacular" such as Pantagruel, "Pierce Plowman," Chaucer, Renard the Fox, and other "merry tales."[105] Yet countless repetitive and uncritical universal histories continued to appear from the first age of printing, adapting the Bible story from Creation or from the Flood and then, following Eusebian precedent, bringing in pagan historians, often including spurious modern fabrications, as convenient. One example was the compendium of universal history by the great critic and polemicist, Jean Leclerc, for whom history was nothing more than a "Catalogue of Errors and Impieties," only Christ being perfect. His book's only claim to originality was that earlier works were either too long or two short; otherwise it followed the tediously familiar pattern of biblical "epochs."[106]

In England one enormously popular contribution was the *History of the World,* composed by Walter Raleigh in prison in the years before his execution on a false charge of treason. His detailed account covered many aspects of human experience and ingenuity from Creation down to 130 B.C. Despite his skepticism in small matters of fact, Raleigh took a very conventional view of the benefits of the art of history, "not the least . . . that it hath made us acquainted with our dead Ancestors," but also that it offers "a policy no lesse wise than eternall; by the comparison and application of other mens forepassed miseries, with our owne like errours and illdeservings."[107] Conventional, too, was his view of the providential course of human experience over time, in which he detected "the infinite spirit of the *Universall,* piercing, moving, and governing all things."

No less influential, though more systematically didactic, was the *Discourse on Universal History,* written half a century later by the Bishop Bossuet, defending his Gallican position against the twin threats of papalism and Protestantism, for the benefit of the eldest son of Louis XIV. Without a knowledge of history and its different stages, Bossuet taught, princes would be dependent for their understanding of human behavior on natural or civil law alone; and so he offered a condensation of the story of religion and empires from biblical beginnings, with distinct "epochs," which marked the pilgrimage of humanity from the Jews and pagans down to the Roman empire.[108]

Bossuet's plan, though based on the parallel columns of Eusebian history, was linear and hybrid, setting the epoch of Troy between those of Moses and Solomon. History is almost liturgical in Bossuet's retelling. It becomes tragedy with the expulsion from Paradise, whose memory had been preserved by poets in the myth of the golden age (which over a century earlier Bodin had ridiculed). It was transformed into civil history in the second epoch, which is that of the Flood (whose memory was also reflected in the myths of many peoples), when the arts of civilization had a new beginning and when the foundations of ancient empires were laid. The culmination came with the Roman Empire, with all the separate national histories gathered into one universal tradition that received divine sanction—and a new epoch—through the Incarnation, which was succeeded by the eleventh and twelfth (Constantine and Charlemagne) epochs, constituting "the seventh and last age of the world" and ending a long concatenation of causes that yet had a providential origin and moreover "encompassed all causes and effects in a single plan."[109]

The idea of the unity of history was expressed in a more rational fashion by Leibniz, who was a historian and archival scholar as well as polymath and philosopher. History, he wrote, "one may compare . . . to the body of an animal, where the bones support everything, the nerves form the connection, the spirit which moves the machine, the humors which consist of nourishing juices, and finally the flesh which gives completion to the whole mass. The past of history corresponds thus: chronology to bones, genealogy to nerves, hidden motives to invisible spirits, and the detail of circumstances to the whole mass of flesh."[110] This organic conceit has been invoked by historians from the time of Polybius down to the present, but theoretical as Leibniz's analogy sounded, he intended to assimilate it to the conventional laws of history. "Since history is a body without life," Leibniz continued, "it is necessary that one try to assert nothing without a basis of fact, and that gradually one purge history of fables, which have crept into it." For Leibniz, a correct understanding of history, as of nature, would ultimately join accidents and particulars with the universal historical organism, and subject the historical process likewise to his famous "law of continuity," though in a more up-to-date philosophical way than the old theological vision preserved by Bossuet.

The foundation of universal history remained chronology, and Christian scholars from the time of Eusebius struggled with the problem of synchronizing the growing number of national traditions, and doing so only on the basis of textual evidence. The result was a vast numerological scholasticism. "What and how many?" (*Quid et quotuplex?*) Bodin had asked about history, and chronologists repeated the catechismal formula. "*Quid est chronologia?*" asked a seventeenth-century textbook, listing, quite uncritically, his many predecessors; and "*Quotuplex?*"[111] Bede had devised a system of Christian chronology, and historians followed his plan for centuries. Chronology was proverbially "the eye of history," or Ariadne's thread (Bodin's conceit) to escape from the historical labyrinth, and innumerable summaries were published in the early modern period. Its foundational importance was insisted on by methodizers of history, such as Bodin and his followers, including La Popelinière and Gaillard, who published both sacred and secular chronologies.[112] Almost eight centuries after Bede, Scaliger revised the whole tradition on the basis of a vastly greater knowledge of languages and sources. His *Opus novum de emendatione temporum* of 1583 and his *Thesaurus temporum* of 1606, which (as Arno Borst put it) opened "the space for a 'prehistory,'" set the science of chronology on its modern foundations.[113]

The concept of time, so essential to the understanding of history, was a huge mystery in Christian tradition, except for those, like Denis Pétau, who identified the two.[114] "If no one asks me, I know," Augustine had confessed; "if I want to explain it to a questioner, I do not know."[115] Some Renaissance scholars, like Bodin, thought that they knew well enough to explain it to their readers. Supporting Plato against Aristotle, Bodin entered into a long and technical metaphysical argument to show, against older sophistries and heresies, the necessity of Creation in time (and out of nothing).[116] But this is the human way of expression, for with God (as Augustine also argued) time was ever present. For Bodin a correct theology was essential for a proper chronology, which allowed historians to determine the "succession of times" and, secondarily, of historians to be read. "Let us then," Bodin concluded, "accept the system of Moses."

Humanist scholars, from Petrarch down to Vico, had a different, and perhaps more Augustinian, sense of time—inclining, as Donald Wilcox has argued, toward a relativist conception which was inseparable from human perception, understanding, and expression.[117] These scholars were concerned not with the cosmological clock but with the shapes taken by time in the perspective of human wisdom and the succession of doctrine, which occurred not sub specie aeternitatis but in the cycles of generations. This was entirely different from modern chronologists who posited a naturalistic and "absolutist" time line, with historical events distributed along it in temporal order (*ratione temporum*, or, in Bodin's phrase, *de temporis universi ratione*) and given meaning and perhaps causal significance in part by their place in the sequence.

For universal and absolute chronology the problem was the need to determine the origin of the world, which meant trying to understand mythical as well as historical time—a hopeless task when undertaken in the pandemonium of learning and riots of religious controversy in Renaissance and Reformation Europe. There were many rival estimates besides that of Scaliger, for whom Creation occurred in 3949 B.C., and in the Anglophone world James Ussher's *The Annals of the World* (1650–54) provided the most conventional dating for Christian believers. Ussher concluded "that from the evening ushering[!] in the first day of the world, to that midnight which began the first day of the Christian era, there was [sic] 4003 years, seventy days, and six temporary hours."[118] Even biblical scholars had questioned this sort of estimate, and the notion of "men before Adam," created but without sin, was a common heretical view in Augustine's time and even before.[119] Such ideas were reinforced both by the fantastic claims of the Egyptian to antiquity, preserved in the Hermetic tradition, and by Neoplatonic theories of the emergence of humanity; and suggestions of these pre-Adamite notions can be found in Renaissance authors like Vives, Paracelsus, Bruno, Campanella, and Raleigh before their radical formulation in the work of Isaac La Peyrère, who cited as evidence not only the ancient Chaldaeans and Egyptians but also the "world newly discovered."[120]

The prehistorical "space" defined by Scaliger was extended in the competition for priority by various national traditions within the Eusebian framework, which all had their partisans and which acted to subvert the scriptural narrative even as they exploited it. The expansion of temporal horizons was encouraged also by a new discipline that emerged in the seventeenth century, the history of philosophy, which continued the search begun by Pico, Ficino, and other humanists for an original philosophy or theology. This quest was promoted by continued fascination with the Hermetic tradition and by the recurring phenomenon of Egyptomania and "philobarbarism" associated with Herodotus and revived by scholars like Athanasius Kircher.[121] Although the antiquity of the Hermetic texts had been challenged by Isaac Casaubon (in 1614), Kircher continued his researches on the premise that they represented an ancient wisdom consistent with Christianity, and he even affected to find visible signs of the Christian trinity in this wisdom. In the next century the French *Encyclopédie* was still reporting the view that the Egyptian priests were the teachers both of Moses and of the Greek wise men and philosophers.[122]

And as Kircher, Otto von Heurne, and others defended the claims of the Egyptians to higher antiquity, so too Vossius (like Bodin before him) defended those of the Chaldeans and Martino Martini those of the Chinese. To many critics such speculations seemed to conceal religious error and atheism — "idolatry" and "mythology" in a pejorative sense, as Theophilus Gale and, later, Bishop Warburton argued — and, most upsetting to the study of history, subversion of Eusebian and Scaligerian chronology. The work of John Marsham, John Spencer, John Toland, and La Peyrère all seemed to lead in this direction and at the same time to transform the temporal horizons of universal history.[123]

This was the drift, too, of Thomas Burnet's *Archaeology of Philosophy or Ancient Doctrine from the Origins of Things* (1694), which traced Western philosophy back to an original and mythical wisdom which he called *philosophia mythologica,* or *sapientia antiquo-barbarica,* and which, emerging from a common nature, represented the source of all later cultural traditions.[124] The analogies which Burnet had in mind were the *Roman Archaeology* of Dionysius of Halicarnassus, which inquired into those obscure ages dismissed by Thucydides as beyond the grasp of historians, and the *Jewish Archaeology* of Josephus, who followed the account of Moses begun after the seventh day of Creation. The tools of this inquiry, it should be added, included all the problematic and conjectural devices of Renaissance scholarship — mythology, textual divination, etymology, and other fellow travelers of the science of philology and Bodinian historical method.

In the very heyday of the new philosophy, the antiquated archaeology and mythistory of traditional learning were still very much alive. Thucydides (translated by Hobbes in 1629) was a popular model in the early modern period because of the literary and analytical qualities of his narrative and his ostensible relevance for political science; but the face of Herodotus became increasingly apparent, especially in connection with the recurring phenomena of Egyptomania and philobarbarism, which looked beyond the classicist and Judeo-Christian traditions for historical origins and for a proper framework for universal history. The conjunction of these impulses with archaeology and anthropology in a modern sense marked the beginning of an enlightened and truly (if in some cases excessively speculative) philosophical history.

9

Philosophical History

History and philosophy are the two eyes of wisdom.
— Christian Thomasius

The Enlightenment conception of history, in its classic form, is based on one of the oldest historical conceits. Humanity is like individual members of the species, and the experience of the human race over time is much like the life of a person, from generation and growth to, presumably if not predictably, corruption and death, whence history, for Ferguson, Lessing, and Condorcet no less than for Florus and Augustine, can be understood as "the education of the human race." Education, or the neologism "culture" (which referred to the same thing in the eighteenth century), was of course seen differently by different scholars — Condorcet taking a Lockean view of psychological progress through sense experience, while Lessing preferred to identify it with revelation, and Ferguson thought in terms of social evolution.[1] Yet the general thesis held all the same, so that, as Ferguson wrote, "the history of the individual is but a detail of the sentiments and the thoughts he has entertained in the view of his species."[2] In any case this biological analogy gave historians a useful conceptual and terminological tool to describe larger patterns of human history, although it also entangled them in all sorts of problems in their efforts of explanation and interpretation.

Philologic

In his defense of Christian tradition against philosophy, published in 1669, Theophilus Gale proposed to trace the "original of human literature," and so wisdom in general, back to Holy Scriptures; and in this textualist project, his doctrinal commitments aside, he laid down a principle of importance for the study of history. "Now the mater of this Discourse is not *Logic* but *Philologic,* touching the spring-head and Derivation of human arts and sciences."[3] In this human arena the fundamental error was not logical fallacy but "Anachronisme," Gale continued, arising from the "confusion of Histories." At certain points, no matter what common sense might suggest or reason demand, positive knowledge originating in areas beyond contemporary experience had to be heeded. "History speaks," in the formula of the great philologist Friedrich August Wolf, and in those cases humanity must listen.[4]

Philosophers — the philosophes of the eighteenth century — were not always disposed to listen. History often remained in the shadows during the self-proclaimed century of Enlightenment. For d'Alembert, writing in the 1750s, his was "the century of philosophy par excellence," which would be known to posterity for the "revolution" of ideas brought by modern science, mathematics, and their offspring.[5] From this self-advertising proclamation, repeated by other philosophes, arose not only the construct of the "philosophical school," as the nineteenth century would refer to the advocates of natural law, but also the notion that this was an "unhistorical century." This is a misconception long since discarded, having been demolished many years ago by Wilhelm Dilthey and especially by Ernst Cassirer in his *Philosophy of the Enlightenment* (1932), even though he began his book by citing at length the revolutionary declaration of d'Alembert and seemed to agree that his century was "imbued with a belief in the unity and immutability of reason."[6] According to Cassirer, eighteenth-century philosophy was based on the belief that nature and history were joined together as "an indivisible unity" and, moreover, that "history bears the torch for the Enlightenment."

But history in what sense? Commonplaces about truth and moral utility, collections of exempla, theories of human development, laborious investigations of source material, or speculations about prehistory and the question of human origins? Formally, eighteenth-century ideas of the nature and value of history were largely commonplace and derivative, though reason did come to play an increasingly important role. For Ephraim Chambers, history was divided after the fashion of Bodin and Bacon, although under the rubric of civil history he admitted additional varieties, including "figurative" — the humanists would have said "elegant" — histories, such as those of Tacitus, de Thou, and Burnet, which are the most useful, representing "a kind of rational *history;* which is without stopping at the shell or outside, or appearance of things; enters into the thoughts, the breasts of the persons concerned therein."[7] Claude-François Menestrier also wrote of "reasoned history," which sought underlying causes, as well as "critical history" and "authorized history," which goes beyond "figured history" to offer documentary proof for its explanations.[8]

As for its uses, history remained philosophy teaching by example, as the deist Lord Bolingbroke repeated, invoking not only Dionysius of Halicarnassus but also Bodin and Bacon.[9] Through history we are "cast back, as it were, into former ages"; we learn of the causal sequence of events, and so are better prepared for action ourselves. Yet at the same time — the arguments of the historical Pyrrhonists had been duly absorbed — history produced no certainty, its "lying spirit" strewing partiality, prejudices, and falsehoods throughout the ages.

Of course history possessed very different meanings in the critical and crisis-ridden eighteenth century, according to various national "prejudices," with Italian, French, British, and German scholars interpreting it according to different tastes and traditions but also to philosophical and ideological disagreements on several levels. In very general retrospect and in terms of the major authors in the historiographical canon, Italian views retained links with the humanist tradition, English and Scottish with empirical and sensationalist philosophy of Baconian and Lockean inspiration, French with Cartesian rationalism as well as Lockean empiricism, and German with Lutheran spiritualism, eclecticism, and what recent scholars regard as a sort of proto- and precursory historicism.

Beyond national allegiances and religious divisions, the wider world of historical scholarship was defined by the republic of letters, in which information and ideas were exchanged, circles, societies, and academies were formed, libraries were opened to researchers, bibliographies and encyclopedias were published, and scholars broadened their horizons directly by more or less institutionalized international voyages, the *itinera italicum, gallicum,* and *germanicum.*[10] Antiquarian and bibliophilic exchanges between Mabillon and the Italians, Muratori and the French, and Leibniz and both Italian and French scholars illustrate the cosmopolitan character of the best of seventeenth- and eighteenth-century historical scholarship.[11]

Some of this made its way into Diderot's *Encyclopédie.* Articles on history ranged from summaries of chronology and periodization to the technicalities of historical methodology and the auxiliary sciences, from the familiar ground of national origins to the exotic history revealed in the wake of discovery. Diderot and his colleagues were shameless in their exploitation of secondary literature, but they continued to preach the humanist theme of "back to the sources." The article on certitude by the Abbé de Prades pointed to oral tradition, eyewitness accounts, later narratives based on these, and "monuments" as the sources of history, leading one scholar to conclude that "whatever man thinks, writes or does becomes a potential historical document for the Encyclopedists."[12]

The late seventeenth and eighteenth centuries were an age of the "normal science" of history (in Kuhn's much used and abused term), when the "great historical enterprises," the pioneering collections of texts and documentary sources, were initiated first by monastic scholars, especially Bollandists and Maurists, and then by the "academic movement," including the Academy of Inscriptions and later the Cabinet of Manuscripts and the projects of individual scholars like La Curne de Saint-Palaye, who continued the antiquarian tradition of Jean du Tillet, Pierre Pithou, and Pierre Dupuy, doing for France what Leibniz was doing for Germany, Muratori for Italy, and Matthew Parker and others for England.[13] The "ancient wisdom" lived on, too, although increasingly suspect and challenged by Deists and orthodox Christians alike in the name of modernizing progress.[14]

In general the objects of research remained the same — classical and Christian antiquity, medieval political and ecclesiastical history, national, legal, and cultural traditions, and "mémoires pour servir à l'histoire" of some well-archived institution or other. To these were added the more exotic histories of the Far East and the New World, such as the Abbé Raynal's "philosophical and political history" of commerce in the East and West Indies, which were expected to shed further light on the study of human nature.[15] The motives for these investigations were also much the same — the defense of the church, the glorification of the state and its interests, and the enhancement of various causes, institutions, or social groups, and yet at the same time disinterested satisfaction of curiosity about the variety and vicissitudes of the human condition. Most fundamental, however, were those venturesome inquiries that promised to raise history to a philosophical or even theological level. The new philosophy of the seventeenth century had been founded on suspicions of and even contempt for history and older traditions of scholarship, yet scholars continued to be fascinated with history in the longest perspectives and from the most challenging sources. Newton himself was an entry in the quest for mythical origins and "the battle of dates."[16]

The eighteenth century, too, was an age not only of philosophy but of philology and the larger goals underlying this humanist science, which was the pursuit of antiquity. What is not apparent, or at least not sufficiently appreciated in most studies of the continental Enlightenment, even that of Cassirer (who, after all, limited his discussion to philosophy in a basically Kantian sense), is the continuing potency of the humanist tradition — philology, criticism, and encyclopedic erudition — during the Enlightenment. D'Alembert wrote the entry on "erudition" (as well as that on "chronology") for the *Encyclopedia,* dividing it into three main parts: the knowledge of history, languages, and books, that is, presumably, bibliography and the history of literature. From this trinity of positive knowledge proceeded "that important part of *erudition* called criticism." *La critique,* in the philological sense of determining the meaning of an ancient author but also in the more philosophical sense of truthfulness, had allowed the exposure of forgeries such as the fables in the saints' lives, the donation of Constantine, Pope Joan, and the miracles reported by Gregory of Tours. Erudition had come in the revival of learning brought in the wake of Dante, Petrarch, Valla, and the Greek exiles from Constantinople and by the time of d'Alembert had become too vast for anyone to master, whence the avalanche of bibliographies, reference works, and handbooks from the seventeenth century. Voltaire mocked pedantry and denied that history could have any certitude; yet he, too, kept abreast of the work of the Academy of Inscriptions and other depositories of unreflective learning, as of course did Diderot and his fellow encyclopedists.[17]

Criticism and *crisis* have the same root, and it is not surprising that the classical age of criticism in Europe, the late seventeenth and early eighteenth century, was also a great age of extraordinary crisis — such is the argument of the seminal 1935 book on "the crisis of European consciousness" from 1680 to 1715 by Paul Hazard, whose intellectual presence is still apparent in recent interpretations of the Enlightenment.[18] In this criticism and accompanying intellectual crisis within the republic of letters, the study of history figured centrally, as every school of thought — not only those laboring unreflectively in the service of the old erudition and those committed to particular doctrines but also devotees of the new science and alleged "atheists" — invoked their own vision of history to legitimize their position and further their hopes and dreams. Even if history were largely a record of crimes and errors, as Bayle and Voltaire believed, it had discernible form and offered exemplary (if largely negative) wisdom for any who would trouble to learn from it.

Debates over origins and the provenance of national cultures continued in similar terms — in France, the Romanist position, to which monastic scholars inclined, was opposed to the Germanism that was urged by champions of the nobility. The debate between Germanists and Romanists, associated with the *Kulturkampf* generated by Tacitus's *Germania* in the sixteenth century, erupted again in the eighteenth century, with advocates of the *thèse nobiliaire* like Henri de Boulainvilliers and the Abbé de Mably seizing on the Germanic conquest as the source of French nationality and upholders of the *thèse romaine* like the Abbé Du Bos and various jurists insisting on continuity with Roman society and institutions, especially with regard to feudalism.[19] In England Sharon Turner carried on the quest for the "Great Ancestors" of modern "Anglo-Saxons."[20] Antiquarianism was thus ridden with ideological motives — partisanship, family and class pride, and chauvinisms of all sorts and levels.

Even without this association of scholarship with political, social, and religious enthusiasm, antiquarianism was not highly regarded in the light of "philosophy" or "good letters." Bolingbroke, for example, would tolerate compilers only if they "neither affect wit nor pretend to reason"; and Gibbon eschewed the technicalities of Mabillon's diplomatic skill and art of criticism while exploiting its achievements. Along with "prejudice," Adrian Baillet observed, "pedantry seems to be the particular vice of critics" — a vice which the French *Encyclopedia* associated with "the baggage of antiquity."[21]

Yet attached to this quasi-professional fascination with antiquities was a higher scientific and professional ideal, illustrated perhaps by that perfect scholar, perennial student, and "Gibbon's mule," Sebastien Le Nain de Tillemont, whose whole life was one of pious, ascetic, and, as Sainte-Beuve wrote, "disinterested study within the sight of God."[22] Denying pleasure in this life, such a scholar could look forward to the immortality conferred by the shelf life of his publications, especially if he could rise above the passions and enticements of the moment. Thus, joining the masculine images of the medieval saint, the Renaissance man, the Baconian man of science, and the enlightened *philosophe* was that of the critical *erudit*, who practiced an almost monkish way of life in the pursuit of historical truth. This *bon académicien* devoted to antiquarian research should be without ambition, free from "intrigue," scornful of wealth, and willing to accept the "voluntary servitude" of a scholarly life.[23] This image, often repeated in the eulogies of the Academy of Inscriptions, was in large part fantasy, but it also suggests, however conventionally, the higher (or lower) epistemological ideal underlying antiquarian labors.

In the later eighteenth century, history and philosophy — each claiming to be critical in a way — were diverging sharply, as a result of the upsurge of idealism in Germany in the time of Kant and also of the Jacobin spirit and later Bonapartist spirit in public life. On the most obvious level this might be seen as another version of the quarrel between Ancients and Moderns — those backward-looking scholars who found their values in the past and those who wanted to escape from the past and change the present on behalf of a better future. And yet it was undeniable that history, like the criticism with which it was associated, offered a documentable sort of truth that was not available to pure reason.

Vico and the New Science

One scholar who aspired to reconcile and to combine "logic" and "philologic" was Giambattista Vico (1668–1744). It has been common, following Croce and Collingwood, to regard Vico as a man either behind or ahead of his age; but as Eugenio Garin has remarked, this judgment is itself a kind of "myth" not unlike some of the anachronisms noted by Vico himself: "Far from being a man out of his time, Vico belongs completely in the center of the great debate of his century, that witnesses the crisis of a 'criticism' of knowledge, and the necessity of distinguishing and organizing the tree of the sciences: to grasp the link between the investigation of nature and the investigation of man; to found and construct the new encyclopedia."[24] This "new encyclopedia," Vico's *New Science,* was the end product of a life journey in quest of a full and historical understanding of humanity throughout all its stages from genesis in nature to decline and fall in civil society — a complete "philosophy of history" in the modern sense of this phrase. This is another example of that ideal of the "indivisible unity" between nature and history attributed by Cassirer to the Enlightenment.

Vico's intellectual journey began in a "trivial" rather than a "quadrivial" mode, with a humanist celebration of the positive learning embodied in "topics" and preserved by memory in contrast to Descartes's abstract method of geometrical analysis. For Vico the ars topica must precede philosophical criticism, and history must precede speculation. Once this balance is restored, Vico concluded, Moderns will be able to "equal the Ancients in the fields of wisdom and eloquence as we excel them in the domain of science."[25] In particular it was the Latin language and Roman law that furnished Vico with the first materials for his project, and to these he later added the Homeric poems as points of entry into the mysteries of prehistory and the foundations of that new science whose first incarnation was philology.

In his treatise *Universal Law* Vico presented his first attempt at periodizing universal history. Characteristically, he accepted the old distinction between sacred and profane history but transformed it by giving it temporal form, mixing biblical and classical history, drawing variously on the schemes of Varro, Polybius, Lucretius, Augustine, Grotius, and especially Roman jurisprudence. Sacred history is the prehistorical time between Creation and Moses, while profane history is divided into five epochs: (1) a theocratic period under Mosaic law, (2) a time of "feudal" organization emerging from the family, (3) the appearance of aristocracy and civil society in the "major nations," (4) the decline of aristocracy and rise of kingship and democracy in the "minor nations," and (5) the age of war, imperial expansion, and the "law of nations" (*jus gentium*), which arises out of violence — war being the driving force of the whole course of history. A crucial turning point in history was reflected in the law of the major and the minor nations, the first being the mythical and violent stage before the founding of cities — the "feral" stage of civilization which provoked such a controversy in the eighteenth century — and the second the civil society reflected most accessibly in the Roman law of the Twelve Tables.[26]

The final expression, or expressions, of Vico's view of history appeared in the successive versions of his *New Science,* which elaborates on the same pattern formulated in the *Universal Law:* the age of the gods, whose relics included the Egyptian hieroglyphs and the oracles; the age of heroes, a period of aristocracy signalized by heroic emblems; and the age of men, organized into monarchies and democracies and communicating in conventional language.[27] Philology and etymology, Vico believed, made it possible to decipher these languages. The faculty not of reason but of imagination — for Vico equivalent, etymologically, and so genetically, to memory — allowed the properly trained scholar to penetrate to the heart of this prehistorical darkness.[28] It was this fusion of philology and philosophy that made possible the construction of the new science in all of its grander aspects.

With many encyclopedic scholars of the seventeenth and eighteenth centuries Vico shared a fascination with the question of origins and the prehistorical ages of myth, barbarism, and a putative state of nature before civil society. For Vico this question had two basic aspects — one the order of ideas and the other the order of things, or institutions, whose nature is "nothing but their coming into being" (*natura* from *nascimento*).[29] These aspects also correspond to the two conceits which Vico warns against — the conceit of nations, which alleges absurdly ancient origins for various peoples, and the conceit of scholars, "who will have it that what they know is as old as the world." A classical statement of this prejudice is the "golden saying" cited by Vico from Diodorus Siculus's *Library of History:* "With respect to the antiquity of the human race, not only do Greeks put forth their claims but many of the barbarians as well, all holding that it is they who are autochthonous and the first of all men to discover the things which are of use in life, and that it was the events in their own history which were the earliest to have been held worthy of record."[30] For Vico this passage illustrated the conceit of nations, and on this basis he rejected what he called "the proud claims of the Chaldeans, Scythians, Egyptians, Chinese, to have been the first founders of the humanity of the ancient world." For him the biblical account invalidated these ancient conceits and chauvinisms and was unassailable, though this holy ground was not itself suitable for purely scientific exploration.

Vico's answer to the question of origins was a combination of traditional orthodoxy and methodological heterodoxy — of Christian and neo-Lucretian theories of the origins of culture. In the first place he returned to the "truth of sacred history," which privileged and gave primacy to the Jews; but in the second place he gave independence to the other, that is, the "gentile," national traditions by arguing (like Bodin, on etymological grounds but to the opposite conclusion) that these nations were indeed autochthonous, self-generated, and self-enclosed and followed similar historical trajectories, of which Rome provided the archetype and much of the evidence.

The *New Science* set out to be the *Principia* of history, expressed in axioms, elements, principles, and corollaries. One of his principles was that "all histories of the gentile nations have had fabulous beginnings" (*favolosi principi*), so that the new science had to be fundamentally a science of "mythology or the interpretation of fable."[31] Vico pursued these mythological inquiries in terms of a trinity of institutional constants — religion, marriage, and burial of the dead — which reinforced his belief in the ultimately divine origin of human history. In general the new science was a many-sided and interdisciplinary construct, purporting to be at once theological, philosophical, political, and historical. Four of its seven aspects were specifically historical: it expressed "principles of universal history" based on a "rational chronology" that transcended the philologically based chronology of Scaliger and other such unphilosophical scholars, a "history of human ideas," a form of "philosophical criticism" which permitted insight into the poetic theology of the earliest ages, and finally "an ideal universal history traversed in time by the histories of all nations."[32]

Perhaps Vico's most fundamental premise, already formulated in philosophical terms in his earlier work *On the Most Ancient Wisdom of the Italians,* was the principle that the true (*verum*) and the made (*factum*) are interchangeable.[33] Historically, this principle was applied to what Vico called "poetic wisdom," the study of which led him to this idea, which was repeated by Michelet, Marx, and other later admirers, according to which "the founders of gentile humanity . . . in a certain sense created themselves."[34] *Poetry* was derived from the Greek *poein,* to make; and it was the poetic remaking of God's Creation that formed both human consciousness (*coscienza*) and its fulfillment in the new science (*scienza*). This notion of "maker's knowledge" suggested to Vico his answer to the Cartesian *Cogito,* which is not "I think, therefore I am," but "I make, therefore I know."[35]

Out of enormous philological learning, ingenious mythology, and inventive (and often credulous) etymology, Vico ascended from historical intuitions to the heights of metaphysical speculation, expressed in his famous theory of the cyclical "course" and "recourse" of the trajectories of national histories. His inquiry began with that condition of human existence known, since ancient times, as "barbarism" (*barbaria, barbarismus,* and vernacular forms). The term *barbarism,* from Herodotus to Machiavelli and beyond, had a fascinating semantic history as a pejorative applied by one nation or party to another, so that it had become not only a careless pejorative but also a conceptual and historical category applied to various periods of unenlightenment.[36] For Vico, however, this idea, or counterideal, became a "first barbarism" (*i tempi barbari primi*), since a second "barbarism of reflection" threatened the end of each turn of the historical cycle.[37]

In these reflections, Vico's major source, conceptually and historically, was Tacitus's *Germania,* together with the massive accumulation of modern commentary.[38] For Vico, *Germania* was a striking representation of an archetype of first barbarism — a way of retracing, or rethinking, one's way historically from culture back to nature, from history to prehistory, and indeed of understanding this primitive stage of civilization in all cultures. If the German songs noted by Tacitus (and by Justinian in the preface to his *Digest*) reflected the poetic wisdom of a society still under the spell of myth and the worship of nature, so reportedly did those of the natives of the New World. "Tacitus in his account of the customs of the ancient Germans," Vico remarks, "relates that they preserved in verse the beginnings of their history, and Lipsius in his notes on this passage says the same thing of the American Indians."[39] Germanic customs such as burial practices permit us, Vico continues, "to conjecture that the same custom must have prevailed among all the other first barbarous nations."[40] In general Vico took the Tacitean stereotypes as illustrations of the *termini a quo* and *ad quem* of the courses of cultural history if not from Genesis to Revelation, then at least from the barbaric age begun by Noah's offspring to the heights and depths of civilization and the emergence of a second barbarism, whose features might also be glimpsed in other works of Tacitus. For Vico, Tacitus seemed to provide materials for a whole philosophy of history.

In the final version of his vision of history Vico argued with erudite virtuosity that every nation lived through three stages: first, divine (myth, poetry, and unwritten custom); second, heroic (history, prose, and written law); third, human (philosophy, science, and civil institutions).[41] But after the cycle comes recycle — after the *corso* comes *ricorso* — and a falling back into a second barbarism, a "barbarism of reflection" (as distinguished from the first "barbarism of sense") arising from the "ultimate civil disease" of a state and from egoistic views epitomized by the "feigned" philosophy of a Descartes, who would reject the past and make a god of himself. By contrast, Vico sought self-knowledge through learned retrospect on human creations throughout the whole world of nations. Knowledge must be genetic — starting with Genesis and with the most profound of Vico's axioms: "Doctrines must take their beginning from that of the matters of which they treat."[42] This may be taken as the very motto and "principle" of Enlightenment historicism. It was an inspiration, too, for the Vichian philosopher Benedetto Croce, whose "new historicism . . . accepts, extends, deepens, and applies the principle that men know only what they do (consequently all they know is their own history)."[43]

Vico may have been very much a man of his times, but he was a prophet neither in his own country nor in his own century. Vico, though Herder knew of him late in life and Coleridge later speaks of him, was little known beyond the Alps; and even in Italy his work was discussed mainly in legal scholarship and in the debate between his disciple Emmanuele Duni and the Dominican G. F. Finetti over the savage ("ferine") origins of religion.[44] The great revival began in France, and with Michelet's abridged translation of the *New Science* in 1827, Vico's genetic and developmental ideas were absorbed and disseminated by Romantic scholars. In this century Vico has become a major figure in the canon of the philosophy of history as well as a prime witness for what Isaiah Berlin has called the "counter-Enlightenment."[45] In his modern incarnation Vico is a prime witness to the coherence and *longue durée* of Western historical thought.

Gibbon and the End of Rome

Rome, in its rise and fall and postmortem existence, furnished the model of historical interpretation for over two millennia, and indeed it still occasionally serves that paradigmatic purpose. In different ways Polybius, Livy, Augustine, the juridical defenders of the translation of empire, Dante, Petrarch, Biondo, Machiavelli, Sigonio, Montesquieu, and Vico all drew on the scholarship and conjectures attending the fortunes of Roman history from pagan expansion to overthrow by barbarism to resurrection at the hands of modern humanists, antiquarians, and archaeologists. Down to the eighteenth century the question of origins was discussed endlessly and usually with little criticism of classical authorities except the general suspicions inspired by historical Pyrrhonism.[46] The fall of Rome had its devoted scholars, too, although they were usually more philosophical — or eschatological and apocalyptic, "when Rome falls, the world will also fall" (*quando cadet Roma, cadet et mundi*) — in their interpretations of the tragic fate of the Roman Empire, which, however, included the providential survival of the Eternal City for a very different sort of universal monarchy.[47]

Attracted to the study of history from the beginning, Edward Gibbon took years before he found himself, his subject, his style, and even his language. *Found* is not quite the right word; Gibbon, the self-professed Historian of the Roman Empire, was very much a construction of a scholarly and literary will — as indeed was "his" empire.[48] Escaping (with the help of Lord Sheffield) from a personal and financial crisis, he turned to a lifework which quite overshadowed both his personal and his public life. Gibbon also escaped from superstition, skepticism, or perhaps a form of "protestantism" like Bayle's, which "protest[ed] indifferently against all systems and all sects," and added enlightened philosophy to his classical learning during his life in Lausanne.[49] Gibbon first "reveal[ed] the measure of his mind" in his *Essai sur l'Étude de la littérature* of 1761, which marked, he said, "the loss of my litterary maidenhead."[50] In this work he celebrated the encyclopedic tradition of literature, which (like Vico) he contrasted to the contempt for learning displayed by Descartes in the name of a false and emaciated *esprit philosophique* for which history seemed to be a mere game: "The new appellation of *Erudits* was contemptuously applied to the successors of Lipsius and Casaubon; and I was provoked to hear (see Mr d'Alembert's Discours preliminaire à l'Encyclopedie) that the exercise of memory, their sole merit, had been superseded by the nobler faculties of the imagination and the judgement."[51] Yet there was no necessary conflict between *l'érudition* and *les lumières* as well as *la critique*. "The antiquarian, who blushes at his alliance with Thomas Hearne," Gibbon remarked, "will feel his profession ennobled by the name of Leibnitz."[52] Gassendi, Bayle, and even Newton had also preserved a balance between learning and reason, and it was in this connection that Gibbon pointed to Tacitus as the ideal *"historien philosophe."*[53]

Gibbon's historical perspective is apparent in his remarks on the ties between political climate and forms of learning: "Thus, metaphysics and logic under the successors of Alexander, politics and eloquence in the days of the Roman republic, history and poetry in the Augustuine age, grammar and jurisprudence under the Lower Empire, scholastic philosophy during the thirteenth century, Belles Lettres down to the time of our fathers have excited by turns the admiration and scorn of mankind."[54] So what about Gibbon's own generation?

Gibbon's mission was to combine erudition and literature, to steer between the Scylla of dilletantism and the Charybdis of antiquarian pedantry. He was indeed a devotee, if not a practitioner, of philology, criticism, and the auxiliary science of history developed from the seventeenth century, including those "monkish historians" scorned by some philosophes, though not on the same scholarly level as his German contemporaries of the Göttingen school.[55] In Lausanne the first installment of his allowance for his "litterary wants" went to the purchase of "the twenty volumes of the Memoirs of the Academy of Inscriptions," which contained the debate, inspired by historical Pyrrhonism, over the "certainty" of the first centuries of Roman history; and his *Memoirs* are filled with his reading not only in the classics and in the works of English friends like William Jones but also of the great Italian and French (but very few German) scholars — Sigonio, Baronios, Muratori, Dupuy, Mabillon, Montfaucon, Freret, Leclerc, Boullainvilliers, Bouquet, Du Bos (before their later falling out), and especially Tillemont, and the authors of many other "dry and dark treatises."[56] But Gibbon also employed travelers' reports and the findings of recent excavations at Herculaneum and Pompeii, in this and other ways transcending the narrow canon of classical historiography and beginning what Momigliano called "the story of how mankind left Rome behind."[57]

Gibbon dramatized his choice of subject as an epiphany produced by his Italian journey of 1764 — the scene of the Franciscan friars singing vespers in the Temple of Jupiter, that is, the church of Santa Maria in Aracoeli, appealing no doubt to his irony as well as to antiquarian sentiment.[58] However, he considered other topics, too, including a history of the liberty of the Swiss, the Republic of Florence, and even a biography of Walter Raleigh, before settling on the post-Tacitean enterprise of describing and explaining "the greatest, perhaps, and most awful scene in the history of mankind."[59] If, as Petrarch said, all history was the praise of Rome, Gibbon meant to write the closing chapters of this long eulogy, and in this project he displayed an extraordinary array of resources, ranging from Tacitus to Tillemont, from Augustine to his favorite French philosophe, Baron Montesquieu. Gibbon appreciated the importance of institutions and included an extraordinary dissertation on Roman law, fully abreast of modern scholarship, that offered a supplementary survey of one dimension of the theme of empire, and discussions of the history of the Near (and even the Far) East. He also ornamented his narrative and carefully crafted footnotes with digressions in social and cultural history; and he suggested other bypaths that needed investigation, such as a historical work "which should lay open the connection between languages and manners of nations."[60]

Some old historiographical habits persisted, such as the geographical introduction which Gibbon assembled for his work, his climatological speculations, and his discussions of the plague. At one point (chapter XLIII, ending with Justinian's death) Gibbon even comments on the prevalence of earthquakes in the reign of Justinian and on the appearance of a comet, which he identified with the great (Halley's) comet of 1680 and which had provoked Bayle's famous *Thoughts on the Comet*.[61] Gibbon does so in a more rational spirit than medieval chroniclers, though he leaves Newton and Halley to the astronomers and draws his "humble science" from d'Alembert's entry in the *Encyclopédie*. Yet Gibbon's focus was primarily political, and Tacitus remained his major guide, supplemented by Tacitus's follower Ammianus Marcellinus, to the extent that uncovering causes, motives, and the "nice and secret springs" of action ostensibly drove his narrative. Gibbon recognized the "empire of Fortune," but he regarded it as merely a disguise for ignorance unworthy of a philosophical historian.

Gibbon's book, treating "the triumph of barbarism and religion" over Rome, was set at the intersections of three stereotypes. He accepted without question what has been called "the myth of Rome" as reflected in historiographical, literary, and legal tradition. This myth had been impressed on him in his early reading and in his personal inspection of the Roman ruins; and he expressed his feelings again in the penultimate chapter of the *Decline and Fall*, citing the words of the Emperor Frederick Barbarossa, who proclaimed that the Roman spirit still lived in his own empire, and finally, in the last chapter, citing the humanist Poggio Bracciolini, who lamented that "the public and private edifices, that were founded for eternity, lie prostrate and broken, like the limbs of a mighty giant."[62] From the beginning the Romans were "incapable of fear and impatient of repose," as Polybius has said. As long as the Eternal City prevailed, the fortunes of the empire were favorable; once the capital was subverted and decentered by foreign influences, and once emperors could be chosen from the provinces, then the old qualities of government under law were lost; for what brought the empire down was not genetic weakness but "immoderate greatness."

The second stereotype was barbarism, which Gibbon saw as a state of society manifested in all the invaders of Rome — Germans, the Goths described by Jordanes ("Jornandes"), the Huns, Lombards, Franks, Bulgarians, Sclavonians, Turks, Avars, Persians, Ethiopians, Britons, Saxons, and others. However, it was Tacitus's portrayal that Gibbon followed, though not uncritically, in his own rendition.[63] Barbarism was defined by the disparity between instinct and reason and by the illiteracy that deprives migratory peoples of the memory of the deeds of their ancestors. As for the Germans, they were products of a cold northern clime that might be compared with the Canada of Gibbon's day. For Gibbon they were free but not, as Tacitus implausibly reported, "indigenous," possessing a sense of honor but also "a supine indolence and a carelessness of futurity," relying on strong beer for their gross debaucheries, being unacquainted with coinage and its civilizing effects, and alternating in their social conduct between sloth and bellicosity. "The introduction of barbarism into the Roman armies," Gibbon concluded, "became everyday more universal, more necessary, and more fatal."[64]

For Gibbon religion meant Christianity, but especially Catholic and more especially Greek Christianity, with all the zeal, idolatry, credulity, superstition, and other unenlightened attitudes which the Romanized church — or rather the Christianized Rome — seemed to have brought to late Roman society, according to pagan and philosophical critics. Romans had fought only over a choice of masters, Gibbon noted (forgetting some of the enthusiasm shown by the last defenders of paganism in the time of Symmachus); Christians, and particularly Byzantine Christians, fought over mysterious ideas. The introduction of monasticism, offspring of that "fruitful parent of superstition," Egypt, and of "New Platonism," tested Gibbon's Tacitean impartiality; and at some points his irony descended into sarcasm: "I must entreat the attention of the reader," he breaks off, wearily and complicitly, in the middle of his attempt to explain the intricate doctrine of the procession of the Holy Ghost.[65]

With Gibbon the question of style is inseparable from his writing of history, which is at once literary and *en philosophe*. What he aimed at was to "hit the middle tone between a dull Chronicle and a Rhetorical declamation."[66] For Gibbon every sentence implied a judgment; every paragraph had a symmetrical shape no matter how confusing or obscure the facts of the matter; and the adjectives, metaphors, and copulas acted to sooth the reader into rational agreement: Walter Bagehot was not entirely wrong when he remarked that "it is not a style in which you can tell the truth."[67] What Bagehot said of style may apply to structure, too, and one literary scholar has argued that Gibbon's erudite epic was intended, consciously or not, to be a prose equivalent of Milton's *Paradise Lost*.[68]

Yet Gibbon — as always the philologist as well as the philosopher — did indeed want to tell the truth, both in small details and in his larger purpose of disclosing the causes of the process of decline and fall. His artful footnotes are filled with particular criticisms of earlier scholars, including the "prejudices" of Voltaire concerning the Greeks and the mistake of Montesquieu in believing that the Goths had abandoned Roman territory after their defeat of Valens at Adrianople (378), whereas in fact it was their continued presence that illustrated "the principal and immediate cause of the fall of the Western Empire of Rome."[69] For Montesquieu the two primary causes of the decline (*decadence*) of the Roman Empire had been the expansion beyond Italy (opening the doors to the admission of non–property holders into the army) and the corruption of the Roman people by their tribunes and by the incursion of foreigners, who finally became generals and even emperors.[70] In his analysis Montesquieu followed chronological order but, writing in the spirit of Machiavelli's reflective discourses on Livy rather than of Biondo's or Sigonio's historical treatment, was concerned not with the details of the historical process but with the bottom line in terms of political, constitutional, and social theory. Montesquieu wrote as a well-informed political scientist, or protosociologist, rather than an erudite and "unprejudiced" historical inquirer.[71]

Gibbon's work was more elaborately and more carefully constructed than Montesquieu's, though it largely avoided system for narrative, not, however, that Gibbon claimed perfection for his creation. Indeed he came late in life to believe that he had made a "terrible mistake" (in the words of Glen Bowersock), on the same order as Montesquieu's, by dating the fall of the empire so late and forgetting earlier periods, such as the tyranny succeeding the death of Augustus.[72] But the realization came too late and in any case had little to do with the substance of his narrative except to qualify his primary structural and explanatory metaphor, that is, the notion of decline and decadence, which he derived from the terminology of the humanists and from his own inspiration.[73]

Nevertheless, the emotional source of this metaphor remained in place. In the last chapter of the *Decline and Fall* he returned to those Roman ruins in Petrarch's day before the "clouds of barbarism were gradually dispelled" in the fifteenth century, and "the map, the description, the monuments of ancient Rome [were] elucidated by the antiquarian and the student" — referring here to the topographical work of Mabillon's successor Montfaucon — and dramatized, finally, by the Historian of the Roman Empire.[74]

Despite the Romanocentric form of his book, Gibbon's horizons were larger than those of Livy, Petrarch, and even Flavio Biondo. He composed his masterpiece with a vision of universal history in mind, a vision which he held in common with his Scottish colleagues, and which — dispensing with the biblical chronology and inclining rather to classical and even Lucretian ideas of human development — presumed a general evolution of man out of a "primitive and universal" condition of savagery not unlike that described by Lucretius through stages of shepherding, agriculture, commercial exchange, and civil society. Referring to the work of Goguet, which summarized the "four-stage theory" of human development, Gibbon continued his celebration of the comedy (in a Dantean sense of the word) of man: "His progress in the improvement and exercise of his mental and corporal faculties has been irregular and various. . . . Yet the experience of four thousand years should enlarge our hopes and diminish our apprehensions: we cannot determine to what heights the human species may aspire in their advance toward perfection; but it may be safely presumed that no people, unless the face of nature is changed, will relapse into their original barbarism."[75] In this paean to the idea of progress, Gibbon showed familiarity with the commonplaces of the philosophes, but he was obviously not aware of, or chose to ignore, the darker and more pious suspicions of Vico.

Gibbon himself did not lack critics to question his accomplishment on philosophical and literary as well as religious grounds. One carping critic complained that his ambition had taken him too far from the conventions of historiography. John Whitaker began his review with a sketch of the stages of history writing, from "wretched annals" to narrative concerned with causal sequences, "such is [Richard] *Baker's Chronicle* among ourselves," and then to a higher literary level drawing on the resources of rhetoric, such as Livy and the best historians of the earlier eighteenth century.[76] "But the activity of the human mind, is always on the wing," Whitaker continued, and strives to "reach the full point of human perfection" in style as well as "ostentatious learning." Unfortunately, "man can easily imagine what he can never execute," so that "we lose in *veracity* what we gain in *embellishments; and the authority* of the narration fades and sinks away, in the lustre of the *philosophy* surrounding it." Such had been the fault of Tacitus, and such was Gibbon's.

Beyond matters purely Roman, Gibbon had a deep sense of the historiographical traditions, learned as well as literary, on which he drew. If his model was Tacitus, "the philosophic historian whose writings will instruct the last generations of mankind," Gibbon also built on the work of Biondo, Sigonio, Lipsius, and the scholars of the previous century. He also valued the modern tradition of vernacular historical writing on which he was a part. He realized that modern history was no less moving than ancient — that, for example, the sack of Rome by Charles V's troops in 1527 (as described by his friend William Robertson) may have been more destructive than that carried out by the Goths in the time of Augustine over a millennium before. The theme of the corruption of religion, too, was carried on by "the noblest historians of the times," most notably Guicciardini, Machiavelli, Sarpi, and Davila. These, Gibbon added, "were justly esteemed the first historians of the modern languages, til in the present age, Scotland arose to dispute the prize with Italy herself."[77] The way to Gibbon's own popular historiographical success had been opened a generation earlier by the Scottish historians, especially Hume and Robertson.

Conjectural History

The Scottish turn to history in the eighteenth century was undertaken in the shadow of a larger plan, which was building a science of human nature, and culminated in the iconoclastic work of Gibbon's "bon David" Hume, "the Tacitus of Scotland."[78] Elaborating on Locke's sensationalist views, Scottish philosophers inquired into the world of man's making, which they called "moral" to distinguish it from the natural world. Reacting to the radical naturalism of Hobbes and Pufendorf, Francis Hutcheson and others sought an impulse to sociability, a "moral sense," that would account not only for human community but also for human progress. This they found in the principle of "common sense," which Vico had defined long before the efforts of Thomas Reid — who also, it may be noted, made language a key in the achievement of social coherence and continuity.[79]

The quest for an understanding of human nature was pursued into the historical realm by a series of Scottish scholars, several of them jurists and writers on natural law, including Lord Kames, Lord Monboddo, the early Adam Smith, James Millar, and most especially Adam Ferguson, William Robertson, and Dugald Stewart. The thrust of the inquiries and investigations of these men was the naturalistic desire — in most radical form in the work of Monboddo and Kames — to project human behavior, and in particular language and religion, back into the state of nature and the animal condition of man. This sort of speculative, evolutionary anthropology furnished a general and secular perspective for more specific explorations of human history, and it substituted for theodicy what Georges Gusdorf calls an "anthropodicy" of history.[80]

For social contract theorists like Hobbes, Locke, and Rousseau the "state of nature" was a hypothetical condition to contrast to civil society; but for Adam Ferguson, professor of moral philosophy at the University of Edinburgh, it was a real stage of barbarism which could be reconstructed — and in effect historicized — with the help of ancient and barbarian historians and ethnographical information from the New World, particularly North America. Questions about human nature were not matters for moral speculation; rather "we are to look for the answer in history." Like Gibbon, Ferguson looked in Roman history, whose fall, brought about by the eruption of barbarism, represents "a mighty chasm in the transition from ancient to modern history."[81] However, Ferguson looked less to national than to universal history for his answers. His *Essay on the History of Civil Society*, published in 1767, was a sort of reasoned history — "conjectural history," as Dugald Stewart would call it — arranged as a sequence of reflections on the rise of humanity from stereotypical origins to heights of civilization achieved by "the polished and commercial nations" in Ferguson's own age.[82]

Like Montesquieu, Ferguson has been regarded as a precursor of modern sociology.[83] With him, and unlike Kames, Ferguson believed that "man was born in society" and was always set apart from animals by his reason, freedom of choice, intellectual powers, and inclination to support the "interest" of himself and of others.[84] All peoples began their history in a pastoral condition and owed their notions of origins to their poets, from whose work one might infer not, to be sure, the facts of history but the mental condition of barbarism. Factors of climate were important for understanding prehistorical development, but more essential was the human potential which expressed itself not only in the accumulation of wealth but also in the history of the arts and literature, including the emergence of historical writing. Here Ferguson's example is Hellanicus, who, even before Herodotus, made an effort "to remove from history the wild representations, and extravagant fictions, with which it had been disgraced by the poets."[85]

Dugald Stewart was Ferguson's successor in the chair of moral philosophy at Edinburgh. After his retirement, he published, for the supplement of the *Encyclopaedia Britannica,* a sketch of intellectual history from the "revival of letters" down to his day.[86] Stewart had planned to follow the "Preliminary Discourse" of d'Alembert for the French *Encyclopédie;* but he found d'Alembert's scheme unsatisfactory for various reasons, including the rigid disciplinary — Baconian — separation between reason, memory, and imagination and the devaluing of this last faculty.[87] The study of history, although it is linked most directly to memory, draws also on reason and imagination if it is to qualify for placement in d'Alembert's encyclopedic tree. Moreover, d'Alembert had operated on the basis of a naive theory of mind and so "does not appear to have paid due attention to the essential difference between the history of the human species, and that of the civilized and inquisitive individual."[88] This was an unfortunate sort of "*conjectural* or *theoretical* history," which obscured rather than clarified the nature of reason and of human nature in its true development. This was not the correct method to be followed by anyone aspiring to be what Stewart called "the historian of Human Mind."[89]

David Hume had no such aspirations — as a historian, at least. Popular in his own day as a historian and suspect as a philosopher, Hume suffered, and enjoyed, a turnabout in both respects. His corrosive skepticism created a watershed in philosophical thinking, whether or not one took the Kantian gambit to elude his critiques of causation and consciousness; and as Friedrich Meinecke argued, it was at least indirectly of major significance for historical thought.[90] Hume had a commonplace view of the utility of history, praising it for a freedom from prejudice and passion that set it above everyday business and for a specificity that set it apart from the cold abstraction of philosophy. What history provided, he wrote, was "materials, from which we may form our observations, and become acquainted with the regular springs of human action and behavior."[91] Duncan Forbes seems to reject the old view that Hume "gave up" philosophy for history, and indeed in this naive form the judgment is surely oversimplified; yet it was no small choice that led to the huge, if philosophically rather humdrum, project of his history of England in the Stuart and Tudor ages.

In any case, it seems clear that in his pursuit of human nature, Hume was drawn from the natural to the moral sphere, and so from speculation to research. His essays are filled with reflections about character, human and national, and the vicissitudes of politics and the arts and sciences. It is true that Hume believed in the essential uniformity of human nature and, like his admired friend Montesquieu, looked for underlying principles. Yet he rejected the notion of the determining force of natural causes, such as climate, seizing instead upon accidents or "moral causes." He also believed that moral principles, unlike speculative opinions (meaning philosophical doctrines) were "in continual flux and revolution"; and he located them in the uncertain realm of custom and opinion, which for him — as philosopher and historian — furnished the true rulers of human behavior. Obviously, the war-torn, party-ridden history of England over the previous two centuries offered a remarkable field for pursuing his notions of human nature in times of "flux and revolution."[92]

In his *History of England,* Hume began — in the spirit both of modern skepticism and of Thucydides, whom he regarded as the "first historian" — with disapproval of the "obscurity, uncertainty, and contradiction" involved in efforts to inquire into the history of remote ages, which are dependent on untrustworthy memory and oral tradition. In any case, "The adventures of barbarous nations, even if they were recorded, could afford little or no entertainment to men born in a more cultivated age."[93] Nor was Hume pleased by the manifestations of those two products of ignorance and unreason, religious zeal and superstition, which informed the centuries between the departure of the Romans and the coming of the Normans, when at least the English were put "in a situation of receiving slowly, from abroad, the rudiments of science and cultivation, and of correcting their rough and licentious manners."[94] But Hume's narrative focused on political conflict (aside from social and cultural matters assigned to appendices), which spread across Europe in the sixteenth century, when all the Christian states "began to unite themselves into one extensive system of policy." This system was broken with the emergence of Luther, whose program owed much to the revival of learning and printing — "not," Hume added, "that reason bore any considerable share in opening men's eyes with regard to the impostures of the Romish church." Hume partook of the characteristic optimism of Enlightenment historiography about the incontrovertible fact of commercial and political progress, but his skepticism led him to more critical conclusions about its causes. He pointed in particular, and paradoxically, to the role of the zealous and superstitious Puritans in the achievement of liberty.[95] For the most part, however, in explaining the process of English history, Hume's emphasis was on the particularities of political and religious experience and of human character, and he rejected mythical constructs such as parliamentary tradition and the ancient constitution. In Hume's own experience, philosophy, by itself, was largely negative and critical; and there was more to learn in a positive way from the moral sphere and still more from the historical record — including, he noted, *"erudition,* which is nothing but an acquaintance with historical facts" — which offered probable truth and palpable insights into human nature, something philosophical reflection could never yield.[96]

William Robertson, who was a public figure in Edinburgh as well as royal historiographer, did not share the philosophical worries of Hume or the anthropological aspirations of Ferguson; but he did have a more focused devotion to historical studies, setting himself in the company of Gibbon, Hume, Ferguson, Voltaire, and Montesquieu. Like Hume, and likewise following the lead of Thucydides, Robertson scorned the prehistorical period of myth, fit only for antiquaries, and devoted himself to periods for which there was written documentation. His concern was historical narrative, and again like Hume he relegated monographic and antiquarian issues to appendices. After publishing his *History of Scotland* in 1769, he went on to his greatest work, the *History of the Reign of Charles V* (1769), which succeeded Guicciardini's history of Italy and Sleidan's Lutheran history as the most comprehensive study of the origins of modern Europe, "the period at which the political state of Europe began to assume a new form."[97] Finally came his *History of America* (1777), which treated Charles's colonial empire and the new global scene of Europe's destiny.

Robertson had still less use than Hume for the period between the fall of the Roman Empire and the formation of the modern state system. He exaggerated the stereotypical Tacitean contrast between furious barbarians and effeminate Romans and the destructive effects of that offshoot of barbarism, feudalism, though in his "proofs and illustrations" Robertson did employ the work of Ducange, Mabillon, Mably, Montesquieu, and other modern érudits in his interpretation of this nemesis of the institution of property. Like Hume, Robertson celebrated the formation of the modern European state system and consolidation of national states, though in his sketch of "the progress of society in Europe" he did not even condescend to mention Luther. Robertson was the chronicler and champion of the history of modern Europe, whose emergence he interpreted as an economic and political triumph — the chief factors being the commercial revival in Italy and the attendant impulse to liberty, followed by the progress of science and cultivation of literature.

Robertson was a Modern, but Scotland did not lack its Ancients. The most striking manifestation of Scottish national and historical enthusiasm was the affair of the Ossianic poems, published by James MacPherson in 1761. Mac-Pherson claimed to have transcribed poems transmitted by oral tradition from the third century, composed under Roman rule and reflecting a state of heroic barbarism before the introduction of Christianity. The poems were preserved by the vanity of Highlanders, he argued, who "loved to place the founders of their families in the days of fable."[98] MacPherson's imposture, though it was soon judged to be such by Samuel Johnson and other English critics, appealed to Celtic primitivism and even to historians like Ferguson; and it acquired a vast following on the Continent, especially in Germany, where it fit in with the sort of fascination with national and "poetic" origins and primitivist patriotism illustrated by the work of Herder, Adelung, and others. For Herder, who wrote an appreciative and credulous essay on "the Scottish bard," Ossian seemed even more valuable than Homer in illustrating the power of myth, magic, and "folksong" in preliterate times. In their "war-cry and lament, battle-song and funeral dirge" they could be compared, he thought, only to the five Indian nations of North America. ("Ossian has replaced Homer in my heart," says Goethe's Werther.)[99] So this neo-Celtic forgery, as most scholars came to view it, became a major factor in the Enlightenment not only in Britain but also in Germany and, converging with Rousseauean pre-Romanticism and reinforced by Diderot's translation, in France.

History of the Human Spirit

The French philosophes of the Enlightenment were in agreement with Robertson's message about the foundational value of history — and more. For them it was not enough to understand the world, it was necessary to improve on it; and this conviction shaped the French view of history as well. In France, history became a dialogue with an often stereotypical past, and the relationship, impelled by the spirit of philosophical criticism, was frankly adversarial. This was the implication of the new phase of the old intellectual feud revived by Charles Perrault's *Parallel of the Ancients and Moderns* in 1688. Perrault pretended to no novelty and indeed invoked an epistle of Horace as the locus classicus, at least for poetry, of the question of the relative value of *antiquitas* and *notivas*, and secondarily of Greeks and their pupils, the mimetic Romans. However, Horace had asked, "If poems are like wine which time improves, I should like to know what is the year that gives to writings fresh value."[100] Must authors then wait a century or more to be appreciated? Should aesthetic worth be gauged by age? And was not everything ancient a novelty once, even among the Greeks?

For the arts each successive age had its own answers to this question, but Perrault intended to go beyond Horace by proposing to examine in detail all the arts and sciences to see what degree of perfection they had achieved in the best times of antiquity, and at the same time to determine what reason and experience had added, especially in his century.[101] What Perrault found was "prodigious progress" over the previous fifty or sixty years, which he described in terms of the old conceit of four ages: infancy from the wars of the Catholic League to Richelieu, adolescence with the founding of the French Academy, maturity the following generation, and perhaps old age beginning in the present age of Louis XIV and Versailles.[102] The reason for this progress toward "perfection" was the enhancement of learning, which was dependent on the principle of authority, by reason and reflection. Nowadays, Perrault argued, authority was still essential to theology and jurisprudence but not to the other sciences and arts of the encyclopedia.

A radical and in a sense historicized version of Perrault's argument was presented in the next century by Louis Dutens, who published in 1766 *An Inquiry into the Origin of the Discoveries Attributed to the Moderns* and who reinforced the case for the Ancients with the help of the old notion of a "perennial philosophy." His purpose, as the subtitle of the French original went on to explain, was to "demonstrate that our most celebrated philosophers have taken their ideas from the works of the ancients and that many important truths about religion were known by the wise men of paganism."[103] For Dutens wisdom was indelibly ancient, and modernism was in large part plagiarism. He wanted "to place in its own native light the share the ancients have in whatever we pretend to know, and even in what has been called modern discoveries" — referring here to Polydore Vergil as well as Perrault and Fontenelle and including in his charge the ideas of Copernicus, Descartes, Locke, Leibniz, Newton, and Buffon. Despite a grain of truth, the argument of Dutens was a reductio ad absurdum of what might, as the counterpart to modernism, be called "antiquism."

In various forms the debate over the Ancients and Moderns, fortified by the "massive unadorned learning" of the seventeenth century, established the framework of the "reasoned history" of the eighteenth century, whose purpose was not merely to chronicle the words and deeds of men but also to reconstruct the "history of the human spirit [i.e., mind]" from barbaric beginnings and ancient phases to the heights of enlightened modernity. In France "the history of the human spirit" (*l'histoire de l'esprit humain — historia intellectus humani* and *Geschichte des menschlichen Geistes* being the Latin and German equivalents) was the key phrase of historical rhetoric from Fontenelle to Condorcet — and beyond.[104] It figured repeatedly in the prefaces that Fontenelle supplied for the annual volumes of the French Academy of Sciences and in the many eulogies he wrote for French savants over his very long life — which constituted indeed a major chapter in the history of the human spirit. Although Fontenelle might praise the historical erudition of a Leibniz or the contributions of Newton to chronology, he had little use for history in a conventional sense, which was "only a spectacle of the perpetual revolutions in human affairs, of the births and deaths of empires, of manners, customs, and opinions which incessantly succeed one another."[105] It was quite different with the sciences; for "if one follows historically the road they have taken, one will be astonished at the rapidity of their progress."

For Fontenelle, as for Vico and others, the story of the progress of the sciences and the human spirit did not begin with modern rational thought, as followers of Descartes or Locke might prefer to believe, but rather with the fables of the "childhood of the human race." These fables were histories as well as myths and stories, science as well as religion; and they constituted "the philosophy of the first ages."[106] For Fontenelle the early history of the human spirit was revealed in these fables, which passed "in debased form" from the Phoenicians and Egyptians to the Greeks and Romans and which began to be dispelled — in history and philosophy, if not literature — by the invention of writing. "So," Fontenelle concluded, "let us not look for anything in the fables except the history of the errors of the human mind," which was nevertheless to say, the first steps toward enlightenment. Like barbarism and civilization, myth and reason were thus given a historicized form.

Tracing "the development of the human spirit" was associated especially with the history of the sciences foundational to enlightened philosophy. Among these histories were Alexandre Savérien's *Histoire des progrès de l'esprit humain dans les sciences exactes* (1766) and J. F. Montucla's extraordinarily detailed history of mathematics (1758). The libraries are filled with histories of battles and wars, said Montucla, but with a few exceptions ignore the real benefactors of humanity. "The history of science, like that of empires, has its beginnings enveloped in darkness and obscurity," he remarked; and it was the office of the historian to restore these "almost effaced remains."[107] In remedying this neglect, moreover, Montucla also hoped to advance his own field of mathematics, for "the history of a Science . . . is a useful work that is capable of contributing to its progresses."

One distinguished French philosopher who, like Hume, turned to history was Abbé Condillac, who realized, as Fontenelle had, that not reason but "the errors of the human spirit" and "revolution of opinions" formed the substance of history and the first stages of "the progresses of the human mind" that led to higher levels of civilization.[108] In his lectures on history compiled for the instruction of the French Dauphin, Condillac also distinguished between philosophical and historical judgment. "If to us he appears obscure," he remarked of Aristotle, "it is owing to the habit we have of judging the customs of antiquity by our own." Condillac was especially sensitive to the social environment of ideas and to the economic base of learning and philosophy. "Commerce brought together people," he wrote, "who exchanged, as well as their opinions and their prejudices, their products, their lands, and their industry."[109] From the Egyptians to the Romans, he concluded, "the revolutions of opinions follow the revolutions of empires."

The most famous French celebration of the history of the human spirit was Voltaire's *Essai sur les moeurs et l'esprit des nations,* from Charlemagne to Louis XIII, which was a contribution to the philosophy of history written for the benefit of Mme. de Châtelet and which began to appear in 1739. "The History of the Human Spirit" would be the best title for this work, Voltaire wrote in 1745, when he was named royal historiographer.[110] "My main idea," he explained, "is to understand as well as possible the manners of men and the revolutions of the human spirit." Formally, he followed the old plan of universal history, beginning with a survey of geography and the origins of nations; but he altered it by employing modern ethnographic knowledge concerning the "savages" from the New World, such as the work of Father Lafitau, and of course dispensing with biblical chronology and fables of the Flood, the fantastically prolific sons of Noah, the Tower of Babel, and such childish stories.[111] For Voltaire, civilization—"the progresses of the spirit"—emerged gradually from savagery, superstition, and theocracy; and this pilgrimage toward Enlightenment took much longer than the few thousand years allotted by orthodox scholars. Nor did he put much stock in the smaller fables related by Herodotus and other classical authors concerning prehistory, or in the miraculous stories of medieval Christian authors, such as Gregory of Tours, who was "our Herodotus" during the centuries of barbarism, ignorance, intolerance, and persecution.[112]

Voltaire was the paradigm of the Whiggish historian (as the term has been employed in recent years), projecting his notions of modern rationality and civilization back into antiquity, deploring the crimes and misdemeanors of humanity, and ethnocentrically celebrating the history of the human spirit. The pattern was that of Lockean psychology, rising from simple sensations to more complex reflections and making history once again an educational process. Voltaire praised in particular these four brilliant ages of Western history: first, the glorious age of Greece, of Philip and Alexander, Pericles, Demosthenes, Aristotle, Plato, and others, when "the rest of the world as then known was barbaric"; second, the age of Caesar, Augustus, Lucretius, Cicero, Livy, Virgil, and Horace; third, the age after the fall of Constantinople, when "the arts [were] once again transplanted from Greece to Italy," and along with them what the Italians called *virtù,* and then extended to France; and finally, the age of Louis XIV and the French Academy, "that one which, of the four, most nearly approaches perfection," not because of the arts but because of the improvement of human reason.[113]

To the writing of history Voltaire brought common sense, reason, a broad cosmopolitanism, and a wit equal to that of Gibbon, though without the latter's subtlety and irony; but he also brought an extraordinary, if deliberate, naïveté and lack of sympathy for earlier ages. His so-called philosophy of history was a mixed bag. Opponent though he was of "prejudice," Voltaire was also, through his often naive skepticism, prejudiced against the learning of the monks and academicians; critical though he was of ignorance, folly, and evil, he was nevertheless curiously uncritical in his approach to history. "Voltaire," wrote Ernest Renan, impelled by his own devotion to philology, "has done more damage to historical studies than an invasion by the barbarians."[114]

There were other efforts, contemporaneous with Voltaire's, to study the history of civilization on a broad scale and in human rather than providential terms, especially Turgot's discourses at the Sorbonne at midcentury and A. Y. Goguet's study of the origin and progress of laws, arts, and science. Speaking for humanity and from the standpoint of universal history, Turgot began his *Philosophical Review of the Successive Advances of the Human Mind* by noting the "ridiculous opinions" which, for the philosophe, marked "our first steps" and then traced the various forms of progress leading up to the cultural heights from which he looked and passed his judgments. "Historical times cannot be traced back further than the invention of writing," he believed, and he was no less practical minded in his ideas on the causes of human progress. Turgot—along with Adam Smith—was one of the formulators of the four-stage theory of cultural development: the ages of gathering, of fishing and hunting, of agriculture, and of commerce underlying the shift from barbarism to full civilization.[115] This thesis also appeared in Goguet's study, which was based on the conviction that "the history of laws, arts, and sciences is, properly speaking, the history of the human spirit," which correlated the manners of peoples in particular epochs not with political arrangements, as Montesquieu had done, but rather with the material bases of society.[116]

The most enthusiastic and highly argued history of the human spirit in eighteenth-century France was Condorcet's *Sketch of a Historical Picture of the Progress of the Human Mind* (1794), which was composed (like Raleigh's universal history) in prison during the last months of his life. Like Bossuet, Condorcet divided universal history into ten epochs; but he followed not biblical chronology but rather a "reasoned" sort of history, analogous again to Lockean psychology and projected onto a collective tabula rasa. Condorcet followed the improvement of social skills, technology, and the concomitant advancement of learning—from tribal, pastoral, and agricultural society, through the ancient and medieval periods, down to the invention of printing, the rise of modern philosophy, and the founding of the French Republic in the age of revolutions. Like Voltaire and other conjectural historians, Condorcet drew on travelers' reports to infer the character of prehistorical humanity. For later periods he shifted to conventional historical materials; and again he treated them en philosophe, following the comparative and "scientific" methods which had been cultivated by Montesquieu and Bodin long before.

After tracing in this reasoned fashion the earlier history of the human spirit, Condorcet turned to his own agenda — "reason, toleration, and humanity" — presented in the form of prophecy, which was but an extension of historical inquiry. He briefly acknowledged the threat of decline due to overpopulation but was convinced that reason could overcome this obstacle, too. "If there is to be a science for predicting the progress of the human race, for directing and hastening it," he wrote, "the history of the progress already achieved must be its foundation."[117] So he made his transition from the ninth to the tenth epoch, which was devoted to "the future progress of the human mind" and represented Condorcet's secular version of the prophetic and eschatological dimensions of Christian tradition.

As the future of humanity depended on reason and "the complete annihilation of prejudice," so it required another sort of historical science, which had to go beyond the mere collection of facts and accounts of individuals to the study of social groups and systematic empirical observation within the framework of the idea of "organic perfectibility." Condorcet lamented that, owing partly to the servility of official historians and partly to the distortions produced "by self-interest, by the spirit of party, by patriotic pride, or merely by the mood of the moment," this "most important chapter in the history of man" had been neglected by historians.[118] "It is only when we come to this final link in the chain," he wrote concerning the ninth epoch, "that our contemplation of historical events and the reflections that occur to us are of true utility." As humanity approaches perfection, we might infer, so history becomes futurology; and such was the heritage taken up by French utopians, positivists, and not a few historians in the next century.[119]

Carl Becker represented the more popular French writings about the past as a "new history," though constructed within the framework of an old, crypto-Christian vision of universal world order.[120] Attempts to discredit Becker's argument comparing medieval Christian and Enlightenment conceptions of human experience in time are based on a naive and literal reading of a thesis that is at once ironic and paradoxical. Voltaire and Condorcet looked out across very different cultural horizons than Augustine and Orosius, and they had of course very different hopes for the future and the "new millennium." Yet they also saw history as a sort of pilgrimage from error to truth, whose higher meaning might be deciphered by men of wisdom and good will. A proud and expansive, if flawed and culpable, humanity remained the center of concern; and while the words of praise, blame, and commemoration may have changed in many respects, much of the old music could still be heard by those who would listen.

Cultural History

The light of reason shone differently in Germany — "In Germany the Enlightenment was on the side of theology," Hegel summed up, "while in France it turned against the Church" — and history took a rather different form, too.[121] Lutheran spirituality gave German *Geist* a very different force than French *esprit* or even English *spirit*. Respect for philosophy and philosophical tradition led Lutheran scholars to avoid both Cartesian skepticism and rationalism and Catholic dogmatism and to find truth by the critical and "eclectic" examination of the legacy of Western learning. As in France, England, and Scotland, the study of history continued to be associated with law and jurisprudence, and ecclesiastical history and theological questions were still approached in historical terms. In very different ways from the French and British, German scholars saw, under the influence of eclecticism, a growing alliance between history and philosophy. The idea was, following the Lutheran history of theology, that in the pursuit of truth, error, too, had to be examined. This was the attitude underlying the aphorism of Christian Thomasius, professor of law at the University of Halle, that "history and philosophy are the two eyes of wisdom, and if one is missing, then one has only half vision" (*einäugy*).[122]

What historical methods brought was a greater concern, at least ostensibly, with human truth, factual and probable if not intellectual and certain. This was the profession in particular of ecclesiastical historians such as Ludwig von Seckendorf, whose history of Lutheranism (1692) was a response to Maimbourg's similar history as well as to Bossuet's *History of the Variations of*

Protestant Churches (1688), and especially Gottfried Arnold in his *Nonpartisan History of the Church and Heresy* (1699), whose "method" was based on the premise that impartiality was the key to historical truth.[123] For this view there was of course good classical authority, but Arnold had a more pious precedent, which was spiritual tradition. Like Flacius Illyricus, he found historical continuity in the thin line of "witnesses to truth" (*Zeugen*) from the earliest writings on Christ onward.[124]

Another prominent Lutheran historian was Johann Lorenz von Mosheim, whose *Ecclesiastical History* (1753) pursued the arguments of Luther and attacks on papal abuses. Mosheim followed the work of Sleidan and Seckendorff, though in a much more partisan way and with attention to both "external" and "internal" history, the former including institutions and events, "calamitous" as well as "prosperous," and the latter including learning, philosophy, theology, heresies, dissensions, and science.[125] For Mosheim the effects of Lutheranism were liberation not only from Romanism but also from servitude to Aristotle, both of which were forms of materialism irreconcilable with the freedom of thought guaranteed by Lutheran tradition; and following the severe Eclectic line, he passed judgments on the doctrinally correct and incorrect.

Mosheim was a founder of the University of Göttingen (1734) and its first chancellor, and it was there that the study of history found its Germanophone center for the rest of the century.[126] The teaching of empirical social science, in the form of cameralism and statistics, gave a practical base for the study of history in more humanistic forms, which inspired dozens of treatises on historical method by eighteenth-century German professors such as F. W. Bierling, J. M. Chladenius, Gottlieb Stolle, J. C. Gatterer, Johannes Müller, and J. C. Adelung — not to mention J. G. Herder and Friedrich Schiller.[127] As in the old *artes historicae* these essays and treatises on *Historik* considered questions of partisanship, objectivity, historical criticism, periodization, the "faith of history," and the history of history as supplements to monographic studies and universal history. In the work of these pious and largely Lutheran champions of historical and empirical methods and frequent critics of natural law, including Gatterer, Justus Möser, and A. L. Schlözer, scholars have seen the early stirrings of German *Historismus* ever since the classic book by Friedrich Meinecke.[128]

Meinecke surveyed this field in terms of the figures most visible to posterity — the "mountaintops" of historical theory — while Peter Reill and other scholars followed his explorations into the foothills and valleys of historical practice. Meinecke also tended to assimilate his chosen forerunners to German nationalism, in violation, perhaps, of the principle of individuality on

which historicism was founded. Some of the scholars he discussed may be
better understood not as protohistoricists but as conservative and backward-
looking scholars concerned more with the people in development than with
the state still unborn. This was the case, for example, with Möser, the historian
of Osnabrück, who was an inquirer into the specificity of the customs and
legal traditions of his land and the "local reason" (*Lokalvernunft*) which
prevailed there.[129] This was in conspicuous contrast to the panoramic universalism of French historians of the human spirit and Scottish practitioners of
conjectural history.

History was indeed "in the air" in Germanophone territories. Historicism
ante litteram found an institutional base both in the universities and in the
academies, and an audience in the academic section of the public sphere
formed by the proliferation of learned journals before 1800 — some 600 of
them (15 percent of the total) being devoted to historical studies.[130] Not only
historians but also philosophers, theologians, and jurists helped to give promi-
nence to historical attitudes and methods; and Swiss scholars such as Isaac
Iselin, J. J. Bodmer, Johannes von Müller, J. G. Sulzer, and Jacob Wegelin
made important contributions. It was in the Göttingen school, however, and
especially in the teaching and writing of Gottfried Achenwall, J. C. Gatterer,
J. M. Michaelis, J. S. Pütter, L. T. Spittler, A. L. von Schlözer, later Karl von
Eichhorn, and Gustav Hugo, godfather of the nineteenth-century historical
school of law, that historicism came to prevail before the Wars of Liberation,
when the center of historicism shifted from Göttingen to the new University of
Berlin, founded in 1807.

One of the largest of Meinecke's precursory mountaintops was Herder, who
of course reached much further into the public sphere than his Göttingen
contemporaries. Herder's contributions, like those of his contemporaries Voltaire and Gibbon, were richer and father reaching than those of any academic.
Herder's path to historical studies was philosophical, literary, encyclopedic;
and at all times the key for him (as, altogether independently, for Vico) was
language, or rather languages, since for him, unlike Locke and Condillac,
language as a general category was virtually, or humanly, meaningless. In an
early essay Herder suggested that "each language has its distinct national
character," which was in turn an expression of local conditions and experiences, and nations possessed no ideas without corresponding words.[131] Moreover, after the natural acquisition of a native tongue, learning foreign and dead
languages was an artificial process which would ever miss the unique spirit in
which meaning, that is, human and historical meaning, lay.

Herder's concern was restoring a connection between humanity and nature,
with language as the primary link between the two. Like Vico, he dismissed

the prejudice of philosophers that, in some spiritual way, concepts preceded words; on the contrary, words were born of human reactions to the material environment and only later acquired conceptual meaning as names.[132] Moreover, "Language is always a function of the general culture"; it grows with the development of kinship groups into nations and is not understandable in universal terms. If historians would consider such factors, they would far surpass the abstract and doctrinaire writings of historians of religion like Mosheim and historians of philosophy like J. J. Brucker.[133]

Herder aimed ultimately at a philosophy of history but had a quite different idea of what was entailed by this coinage of Voltaire, which for some scholars seemed an oxymoron. "A historian is not a philosopher," wrote Adelung, "who spins out of himself like a spider and who . . . would write not history but a novel."[134] While Voltaire thought mainly in terms of extracting the enlightened aspects of history as a background for his own agenda, Herder (again like Vico, though again independently) aspired to a larger vision of human nature and a fundamental critique, or rather a metacritique, of reason and philosophy as understood in the eighteenth century. Herder wanted indeed to understand the human spirit and its history, but it was the "unique spirit" that concerned him, and this led him to the new discipline that emerged in precisely those years in which he was formulating his philosophy of history — namely, cultural history.

The terminological shift is precise and significant. In 1770 Herder had written of culture in a modern, that is, a social rather than a pedagogical, sense, but his usual term was still *spirit*. In 1774 his *Yet Another Philosophy of History* told the story of the development of the human spirit (*menschliches Geist*), employing the ancient and Augustinian conceit of the ages of man, from its appearance in the state of nature to the emergence of the *Volk*.[135] "Only through spirit," Herder later wrote, "which brings to history and draws from it, do we participate in the history of humanity and people."[136] It was this "spiritual" and philosophical approach to universal history that led to his notions of the *Volksgeist* and *Zeitgeist* and the historicist belief that "you must enter the spirit of a nation before you can share even one of its thoughts and deeds."[137] The terms *spirit* and *human spirit* in a Herderian sense inform this whole effort to formulate "another philosophy of history."

Ten years later, Herder resumed his theme on a much larger scale in his *Ideas for the Philosophy of History of Mankind*, this time shifting to the new terminology of *culture*, and *history of culture*, in the sense of the collective cultivation of intellectual and linguistic attributes.[138] Not *Geist* but *Kultur*, not *Geschichte des menschlichen Geistes* but *Kulturgeschichte* became the words to conjure with in Herder's *retractatio* of the question of the philosophy of history. This is the terminology that would seize the attention and imagination of scholars for the next two centuries.[139]

In fact, Herder denied that "by employing a few figurative expressions, the *childhood, infancy, manhood,* and *old age* of our species," he had presumed to formulate a general "history of culture" (*Geschichte der Kultur*) and still less a general philosophy of history, "which follows the chain of tradition" and is equivalent to "the education of the human race," invoking here Lessing's famous title. Even in this second book he offered only ideas toward these conceptual goals — of which one of the most important was joining the four-stage theory to that of the organic development of *Kultur.*[140] Herder's point was that in contrast to the *civilization* of scholars and philosophers, *culture* could involve the whole people (*Kultur des Volkes*) and so represented the best road to an understanding not only of history but also of human nature.[141] In opposition to idealistic philosophy, Herder believed that the object of criticism as well as historical inquiry must be human, not "pure," reason, that this involved analysis not of transcendent spirit but of its concrete cultural man-ifestations, especially those of language, and that it required the study of the culture of reason (*Kultur der Vernunft*) and the whole historical process which had produced it.[142] Kant proclaimed his to be an "age of criticism," but in a rationalist sense, to which Herder felt bound to react with a metacriticism that reasserted the centrality of language and historical experience; and in the spirit of this *Metakritik* came his second *Philosophy of History.*

Herder worked within the genre of universal history in a modernized form which expressed the experience of humanity in terms not of a pilgrimage but of organic and evolutionary development, but this view was severely qualified by his sense of individuality and relativity. "People who are ignorant of history and know only their own age," he had written in an early fragment, "believe that the present taste is the only one, and so necessary that nothing else besides it is even thinkable."[143] He accepted the French notions of progress and per-fectibility, but neither could be expressed as a constant or universal, since both could only occur in a specific cultural context: "Each form of human perfec-tion then, is, in a sense, national and time-bound and, considered most specifi-cally, individual."[144] As for progress, it was not only irregular, but it had many "costs"; and Herder waxed sarcastic at the national and temporal chauvinism of complacent Moderns who were incapable of looking back to earlier stages of the human condition.

Herder's first principle, like that of Vico, was the essential historicity of humanity, and this is what gave "anthropology" priority over philosophy. "Thus the history of man is ultimately a theatre of transformations, which he alone can review, who animates all these figures, and feels and enjoys in them all."[145] Invoking this same theatrical topos, medieval and Renaissance scholars placed man, epistemologically, at the midpoint of the universe — between the two horizons of the earthly and the heavenly, as Dante has said — which (as Baudouin had pointed out in his *Institution of Universal History* two centuries earlier) was an ideal vantage point from which to view the universe. What Herder did was to temporalize this conceit and turn the Great Chain of Being into a "chain of change" — a Chain of Becoming — so that "in every age, thus, every human being stands, so to speak, at a midpoint . . . [and] is able to surround himself with the vanished images of his ancestors . . . [and] also to cast a prophetic glance into future ages beyond the grave and, so to speak, see children and grandchildren treading upon his ashes."[146]

Other scholars followed Herder in this cultural turn, for example, Christoph Meiners, professor of "secular learning" at Göttingen and one of the most prolific historians of the century. Like Herder, Meiners was not content with Kant's answer to the question of "What is enlightenment?" "Was ist *wahre* Aufklärung?" is the way the Meiners rephrased it in historical terms, which for him was the historical question "How has enlightenment come about?" Like Herder, he sought the answer to his question in the light not of pure reason but rather of the universal history of humanity and its culture.[147] This genetic approach led Meiners to questions of the economic, social, and even sexual base (e.g., Greek homosexuality) of culture. His *History of Humanity* (1775) presented a manifesto of cultural history, which for him included the bodily needs — clothing, cooking, lodging, tools, and the other aspects of material culture, as it was already called — of people presupposed by the progress and "revolutions" of the human spirit. This was the legacy passed on by the old cultural history to a whole series of "new" cultural histories of the nineteenth, twentieth, and (if history is any guide) twenty-first centuries.[148]

IO

Modern Historiography

The last stage of history, of our world, of our time . . .
— G. W. F. Hegel

By the end of the eighteenth century, the study of history had achieved the status not only of a literary genre, discipline, and "science," with its own complex history, but also of a profession. There were established chairs of history in the universities of Europe, especially in England, France, and Germany, as well as official historiographers, official collections of documents, and other kinds of private and public support for practitioners of history.[1] What was new in the Enlightenment was the encounters between history and philosophy, which had likewise, and even earlier, emerged as a professional field with an academic base. The confrontations and rapprochements between these two old rivals, which occurred in a variety of cultural contexts and on several levels, were central to the "Enlightenment project" and to the rise of modern historicism and have been central to Western historical studies down to the present. They are central, too, to more recent debates over modernity and postmodernity and over the "end of history."

New Faces of History

Two and a quarter millennia after the nominal beginnings of the Western historiographical tradition, the visages of Herodotus and Thucydides were still visible. They could still be seen, on the one hand, in the learned and anthropological history concerned with cultural values and human self-knowledge on a world scale and, on the other, in the pragmatic history devoted to questions of local politics and power. Beyond the investigative tourism in the amateurish style of Herodotus, however, there was a vast accumulation of ethnographic information based on encyclopedic erudition, voyages of discoveries, and excavations; beyond Thucydidean narrative, there was also a great tradition of Tacitean and Machiavellian political and didactic analysis; and beyond both there was a drive to make historical understanding transcend its empirical foundations and become philosophical in a global sense, extending the old tradition of universal history into the larger cosmos that modern science was revealing. Of course, all of this was carried on under new conditions of understanding, communication, and social and political life in an age of science, commercial progress, revolution, and — as Herodotus and Thucydides could well appreciate — periodic wars of conquest and expansion.

The study of history had also come — in what Hegel called a "fragmentary" way — to inform other disciplinary traditions, beginning especially with the history of literature, which since the sixteenth century had itself become both discipline and genre. In Germany the history of literature (*historia literaria; Historie der Gelahrheit*) included all the "liberal arts" and higher "sciences," each of which also had its own history and bibliography. Most prominent was the history of philosophy (*historia philosophica*), which had itself become a science and, as in the standard handbook of Gottlieb Stolle (1718), was subdivided into logic, psychology (*Pneumatik* or *Geisteslehre*), natural law, and moral philosophy.[2] History still found a place under the last rubric, but it also achieved a larger interdisciplinary status. From the sixteenth century there were histories of science and of particular sciences, of art and of particular arts, of law and of particular legal traditions, of moral philosophy, political economy, social formations, and institutions; and these were all part of the larger areas of cultural history as explored variously by Vico, Voltaire, Ferguson, Herder, Meiners, Iselin, and many others.

What is more, Western historiography could now look back on itself self-consciously and reflexively, opening up further the history of history and creating both a taxonomy of historiographical forms and a canon of historical works through ancient, medieval, and modern times — the threefold periodization which had long been conventional since the work of Christoph Cellarius in the previous century.[3] Following the lead of Bodin, La Popelinière, and many others, Lenglet du Fresnoy published the *Method for the Study of History* (1713), which enjoyed several editions and translations and offered one of many summaries of historical writings, expansions of the reading list appended to Bodin's *Method* and likewise arranged both chronologically and topically.[4] The old distinction, now become a progression of annal, chronicle, history, and "perfect history," was also preserved, and indeed enhanced, by various forms of philosophical history—giving modern and enlightened fulfillment to the ancient rhetorical notion of history as philosophy teaching by example and the Renaissance ideal of perfect history.

Archaeololatry and historiogenesis were as much in evidence as ever, although questions of origins were posed within different and rapidly changing cultural horizons for those who, like Vico and Herder, chose to evade theological convention or even, like Voltaire and Condorcet, to reject it. Mythology remained in a speculative stage—a sort of "spiritual archaeology," as Gusdorf calls it—subject to various theories of human nature, primitive psychology, oral tradition, and literary composition.[5] Such was the case with Friedrich Creuzer's massive collections of myths (1810–11), which provided a larger base for comparative mythology but which came under fire by more "scientific" mythologists in the nineteenth century.[6] Specific focus on the "Homeric question," from Vico's "discovery of the true Homer" in the early part of the eighteenth century to F. A. Wolf's iconoclastic *Prolegomenon to Homer* at the end (1795), provided a more concrete field of investigation, though not—then or later—a basis for scholarly consensus.[7]

The question of linguistic origins had gone beyond the Psammeticus stage of inquiry, although, to judge from Condillac's statue of natural man, the Adamic and antihistorical "epistemological myth of the first man" (in the phrase of Gusdorf) still seemed a useful hypothesis for speculation.[8] Of much greater significance were the investigations of Gibbon's friend William Jones and others into oriental languages and the revelations concerning the links between Sanskrit and classical Western languages.[9] A similar contrast can be seen between natural law theories of social contract and "first occupant" rights and the scholarly studies of Vico, Terrasson, and others into the Twelve Tables and other monuments of ancient legislation, which had been the object of erudite inquiry by historians and jurists for several centuries.[10] These lines of inquiry, which were begun by old-regime scholars, constitute separate chapters in the later story of modern historical study, which is a continuation of the present account (and which still needs telling in a coherent way).

However, it was not only the more intensive and systematic examination of traditional sources and expansion of cultural horizons that set new expressions on the faces of history; it was also the infiltration of new information and attitudes, especially from the embryonic disciplines of anthropology and archaeology. *Anthropology* was nominally a field of study from the early sixteenth century, but the term referred to the study of human nature in a physiological or philosophical sense, as Kant and later idealists continued to do. In the eighteenth century the field was extended through the accumulation of ethnographic information by travelers and missionaries, such as the Jesuit Lafitau, and later by government-supported expeditions, such as that conceived by Baron Degérando for the *Société des observateurs de l'homme* at the turn of the nineteenth century.[11] This, too — like La Popelinière's wild project two centuries earlier — was in the service of "the proper study of mankind" (Degérando, citing Pope's famous formula), self-knowledge, and a systematic "science of human nature," but it also helped to reshape the study of history.

Archaeology also had a long semantic history, being associated first with Greek prehistory and later with early modern "antiquities." By the eighteenth century, however, archaeology had achieved disciplinary form, thus adding the study of things to that of words in the inventory of historical sources.[12] There had been important Renaissance precedents, especially in the study of art history, heralding the more reflective work of Winckelmann and others in the Enlightenment, just as folkloric studies of the Romantic period continued literary history. Winckelmann himself approached art history and archaeology as ideal expressions of cultural history as a whole.[13] As for excavations, digs, and material finds, this impulse can also be seen in the "cabinets of curiosities" and museological collections of the Renaissance, which included both human and natural history. From the seventeenth century, government-sponsored investigations were mounted in Scandanavia, Russia, Germany, England, and elsewhere. A chair of antiquities was established at the University of Uppsala as early as 1662, and the beginnings of the London Society of Antiquaries can be traced back to 1707. A treatise published by A. A. Rhode in 1719 attempted to establish rules for proper excavation of burial sites, which he regarded as more important for German prehistory than all of Tacitus's *Germania*.[14] Not that ideological factors were eliminated from prehistory; rather they were shifted to another intellectual battleground.

In Germany the *ars historica* (*die historische Kunst*) was again, as in the sixteenth century, raised to the level of science (*Geschichtswissenschaft*), though more systematically. Again a primary agent was philology, which became the subject of a pioneering seminar in Halle from 1737 and which continued to develop critical methods essential to the science of antiquity (*Altertumswissenschaft*).[15] Of primary importance were C. G. Heyne, who founded the Göttingen seminar in 1763 and brought to it an interest in art history and mythology, and his followers J. G. Eichhorn and F. A. Wolf, students respectively of the Old Testament and of the Homeric poems.[16] The older fields of chronology, geography, heraldry, genealogy, paleography, diplomatics, epigraphy, and numismatics were joined to the academic study of history as "auxiliary sciences" (*Hilfswissenschaften*); and to these were added statistics, a quantitative

Staatswissenschaft which itself was identified with history in the sense of empirical knowledge.[17] In German universities this conglomerate of historical disciplines was organized (like the fields of philosophy, philology, law, and others) into a pedagogical "encyclopedia" that reinforced the scientific status of history.[18]

Universal history, a medieval and Renaissance genre still taught as such in German universities, and the "conjectural history" of French and British scholars were transformed by these new revelations and by other discoveries made in geology, paleontology, and biology. Fossils had long presented a theoretical problem, but not until the early nineteenth century were discoveries acknowledged to have discredited the assumptions of biblical chronology.[19] Eighteenth-century evolutionism, adopted by Herder, Ferguson, and others, expanded temporal horizons further; and while fundamentalists kept the debate going both in geology and in biology, nineteenth-century cultural history was, long before Darwinism, grounded on the deep evolutionary perspective suggested by that alliance between nature and history which Cassirer regarded as so fundamental to the philosophy of the Enlightenment.

In this expanding and panoramic perspective narrow questions of causation seemed inadequate, and other sorts of analogy, or metaphor, were introduced to express historical change, most notably the notion of influence. Originally a medico-astrological term, *influence* is represented mainly in this sense in the *Encyclopédie* entry. More generally, however, *influence* was "a term which is used to explain the connection between soul and body," and so it was easy to extend it to questions of "spirit" in a social and cultural, as well as a psychological, sense. This is strikingly illustrated by several of the prize questions posed by eighteenth-century academies. "What has been the reciprocal influence of the opinions of a people on its language and language on opinions?" asked the Berlin Academy in 1757; and again in 1780, "What has been the influence of government on literature among peoples in which it has flourished, and the influence of letters on government"; and that posed by the French Institute in 1802 concerning "the spirit and influence of the Reformation of Luther" on the various states of Europe.[20] Such questions provided inspiration for various historical works, including (for the first of these questions) that of Condillac and (for the last) the French émigré Charles de Villers, whose work was a manifesto for what he called the "gradual cultivation [*culture*] of the human race" and "the successive progresses of enlightenment."[21]

To many of the revolutionary generation, as to Louis Le Roy more than two centuries before, the "road [was] open." Reason, Justice, Humanity — this was Condorcet's prescription in his account and prediction of the "progress of the human mind," though he did entertain Malthusian doubts about the demographic problems. Development, Progress, Modernization—this might be taken as the motto of European historiography at the turn of the nineteenth century. Whether these values would take the form of revolutionary or evolutionary change depended on factors beyond the vision of historians and even prophets like Condorcet, but this did not prevent speculators like Kant and Hegel from offering their unrigorous, metahistorical conclusions about the shape of the future as well as the past. Millennialist habits die hard, as is again becoming apparent in the waning years of this millennium and (some would say) posthistorical age.

New Contexts of History

Historical inquiry has had different "scenes" as well as "fortunes" (in the terms of Nicholas Jardine), that is, different contexts in which the forms of Western historiography have been shaped.[22] The largest intellectual context was that defined by print culture, which appeared just in time, as historians have often noticed, to accommodate the first stages of Renaissance learning, the humanist republic of letters, the Protestant Reformation, the growing demand for textbooks in schools and universities, the public arena of religious, social, and political controversy, emergent commercial interests, the various branches of natural and human sciences and vernacular literatures, and the complex process of state building. With each of these phenomena historical writing was associated in one way or another, and it came to record and to interpret them, usually—except by skeptics or defenders of an old orthodoxy—in terms of the mythology of modernity and progress of the human spirit.

Other scenes of inquiry were provided by the monastic orders, which manifested their piety through antiquarian studies; the universities, which shaped history to pedagogical, religious, and social needs; the academies, which brought scholars together for cooperative and competitive scholarship; the educated reading public, which made aesthetic taste a major factor in historical writing; the learned journals, which were addressed to this public; the libraries, public as well as private, which brought together and made available the researches of earlier generations; and the archives, national, provincial, and ecclesiastical, which were open to researchers and given privileged position as a source of information second only to Herodotean autopsy.[23] In all of these contexts the ancient ideals of historical study were maintained, at least nominally; but of course partisanship of one sort or another was inseparable from all of these institutional contexts, especially those touching on religious passions and political interests—passions and interests which would be much magnified in an age of revolution, nationalism, and world war, in which history, too, would be conscripted — or, as in the case of Jacobinism and Utilitarianism, rejected as unfit for service.

Economic conditions were not only part of the context but a favorite target of inquiry by Enlightenment historians. From antiquity, historians had been aware of the connections between civilization and wealth, usually in the patronage offered by generous princes to scholars and artists; and this topos was continued by humanists as a way both of celebrating and of appealing for royal generosity. In the eighteenth century, however, this small connection was expanded to a general principle positing economic surplus and "luxury" as necessary preconditions for high culture. Christoph Meiners, who wrote extensively on the rise of the sciences in classical Greece, also investigated the related phenomenon of *Luxus*.[24] A century later, one of Meiners's successors in the field repeated the argument as an axiom of cultural history, that "Ohne Luxus kein Kultur," without material base no cultural superstructure.[25]

Despite the universalist ideals of many eighteenth scholars, it is difficult to generalize about the new history of that age. National styles of historiography were divergent according to the political divisions of later eighteenth-century Europe. In France history was geared increasingly to an ideology of progress, promoted by the earlier "prophets of Paris," starting with Turgot and carried on by Condorcet, the Saint-Simonians, and the Positivists. However, the scientism, and social scientism, of Condorcet and the ideologues operated to give history a subordinate role.[26] For the latter, history was to be studied only *after* the inculcation of rational principle, its basic function being, like that of anthropology, to supply facts about human nature for more theoretical and systematic studies carried out on a higher level. It was partly in reaction to this — as well as to the unhistorical attitudes of natural law, the Philosophical School, as it was called, and revolutionary radicalism — that the "new history" of Restoration France would turn back again, in scholarly if not necessarily in political terms, to the old regime and the social and cultural background of revolution, restoring to historical studies their foundational position.

In Germany history was concerned especially with the culture of the *Volk* and later with the new nation which might arise from the Napoleonic wars and its destructive cultural and political intrusions. *Kulturgeschichte* flourished in the generation after Herder and indeed throughout the next century, though not in a professional or academic form until the efforts of Karl Lamprecht; and the literary and linguistic thrust of Herder's approach to culture would be continued and reinforced by Romantic scholars like Humboldt, the Schlegels, and the Grimms.[27] However, as the center of historical studies shifted from Göttingen to the new University of Berlin, founded in 1807, a new generation of German scholars would turn to the Thucydidean and Machiavellian questions of politics and power — questions which would preoccupy Ranke and his school in the generation before German unification. They would also turn back to the project of formulating the longer historiographical canon of which they claimed to be the culmination.[28] This retrospective inventorying of the historiographical canon was the work begun by Friedrich Creuzer and Ludwig Wachler, and continued by other scholars in the nineteenth century, who celebrated their forefathers — those "brave men before Agamemnon" studied by F. X. von Wegele and others.[29] It was on this scholarly foundation that Eduard Fueter's classic handbook was based.[30]

In England, modern historical writing remained for the most part in conventional channels, often associated with the sort of political conservatism represented by Edmund Burke, who indeed celebrated reason, but only "the collected reason of ages." "In history," declared Burke, drawing on the commonplaces of the *ars historica* tradition, "a great volume is unrolled for our instruction, drawing the materials of future wisdom from past errors and infirmities of mankind."[31] Society was indeed a contract, but one made not in nature but set between generations over time. The myth of the "ancient constitution" was still in place among historians as well as common lawyers, its latest application being the argument that these traditions had preserved England from revolutionary upheaval and despotic repercussions. And English historical writing has for the most part remained in this exceptionalist, if not insular, mode, which radically localizes and atomizes historical experience, even in recent "revisionist" forms.

In the last decade of the century, the French Revolution became the center of attention for questions about historical change, marking as it did, according to defenders and prosecutors alike, an apparent break with the past and with the nature of history as conceived by writers for centuries. The revolution presented an enormous challenge to conventional approaches to causal analysis, and a century later Lord Acton, reviewing the extraordinary range of explanations, admitted that he had no "deciding evidence."[32] Nor has the century since Acton's review brought scholars nearer consensus. Instead, the number of theories has grown — from which we should be able to learn something about the nature of modern historical thinking as it has taken shape since the eighteenth century, which is that it advances, or at least changes, as much by debate as by inquiry.

It is clear that revisionism is built into the structure of historical inquiry and interpretation, and yet it is often a sort that rejects a modern view for an earlier, formerly superseded position. Historians not only repeat one another; they also reject one another, according to a dialectical pattern that has generational and ideological aspects. For example (not to enter into the never-ending disputes about the revolution), jurists from the thirteenth century, and historians from the sixteenth century, debated the provenance of feudal institutions in terms of Roman and German origins, and the controversy persisted into the eighteenth century still more passionately. One underlying issue was still whether the "common law" of France was to be identified with Roman law or with feudal custom, and in particular that of Paris.[33] For lawyers it was a matter of authority, and — like the antiquaries in the time of James I of England — historians were warned not to inquire too curiously into incendiary and perhaps indemonstrable questions of origins. Montesquieu (with defenders of the *thèse nobiliaire* generally) was essentially on the side of the Germanists in this *Kulturkampf;* although (to judge from the Napoleonic Code) the Romanists ultimately triumphed in juridical terms, the historiographical debate has continued down to the present century.

No less than the Reformation, the Age of Revolution inspired and distorted historical studies and at the same time questioned their social and cultural value. As Galilean science and Cartesian philosophy had both in effect rejected history as irrelevant to a proper method, so too French revolutionaries in the first flush of constitutional — and second flush of republican — euphoria rejected it as a social burden to be thrown off. "Erudition," writes Sophie-Anne Leterrier, "was decapitated by the French Revolution."[34] The results of enthusiasm included destruction of the corporate structure of the old regime, with spillover fury directed against history itself in the form of the archival records of the monarchy and its "feudal" base. Peasants in the summer of 1789 set about burning the hated "feudal" charters; and on the second anniversary of the famous night of 4 August, more documents were destroyed in the republican celebration.[35] Reaction to such extremism came soon, and indeed it was the government of the revolutionary period that, in the summer of 1794, revived the old enterprise of reorganizing the national archives. Historical consciousness was not something to be wiped away, as radicals (perhaps in the spirit of Condorcet) came to understand, but rather to be controlled, revised, and directed — as indeed were its various "contexts." This began another phase of antiquarian effort in France and a new appreciation for the national past.[36]

History and Philosophy

History and philosophy, like rhetoric and philosophy, have had a running battle over the centuries, the fundamental difference being that the former dealt with universals and the latter with particulars — the former "nomothetic," in Wilhelm Windelband's sociological version of this old binomial, and the latter "idiographic."[37] This is a distinction that has been embedded in historiographical premises and practice from the beginning down to the present, making most professional historians suspicious of general and even middle-range concepts. Of course even simple narrative historians cannot avoid questions of the meaning of the materials that they assemble and to which they give shape, but claiming philosophic status for their inquiries is more difficult and, even if desirable, debatable.

Yet this is what Enlightenment historians like Vico, Voltaire, Condorcet, and Herder seem in retrospect to be doing—laying foundations for a never-completed structure called the philosophy of history, which emerged just as *history* in a singular form was supplanting particular histories.[38] Vico's life-work was an original attempt to resolve the problem of universals by joining the particularity of philology with the universality of philosophy and at the same time to resolve the problem of permanence and change by making a science out of history, broadly understood as the cultural past of humanity. In his contribution to universal history, Voltaire had the more modest aim of searching this cultural past for examples and models of rationality and civility, while Condorcet set about tracing the progress of enlightenment through conventional, if secularized, historiographical epochs. The project of Herder and other cultivators of *Kulturgeschichte* was to establish a philosophy more critical than that of Kant, who (according to Herder) never asked the crucial question, "How did human concepts of understanding arise and develop?" So Herder set about examining not merely the "pure," reflective reason of academic philosophers but the full development of human reason from the beginning of collective human experience.[39]

Hegel, too, devoted himself to the history of philosophy and to the "philosophy of history"—in neither of which projects, however, did historical inquiry itself play a primary role. Hegel distinguished three levels of historical inquiry. The first was the "original history" of naive historians like Herodotus and Thucydides, who merely described what was, directly or indirectly, before their eyes. The second, "reflective history," was of four types: one which, as in Livy and Diodorus Siculus, transcended immediate experience and reached out for a universal perspective; a second which sought in a "pragmatic" way to bring a dead past to life; a third which tried to look in a "critical" way beyond the sources; and fourth, the "fragments," that is, the histories of disciplines. Last came the "philosophical" type, which assimilated history to mind, the real to the ideal, and told the story of humanity as a "history of ideas," that is, a theodicy of reason and human freedom. While Herder, in effect, assimilated philosophy to history, Hegel sought instead to assimilate history to philosophy — as hundreds of medieval chroniclers had assimilated it to theology — and the result was indeed an example of the "end of history."[40]

Hegel's line of argument, like Kant's, was in a sense a repudiation of uncommitted historical inquiry and also of historical experience. Both idealist philosophers and cultural historians appealed to experience, but they had very different things in mind. Neither the geometric space nor the absolute time of the new science, with its ideal of knowledge as measurement, corresponded to human perception and thought. In books of history the sun still rose and set, human memory was bound to a sense of time that changed with private and public circumstances, human vision was limited to finite horizons, and death always waited on the edges. Not that historians were incapable of global hypotheses that transcended the human condition, its follies and its limits; but these hypotheses were projected on a philosophical level which was not accessible to — and so not directly meaningful in terms of — life experience.

One point of contention between philosophy and history was the problem (analyzed most memorably by Rousseau) of what Herder called the costs of cultures. Historians had often to confront examples of folly, error, and wickedness; and writers like Gibbon and Voltaire could not easily imagine a historical process devoid of these unfortunate byproducts of human nature, while philosophers, from Leibniz to Kant and Hegel, translated this aspect of the human condition into a philosophical "problem of evil" (a problem, like that of poverty, to be resolved, presumably, by reason). Eighteenth-century philosophy and progressivist "social science" based on these enlightened premised envisaged an ever brighter future, while historians, looking around as well as back, saw the tragic aspects of the human past. The question posed by Meiners was "whether we may hope for progress toward the good or must fear a decline into evil."[41] We, humanity, may indeed have made the world in which we live, but along with genius and heroism have come war and destruction. Condorcet had entertained the possibility that increased population would entail increased poverty but dismissed it in the conviction that policy based on reason, which was always more important to him than historical understanding, would ultimately resolve such difficulties.[42]

Another area of intersection between history and philosophy in the eighteenth century was the new "science" of aesthetics, which A. G. Baumgarten and then Kant sought to subsume under philosophy.[43] The basic question was whether taste — associated also with the "common sense" of Shaftesbury and the "moral sense" of Hutcheson — was governed by rules and universal reason or was variable, relative, and so subject to the uncertainties of imagination and desire. "Men will always be fonder of books that move them, than of those that instruct them," wrote the Abbé Du Bos, testifying to the role of emotions in judgment and insisting that there were "moral" as well as "physical" causes operative in human experience and changing tastes, which accounts for the need to distinguish particular ages in history.[44] The division of opinion over questions of taste reflected the opposition, ultimately, between Classic and Romantic, and even objective and subjective; but at issue, too, was what aesthetic "criticism" and the judgment which it entailed were and how they related to sense and reflection. Classicist and Grecophile though he was, Winckelmann opposed the philosophical approach to art represented by Baumgarten and turned to history for an understanding of art, and for this he gained the deep admiration of Herder.[45] The fact that taste was obviously, if deplorably, time bound — and romantically if not classically beyond dispute — ties aesthetics to the sense of history, and indeed (in the work of Vico) to historicism, which is also part of the Enlightenment legacy.[46]

What historians perceived more clearly than ever in the Age of Enlightenment was the plurality of human forms, languages, traditions, and epistemologies, and the vast distance between this cultural abundance and the idea of a uniform theory or science of human nature. The principle of plenitude which Arthur Lovejoy traced remained in place, but without the support of hierarchy except for a generalized evolutionism.[47] Reinforcing this sense of the variety and instability of "human nature" was the growing awareness that nature itself had a history and that the developmental and dialectical science of biology, rather than physics and astronomy, furnished the best framework for an understanding of universal and national history. These insights were all in keeping with the notion, expressed for example by Justus Möser, of the importance of "local reason" (*Lokalvernunft*) — anticipating the "local knowledge" recommended by Clifford Geertz for an understanding of culture — which suggests another criticism of Enlightenment universalism.[48]

In general, there is a vast and still growing literature on the "Enlightenment project" — the "unfinished Enlightenment project" or the "failed Enlightenment project," as it is variously called by its adherents or critics.[49] As scholars have come to understand, or to recall, however, the Enlightenment project included history as well as philosophy. The "popular philosopher" Friedrich Nicolai wrote in 1782, "An enlightenment without grounds, a historical Enlightenment without documents, is no Enlightenment at all."[50] As always, history is the source of contradictions not yet resolved by reason. The Enlightenment was an age not only of reason and criticism in a Kantian sense but also of erudition, relativism, and historicism in a Vichian or Herderian sense — whence the grounds for the critique of Enlightened reason and what Isaiah Berlin has (with special reference to Vico, Herder, Hamann, and De Maistre)

famously called the "Counter-Enlightenment," which created new myths, attitudes, and questions underlying "the great river of romanticism" and the
heyday of historicism.[51] The harvest time came in the nineteenth century, and
the result, as Auguste Comte wrote, was an "irrevocable preponderance of
history in philosophy, in politics, and even in poetry."

History and Hermeneutics

Historians have seldom been profound thinkers — continuing unreflectively to repeat the ancient commonplaces which passed for a theory of history — but with their gazes turned toward the long term, their inquiries have
sometimes had profound implications. What the profundity conceals, however, is not the explanatory power of theory but rather the more humble
insights of wisdom. What historians confront is the question not of Being or
even Becoming but of Doing, and they work within the limits of these human
doings. At least inadvertently, they are the philosophers of difference, and so in
a way antiphilosophers, turning their gazes not inward to ask reflectively
"Who are we?" but rather outward, and especially backward, to ask "What
have we made?" and then to question the idea, the reality, and the history of
this "we."[52]

The problem of historical knowledge as it has emerged from the Enlightenment is in what depth of understanding could be attained not only of this "we"
but also of the "other" of alien encounters, and the extent to which both could
be assimilated to a common "humanity." In the eighteenth century there were
two basic models of understanding, though neither can be found in a pure
form. One was hermeneutical, that is, interpretation on the analogy of reading
a text in its literary and philological fullness (as distinguished from logical
analysis), or even translating it; and the other was analytical (*analysis* being
basically a mathematical and logical term), requiring the selection and isola-
tion of factors, political or economic, which were given privileged explanatory
status. History drew on both of these models, but modern historicism and the
historical schools of the nineteenth century inclined toward the former.[53]

The issue may be illustrated with reference to one of the oldest of topoi,
which represents history as a mirror. The most conventional and backward-
looking view is that of simple historiographical imitation or reproduction.
According to Lucian, for example, the writer of history should have a mind
brightly reflecting, like a mirror, while for Vincent of Beauvais history was
itself a mirror, displaying the whole providential plan for humanity.[54] For
promoters of secular progress like Condorcet and Marx, history is rather like a
rear-view mirror, which indeed shows where we have been but only from the

point of view of where we are going (leaving aside the question of who "we" are). What a hermeneutical view adds to the conceit is a consideration of the observer looking into the mirror, his or her qualities, point of view, and focus, and the representations derived from the process of observing fast-receding scenes. History was a matter not of seeing, as tradition and etymology would have it, but rather of reading, deciphering, and interpreting.

It is in this sense that history converged with hermeneutics in the eighteenth century. The *ars hermeneutica,* an aspect of philology devoted to the theory and practice of interpretation, was most prominent in law, theology, and philosophy, but in the eighteenth century its implications for history were also becoming apparent. In his *Allgemeine Geschichtswissenschaft* (1752), Johann Martin Chladenius claimed for hermeneutics the status of a discipline and raised the level of discussion from methodology to epistemology and established the grounds for historical knowledge (*historische Erkenntniss*), introducing, by analogy with Leibniz's monadology, the idea of "point of view" (*Sehepunkt*).[55] Friend and foe, high and low social standing, learned and illiterate, civilized and barbarian — all were conditions of the observer (*Zuschauer*) and his or her situation (*Zustand*), interior as well as exterior, and so affected the quality and truth of historical narrative, "because every account has its own specific place, particular people and certain time, and because it is the knowledge of these things which enables us to comprehend it."[56] These insights, which admitted the historian into the interpretive process of historical knowledge and writing, reinforced the relativism and historicism long associated with historical scholarship. According to Joachim Wach, Chladenius's works represents an early contribution to that post-Kantian project known as "the critique of historical reason."[57]

Like historicism and philosophical idealism, the "new science" of hermeneutics was a product of late eighteenth-century German academe. A later stage of this "hermeneutic turn" was made by Friedrich Schlegel, who also lectured on the philosophy of history.[58] Schlegel saw hermeneutics as surpassing traditional philology and criticism and approaching a "higher criticism," which was again based on an alliance of history and philosophy, the letter and the spirit. Friedrich Schleiermacher, among others, continued this Romantic project of inquiring into the dark areas of the past and haunts of cultural and linguistic Others — a project analogous, if not identical, to historicism.

In general a hermeneutical approach to history requires the adoption of a language model rather than a science model. According to this model, history is not a process to be explained — not the "fiction," as Jauss calls it, "of a complete unfolding of a course of events" — but a field of bygone activity which can only be represented through the interpretation of linguistic and material traces.[59] History is a matter not of demonstration but, in Huizinga's phrase, "a rendering account to oneself."[60] It is not propositional but narrative, not apodictic but heuristic, not rational but commemorative and imaginative; and there is no Archimedean point from which to view, still less to move, humanity in its passage. We may pose questions, but we cannot penetrate the subjects of history, nor can we link cause and effect in any rigorous way. We may tell many stories, true or probable, about the past; but we can never tell *the* story, the whole truth, the metanarrative, as scientific, philosophical, and theological historians used to do, and, indeed, some of them are still doing.[61]

Hermeneutics implies a kind of irony on the part of the historian — not quite irony in the ancient sense of concealed meaning or the opposite of intended meaning, but irony in the sense of an author's awareness of his rhetorical and judgmental role and of the relativism that such an awareness implies.[62] Historical meaning depends on the res gestae which are written about and on the author's point of view, on context, and on the values brought by the writer to his material. In a sense such irony was inherent in historiography from the beginning, and there was indeed both a Socratic and a Herodotean sort of irony that brought the historian into the process while at the same time distancing him from it; but in the eighteenth century a theoretical dimension was added by hermeneutics and the acknowledgment that meaning, like taste, would always (ironically speaking) be subjects of debate — as indeed would the subjective center of judgment itself.

A central aim of Romantic hermeneutics was "to understand an author better than he understood himself" (*Besserverstehen*, a modern variant of a topos of Homeric scholarship), and one can understand the advantages of hindsight and information not accessible to the "original author."[63] Yet this optimistic conception of the potential of imaginative empathy has not survived criticism; for what, asks Ernst Behler, is the *meaning* of the understanding — of the meaning — in question? The meaning of the author is lost forever, and indeed hardly retrievable by the author himself, while the meaning of the *Besserversteher* is a construct of a very different order within very different, but likewise impermanent, cultural horizons.

Like recovering the mentality of an author, unmasking ideology, revealing hidden patterns of collective behavior, and "getting behind the back of language" are noble aims; but can history, or historicism, really reach so high, or so deep? Critical insights are always admirable, but can criticism afford to forget the lessons of skepticism? As Nietzsche remarked, "The historian looks backwards; at last he also *believes* backwards."[64] Yet can we escape the prejudices and forestructures of language and local culture? Yes, of course, was the answer of rational critics and philosophes like Voltaire and Condorcet, who associated historical understanding with ideals whose realization is located in the future and perhaps beyond local cultures. The conditions of hermeneutics are such that meaning cannot be found in a bygone original intention or original context, nor by looking "behind the back of language"; nor is reading between the lines a historical license recognized by all critics. Historical meaning must always be a present construction based on the historian's knowledge and imagination. To this extent we have not gone beyond the reasoned history or historicism of the Enlightenment, or indeed of the classical tradition. Again, while the words change, the music remains curiously familiar.

Historicism

What Paul Ricoeur calls a "hermeneutics of tradition" accepts "prejudice" and "authority," in the sense of the forestructures of understanding embedded in language and culture, as essential to understanding; and such a premise may well seem conservative and backward looking in contrast to a "hermeneutics of suspicion," which aspires to analyze and to "unmask" human behavior and social structures in the hope not only of understanding but also of changing the direction of history.[65] Thus it was at the end of the eighteenth century, an age when revolution claimed philosophy as its mother and history as its enemy. To many of that generation, the study of the past seemed to be an expression of reaction and counterrevolution. As Lord Acton remarked, "The romantic reaction which began with the invasion of 1794 marked the revolt of outraged history"; and shortly thereafter "a movement began in the world of minds which was deeper and more serious than the revival of ancient learning" — by which he meant "the renovation of history" and "that influence for which the depressing names historicism and historical-mindedness have been devised."[66]

Historicism is basically a nineteenth-century term and concept, appearing first, it seems, in a notebook of Friedrich Schlegel, "On Philology," referring to a concern for the spirit behind the letter of a text — "one must insist on *historism* that is necessary to philology."[67] Like Vico, Schlegel wanted to raise philology to a philosophical level. Contemporaneously, Novalis associated historism, no doubt pejoratively, with mysticism and "the system of confusion," while offering a miscellaneous listing of systematic methods (Fichte's, Kant's, chemical, mathematical, artistic, and so on). Later, the term was occasionally used in philosophical polemics, especially regarding the question of the value of history for philosophy — a question often answered in the negative by academic philosophers.[68] In the late nineteenth century, for example, Felix Dahn argued that "historicism is above all a methodological moment, not a speculative principle . . . ; its goal is [not philosophy but] life"; Christlieb Julius Braniss opposed it to the reductionist and deterministic philosophy of "naturalism"; and in 1879 Karl Werner applied the phrase "philosophical historicism" to the work of Vico, a connection which was later popularized by Benedetto Croce, Friedrich Meinecke, Erich Auerbach, and others.[69]

In the hands of some philosophers and historians of ideas, however, historicism (or historism) has also been refashioned into a doctrine and even a theory. The classic work of Meinecke reduces *Historismus* to a formula: "The essence of historism is the substitution of a process of *individualising* observation for a *generalising* view of human forces" (a modern version of the stock philosophical argument that assigns history to particulars and philosophy to generalities).[70] "The idea of individuality, and the idea of development" are the ingredients of historicism; and under this definition, qualified by assignments of Platonism and other intellectual forces, Meinecke traced a process through a canon of forerunners (*Vorbereiter*), who heralded a "future historism" (*kommende Historismus*) and a full historicism leading to Ranke and his disciples, including Meinecke himself.

Many of these forerunners, including Shaftesbury, Leibniz, Gottfried Arnold, Vico, Montesquieu, and the "pre-Romantic" Burke, were not historians and were included by Meinecke simply because they variously exemplified one or both of these two attributes. Leibniz was a "torchbearer" of protohistoricism because of his metaphysics (his "law of continuity" and monadological individualism), Shaftesbury for his moral and aesthetic views, Arnold because he "moved the human soul into the center of history," and Montesquieu in a more qualified way for his relativism, his awareness of irrational and climatological factors, and his Germanist view of French origins. Among the Germans, Meinecke (in addition to noting the importance of the Göttingen school) included Lessing, Winckelmann, Möser, and Herder, who, following Florus, Augustine, and Isaac Iselin, adopted the "stage of life" theory and mystical ideas of the *Volksgeist* and progress as well as his criticism of the "national madness" of the French Revolution. The culmination of this historicism came with Goethe's developmental views of nature and his dictum, which Meinecke took, from Goethe, as the motto of his own book: *Individuum est ineffabile*.[71]

One point is clear about attitudes of historicism, and that is its hostility toward "the pattern based upon Natural Law, which," according to Meinecke, "delighted in deriving the essence of things from their finished and fully rounded forms."[72] Jusnaturalists often ignored variability and development in their search for general laws of human nature in an idealized form, and they argued from a fictitious state of nature, as if humankind could ever be found outside social groupings and without culture of some sort. Like Vico, Herder adhered in his own way to the idea of "maker's knowledge," settled on language as the model of the process of human self-creation, and on this basis went on "to forge his chain of universal history."[73]

Later German epigones have extended Meinecke's line of argument and multiplied examples of historicism. Pushing the historicist cast of mind back to the sixteenth century, Erich Hassinger finds four stages of "empirical-rational historicism," from Guicciardini to Saint-Evremond, beginning with, first, the segregation of a cultural world from a natural one (Baudouin, Bodin, La Popelinière, and others); second, the appearance of comparative method (Le Roy, Vignier, and others); third, the quarrel of Ancients and Moderns (Le Roy, Bacon, and others); and finally the modern sense of history.[74] In a still more schematic way, Ulrich Mulbach has traced the "prehistory of historicism" back to Renaissance humanism.[75] The most impressive and doctrinaire treatment has been that of Horst Blanke, which, supplemented by detailed investigations into the teaching of history in eighteenth-century German universities, defines historicism as a Kuhnian paradigm of historical method (*Historik*).[76]

Despite the accumulation of valuable detail about the history of history, these works represent a progressive narrowing of historicism, from Meinecke's formulaic approach to Blanke's identification of the concept with the professional tradition of history in Germany. What has emerged is a scholasticism that generates debate through disagreement about the definition of historicism and its exclusively German character. The historical reality seems to be a detectable inclination to historical interpretation, with attendant individualizing, developmental, relativist, and constructivist attitudes in many areas of historical study — historiography being perhaps the least conspicuous of these. History is always "historicist" in some rudimentary sense; it was the study of literature, philosophy, other arts and sciences, and indeed the whole encyclopedia of disciplines that, from the Renaissance on, has turned to history for self-understanding, self-advertisement, and legitimation; and this impulse, manifested especially in the historical schools of law, political economy, and literature, rather than adoption of particular concepts, is the essence of historicism.

Like history, historicism has shown many faces. The term has been much used and misused, and it is probably too late to correct misunderstandings.[77] The semantic range is very wide: from a specific historical movement arising in late eighteenth-century Germany and culminating in the *Geschichtswissenschaft* of Ranke and the *Ideengeschichte* of his admirer (and critic) Meinecke, to a general pattern of thought, a sense of history and cultural change, manifested not only in Renaissance humanism but also in classical forerunners like Varro and Alexandrine philology. The problems and disagreements come in the construction of, and assignment of particular authors to, a tradition, especially those who were not aware of any such intellectual tradition.

Whatever the appropriate terminology, a turn to history was apparent in many areas of thought and inquiry in the later eighteenth century — indeed throughout the whole encyclopedia of arts and sciences, including the imperial discipline of philosophy itself. "Was history necessary for philosophy?" was the common topic of debate in what has, for two centuries, been called *Philosophie der Philosophiegeschichte.*[78] One of those who answered in the affirmative was Hegel, and Frederick Beiser has lamented his neglect in most discussions of historicism.[79] Hegel, however, wanted not to historicize philosophy (except in a wholly theoretical way) but to philosophize history, in contrast to Herder and other cultural historians, who wanted to supplant philosophy by history as the foundational discipline of the science of human nature and criticism of reason.

From the standpoint of this book, historicism began as and remains a way of characterizing the cast of mind that carries on historical inquiry in the spirit especially of Herodotus, that is, the art of asking perhaps naive (if not objective) questions about human behavior in time. In the spirit of Herodotus, too, historicism was concerned not only with the headline news of politics and war but also, and more intensively, with matters of culture and society. The historical school of law was founded by Savigny on a critical review of Western legal traditions in all their "individuality" and "development" in a spirit quite opposed to philosophes and Aufklärer; and the same went for the methods applied to the history of language by Savigny's disciples, the brothers Grimm, and to the history of economics by Wilhelm Roscher. Rooted in Germany, these attitudes and ideas were extended to the rest of Europe, especially France.[80] To these might also be added the inflammatory application of a historical and mythological approach to the study of the Bible itself; for David Friedrich Strauss — whose revolutionary book opens up a whole world of forgotten eighteenth-century biblical scholarship — also belongs in Meinecke's pantheon of historicists.[81]

The spirit of Herodotus presided over modern historicism. Collingwood begins with the Herodotean position that "history is a kind of research or inquiry," treats "human actions done in the past," and "proceeds by the interpretation of evidence." The hard question, not posed by Herodotus, is the purpose of history, and Collingwood gives a commonplace answer embedded deep in the Western idea of history. "What is history for? . . . My answer is that history is 'for' human self-knowledge."[82] But as Hume showed, the human self is not a stable target, and in historical and collective terms it seems even less susceptible of definition in terms of philosophy, or philosophy of history.

So we return to the point of origin: history is indeed a way of asking questions; its answers, however, must be local and provisional; and while they may be improved on or replaced as geographic and temporal horizons are extended or techniques are improved, they can never be complete until history becomes truly universal and is capable of prediction as well as retrodiction — and this is indeed a millennialist hope. History is a matter not of "endings" but of "beginnings," not of doctrinal closure but (as philosophy started out to be) of exploratory pursuit and disclosure; and historicism, too, should be understood in such historicizing terms.[83]

Posthistoricism

Historical learning is both a source and a solvent of philosophical schemes and systems, which periodically reject and then return to historical study — just as history periodically rejects and then returns to philosophy, in one way or another. Once perfected, philosophy has no need of history; once committed to radical skepticism or empiricism, history has no need of philosophy. This was apparently the view of Kant, who was, concludes one scholar, "the first philosopher of the 'end of philosophy' in the *historical* sense of the word."[84] To speak of ending was, of course, ambiguous, since it might be a sign of optimism or pessimism — the achievement of perfection or the coming of death. When Lessing declared that the "time of perfection" (*die Zeit der Vollendung*) would surely come, he meant the former; when J. C. A. Grohmann wrote in 1797 that "the history of philosophy is the end of all philosophizing," he was expressing the latter, meaning that the pedantic involvement in the opinions of the past — literary and perhaps cultural history — prevented a critical pursuit of the truth.[85] Hegel agreed with both authors, seeing in that world-shattering age the end both of philosophy and of history. As he declared at the end of his lectures on the philosophy of history, the revolution, having received its first impulse from philosophy, marked the end of the theodicy of reason and the achievement of freedom: "the last stage of history, of our world, of our time."[86]

This was not the first time, nor would it be the last, that the end of history was announced. Convinced that enlightened understanding was possible only at the end of the historical process, Hegel was deeply in debt to theological tradition, and his philosophical terminalism was in one sense a secularized version of old-fashioned millennarianism — as indeed were those versions of both the right and the left Hegelians of a later generation. Yet philosophy was not over; it only moved to a more positive and activist level in the wake of revolutionary dreams and disappointments. Nor did history perish in the waves of the radical and terrorist rhetoric of Jacobins and Bonapartists; on the contrary, it had a new birth in the "new history" of the Romantic period, while the French Revolution itself became — as indeed it remains — the target of intensive historical investigation and interpretation.

But modern authors have sought to go beyond, or beneath, the complacent search for historical truth in the deeds and words of men and have envisioned metahistorical patterns comparable to the "secret springs" of action sought by classical historians or the providential master narrative of Christian historiography. Following Hegel as well as the stadial schemes of the Enlightenment, Marx announced the "end of philosophy" and sought to decipher the book of human history with the key concept of "ideology," class analysis, and an implicitly reductionist idea of dialectical materialism. In heuristic terms, this was a fruitful theory which led to a wide range of questions expanding the horizons of historical investigation, although the Marxian system itself generated endless revisionisms and a huge scholasticism that continues and, despite recent setbacks, will continue into the next millennium. Late in life Marx himself came to appreciate anthropology and cultural history and the implications of these fields for Eurocentric class analysis and the reductionist ideals which he inherited from Enlightenment social science and historiography (including Vico and Condorcet); but Marxists of many revisionist stripes have continued for the most part to follow the original analytical and unmasking line.[87]

In search of an "archaeology" of knowledge, Foucault rejected the commonplaces of historicist rhetoric — tradition, influence, development, evolution, spirit, given unities and links, familiar divisions and groupings, the oeuvre, origins, and the "already said."[88] As a professed historian of ideas, Foucault sought to decipher or unmask the human structures or practices beneath the surface of the discourses based on such conventions, and at first his notion of "episteme" seemed to offer a way beyond the languages of man and toward a fundamental critique of reason; but no more than Marxist dialectic does Foucault's archaeology shut off questions provoked by history about the mysteries of the subject that produces narratives and analyses and the historical continuity that inheres in language, discourse, and practices.

Nor is Foucault persuasive in declaring a late seventeenth-century discontinuity in the practice of historiography, between an occultist effort to find hidden meaning in words and a modern taxonomic realism which reverts to the original Greek notion of ocular inquiry, "gathered in smooth, neutralized, and faithful words."[89] On érudits, at least, an education in classical languages and rhetoric left the stamp of a prescientific mentality and logocentric habits; and even pretensions to novelty, revolution, and other "breaks" with the past could find good classical and biblical authority. If historical continuity can be seen anywhere, it is in Western historiographical practice — right across the epistemic caesura of modern science — whose discourse is a palimpsest of discourses of divination, myth, honest questioning of the "faith" of history, and a search for a language which would both tell the truth and spiritually resurrect bygone ages, whether revered, hated, or merely "interesting."

But in order to have meaning, history must have a sense of the future as well as the past. Its Janus posture is preserved in the need for its practitioners to look back into the past yet at the same time, for the sake of understanding, to break with it and to "make it new." "Are you saying the same old things, Socrates, that I heard you saying long ago," asked Hippias the Sophist; "I always try to say something new." Not only philosophy but also history has been informed by the rhetoric of novelty,[90] from the new history of La Popelinière, Voltaire, and Augustin Thierry to that of James Harvey Robinson, Carl Becker — who pitched the new history of that generation back to the Enlightenment — and the self-proclaimed new cultural history and new historicism of recent vintage, though already aging.[91] The new historicism is based on political and generational disagreement rather than serious difference in historical method. New historicists have continued to make assumptions about shaping intentions in literary and political behavior and connectedness in cultural phenomena — between discourse and power, for example — which beg rather than answer historical questions and which evade the Humean malady by maintaining, as Brook Thomas notes, "an older historicist's faith in the progressive emergence of truth through history."[92] What Louis Montrose remarks about the new historicism, that it reveals at once the historicity of the text and the textuality of history, might well be said about older historicists who had taken their own version of the linguistic turn.[93]

Another current form of generational one-upping is the "postist" phenomenon, centering on that most unreflective, presumptuous, and playful offshoot of modernism — and form of historicism — "postmodernism." Postmodernism, too, has its precursors, as its promoters admit, and will be certainly be assimilated to historical perspective in its turn. Nor are these precursors limited to Nietzsche, for they also exist, though not yet identified, in the often conceptually inarticulate realm of historical inquiry. Thus Herder, in his metacriticism of Kantian rationalism, questioned the function of the original author in his conception of culture and the creative role of tradition and the Volk. Following Herder, other cultural historians also inquired into the limits and conditions of knowledge and possibility or accessibility of "truth" as philosophers had for centuries conceived it; and they explored in particular the mysteries of myth, which were undoubtedly human creations but which seemed remote from the rational processes of historians and philosophers alike. Yet it was in ancient stages of culture rather than in modern reason — so Herder, Hamann, and others believed — that a true understanding of human nature was to be sought.

Hume's skeptical line of inquiry was perhaps more radical, undermining as it did the continuity over time of personal identity and a stable self. He also denied the possibility of causality, and so dissolved the continuity on which historical explanation depended.[94] Long before Foucault, Hume rejected both the "founding subject" and the continuous history dependent on it — not to mention other sorts of rationalist and intentionalist assumptions (or fictions, as Hume would say) unsuitable or irrelevant to collective history. But unlike Foucault, Hume did not pretend to find a neutral point from which to judge history, instead leaving history in the literary arena of opinion, probability, "moral certainty," practical judgment, conjecture, and empirical inquiry.[95] Losing faith in the value of internal reflection, he turned to the doings of humanity within his own national tradition, where practical knowledge and cultural meaning were to be found.

Among the myriad "post" terms in circulation these days is, inevitably, "posthistory."[96] This terminalist rhetoric also has precedents, of course, not only in loose talk about the end of the novel and the death of the author (not to mention God) but also in eighteenth-century worries about the end of philosophy (produced by history) — and, in one of the paradoxes of Hegelian dialectic, vice versa. This debate persists in recent sensationalist, if hardly novel, forms, positing ruptures in historical experience largely on the basis of political transformations, the consequences of recent economic and technological modernization, and the disappointments arising for adherents of particular ideological positions. But ideological or philosophical closure does not bring an end to history as conceived by Herodotus, Thucydides, and their intellectual progeny. To the asking of questions, which is history's function — and indeed to the search for wisdom, which is philosophy's — there is no end.

Epilogue

This book ends where most accounts of the modern study of history begin — that is, with the rise of historicism, the academic and professional organization of history, and the classics of nineteenth-century historical narrative. Even for Lord Acton, who was well aware of the "brave men who lived before Agamemnon," the postrevolutionary period began a new era, an era that was more significant than the revival of learning in the Renaissance. Yet the three marks of novelty for Acton — exploitation of archives, application of historical criticism, and attainment of impartiality — were all claims which historians had made across many centuries. This is not to deny the striking accomplishments of the "new history" of the French Restoration and the "historical science" of the German schools which Acton celebrated, but only to recall the persistent tendency of historians to prize and to advertise their own innovations and departures from tradition and to undervalue the accomplishments of predecessors — as, indeed, contemporary historians are still doing.

Historical studies in the twentieth century have larger claims to novelty, in terms especially of technical and quantitative methods; obviously, there are no clear precedents for cliometrics, for example, or for computer technology and radiocarbon dating. Yet again, on a more general intellectual level, many of the grounds for the "new" histories of the twentieth century had been charted by earlier explorers. The complexities of material culture, the value of making interdisciplinary contacts, the uses of comparative methods, the rhetorical structure of historical narrative and analysis, and speculations about the end of history, for example, have been familiar topics of discussion for centuries.

The facts of technical progress are not in question, but from one point of view they do not fundamentally alter the historical and generational patterns of the history of history. For centuries, Moderns, in one way or another, struggled against Ancients, though not without a certain sense of the historical place of their rivals. And the pattern continues, even if the terms have changed so that Moderns are pitted against Postmoderns and history itself has ostensibly been placed at issue — at least "posthistorically."

From the eighteenth century, history continued to serve as recorder and celebrator of many conflicting interests and traditions. With regard to the canon in general, it seemed to become, above all, an advocate and conveyor of modernity, and even modernism — the Enlightenment Project, as it has been called, which celebrated science, rationality, national states, and the secular progress that accompanied these modernizing creations. In many ways, history itself became a science and a modernist project, chronicling and glorifying these attributes of Western progress and adapting to them its own qualities of truth, social utility, and critical and impartial inquiry. Yet at the same time, in part as a result of these qualities, history became a critique of the Enlightenment and its progressivist ideologies. This was the implication of historicism, which reflected the darker and more skeptical side of Enlightenment and was employed by some authors to undermine it.

History continues to play a critical role, as intellectuals struggle to escape the inertial forces of the past and to exert influence on the future. In the late twentieth century, however, the critical power of historical study turned inward, as doubts were cast on the old projects of understanding "the past" in a global way and of finding the "great story" of Polybian, Augustinian, Hegelian, or Marxist aspirations. Despite the extraordinary expansion of methods, sources of information, and range of legitimate questioning, historical inquiry has become increasingly fragmented, pluralized, and controversial. Yet such developments are not necessarily to be lamented, since they are themselves the product of historical inquiry and constitute an expression of wisdom. The form of this wisdom may be distressing and postmodern, but it is not posthistorical; for the questions continue to appear, even if we do not always like the answers. It is pleasant to think that Herodotus and perhaps Thucydides would not be disappointed in their remote progeny.

Notes

Chapter 1: Mythistory

1. Michel de Certeau, *The Writing of History,* tr. Tom Conley (New York, 1988), 21.

2. David Hume, *A Treatise of Human Nature,* I, iv, 2.

3. Hans Blumenberg, *Work on Myth,* tr. R. M. Wallace (Cambridge, 1985), 19.

4. Fredric Jameson, *The Political Unconscious* (London, 1981), 9: "Always historicize!"

5. Gisela M. A. Richter, *The Portraits of the Greeks,* rev. R. Smith (Ithaca, 1984), 132. Also reproduced, e.g., in Jacob Burckhardt, *History of Greek Culture,* tr. Palmer Hilty (New York, 1963), and on the cover of the paperback edition of my *Versions of History.* On the Janus myth, see Macrobius, *Saturnalia* 1.9; and Augustine, *De Civitate Dei* 7.8.

6. The first by Cicero and the second by Juan Luis Vives.

7. See T. P. Wiseman, "Lying Historians: Seven Types of Mendacity," in *Lies and Fiction in the Ancient World,* ed. Christopher Gill and T. P. Wiseman (Austin, 1993), 122–46.

8. F. M. Cornford takes the Thucydidean term for the title of his *Thucydides Mythistoricus* (London, 1907), as does William McNeill for a collections of his world-historical essays, *Mythistory and Other Essays* (Chicago, 1986).

9. See K. Keuck, *Historia: Geschichte des Wortes und seiner Bedeutung in der Antike und in den romanischen Sprache* (Emsdetten, 1934); F. Muller, "De 'historiae' vocabulo atque notione," *Mnemosyne* 54 (1926), 234–57; and "Geschichte," in *Geschichtliche Grundbegriffe,* 8 vols., ed. Otto Brunner, Werner Conze, and Reinhard Koselleck (Stuttgart, 1972–92).

10. The term *canon* (*kanon*) in this sense of a selective list is a modern coinage of David Ruhnken, who applied it to the chosen subjects of his "critical history of Greek orators" — whether or not with the judgmental connotation of ethical "canons" in the sense of rules. See Rudolph Pfeiffer, *History of Classical Scholarship* (Oxford, 1968), 207.

11. See, e.g., Friedrich Meinecke, *Die Entstehung des Historismus*, ed. Carl Hinrichs (Munich, 1939); and see below, ch. 9 at n. 128, and ch. 10 at n. 70.

12. J. R. Green, *A Short History of the English People* (London, 1874).

13. In a vast literature, see Arnaldo Momigliano, *The Development of Greek Biography* (Cambridge, 1971); Thomas Mayer and Daniel Woolf (eds.), *The Rhetoric of Life-Writing in Early Modern Europe* (Ann Arbor, 1995); and the monumental, unfinished work of Georg Misch, *Geschichte der Autobiographie*, 3d ed. ([1905–] 1949–62).

14. Nicholas Jardine, *Scenes of Inquiry* (Oxford, 1991).

15. See introduction to Simon Hornblower (ed.), *Greek Historiography* (Oxford, 1994), 71.

16. Paul Ricoeur, *Interpretation Theory* (Fort Worth, 1976), 25.

17. "Effigiam meam . . . sed carmina maior imago" — "ten kreitto ta synggrammata deizei"; see Lisa Jardine, *Erasmus, Man of Letters* (Princeton, 1993), 36; and cf. Proust, *Contre Sainte-Beuve* (Paris, 1909).

18. Hans-Georg Gadamer, *Truth and Method*, tr. Garrett Barden and John Cumming (New York, 1975), 310ff.

19. See Harold Bloom, *A Map of Misreading* (Oxford, 1975); and his own precursor, W. Jackson Bate, *The Burden of the Past and the English Poet* (Cambridge, Mass., 1970); and on *Rezeptionsgeschichte*, see Robert C. Holub, *Reception Theory: A Critical Introduction* (London, 1984).

20. Many of these views are collected in my anthology of the historiographical canon, *Versions of History* (New Haven, 1991).

21. Bruno Neveu, *Erudition et religion aux XVIIe et XVIIIe siècles* (Paris, 1994), 365; Voegelin, *Order and History*, VI, *The Ecumenic Age* (Baton Rouge, 1974), 59.

22. See Hans Robert Jauss, *Question and Answer: Forms of Dialogic Understanding*, tr. Michael Hays (Minneapolis, 1989), 197.

23. See below, ch. 8 at n. 23.

24. Henri Berr, *Writing History: Essay on Epistemology*, tr. Mina Moore-Rinvolucri (Middletown, 1984), 63.

25. See below, ch. 3 at n. 91.

26. See David Lowenthal, *Possessed by the Past: The Heritage Crusade and the Spoils of History* (New York, 1996).

27. See A. J. Woodman, *Rhetoric in Classical Historiography* (London, 1988).

28. Dionysius of Halicarnassus, *De arte rhetorica* 11.2; and see ch. 8 at n. 7, and ch. 9 at n. 9.

29. See below, ch. 8 at n. 34.

30. Marcel Detienne, *The Masters of Truth in Archaic Greece,* tr. Janet Lloyd (New York, 1996).

31. See Bonnie Smith, *Gender and the Mirror of History* (Cambridge, Mass., 1998).

32. See Steve Shapin, *The Social History of Truth* (Chicago, 1994).

33. See Emile Benveniste, "De la subjectivité dans le langage" and other essays, in *Problèmes de linguistique générale* (Paris, 1966).

34. See Jacques Le Goff, *History and Memory*, tr. Stephen Redall and Elizabeth Claman (New York, 1992).

35. See Henri-Jean Martin, *The History and Power of Writing*, tr. Lydia G. Cochrane (Chicago, 1944).

36. See ch. 8, "The Art of History."

37. This is the thrust of R. G. Collingwood's influential *The Idea of History*, rev. ed. (Oxford, 1993); and cf. Gaillard (ch. 8 at n. 24).

38. See Roland Bainton et al., *The Idea of History in the Ancient Near East*, ed. Robert C. Dentan (New Haven, 1955); Herbert Butterfield, *The Origins of History* (New York, 1981); and Gerdien Jonker, *The Topography of Remembrance: The Dead, Tradition and Collective Memory in Mesopotamia* (Leiden, 1995).

39. *Timaeus* 22b. Walter Burkert, *The Orientalizing Revolution: Near Eastern Influence on Greek Culture in the Early Archaic Age*, tr. Margaret E. Pinder and Walter Burkert (Cambridge, Mass., 1992), is more authoritative but presents a line of argument similar to that of Martin Bernal, *Black Athena: The Afroasiatic Roots of Classical Civilization* (New Brunswick, 1987).

40. On lists see Jack Goody, *The Logic of Writing and the Organization of Society* (Cambridge, 1980), 37ff.

41. *Manetho*, tr. W. G. Waddell (London, 1944); and see Garth Fowden, *The Egyptian Hermes: A Historical Approach to the Late Pagan Mind* (Princeton, 1986).

42. From Miriam Lichtheim (ed.), *Ancient Egyptian Literature: A Book of Readings* (Berkeley, 1973), I, 58.

43. Lichtheim, 62–65.

44. Lichtheim, 99.

45. See J. A. S. Evans, *Herodotus: Explorer of the Past* (Princeton, 1991), 105; and Michael Grant, *The Ancient Historians* (New York, 1970), 19.

46. See Anthony Grafton, *Forgers and Critics: Creativity and Duplicity in Western Scholarship* (Princeton, 1990).

47. As Fustel de Coulanges wrote of the ancient Greeks and Romans, "In their thoughts the dead were gods" (*The Ancient City: A Study on the Religion, Laws, and Institutions of Greece and Rome* [New York, n.d.], 21).

48. J. B. Bury, *The Ancient Greek Historians* (New York, 1958); and see his "Science of History" (1902), in Fritz Stern (ed.), *The Varieties of History* (New York, 1972), 214–23.

49. *The Classical Foundations of Modern Historiography* (Berkeley, 1990).

50. "German Schools of History," in *Selected Writings of Lord Acton*, II: *Essays in the Study and Writing of History*, ed. J. Rufus Fears (Indianapolis, 1985), 325.

51. *History* 2.53.

52. See below, ch. 2 at n. 18.

53. J.-P. Vernant, *Myth and Society in Ancient Greece*, tr. Janet Lloyd (London, 1982), 205.

54. B. G. Niebuhr, *The History of Rome*, tr. J. C. Hare and C. Thirlwall (Philadelphia, 1835), I, 1.

55. George Grote, *Greece,* 2d ed. (New York, 1899), I, viii and 351, referring to the views of Vico, "no less correct than profound."

56. Blumenberg, *Work on Myth.*

57. Bury, *Ancient Greek Historians,* 41–42.

58. Robert Lambertson, *Homer the Theologian* (Berkeley, 1986).

59. *Iliad* 12.176, 2.484.

60. Fritz Stern, *The Varieties of History,* 2d ed. (New York, 1973), 209ff, 207ff.

61. See Robert Lamberton, *Hesiod* (New Haven, 1988).

62. Jacob Burckhardt, *Force and Freedom: An Interpretation of History,* tr. James Hastings Nichols (New York, 1955), 137.

63. T. S. Eliot, "The Rock," I.

64. See below, ch. 2, at n. 124.

65. See below, ch. 10, at n. 37.

66. Martin Nilsson, *A History of Greek Religion,* 2d ed., tr. F. J. Fielden (Oxford, 1949), 42n.

67. In G. S. Kirk, J. E. Raven, and M. Schofield, *The Presocratic Philosophers,* 2d ed. (Cambridge, 1983), 188, 179.

68. Marcel Detienne, *The Creation of Mythology,* tr. Margaret Cook (Chicago, 1986); and Blumenberg, *Work on Myth,* 627.

69. Martin Nilsson, *The Mycenaean Origin of Greek Mythology* (New York, 1963), 4.

Chapter 2: Greek Horizons

1. On Greek historiography in general, see esp. Arnaldo Momigliano, *Classical Foundations of Modern Historiography* (Berkeley, 1990); Gordon S. Shrimpton, *History and Memory in Ancient Greece* (Montreal, 1997), Charles William Fornara, *The Nature of History in Ancient Greece and Rome* (Berkeley, 1983); Michael Grant, *The Ancient Historians* (New York, 1970); Kurt von Fritz, *Die Griechische Geschichtsschreibung* (Berlin, 1967); Chester Starr, *The Awakening of the Greek Historical Spirit* (New York, 1968); François Chatelet, *La Naissance de l'histoire* (Paris, 1962); F. Jacoby, *Griechische Historiker* (Stuttgart, 1956); J. R. Shotwell, *The Story of Ancient History* (New York, 1961); and J. B. Bury, *The Ancient Greek Historians* (New York, 1958 [1909]).

2. Diodorus Siculus, *The Library of History,* tr. C. H. Oldfather (Cambridge, Mass., 1989), 4.7.

3. Henry R. Immerwahr, *Form and Thought in Herodotus* (Cleveland, 1966).

4. Herodotus, *The Persian Wars,* tr. George Rawlinson (New York, 1947), 1.1. J. A. S. Evans, *Herodotus: Explorer of the Past* (Princeton, 1991), 3, prefers "public exposition" to "publication."

5. Mabel Lang, *Herodotean Narrative and Discourse* (Cambridge, Mass., 1984), ch. 3, "How Could Herodotus Imitate Homer?"

6. See Stewart Flory, *The Archaic Smile of Herodotus* (Detroit, 1987); and Donald Lateiner, *The Historical Method of Herodotus* (Toronto, 1989).

7. Myres, *Herodotus: Father of History* (Oxford, 1953), 16.

8. Herodotus, tr. A. D. Godley (London, 1920), 1.30–34.

9. Herodotus, 1.60; and see Edith Hall, *Inventing the Barbarians: Greek Self-Definition through Tragedy* (Oxford, 1988).

10. Herodotus, 1.134.

11. See Walter Burkert et al., *Hérodote et les peuples non Grecs* (Geneva, 1988); and A. B. Breebart, "The Figure of Anacharsis in Herodotus," in *Clio and Antiquity: History and Historiography of the Greek and Roman World* (The Hague, 1987), 32–39.

12. Herodotus, 1.182, *"emoi ou pista legontes"*; and cf. 4.5.

13. Alan B. Lloyd, *Herodotus Book II*, 3 vols. (Leiden, 1975), 1.66.

14. Lloyd, 2.7; and see Antoni Sulek, "The Experiment of Psammetichus: Fact, Fiction, and Model to Follow," *Journal of the History of Ideas* 50 (1989), 645–51.

15. Herodotus, 2.53.

16. Herodotus, 2.100.

17. Herodotus, 2.77, 100; cf. Plato, *Timaeus* 22b.

18. Paul Veyne, *Did the Greeks Believe Their Myths?* tr. Paula Wissing (Chicago, 1988), 13; cf. Marcel Detienne, *The Creation of Mythology*, tr. Margaret Cook (Chicago, 1986).

19. Herodotus, 2.123.

20. Herodotus, 7.152.

21. Myres, *Herodotus*, 43; Momigliano, *Classical Foundations*, 37.

22. Herodotus, 3.38.

23. W. W. How and J. Wells, *A Commentary on Herodotus* (Oxford, 1912), I, 278: "This passage is the beginning of Greek political philosophy."

24. Herodotus, 3.80–83.

25. Herodotus, 4.5.

26. James S. Romm, *The Edges of the Earth in Ancient Thought* (Princeton, 1992).

27. François Hartog, *The Mirror of Herodotus: The Representation of the Other in the Writing of History*, tr. Janet Lloyd (Berkeley, 1988), 11.

28. Herodotus, 4.76.

29. Herodotus, 5.78.

30. Herodotus, 7.11.

31. Herodotus, 7.46.

32. Herodotus, 7.104.

33. Herodotus, 8.26.

34. Herodotus, 7.139, 213.

35. Herodotus, 8.68.

36. Virginia Hunter, *Past and Process in Herodotus and Thucydides* (Princeton, 1982), 50.

37. *Lives of Eminent Philosophers*, tr. R. D. Hicks (Cambridge, Mass., 1980), I, 1.

38. See the problematic listing in Dionysius of Halicarnassus, *De Thucydide*, 5; Fornara, *The Nature of History*, ch. 1, and Lionel Pearson, *The Local Historians of Attica* (Philadelphia, 1942).

39. See Clarence J. Glacken, *Traces on the Rhodian Shore: Nature and Culture in Western Thought from Ancient Times to the End of the Eighteenth Century* (Berkeley, 1967), 82.

40. James S. Romm, *The Edges of the Earth.*

41. See below, ch. 8, at n. 10.

42. Detlev Fehling, *Herodotus and His "Sources": Citation, Invention and Narrative Art,* tr. J. G. Howie (Leeds, 1989), 240. See also J. L. Moles, "Truth and Untruth in Herodotus and Thucydides," in *Lies and Fiction in the Ancient World,* ed. Christopher Gill and T. J. Wiseman (Austin, 1993), 88–121.

43. *The Idea of History,* 30. In general, see W. Robert Conner, *Thucydides* (Princeton, 1984); F. E. Adcock, *Thucydides and His History* (Cambridge, 1963); John H. Finley Jr., *Thucydides* (Cambridge, Mass., 1942); Louis E. Lord, *Thucydides and the World War* (Cambridge, Mass., 1945); and Francis Cornford, *Thucydides Mythistoricus* (London, 1907).

44. Conner, *Thucydides,* 9.

45. Jacqueline de Romilly, *Thucydides and Athenian Imperialism,* tr. Philip Thody (New York, 1979).

46. See Philip Stadter (ed.), *The Speeches in Thucydides* (Chapel Hill, 1973).

47. Herodotus, 3.122; cf. *Thucydides,* tr. Charles Foster Smith (Cambridge, 1951), 1.4; *VH.*

48. See Bury, *Ancient Greek Historians,* 13; and Momigliano, *Classical Foundations,* 32ff.

49. Thucydides, 2.36.

50. Adcock, *Thucydides.*

51. Paideia: *The Ideals of Greek Culture,* 3 vols., tr. Gilbert Highet (Oxford, 1945), I, 384.

52. *Thucydides Mythistoricus,* xi.

53. See Macaulay, "History," in *Critical, Historical, and Miscellaneous Essays* (New York, n.d.), 272, 281.

54. See esp. Arthur M. Eckstein, *Moral Vision in the Histories of Polybius* (Berkeley, 1995); Klaus Stiewe (ed.), *Polybios* (Darmstadt, 1982); Paul Pédech, *La Méthode historique de Polybe* (Paris, 1964); and Frank Walbank, *Polybius* (Berkeley, 1972).

55. *The Histories,* tr. W. R. Paton (Cambridge, Mass., 1992), 1.1; *VS.*

56. See F. W. Walbank, "Polybius between Greece and Rome," *Entretiens Hardt XX* (Geneva, 1973), 1–31; and Arnaldo Momigliano, "The Historian's Skin," in *Sesto Contributo alla storia degli studi classici e del mondo antico* (Rome, 1980), I, 78–88.

57. Polybius, *The Histories,* tr. W. R. Paton (Cambridge, 1960), 3.32.

58. Polybius, 3.57.

59. Polybius, 36.12; and see Peter Dero, "Historical Explanation: Polybius and His Predecessor," in *Greek Historiography,* ed. Simon Hornblower (Oxford, 1994), 73–90.

60. See Polybius, 1.42, e.g., in order to explain the earlier stages of the formation of the Achaean League; cf. 38.5–6.

61. Polybius, 15.34.

62. Polybius, 9.1.

63. Polybius, 6.47.

64. Polybius, 1.41, 3.58, 4.21.

65. Polybius, 3.29, 12.25, 15.7, e.g., and see Pédech, *La Méthode.*

66. Polybius, 3.22 and 26.

67. Polybius, 15.36.

68. Polybius, 3.31.

69. Polybius, 7.7, 15.34.

70. Polybius, 3.22, 12 passim.

71. Polybius, 1.14; and see Walbank, *Polybius*, 43.

72. Polybius, 3.6; and see Pédech, *La Méthode*, 78.

73. Polybius, 38.2, 1.58.

74. Polybius, 6.57.

75. Polybius, 29.21

76. Polybius, 1.39, 38.22.

77. Polybius, 6.56, on which see T. R. Glover, *The Conflict of Religions in the Early Roman Empire* (Boston, 1960), 3–4.

78. Polybius, 5.31, 8.2.

79. Polybius, 1.3, 5.31.

80. Polybius, 12.25.

81. See Kurt von Fritz, *The Theory of the Mixed Constitution in Antiquity: A Critical Analysis of Polybius' Political Ideas* (New York, 1954).

82. Polybius, 6.11; and see Claude Nicolet, "Polybe et les institutions romaines," *Entretiens Hardt XX*, 147–200.

83. Polybius, 6.7–9; see G. W. Trompf, *The Idea of Historical Recurrence in Western Thought from Antiquity to the Reformation* (Berkeley, 1979).

84. See Kenneth Sacks, *Diodorus and the First Century* (Princeton, 1990).

85. Diodorus, 1.1; *VH*. See Anne Burton, *Diodorus Siculus, Book I: A Commentary* (Leiden, 1972).

86. Fornara, *The Nature of History*, 38; and see Michael Attyah, *Theopompus of Chios: History and Rhetoric in the Fourth Century B.C.* (Oxford, 1994); and esp. Gordon S. Shrimpton, *Theopompus the Historian* (Montreal, 1991).

87. Diodorus of Sicily, *The Library of History*, tr. C. H. Oldfather (Cambridge, 1960), 1.2, "*de tou koinou genous ton anthropon*," a passage from Posidonius, according to M. L. W. Laistner, *The Greater Roman Historians* (Ithaca, 1963), 20.

88. See A. J. Woodman, *Rhetoric in Classical Historiography* (London, 1988).

89. Diodorus, 1.3.

90. Diodorus, 1.8; Sacks, *Diodorus*, 55.

91. Diodorus, 1.9.

92. Diodorus, 1.10ff.

93. See E. R. Dodds, *The Ancient Concept of Progress* (Oxford, 1973), 10.

94. Diodorus, 1.37.

95. Diodorus, 4.8.

96. Dionysius of Halicarnassus, *The Roman Antiquities*, tr. Edward Cary (Cambridge, 1968), 1.7.; *VH*. See Emilio Gabba, *Dionysius and the History of Archaic Rome* (Berkeley, 1991).

97. Dionysius, 1.1.

98. *Nemean Odes* 4.346.

99. Dionysius, 1.3.

100. See Felix Jacoby, *Atthis: The Local Chronicles of Athens* (Oxford, 1949).

101. Dionysius, 1.10.
102. Dionysius, 1.33.
103. Dionysius, 1.35.
104. Dionysius, 1.48.
105. Dionysius, 1.60.
106. Dionysius, 1.73.
107. Dionysius, 1.89.
108. Dionysius, 2.3–6.
109. Dionysius, 2.20.
110. Dionysius, 2.24.
111. Dionysius, 2.25–27.
112. Dionysius, 2.62.
113. Dionysius, 2.68.
114. The classic study is Werner Jaeger, *Paideia*, III, 46–70.
115. A useful collection is Arnold J. Toynbee (ed.), *Greek Historical Thought* (New York, n.d.).
116. Plato, *Greater Hippias* 285d; and see Rudolf Pfeiffer, *History of Classical Scholarship: From the Beginnings to the End of the Hellenistic Age* (Oxford, 1968), 51–52.
117. See below, ch. 8.
118. The old argument of Werner Jaeger, *Aristotle: Fundamentals of the History of His Development*, tr. Richard Robinson (Oxford, 1934), has been taken up in a critical way by John Rist, *The Mind of Aristotle: A Study in Philosophical Growth* (Toronto, 1989).
119. *The Geography*, tr. Horace Leonard Jones (London, 1917); VH.
120. *Geography* 8.3.9.
121. *Geography* 3.4.19.
122. *Geography* 2.8.
123. *Traces on the Rhodian Shore*, 99.
124. *Poetics* 1451ᵇ5–7; VH. See Chatelet, *Naissance de l'histoire*, 339; Starr, *Awakening*, 9; and G. E. M. de Ste.-Croix, "Aristotle on History and Poetry," in *The Ancient Historian and His Materials*, ed. Barbara Levick (Westmead, 1975), 45–58.
125. *Poetics* 1459ᵃ.
126. See esp. Brian Vickers, *In Defense of Rhetoric* (Oxford, 1988); Thomas M. Conley, *Rhetoric in the European Tradition* (Chicago, 1990); and George Kennedy, *The Arts of Persuasion in Greece* (Princeton, 1963), *The Arts of Rhetoric in the Roman World* (Princeton, 1972), *Greek Rhetoric under Christian Emperors* (Princeton, 1983), and *Classical Rhetoric and Christian and Secular Tradition from Ancient to Modern Times* (Chapel Hill, 1980).
127. Diodorus, 1.2.
128. *On Thucydides*, tr. W. Kendrick Pritchett (Berkeley, 1975), ch. 10; VH.
129. *On Thucydides* 42.
130. R. H. Barrow, *Plutarch and His Times* (Bloomington, 1967), 157.
131. *The Malice of Herodotus*, tr. Anthony Bowen (Warminster, 1992), 21; VH.
132. *The Malice of Herodotus*, 13.
133. See Momigliano, *The Development of Greek Biography* (Cambridge, Mass., 1993).

134. "Superstition" and "Isis and Osiris," *Moralia*, tr. F. C. Babbitt, II and V (Cambridge, Mass., 1928, 1936).

135. Plutarch, *Theseus* 1; cf. *The Roman Questions*, tr. H. J. Rose (Oxford, 1924).

136. Plutarch, *Pericles* 13.

137. C. P. Jones, *Culture and Society in Lucian* (Cambridge, Mass., 1986), 65; and see Barry Baldwin, *Studies in Lucian* (Toronto, 1973); and Gert Avenarius, *Lukians Schrift zur Geschichtsschreibung* (Meisenheim, 1956).

138. *How to Write History*, tr. K. Kilburn (Cambridge, Mass., 1959), 45ff; *VH*.

139. See the classic statement by Eduard Meyer, *Thukidides und die Entstehung der wissenschaftlichen Geschichtsschreibung* (Vienna, 1913).

Chapter 3: Roman Foundations

1. See esp. M. L. W. Laistner, *The Greater Roman Historians* (Berkeley, 1963); Michael Grant, *The Ancient Historians* (New York, 1970); T. A. Dorey (ed.), *Latin Historians* (New York, 1966); Stephen Usher, *The Historians of Greece and Rome* (London, 1969); and Dieter Flach, *Einführung in die römische Geschichtsschreibung* (Darmstadt, 1985).

2. Raymond Bloch, *The Origins of Rome* (New York, 1960), 124.

3. *Epistles* 2.1.156.

4. *De republica* 2.33.

5. *Rome: The Book of Foundations*, tr. Felicia McCarren (Stanford, 1991), 13; and see Jean Bayet, *Histoire politique et psychologique de la religion romaine* (Paris, 1957).

6. See D. R. Kelley, *The Human Measure: Social Thought in the Western Legal Tradition* (Cambridge, Mass., 1991), ch. 3.

7. "De origine iuris civilis" (*Digest* 1.2); *VH*.

8. *Conflict of Religions in the Early Roman Empire* (London, 1909), 8.

9. *On the Latin Language*, tr. Roland G. Kent (Cambridge, 1958), 98.2–6.

10. See Arnaldo Momigliano, *Classical Foundations of Modern Historiography* (Berkeley, 1990), 68.

11. Aulus Gellius, *The Attic Nights*, tr. John C. Rolf (Cambridge, 1984), 17.21; *VH*.

12. Leofranc Holford-Stevens, *Aulus Gellius* (Chapel Hill, 1989).

13. Aulus Gellius 14.6, citing *Odyssey* 4.392.

14. Aulus Gellius, 3.11, 15.23, 17.21.

15. Aulus Gellius, 1.10.4.

16. Aulus Gellius, 1.18.

17. Aulus Gellius, 16.10.

18. Aulus Gellius, 20.1.

19. Aulus Gellius, 5.18.8.

20. Aulus Gellius, 11.18.

21. Livy, *From the Founding of the City*, tr. B. O. Foster (Cambridge, 1976), 1.44.2; and see esp. E. Badian, "The Early Historians," in Dorey, *Latin Historians*, 1–38.

22. See *Classical Foundations*, 88–108.

23. Cicero, *Tusculan Disputations*, tr. J. E. King (Cambridge, 1942), 1.2.1, 4.2.3, on the *carminae*.

24. See T. A. Dorey, "Caesar: the 'Gallic War,' " in Dorey, *Latin Historians,* 65-84; and G. M. Paul, "Sallust," in ibid., 85-113.

25. *The War with Cataline,* tr. J. C. Rolfe (Cambridge, Mass., 1931), 3; cf. Aulus Gellius 4.15.

26. *The War with Jugurtha,* tr. J. C. Rolfe (Cambridge, Mass., 1931), 10.6.

27. *The War with Cataline,* 1.1; cf. *The War with Jugurtha,* 1.1.

28. Beryl Smalley, "Sallust in the Middle Ages," in *Classical Influences on European Culture,* A.D. 500-1500, ed. R. R. Bolgar (Cambridge, 1972), 165-76.

29. *De rerum natura,* tr. W. H. D. Rouse (Cambridge, 1982), 5.1012; and see below, ch. 9 at nn. 26 and 75. See also Howard Jones, *The Epicurean Tradition* (London, 1989), esp. 64ff; Pierre Boyancé, *Lucrèce et l'épicuréanisme* (Paris, 1963); and Clarence J. Glacken, *Traces on the Rhodian Shore* (Berkeley, 1967), 134ff.

30. Lucretius, 5.1141.

31. Lucretius, 5.1457.

32. See below, ch. 9 n. 31.

33. *Georgics* 2.489: "Felix qui potuit rerum cognoscere causas." See Philip P. Hardie, *Virgil's Aeneid: Cosmos and Imperium* (Oxford, 1986); and Francis Cairns, *Virgil's Augustan Epic* (Cambridge, 1989).

34. *Aeneid* 1.21. See Richard Waswo, *The Founding Legend of Western Civilization: From Virgil to Vietnam* (Hanover, N.H., 1997).

35. *Aeneid* 1.278.

36. *Aeneid* 6.851-53.

37. Livy 1.19; *VH.*

38. See J. Wight Duff, *A Literary History of Rome* (London, 1960), I, 464: "His prose-epic is own sister to the *Aeneid.*"

39. Hermann Tränkle, *Polybios und Livius* (Basel, 1977).

40. See esp. P. G. Walsh, *Livy: His Historical Aims and Methods,* 2d ed. (Bristol, 1989); T. J. Luce, *Livy: The Composition of His History* (Princeton, 1977); T. A. Dorey (ed.), *Livy* (London, 1971); and Erich Burck (ed.), *Wege zu Livius,* 2d ed. (Darmstadt, 1977).

41. Livy 4.4, 28.28; and see Gary B. Miles, *Livy: Constructing Early Rome* (Ithaca, 1995); and Michael Grant, *Roman Legends* (London, 1971).

42. Miles, *Livy,* 63.

43. "History," in *Critical, Historical and Miscellaneous Essays and Poems* (New York, n.d.), I, 288.

44. Ennius, in *Remains of Old Latin,* tr. E. H. Warmington (Cambridge, 1935), 1.390: "Moribus antiquis stat res Romana virisque."

45. *The Republic,* tr. Clinton Walker Keyes (Cambridge, 1988), 2.2.

46. See Lidia Mazzolani, *Empire without End* (New York, 1972).

47. Livy, 1.16.

48. Livy, 1.18.

49. Livy, 3.23.

50. Livy, 3.33.

51. Livy, 5.18ff.

52. Livy, 5.1.

53. Miles, *Livy*, 75–109.

54. *Epitome of Roman History*, tr. E. S. Forster (London, 1947), I, intro.

55. See esp. Ronald Syme, *Tacitus*, 2 vols. (Oxford, 1958); also Ronald Martin, *Tacitus* (Berkeley, 1981); Ronald Mellor (ed.), *Tacitus: The Classical Heritage* (New York, 1995); T. A. Dorey (ed.), *Tacitus* (New York, 1969); and Viktor Pöschl (ed.), *Tacitus* (Darmstadt, 1969).

56. Syme, *Tacitus*, I, 117; *VH*.

57. See B. Walker, *The Annals of Tacitus: A Study in the Writing of History* (Manchester, 1952), 74, 156–57; and Frederick M. Ahl, *Lucan: An Introduction* (Ithaca, 1976), 18.

58. *Dialogue on Oratory*, in *The Complete Works of Tacitus*, tr. Alfred John Church and William Jackson Brodribb (New York, 1942), 32. See Brian Vickers, *In Defense of Rhetoric* (Oxford, 1988), 44–47; and George A. Kennedy, *A New History of Classical Rhetoric* (Princeton, 1994), 173–74.

59. *Dialogue* 28.

60. *Ancient Historians*, 295.

61. *Germany* 7.

62. *Germany* 19.

63. *The Annals*, tr. John Jackson (Cambridge, 1956), 2.88.

64. *The Histories*, tr. Clifford H. Moore (Cambridge, 1956), 1.2; cf. *Annals* 16.16 ("monotony of disasters").

65. *Histories*, 1.4.

66. *Histories*, e.g., 2.38, 14.12.

67. *Histories*, 5, passim.

68. *Annals*, 1.4.

69. *Annals* 3.54.

70. *Annals* 3.60.

71. See Patrick Sinclair, *Tacitus the Sententious Historian: A Sociology of Rhetoric in Annales 1–6* (University Park, 1995).

72. *Tacitus* II, 529.

73. *Annals* 16.22.

74. *Annals* 4.33.

75. *Classical Foundations*, 117.

76. *Annals* 3.26–27.

77. *Annals* 11.27, 3.65.

78. See ch. 8 at n. 37 and ch. 9 at n. 7.

79. *Annals* 14.14–15, 11.14. See below ch. 6 at n. 86.

80. Ammianus Marcellinus, tr. John C. Rolfe, 3 vols. (Cambridge, 1982–86), 31.16; *VH*. See E. A. Thompson, *The Historical Work of Ammianus Marcellinus* (Cambridge, 1947); Ronald Syme, *Ammianus and the Historia Augusta* (Oxford, 1968); and Arnaldo Momigliano, "The Lonely Historian Ammianus Marcellinus," in *Sesto Contributo alla storia degli studi classici e del mondo antico* (Rome, 1980), I, 143–57.

81. Ammianus, 26.1.

82. Ammianus, 15.1.

83. Ammianus, 14.6, 19.10, 28.1 and 4.

84. John Matthews, "Ammianus and the Eternity of Rome," in *The Inheritance of Historiography*, ed. Christopher Holdsworth and T. P. Wiseman (Exeter, 1986), 18.

85. Ammianus, 16.12.

86. *How to Write History*, tr. K. Kilburn (Cambridge, Mass., 1959), 45ff.

87. G. M. Paul, "Sallust," in *Latin Historians*, 105ff; P. G. Walsh, *Livy*, 129ff; Syme, *Tacitus*, I, 340ff; Martin, *Tacitus*, 214ff; Robin Seager, *Ammianus Marcellinus: Seven Studies in His Thought and Language* (Columbia, Mo., 1986).

88. *De oratore*, tr. E. W. Sutton (Cambridge, 1988), 1.5; *VH*.

89. *De oratore* 2.9.

90. *De Inventione*, tr. H. M. Hubbell (Cambridge, 1959), 1.27: "historia est gesta res ab aetatis nostrae memoria remota."

91. *De oratore* 2.15.

92. *De legibus* 1.1.

93. *De oratore* 2.13; and see *De legibus* 1.5.

94. *The Letters*, tr. William Melmoth (London, 1915), 5.8; *VH*.

95. *Letters* 7.33.

96. Quintilian, *The Institutio oratoria*, tr. H. E. Butler (Cambridge, 1989), 2.4.2; *VH*.

97. Quintilian, 1.6.

98. Quintilian, 3.8.

99. Quintilian, 1.9.

100. Quintilian, 1.10. He remarks that "historians have been taken to task by geometricians for believing the time taken to circumnavigate an island to be a sufficient indication of its size."

101. Quintilian, 2.4, 4.2.

102. Quintilian, 9.4.

103. Quintilian, 10.1.

104. Quintilian, 2.4.18; and see Frank Borchart, *German Antiquity in Renaissance Myth* (Baltimore, 1971), 45.

105. Quintilian, 10.1.73.

106. *Agricola* 10, in *The Complete Works*, 4 vols. (Cambridge, Mass., 1920–22), 682; and see Syme, *Tacitus*, I, 179.

107. Gerhard Ladner, *The Idea of Reform: Its Impact on Christian Thought and Action in the Age of the Fathers*, 2d ed. (New York, 1967), 119–21.

108. Edward Kennard Rand, *Founders of the Middle Ages* (New York, 1857), 14–21; also H. Bloch, "The Pagan Revival in the West at the End of the Fourth Century," in *The Conflicts between Paganism and Christianity in the Fourth Century*, ed. Arnaldo Momigliano (Oxford, 1963), 193–218; and *Der Streit un den Victoriaalter*, ed. and tr. Richard Klein (Darmstadt, 1972).

109. *A Reply to the Address of Symmachus*, tr. H. J. Thomson (Cambridge, Mass., 1949), II, 45.

110. *The Age of Constantine the Great*, tr. Moses Hadas (New York, 1949), 151.

111. *History of the Later Roman Empire* (New York, 1958), II, 369.

112. "Byzantine" is a seventeenth-century French coinage; the empire of Constantine and his successors had continued to be "Roman."

113. For introductions to this large, and largely independent, story, see Karl Krumbacher, *Geschichte der byzantinischen Literatur von Justinian bis zum Ende des oströmischen Reiches, 527–1453*, 2d ed. (Munich, 1897), 219–408; and Robert Browning, "Byzantine Literature," and Averil Cameron, "Historiography, Byzantine," *Dictionary of the Middle Ages*, ed. Joseph R. Strayer (New York, 1983), II, 511–19, and VI, 242–48.

114. *History of the Wars, Secret History*, and *Buildings*, tr. Averil Cameron (New York, 1967), 3; VH.

115. *The Anecdota, or Secret History*, H. B. Dewing (London, 1914), 8.22.

116. *Fourteen Byzantine Rulers: The "Chronographia" of Michael Psellus*, tr. E. A. R. Sewter (Baltimore, 1966), 64.

117. *The History of Theophylact Simocatta*, tr. Michael Whitby and Mark Whitby (Oxford, 1986), 3–5; VH.

118. Cited by Deno John Geanakoplos (ed.), *Byzantium: Church, Society, and Civilization Seen through Contemporary Eyes* (Chicago, 1984), 397.

119. *The "Alexiad" of Anna Comnena*, tr. E. R. A. Sewter (New York, 1969), 17; VH.

120. *O City of Byzantium: Annals of Niketas Choniates*, tr. Harry J. Margoulias (Detroit, 1984), xvi, 3.

121. Niketas, 319.

122. Gibbon, *Decline and Fall*, ch. LX; and see Villehardouin in *Memoirs of the Crusades*, tr. F. Marzials (London, 1908), 65.

123. *Byzantina historia*, cited in Geanakoplos, *Byzantium*, 382.

124. *Decline and Fall*, ch. LXVIII, n. 65; and on Chalkokondylas and others, see *The Siege of Constantinople, 1453: Seven Contemporary Accounts*, tr. J. R. Melville Jones (Amsterdam, 1972).

125. *Decline and Fall*, ch. LXVIII, n. 57; and see Donald M. Nicol, *Immortal Emperor: The Life and Legend of Constantine Palaeologos, Last Emperor of the Romans* (Cambridge, 1992), 67.

126. *The Fall of the Byzantine Empire: A Chronicle by George Sphrantzes, 1401–1477*, tr. Mario Philippides (Amherst, 1980), 133.

127. *Decline and Fall of Byzantium to the Ottoman Turks*, tr. Harry J. Margoulias (Detroit, 1975), 57–59.

128. See R. R. Bolgar, *The Classical Heritage and Its Beneficiaries: From the Carolingian Age to the End of the Renaissance* (Cambridge, 1954), 435, 461ff; and N. G. Wilson, *Scholars of Byzantium* (Baltimore, 1996) and *From Byzantium to Italy: Greek Studies in the Italian Renaissance* (Baltimore, 1992).

129. See Cyril Mango, *Byzantium: The Empire of New Rome* (London, 1980), 242.

Chapter 4: The Education of the Human Race

1. *City of God* 10.14.

2. See below, ch. 9, at nn. 1 and 140.

3. *The Origins of History* (New York, 1981), 86. See also Norman Cohn, *Noah's Flood: The Genesis Story in Western Thought* (New Haven, 1996); and the interpretation of Eric Voegelin, *Order and History*, I: *Israel and Revelation* (Baton Rouge, La., 1956).

4. *The Idea of History in the Ancient Near East* (New Haven, 1955), 107.

5. *Historism: The Rise of a New Historical Outlook,* tr. J. E. Anderson (London, 1972), lv.

6. Daniel 4.17; *VH.*

7. Daniel 2 and 7. See Arnaldo Momigliano, "Daniel and the Greek Theory of Imperial Succession," in *Essays on Ancient and Modern Judaism,* ed. Silvia Berti and tr. Maura Masella-Gayley (Chicago, 1994), 29–35; and, more generally, John J. Collins, *Daniel* (Minneapolis, 1993), with full bibliography.

8. *Shapes of Philosophical History* (London, 1965), 16.

9. See also Katharine R. Firth, *The Apocalyptic Tradition in Reformation Britain, 1530–1645* (Oxford, 1979).

10. Ecclesiastes 10.8.

11. Josephus, *The Life,* tr. H. St. J. Thackeray (Cambridge, 1993), 1ff.

12. *Jewish Antiquities,* tr. H. St. J. Thackeray (Cambridge, Mass., 1991); *VH.*

13. *The Jewish War,* tr. H. St. J. Thackeray (Cambridge, Mass., 1927), 5.9.

14. *Jewish Antiquities* 1.34.

15. *Jewish Antiquities* 1.118; and see Arno Borst, *Der Turmbau von Babel: Geschichte der Meinungen über Ursprung und Vielfalt der Sprachen und Völker,* 4 vols. (Stuttgart, 1957–63).

16. *Jewish Antiquities* 1.120.

17. *Jewish Antiquities* 3.81.

18. *Against Apion,* tr. H. St. J. Thackeray (Cambridge, Mass., 1993), 1.1; *VH.*

19. *Against Apion* 1.165.

20. *Against Apion* 1.16.

21. *Against Apion* 1.26.

22. *Exhortation to the Greeks,* tr. G. W. Butterworth (London, 1982), 1. See R. L. P. Milburn, *Early Christian Interpretations of History* (London, 1954); T. R. Glover, *The Conflict of Religions in the Early Roman Empire* (London, 1909), 262–304; and on "the Greek Apologists" and "early Christian speculation," Etienne Gilson, *A History of Christian Philosophy in the Middle Ages* (New York, 1955).

23. The Epistle of Barnabas 2.4, 19.1, in *The Apostolic Fathers,* tr. Kirsopp Lake (London, 1925), I, 345, 401; and see Johannes Quasten, *Patrology* (Westminster, Md., 1950), I.

24. *Paul: Apostle to the Gentiles,* tr. O. C. Dean Jr. (Louisville, Ky., 1993), 57–58.

25. Daniel 7.16, 19; but cf. 5.37.

26. Titus 1.14: "Not giving heed to Jewish fables, and commandments of men, that turn from the truth."

27. *Patrology,* I, 196.

28. *Apology* 1.46.

29. *Exhortation to the Greeks,* tr. Thomas B. Falls (New York, 1948), 384ff.

30. *Oratio ad Graecos,* tr. Molly Whittaker (Oxford, 1982), 1–2.

31. *Stromateis, Books One to Three,* tr. John Ferguson (Washington, D.C., 1991), I, 16; *VH.*

32. *Stromateis* 1.25 and 23; cf. Clement, *Exhortation to the Greeks,* tr. G. W. Butterworth (Cambridge, Mass., 1982), 159.

33. *Stromateis* 1.36.

34. Colossians 2.8.

35. *Stromateis* 1.138, 144.

36. *Song of Songs: Commentary and Homilies,* tr. R. P. Lawson (London, 1957), 221.

37. Jerome, cited by G. W. Butterworth in his introduction to *Origen on First Principles* (New York, 1966), xxiii.

38. *First Principles* 1.1.2, 2.7.1; *VH.* See John Clark Smith, *The Ancient Wisdom of Origen* (Lewisburg, NY, 1992).

39. *First Principles* 2.3.6. See below ch. 9, at n. 14.

40. See Glover, *Conflict of Religions,* 239–61.

41. *Contra Celsum,* tr. Henry Chadwick (Cambridge, 1953), 17.

42. *On the True Doctrine: A Discourse against the Christians,* tr. R. Joseph Hoffman (New York, 1987), 53ff, 79.

43. *The Apology,* tr. T. R. Glove (London, 1931); *VH.*

44. *Apology* 50.13.

45. *A Select Library of Nicene and Post-Nicene Fathers of the Christian Church,* ed. P. Schaff and H. Wace, 2d ser. (New York, 1893), VI, 149 (Ep. 70); *VH.*

46. *The Deaths of the Persecutors* (De mortibus persecutorum), in Lactantius, *The Minor Works,* tr. Mary Frances McDonald (Washington, 1965), 61–203.

47. *The Rise of Christianity* (Philadelphia, 1984), 240.

48. Quoted by Eusebius, *History of the Church,* 5.26; *VH.* Quasten (*Patrology,* I, 242) associates Melito's petition with Marcus Aurelius.

49. *History of the Church* 2.3.

50. *History of the Church* 2.1. In general, see Robert M. Grant, *Eusebius as Church Historian* (Oxford, 1980).

51. *History of the Church* 8.2.

52. Cf. Acts 7.22: "And Moses was learned in all the wisdom of the Egyptian priests, and was mighty in words and in deeds."

53. Grant, *Eusebius,* 45ff.

54. See Alden S. Mosshammer, *The Chronicle of Eusebius and Greek Chronographic Tradition* (Lewisburg, Pa., 1979), 128ff; and Brian Croke, "Porphyry's Anti-Christian Chronicle" and "The Origin of the Christian World Chronicle," in *Christian Chronicles and Byzantine History, 5th–6th Centuries* (London, 1992).

55. See R. A. Markus, "Chronology and Theology: Prosper of Aquitaine," in *The Inheritance of Historiography, 350–900,* ed. Christopher Holdsworth and T. P. Wiseman (Exeter, 1986), 38.

56. Brian Croke, "A.D. 476: The Manufacture of a Turning Point," in *Christian Chronicles and Byzantine History* (London, 1992).

57. Julius Africanus, cited in Mosshammer, *The Chronicle of Eusebius,* 148.

58. *Ecclesiastical History,* in *A Select Library of Nicene and Post-Nicene Fathers,* 2d ser., III, 33.

59. Jill Harries, "Sozomen and Eusebius: The Lawyer as Church Historian in the Fifth Century," in Holdsworth and Wiseman, *Inheritance of Historiography,* 17–29; and Momigliano, *Classical Foundations,* 137ff.

60. *History of the Church* (London, 1853), VI, preface.

61. M. L. W. Laistner, "The Value and Influence of Cassiodorus' Ecclesiastical History," in *The Intellectual Heritage of the Early Middle Ages,* ed. Chester G. Starr (Ithaca, 1957), 22–39.

62. Cyril Mango, *Byzantium: The Empire of New Rome* (London, 1980).

63. Karl Heinrich Krüger, *Die Universalchroniken* (Turnhout, 1976), 37.

64. Theodosian Code 16.1.2; and see Charles Norris Cochrane, *Christianity and Classical Culture* (Oxford, 1940), 327.

65. Gerhard B. Ladner, *The Idea of Reform: Its Impact on Christian Thought and Action in the Age of the Fathers* (Cambridge, Mass., 1959), 18ff; and Yves M. J. Congar, *Tradition and Traditions: An Historical and a Theological Essay,* tr. Michael Naseby and Thomas Rainborough (New York, 1967), 53ff.

66. *City of God* 7.8.

67. Henri-Irénée Marrou, *Saint Augustin et la fin de la culture antique* (Paris, 1949); Peter Brown, *Augustine of Hippo* (Berkeley, 1969); John Rist, *Augustine* (Cambridge, 1994); and also William M. Green, "Augustine on the Teaching of History," *University of California Publications in Classical Philology* 21 (1944), 315–32.

68. Cited by Laistner, *Thought and Letters in Western Europe A.D. 500–900,* 2d ed. (London, 1957), 71.

69. *Autobiography* 10.14. And see Donald J. Wilcox, *The Measure of Times Past: Pre-Newtonian Chronologies and the Rhetoric of Relative Time* (Chicago, 1987), 119ff.

70. *City of God* 12.10; *VH.*

71. *City of God* 1, preface; 2.18.

72. *City of God* 2.3.

73. Ladner, *Idea of Reform,* 196.

74. *City of God* 10.14. See Theodore E. Mommsen, "St. Augustine and the Christian Idea of Progress: The Background of the City of God," in *Medieval and Renaissance Studies,* ed. Eugene Rice (Ithaca, 1959), 265–98.

75. *City of God* 19.7.

76. *City of God* 18.2. See below, ch. 5 at nn. 87 and 115, ch. 6 at n. 119, ch. 7 at n. 29, and ch. 8 at n. 41.

77. *City of God* 22.30. See Ladner, *Idea of Reform,* 222–38; Elizabeth Sears, *The Ages of Man: Medieval Interpretations of the Life Cycle* (Princeton, 1986); and J. A. Burrow, *The Ages of Man: A Study in Medieval Writing and Thought* (Oxford, 1986).

78. *The Seven Books against the Pagans,* tr. Roy J. Deferrari (Washington, D.C., 1964), I, prologue; on the fire, 7.7; *VH.* Cf. Tacitus, *Annals* 15.83, and Suetonius, "Nero," 38. See Mommsen, "Orosius and Augustine," in Rice, *Medieval and Renaissance Studies,* 325–48; H. W. Goetz, *Die Geschichtstheologie des Orosius* (Darmstadt, 1980); and B. Lacrois, *Orose et ses idées* (Montreal, 1965).

79. *Seven Books,* 2.2–4.

80. *Seven Books* 3.7.

81. *Seven Books* 3.20.

82. *Seven Books* 3.2.

83. *Seven Books* 7.2.

84. *Seven Books* 3, preface.

85. *Seven Books* 6.22.

86. *Seven Books* 7.7.
87. *Seven Books* 6.2; *Aeneid* 2.351–52.
88. *Seven Books* 7.37; Augustine, *City of God* 5.23; and cf. Gibbon, *Decline and Fall*.
89. "Sallust in the Middle Ages," in *Classical Influences on European Culture, A.D. 500–1500,* ed. R. R. Bolgar (Cambridge, 1972), 165–76.
90. Green, "Augustine on the Teaching of History."
91. See Rita Copeland, *Rhetoric, Hermeneutics, and Translation in the Middle Ages: Academic Traditions and Vernacular Texts* (Cambridge, 1991).
92. "On Interpreting Scripture," in *Origen: Spirit and Fire,* tr. Hans Urs von Balthasar (Washington, D.C., 1984), 100.
93. Laistner, *Thought and Letters,* 65; and see Jean Daniélou, *Origen,* tr. Walter Mitchell (New York, 1955).
94. Origen, *On First Principles,* tr. G. W. Butterworth (Gloucester, Mass., 1973) 3.3.
95. *On First Principles* 2.11.
96. *Le Temps de l'histoire* (Monaco, 1954), 89.
97. See Lane Cooper, *A Concordance to Boethius* (Cambridge, Mass., 1928), 90ff.
98. Beryl Smalley, *The Bible in the Middle Ages,* 3d ed. (New York, 1980), 245; and see Marie-Dominique Chenu, "Histoire et allégorie au douzième siècle," *Festgabe Joseph Lortz* (Baden-Baden, 1958), II, 59–71.
99. Smalley, *The Study of the Bible*.
100. *The Idea of History* (Oxford, 1946), 56. See below, ch. 9.
101. Manuel, *Shapes of Philosophical History*.

Chapter 5: History in the Medieval Mirror

1. *Speculum maius* (Douai, 1624), IV. See Monique Paulnier-Foucart, "La Compilation dans le Speculum Historiale de Vincent de Beauvais: le cas Hugues de Fleury," in *L'Historiographie médiévale en Europe,* ed. Jean-Philippe Genet (Paris, 1991), 51–66. See also Franz-Josef Schmale, *Funktion und Formen mittelalterlichen Geschichtsschreibung: Eine Einführung* (Darmstadt, 1985); Walter Lammers (ed.), *Geschichtsdenken und Geschichtsbild im Mittelalter* (Darmstadt, 1965); Denys Hay, *Annalists and Historians: Western Historiography from the Eighth to the Eighteenth Century* (London, 1977); A. Scherer and Georg Scheibelreiter (eds.) *Historiographie im frühen Mittelalter* (Munich 1994); and esp. Bernard Guenée, *Histoire et culture historique dans l'occident médiéval* (Paris, 1980), with further bibliography.
2. *An Introduction to Divine and Human Readings,* tr. Leslie Webber Jones (New York, 1946), 1.17; *VH.*
3. Patrides, *The Grand Design of God: The Literary Form of the Christian View of History* (London, 1972); Karl Heinrich Krüger, *Die Universalchroniken* (Turnhout, 1976); Rolf Sprandel, *Chronisten als Zeitzeugen* (Cologne, 1994); Martin Haeusler, *Das Ende der Geschichte in der mittelalterlichen Weltchronistik* (Cologne, 1980); Ernst Schulin (ed.), *Universalgeschichte* (Cologne, 1974); Fritz Landsberg, *Das Bild der alten Geschichte in mittelalterlichen Weltchroniken* (Berlin, 1934); and Genet, *L'Historiographie,* esp. the papers by Paolo, Prezzi, Patrick Gautier-Dalché, and Hans-Werner Goetz.

4. See Joachim Knape, *Historie in Mittelalter und früher Neuzeit* (Baden-Baden, 1984), 52ff.

5. *The Metalogicon,* tr. Daniel D. McGarry (Berkeley, 1962), 1.13. See the studies in *The World of John of Salisbury,* ed. Michael Wilks (Oxford, 1984); and H. Wolter, "Geschichtliche Bildung in Rahmen der Artes Liberales," in *Artes Liberales von der antiken Bildung zur wissenschaft des Mittelalters,* ed. Josef Koch (Leiden, 1959), 50–83.

6. *The Marriage of Philology and Mercury,* tr. William Harris Stahl and Richard Johnson (New York, 1977), 5.550.

7. *The Didascalion of Hugh of St. Victor,* tr. Jerome Taylor (New York, 1961), 1.6.

8. Cited by Jean Leclerc, *The Love of Learning and the Desire for God,* tr. Catharine Misrahi (New York, 1961), 157.

9. See Charles Homer Haskins, *The Renaissance of the Twelfth Century* (New York, 1957), ch. VIII.

10. Marie Schulz, *Die Lehre von der historischen Methode bei den Geschicht-schreibern des Mittelalters (VI.–XIII. Jahrhundert* (Berlin, 1909), 10, 11, 30.

11. Cited in Henry of Huntingdon, *Historia Anglorum,* ed. T. Arnold (London, 1879), 2.

12. Alison Goddard Elliott, *Roads to Paradise: Reading the Lives of the Early Saints* (Hanover, 1987), esp. 215ff; and Thomas F. X. Noble and Thomas Head (eds.), *Saints and Saints' Lives from Late Antiquity and the Early Middle Ages* (University Park, Pa., 1995).

13. *Etymologiarum sive originum libri XX,* ed. W. M. Lindsay (Oxford, 1911), 1.41–44. Cf. Skeat and Partridge: root=*weid.*

14. *Etymologiae,* I, 98ff.

15. *Bibliophilion,* tr. E. C. Thomas (Oxford, 1970), 17.

16. *Bibliophilion,* 151.

17. In general, see Bernard Guenée, "L'Historien par les mots," in *Le Métier d'historien au moyen âge: Etudes sur l'historiographie médiévale,* ed. Bernard Guenée (Paris, 1977), 19–30.

18. *Historia Pontificalis,* tr. Marjorie Chibnall (London, 1956), 86; *VH.* See *Fäl-schungen im Mittelalter,* Internationales Kongress MGH, Munich 1986 (Hanover, 1988); also D. R. Kelley, "Clio and the Lawyers: Forms of Historical Consciousness in Medieval Jurisprudence," *Medievalia et Humanistica,* n.s., 5 (1974), 25–49; repr. in Kelley, *History, Law, and the Human Sciences* (London, 1984); and Marcia Colish, *Peter Lombard* (Leiden, 1994), I, ch. 3 and 4.

19. Cited by J. M. Salgado, "La Méthode d'interprétation en usage chez les ca-nonistes," *Revue de l'Université d'Ottawa* 21 (1951), 209.

20. *Letters,* 130.

21. *Lives and Opinions of Eminent Philosophers,* tr. R. D. Hicks (Cambridge, Mass., 1980), 1.1.

22. See T. R. Glover, *The Conflict of Religions in the Early Roman Empire* (Boston, 1909), 240ff.

23. M. L. W. Laistner, "Some Reflections on Latin Historical Writing in the Fifth Century," in *The Intellectual Heritage of the Early Middle Ages,* ed. Chester G. Starr (Ithaca, 1957), 3–21; and G. K. von Andel, *The Christian Concept of History in the Chronicle of Sulpicius Severus* (Amsterdam, 1976).

24. Salvian, *On the Government of God,* tr. Eva M. Sanford (New York, 1930), 147, 223.

25. *History of the Kings of the Goths,* tr. Kenneth Baxter Wolf in *Conquerors and Chroniclers of Early Medieval Spain* (Liverpool, 1990), 81ff; and also Isidore of Seville, *History of the Goths, Vandals, and Suevi,* tr. Guido Donini and Gordon B. Ford Jr. (Leiden, 1970), 1ff.

26. *Seven Books* 3.20; see above, ch. 4 at n. 78.

27. *History of the Goths,* 68, 15–16.

28. *History of the Goths,* 84, 92.

29. Cassiodorus, *Variarum,* IX, 25; cited by Thomas Hodgkin, *Italy and Her Invaders,* 2d ed. (Oxford, 1892), I, (1), 27.

30. Walter Goffart, *The Narrators of Barbarian History,* A.D. *550–800: Jordanes, Gregory of Tours, Bede, and Paul the Deacon* (Princeton, 1988), 105.

31. *The Gothic History of Jordanes,* tr. Charles C. Mierow (Princeton, 1915), 25; *VH.*

32. *Gothic History,* 68.

33. *Narrators,* 55, 68.

34. *Gothic History,* 78.

35. *Gothic History,* 40.

36. *Gothic History,* 316.

37. Martin Heinzelmann, "Gregory of Tours: 'Père de l'histoire de France'?" in *Histories de France, historiens de la France,* ed. Yves-Marie Bercé and Philippe Contamine (Paris, 1994), 19–45; and see also Adriaan H. B. Breukelaar, *Historiography and Episcopal Authority in Sixth-Century Gaul: The Histories of Gregory of Tours Interpreted in Their Historical Context* (Göttingen, 1994).

38. See Giselle de Nie, *Views from a Many-Windowed Tower: Studies of Imagination in the Works of Gregory of Tours* (Amsterdam, 1987).

39. *The History of the Franks,* tr. Lewis Thorpe (New York, 1974), I, intro., 41; *VH.*

40. *History of the Franks,* 1.41.

41. See Wilcox, *The Measure of Times Past* (Chicago, 1987), 138–39.

42. *History of the Franks,* 2.9.

43. *History,* 3.1.

44. *Narrators,* 197; see also 183, 229.

45. *History,* 10.31.

46. See Peter Hunter Blair, *The World of Bede* (Cambridge, 1990).

47. *A History of the English Church and People,* tr. Leo Sherley-Price (Baltimore, 1955), preface; *VH.* See below ch. 8 at n. 71.

48. *History,* 5.23.

49. *History of the Lombards,* tr. William Dudley Foulke (Philadelphia, 1907); *VH.*

50. *Narrators,* 399.

51. *The Works of Gildas,* in *Six Old English Chronicles,* tr. J. A. Giles (London, 1848), 307. In general, see Robert Hanning, *The Vision of History;* and Thomas D. O'Sullivan, *The "De excidio" of Gildas: Its Authenticity and Date* (Leiden, 1978); and Antonia Gransden, *Historical Writing in England, c. 550 to c. 1307* (Ithaca, 1974).

52. *History of the Britons,* in *Six Old English Chronicles,* 385.

53. Antonia Gransden, "Bede's Reputation as an Historian in the Middle Ages," in *Legends, Traditions and History in Medieval England* (London, 1992), 1–30.

54. *The Anglo-Saxon Chronicle,* tr. Dorothy Whitelock et al. (New Brunswick, N.J., 1961), 202.

55. See Joan Gluckauf Haahr, "William of Malmesbury's Roman Models," in *The Classics in the Middle Ages,* ed. Aldo S. Bernardo and Saul Levine (Binghamton, N.Y., 1990), 79–94; and Gransden, *Historical Writing,* 166; *VH.*

56. *The Annals of Roger de Hoveden,* tr. Henry T. Riley (London, 1853), 2; *VH.*

57. In general, see Auguste Molinier, *Les Sources de l'histoire de France,* I: *Epogue primitive, mérovingien et carolingien* (Paris, 1901).

58. *The Fourth Book of the Chronicle of Fredegar, with Its Continuations,* tr. J. M. Wallace-Hadrill (London, 1960), xi; *VH.* See Marie Tanner, *The Last Descendant of Aeneas: The Habsburgs and the Mythic Image of the Emperor* (New Haven, 1993), 75ff; Gilbert Highet, *The Classical Tradition* (Oxford, 1949), 51ff; and Richard Waswo, *The Founding Legend of Western Civilization: From Virgil to Vietnam* (Hanover, N.H., 1997).

59. Gabrielle M. Spiegel, *The Chronicle Tradition of Saint-Denis* (Brookline, Mass., 1978); "Laurent Theis, Dagobert, Saint-Denis et la royauté française au Moyen Age," in Guenée, *Le Métier d'historien,* 19–30; and Bernard Guenée, "Les *Grandes Chroniques de France,*" in *Les Lieux de mémoire,* II, *La Nation,* ed. Pierre Nora (Paris, 1986), 185–214; and more generally Carlrichard Brühl, *Deutschland-Frankreich die Geburt zweier Völker* (Vienna, 1990).

60. See Heinrich Fichtenau, *Living in the Tenth Century: Mentalities and Social Orders,* tr. Patrick J. Geary (Chicago, 1991), 296.

61. *France before Charlemagne: A Translation from the "Grandes Chroniques,"* tr. Robert Levine (Lewiston, 199), 11. See Gabrielle M. Spiegel, *Chronicle Tradition,* and *Romancing the Past: The Rise of Vernacular Prose Historiography in Thirteenth-Century France* (Berkeley, 1993); Hélène Charpentier, "Louis VI–Louis VII: Chronique nationale et biographies royales dans *Les Grandes Chroniques de France,*" in *Chroniques nationales et chroniques universelles,* ed. Danielle Buschinger (Göppingen, 1990), 35–48; and Robery-Henri Bautier, "L'Ecole historique de l'Abbaye de Fleury d'Aimon à Hugues de Fleury," in Bercé and Contamine, *Histoire de France,* 59–72; *VH.*

62. Colette Beaune, "Saint Clovis: Histoire, religion royale et sentiment national en France à la fin du moyen age," in Guenée, *Le Métier d'historien,* 139–56; and on the question of "national origins" more generally see Brühl, *Deutschland-Frankreich.*

63. Spiegel, *Romancing the Past,* 315.

64. *Grandes Chroniques,* 102.

65. Robert Folz, *Le Souvenir et la lègende de Charlemagne dans l'empire germanique médiéval* (Paris, 1950); Brühl, *Deutschland-Frankreich;* and esp. Robery Morissy, *L'Empereur à la barbe fleurie: Charlemagne dans la mythologie et l'histoire de France* (Paris, 1997).

66. Einhard and Notker the Stammerer, *Two Lives of Charlemagne,* tr. Lewis Thorpe (Baltimore, 1969), 93.

67. Werner Goez, *Translatio Imperii* (Tübingen, 1958). See the polemical collection, *Karl des Grosse oder Charlemagne? Acht Antworten deutschen Geschichtsforscher* (Berlin, 1935).

68. See Heinz Thomas, "Warum hat es im deutschen Mittelalter keine nationale Ge-

schichtsschreibung gegeben?" in Buschinger, *Chroniques nationales,* 35–48; and Brühl, *Deutschland-Frankreich.*

69. *Rerum gestarum Saxonicarum libri tres,* 5th ed., ed. Paul Hirsch (Hannover, 1935).

70. *Chronicon,* ed. Robert Holtzmann (Berlin, 1935).

71. *History of the Archbishops of Hamburg-Bremen,* tr. F. J. Tschan (New York, 1959).

72. *Medieval Foundations of Renaissance Humanism* (London, 1977), 63. Lambert of Herzfeld, *Annales,* in *Opera,* ed. O. Holder-Egger (Hannover, 1894).

73. *Chronica,* ed. F. Schmale and I. Schmale-Ott (Darmstadt, 1972).

74. *Sächsische Weltchronik,* ed. Ludwig Weiland (*MGH, Deutsche Weltchroniken* (Munich, 1980 [1877]), II, 280ff.

75. *Deutsche Chroniken,* I, pt. 1, *Kaiserchronik einer Regensburg Geistlichen* (Zurich, 1969 [1892]).

76. *The Renaissance of the Twelfth Century* (Cambridge, Mass., 1927), ch. VIII; and see Karl F. Morrison, *History as a Visual Art in the Twelfth-Century Renaissance* (Princeton, 1990).

77. *The Deeds of Frederick Barbarossa,* tr. Charles C. Mierow (New York, 1953), 24; *VH.*

78. *Deeds,* 144.

79. *Deeds,* 25.

80. *Deeds,* 147.

81. *The Book of the Popes,* tr. Louise Ropes Loomis (New York, 1916); *VH.*

82. *Historia Pontificalis,* tr. Marjorie Chibnall (London, 1956), 2.

83. See B. Sanchez Alonso, *Historia de la historiografía española* (Madrid, 1947), I, 127.

84. *Deutschland-Frankreich,* 82.

85. Hans Blumenberg, *Work on Myth,* tr. Robert M. Wallace (Cambridge, Mass., 1985).

86. Bernard Guenée, *Histoire et culture historique,* and "Histoire, annales, chroniques: Essai sur les genres historiques au Moyen Age," *Annales* 28 (1973), 997–1016; Fritz Landsberg, *Das Bild der alten Geschichte in mittelalterlichen Weltchroniken* (Berlin, 1934); and Reginald L. Poole, *Chronicles and Annals* (Oxford, 1926).

87. *Studien zur lateinischen Weltchronistik bis in das Zeitalter Ottos von Freising* (Düsseldorf, 1957); and see Krüger, *Die Universalchroniken,* 37–45.

88. In E. Goldschmidt, *Medieval Texts and Their First Appearance in Print* (London, 1943), 174.

89. *The Shape of Medieval History: Studies in Modes of Perception* (New Haven, 1966).

90. See Brandt, *Shape of Medieval History,* 47; and cf. Paul Veyne, *Writing History: Essay on Epistemology,* tr. Mina Moore-Rinvolucri (Middletown, Conn., 1984).

91. See Johannes Spörl, *Grundformen hochmittelalterlicher Geschichtsanschauungen: Studien zum Weltbild der Geschichtsschreiber des 12 Jahrhunderts* (Munich, 1935).

92. Quoted in the introduction to *Anglo-Saxon Chronicle,* tr. G. N. Garmonsway (London, 1953), xviii; and see Reginald L. Poole, *Chronicles and Annals* (Oxford, 1926).

93. *Chronicle,* xviii.

94. Introduction to *The Chronicle of Benedict of Peterborough,* ed. William Stubbs (London, 1867), I, xii.

95. See Antonia Gransden, *Legends, Traditions and History in Medieval England* (London, 1992), 125–51.

96. Ernst Robert Curtius, *European Literature and the Latin Middle Ages,* tr. Willard R. Trask (Princeton, 1953), 407.

97. *History of Recent Events in England,* tr. Geoffrey Bosanquet (London, 1964), preface; *VH.*

98. *Polychronicon Ranulphi Higden monachi cestrensis,* ed. Churchill Babington (London, 1865).

99. *The Chronicle of Richard of Devizes of the Time of Richard the First,* ed. and tr. John T. Appleby (London, 1963), 2–3.

100. *Gesta Dei per Francos,* in *Recueil des historiens des croisades* (Paris, 1879), IV, 115–263; *VH.*

101. *Chronicle of the Crusade of St. Lewis,* tr. Frank T. Marzials (London, 1951), 326.

102. *Romancing the Past,* 3.

103. See above, n. 56.

104. *The History of English Affairs,* ed. and tr. P. G. Walsh and M. J. Kennedy (Warminster, 1988), 32–33; *VH.* See T. D. Kendrick, *British Antiquity* (London, 1950), ch. 1.

105. *Polychronicon,* I, 3.

106. *Pontifical History,* 4.

107. *Historia Anglorum: The History of the English People,* ed. and tr. Diana Greenway (Oxford, 1996), 4–5; *VH.* See Diana Greenaway, "Henry of Huntingdon and Bede," in Genet, *L'Historiographie,* 43–50; and Gransden, *Historical Writing,* 193.

108. See above, n. 1.

109. *The Two Cities: A Chronicle of Universal History to the Year 1146 A.D.,* tr. Charles C. Mierow (New York, 1928), 87, 89; *VH.* See Hans-Werner Goez, *Das Geschichtsbild Ottos von Freising* (Cologne, 1984).

110. *The Deeds of Frederick Barbarossa,* tr. Charles C. Mierow (New York, 1953), 31ff.

111. *Two Cities,* 154.

112. *Two Cities,* 271.

113. *Two Cities,* 220; and in general see Johannes Spörl, "Das Alte und das Neue in Mittelalter: Studien zum Problem des mittelalterlichen Fortschrittsbewusstsein," *Historisches Jahrbuch* 50 (1930), 297–341, 498–524.

114. *Two Cities,* 221.

115. *Two Cities,* 358; and see above, n. 67.

116. *Two Cities,* 97.

117. *Two Cities,* 272.

118. *Deeds of Frederick Barbarossa,* 28, 252.

119. *The Two Cities,* 454.

120. See Marjorie Reeves, *Joachim of Fiore and the Prophetic Future* (New York, 1976), 2; *VH.*

121. Reeves, *Joachim of Fiore,* 14, and *The Influence of Prophecy in the Later Middle*

Ages: A Study in Joachimism (Oxford, 1969); also Bernard McGinn, *The Calabrian Abbot: Joachim of Fiore in the History of Western Thought* (New York, 1985).

122. *The Chronicle of Salimbene de Adam*, tr. Joseph L. Baird (Binghamton, 1986), 230.

123. *Translatio imperii*, in *Schriften*, ed. H. Grundmann and H. Heimpel (Stuttgart, 1958), ll. 124–28; *VH*.

124. *Cligès*, ll.30–35.

125. *The Book of the City of Ladies*, tr. Jeffrey Richards (New York, 1982), 59; *VH*.

126. *Life in the Middle Ages*, 4 vols. (Cambridge, 1928), II, 3.

127. *Polychronicon*, I, 19, 21.

128. "A Definition of the Concept of History," in *Philosophy and History*, eds. R. Klibansky and H. Paton (Oxford, 1936), 5.

Chapter 6: Renaissance Retrospection

1. *Epistolae metricae*, 3.33; *VH*. See Theodore E. Mommsen, "Petrarch's Conception of the 'Dark Ages,' " in *Medieval and Renaissance Studies*, ed. Eugene F. Rice (Ithaca, 1959), 106–29; and August Buck, *Das Geschichtsdenken der Renaissance* (Krefeld, 1957).

2. Cited in Mommsen, "Petrarch's Conception," 122.

3. *Africa*, tr. Thomas G. Bergin and Alice S. Wilson (New Haven, 1977), 231–32; and see Aldo S. Bernardo, *Petrarch, Scipio and the "Africa": The Birth of Humanism's Dream* (Baltimore, 1962).

4. *Africa*, 239.

5. *Petrarch's Sonnets and Songs*, tr. Anna Maria Armi (New York, 1968), 513, poem no. 365, the last.

6. See *Petrarch's Secret*, tr. William H. Draper (Chicago, 1911), his dialogues with Augustine, and (below, n. 22) his fictitious correspondence with Cicero.

7. Trans. in Benjamin Kohl, "Petrarch's Prefaces to *De viris illustribus*," *History and Theory* 13 (1974), 132; *VH*.

8. See Eckhard Kessler, *Petrarch und die Geschichte: Geschichtsschreibung, Rhetorik, Philosophie in Übergang von Mittelalter zur Neuzeit* (Munich, 1978); Werner Handschin, *Francesco Petrarca als Gestalt der Historiographie* (Bagel, 1964); also Timothy Hampton, *Writing from History: The Rhetoric of Exemplarity in Renaissance Literature* (Ithaca, 1990).

9. *Rerum familiarum, Libri I–VIII*, tr. Aldo S. Bernardo (Albany, 1975), I, 4; and, in general, see Denys Hay, "Italy and Barbarian Europe," in *Italian Renaissance Studies*, ed. E. F. Jacob (London, 1960), 48–68.

10. Giuseppe Billanovich, "Petrarch and the Textual Tradition of Livy," *Journal of the Warburg and Courtauld Institutes* 14 (1951), 137–208; and Eckhard Kessler, "Petrarcas Philologie," *Petrarca, 1304–1374: Beiträge zu Werk und Wirkung*, ed. Fritz Schalk (Frankfurt, 1975), 97–112.

11. "Petrarch's Prefaces to *De viris illustribus*," 13; and see Ernest H. Wilkins, *Petrarch's Later Years* (Cambridge, Mass., 1959), 283; also Peter Burke, *The Renaissance Sense of the Past* (London, 1968).

12. Angelo Mazzocco, "Petrarch, Poggio, and Biondo: Humanism's First Interpreters of Roman Ruins," in *Francesco Petrarch: Six Centuries Later,* ed. Aldo Scaglione (Chicago, 1975), 355. See Petrarch, *Rerum memorandarum libri,* ed. G. Billanovich (Florence, 1945).

13. *Rer. fam.,* 6.2; and see Mommsen, "Petrarch's Conception," 115.

14. See Philip Jacks, *The Antiquarian and the Myth of Antiquity: The Origins of Rome in Renaissance Thought* (Cambridge, 1993).

15. *Africa,* 58.

16. *Rerum familiarum, libri IX–XVI,* tr. Aldo S. Bernardo (Baltimore, 1982), XVI, 9.

17. Mario Emilio Cosenza, *Francesco Petrarca and the Revolution of Cola di Rienzo* (Chicago, 1913).

18. See Thomas M. Greene, *The Light in Troy: Imitation and Discovery in Renaissance Poetry* (New Haven, 1982), 81ff.

19. *Four Dialogues for Scholars,* tr. Conrad H. Rawski (Cleveland, 1967), 48–54.

20. *Rer. fam.,* 1.1.

21. *Rerum senilium, libri I–XVIII,* tr. Aldo S. Bernardo, Saul Levin, and Reta A. Bernardo (Baltimore, 1992), XVIII, 1; VH.

22. *Petrarch's Letters to Classical Authors,* tr. Mario Emilio Cosenza (Chicago, 1910); VH.

23. See *Petrarch's Testament,* ed. and tr. Theodor E. Mommsen (Ithaca, 1957).

24. Reported in contemporary letter by Manzini de la Motta, cited by James Harvey Robinson, *Petrarch: The First Modern Scholar and Man of Letters* (New York, 1898), 428.

25. "Life of Petrarch," in *The Humanism of Leonardo Bruni,* tr. Gordon Griffiths, James Hankins, and David Thompson (Binghamton, N.Y., 1987), 97; VH.

26. Cited in Lewis Spitz, *The Religious Renaissance of the German Humanists* (Cambridge, Mass., 1963), 22; cf. *La Storiografia umanistica* Messina, 1987).

27. See Eric Cochrane, *Historians and Historiography in the Italian Renaissance* (Chicago, 1981).

28. Poem of 1087, cited in Hans Baron, *In Search of Florentine Civic Humanism: Essays on the Transition from Medieval to Modern Thought* (Princeton, 1988), I, 47.

29. *Villani's Chronicle,* tr. Rose E. Selfe (London, 1906), 8.36; VH.

30. *Villani's Chronicle,* I–II.

31. *Chronica de origine civitatis,* ed. O. Hartwig (Santini, 1903).

32. Louis Green, *Chronicle into History: An Essay on the Interpretation of History in Florentine Fourteenth-Century Chronicles* (Cambridge, 1972).

33. *The Chronicle of Dino Compagni,* tr. Else C. M. Benecke (London, 1906), I, 1; VH.

34. Cited by Green, *Chronicle into History,* 139.

35. "The New Cicero," in *Humanism of Leonardo Bruni,* 187–88. On this whole theme of "civic humanism," see the work of Hans Baron, the summary of Albert Rabil in Vol. I of *Renaissance Humanism: Its Sources, Forms and Legacy,* ed. Albert Rabil (Philadelphia, 1988); and James Hankins, "The Baron Thesis after Forty Years and Some Recent Studies of Leonardo Bruni," *Journal of the History of Ideas* 56 (1995), 309–38.

36. "Life of Petrarch," 96.

37. *History of Florence,* in *Humanism and Liberty: Writings on Freedom from Fifteenth-Century Florence,* tr. Renée Neu Watkins (Columbia, S.C., 1978), 27; VH.

38. "On the Study of Literature," in *Humanism of Leonardo Bruni,* 245.

39. See Eduard Fueter, *Geschichte der neueren Historiographie,* 2d ed. (Berlin, 1936).

40. *The Treatise of Lorenzo Valla on the Donation of Constantine,* tr. C. B. Coleman (New Haven, 1922), 25; *VH.* See "Lorenzo Valla: A Symposium," *Journal of the History of Ideas* 57 (1996), 1–86, esp. the papers by Salvatore Camporeale, Ronald Delph, and Riccardo Fubini.

41. *The Elegancies of the Latin Language,* in *The Portable Renaissance Reader,* ed. and tr. J. B. Ross and M. M. McLaughlin (New York, 1953), 131; *VH.*

42. See Donald J. Wilcox, *The Development of Florentine Humanist Historiography in the Fifteenth Century* (Cambridge, 1969).

43. Cited in Robert Black, *Benedetto Accolti and the Florentine Renaissance* (Cambridge, 1985), 290.

44. See Denys Hay, "Flavio Biondo and the Middle Ages," *Proceedings of the British Academy* 45 (1959), 97–125.

45. See D. R. Kelley, "Humanism and History," in Rabil, *Renaissance Humanism,* III, 236–70.

46. *The Chronicles,* tr. Thomas Johnes (London, 1867), I, 1.

47. See Jean-Claude Delclose, *Le Témoignage de Georges Chastellain: Historiographe de Philippe le Bon et de Charles le Téméraire* (Geneva, 1980); and Michael Zingel, *Frankreich, das Reich und Burgund im Urteil der burgundischen Historiographie des 15. Jahrhunderts* (Sigmaringen, 1996).

48. *The Memoirs of Philippe de Commynes,* ed. Samuell Kinser, tr. Isabelle Cazeaux (Columbia, S.C., 1969). See Auguste Molinier, *Les Sources de l'histoire de France* (Paris, 1904), V, 5–22.

49. *The Monarchy of France,* tr. J. H. Hexter, ed. D. R. Kelley (New Haven, 1981), 13.

50. See introduction and further bibliography to *Monarchy of France.*

51. *Lhystoire de Thucydide Athenien, de la guerre, qui fut entre les Peloponesiens et Atheniens* (Paris, 1527). In general, see Glyn P. Norton, *The Ideology and Language of Translation in Renaissance France and Their Ancient Antecedents* (Geneva, 1984).

52. Seyssel, proem to Appian, *The Deeds of the Romans,* tr. Michael Sherman, in *Monarchy of France,* 170.

53. *La Défense et illustration de la langue française,* ed. Henri Chamard (Paris, 1948).

54. Exordium to Justin's *History,* tr. Michael Sherman, in *Monarchy of France,* 166.

55. *Les Louanges du Roy Louis XIIe de ce nom* (Paris, 1508); and see Michael Sherman, "The Selling of Louis XII," (Ph.D. diss., Madison, 1975).

56. *Les Monarchiques* (Paris, 1570).

57. *Compendium de origine et gestis Francorum* (Paris, 1500–1501), on which see Franck Collard, *Un Historien au travail à la fin du XVe siècle: Robert Gaguin* (Geneva, 1996).

58. The best study is still Katherine Davies, "Late XVth Century French Historiography, as exemplified in the *Compendium* of Robert Gaguin and the *De rebus gestis* of Paulusm Aemilius" (diss., Edinburgh, 1954); also C. Vivanti, "Paulus Aemilius condidit historias?" *Annales,* 19 (1964), 117–24.

59. *De rebus gestis Francorum, libri X* (Paris, 1555), fol. 9ᵛ.

60. *Dix ans d'études historiques,* 11th ed. (Paris, 1968).

61. *Prince,* ch. 14.

62. *Discourses*, I, introduction; *VH*. See Felix Gilbert, *History: Choice and Commitment* (Cambridge, Mass., 1977), 115–34, and *Machiaveli and Guicciardini: Politics and History in Sixteenth-Century Florence*, 2d ed. (Princeton, 1984).

63. Peter Burke, "A Survey of the Popularity of Ancient Historians, 1450–1700," *History and Theory* 5 (1966), 135–52; and Momigliano, "Polybius' Reappearance in Western Europe," *Sesto Contributo*, I, 103–23.

64. Youthful poem quoted by Sebastian de Grazia, *Machiavelli in Hell* (Princeton, 1989), 207.

65. *Discourses*, I, 2; and, in general, see G. W. Trompf, *The Idea of Historical Recurrence in Western Thought from Antiquity to the Reformation* (Berkeley, 1979).

66. *Discourses*, I, 2.

67. *Discourses*, I, 39.

68. To Soderini (Jan. 1513), in *The Letters of Machiavelli*, tr. Allan Gilbert (New York, 1961), 99.

69. *Florentine Histories*, tr. Laura F. Banfield and Harvey Mansfield (Princeton, 1988), I, 5; *VH*. See Gilbert, *History*, 135–53; and Mark Phillips, "Machiavelli, Guicciardini, and the Tradition of Vernacular Historiography in Florence," *American Historical Review* 84 (1979), 86–105.

70. *Florentine Histories*, I, 9.

71. *Florentine Histories*, II, 2.

72. *Florentine Histories*, V, 1.

73. *Florentine Histories*, II, 20.

74. *Florentine Histories*, V, 1.

75. *Florentine Histories*, VIII, 36.

76. *The History of Florence*, tr. Mario Domandi (New York, 1970), 88–89; *VH*. See Vittorio de Caprariis, *Francesco Guicciardini: Della politica alla storia* (Florence, 1950); and Mark Phillips, *Francesco Guicciardini: The Historian's Craft* (Toronto, 1977).

77. J. H. Hexter, *The Vision of Politics on the Eve of the Reformation* (New York, 1973), on Thomas More and Seyssel as well as Machiavelli.

78. In *Maxims and Reflections of a Renaissance Statesman*, tr. Mario Domandi (New York, 1965), 123 (no. 114); *VH*.

79. *Maxims*, 131 (no. 146).

80. Phillips, *Guicciardini*, 141.

81. Gilbert, *Machiavelli and Guicciardini*, 203ff; and Rudolf von Albertini, *Das Florentinische Staatsbewusstsein in Übergang von der Republik zum Principat* (Bern, 1955).

82. Alessandro Benedetti, *Diaria de bello Carolino*, tr. Dorothy M. Schullian (New York, 1967), 61.

83. Hobbes, "To the Readers," introduction to Thucydides, *The Peloponnesian War* (Chicago, 1959), xxi; *VH*.

84. *Renaissance Princes, Popes, and Prelates: The Vespasiano Memoires — Lives of Illustrious Men of the XVth Century*, tr. William George and Emily Waters (New York, 1963); *VH*.

85. Cochrane, *Historians and Historiography*, 368, 408, 412; and see *Atti del convegno Paolo Giovio: Rinascimento e la memoria* (Como, 1983).

86. *The Value of History*, tr. George W. Robinson (Cambridge, Mass., 1943), 14–15.

87. On all this, see D. R. Kelley, "The Rise of Legal History in the Renaissance," *History and Theory* 9 (1970), 174–94.

88. "De initiis, sectis, et laudibus philosophiae" (1518), in *Opera omnia* (Valencia, 1782), 3ff.

89. *De scribenda vniversitatis rervm historia libri gvingve* (Basel, 1551), 134; and see D. R. Kelley, "Writing Cultural History in the Sixteenth Century: The Project of Christophe Milieu," *Renaissance Quarterly* (forthcoming).

90. *De scribenda,* 11.

91. *De scribenda,* 69.

92. *De scribenda,* 16–17.

93. *De scribenda,* 313.

94. *De scribenda,* 186.

95. *De scribenda,* 30, 304.

96. *La Vicissitude ou varieté des choses en l'univers* (Paris, 1575); *VH.* See Philippe Desan, *Penser l'histoire à la Renaissance* (Caen, 1993); and Hans Baron, "The *Querelle* of the Ancients and Moderns as a Problem for Present Renaissance Scholarship," *Journal of the History of Ideas* 20 (1959), repr. in *Renaissance Essays,* ed. P. O. Kristeller and Philip P. Wiener (Rochester, 1992); and Baron, *In Search of Florentine Civic Humanism* (Princeton, 1988), II, 72–100.

97. *The Idea of Progress: An Inquiry into Its Growth and Origin* (London, 1932); see also the pioneering work of A. Javary, *De l'idée de progrès* (Paris, 1851).

98. *La Vicissitude,* fol. 98ᵛ.

99. *Historia de rebus Hispaniae libri XXX,* XXVI, ch. 3; and see Georges Cirot, *Mariana historien: Etudes sur l'historiographie espagnole* (Bordeaux, 1905).

100. *La Historia general de las Indias* (Antwerp, 1554), ch. ccxiv.

101. *"De orbe novo": The Eight Decades of Peter Martyr d'Anghera,* tr. F. A. MacNutt (New York, 1912), II, 331.

102. D. R. Kelley, "New World, Old Historiography," in *Changing Identities,* ed. Michael Wolfe (Durham, N.C., 1997), 275–93. In general, see B. Sánchez Alonso, *Historia de la historiografía española,* 3 vols. (Madrid, 1944–50); A. Curtis Wilson, *The Historiography of Latin America: A Guide to Historical Writing, 1500–1800* (Metuchen, N.J., 1975); Georges Cirot, *Mariana historien;* Edmundo O'Gorman, *Cuatro historiadores de Indias: Siglo XVI* (Mexico City, 1972); Anthony Grafton, *New Worlds, Ancient Texts: The Power of Tradition and the Shock of Discovery* (Cambridge, Mass., 1992); and Angel Delgado-Gomez, *Spanish Historical Writing about the New World 1493–1700* (Providence, 1992).

103. See esp. C. A. Patrides, *The Grand Design of God* (London, 1972).

104. Juan Luis Vives, *On Education,* tr. Foster Watson (Cambridge, 1913), 236.

105. Luis Cabrera de Córdoba, *De historia para entenderla y escribirla* (Madrid, 1948 [1611]), 28; and see Urbano Gonzalez de la Calle, *Sebastián Fox-Morcillo: estudio histórico-crítico de sus doctrinas* (Madrid, 1903).

106. See José Antonio Maravall, *El Concepto de España en la edad media,* 2d ed. (Madrid, 1964); and Gaines Post, *Studies in Medieval Legal Thought: Public Law and the State, 1100–1322* (Princeton, 1964), 482–93.

107. The formula is in Alfonso's code of laws, the *Siete partidas,* II, 1.

108. See Anthony Pagden, *Spanish Imperialism and the Political Imagination* (New Haven, 1990), 43, and *European Encounters with the New World* (New Haven, 1993).

109. *Historia de las Indias,* ed. Agustín Millares Carlo (Mexico City, 1951), 8: "testigo de los tiempos, maestra de la vida, vida de la memoria, luz de la verdad y de la antigüedad mensajera."

110. *Methodus ad facilem historiarum cognitionem,* ed. and tr. Pierre Mesnard (Paris, 1951), 367: "geographistorici universales."

111. *O Strange New World: American Culture — The Formative Years* (New York, 1952).

112. *De orbe novo,* I, 174.

113. E.g., Juan de Torquemada, *Monarquia Indiana* (Mexico City, [1615] 1969), XI, 116.

114. *History of a Voyage to the Land of Brazil, Otherwise Called America,* tr. Janet Whatley (Berkeley, 1990), xli.

115. *History of a Voyage,* 218.

116. Milieu, *De scribenda,* 183; and Le Roy, *La Vicissitude,* 98.

117. *De orbe novo,* I, 184.

118. *Historia general,* ch. 224.

119.   Quatro coronas tienes,
     ... en Africa y Europa
     en Asia y en America triunfante.

120. *De rerum inventoribus,* III, 15; *VH.* See Brian P. Copenhaver, "The Historiography of Discovery in the Renaissance: The Sources and Composition of Polydore Vergil's *De inventoribus rerum,* I–III," *Journal of the Warburg and Courtauld Institutes* 41 (1978), 192–214.

Chapter 7: Reformation Traditions

1. "Martinus Lutherus pio lectori in Christo," preface to Barnes, *Vitae romanorum pontificum* (Basel, [1535]), and Barnes's dedication to Henry VIII ("ex fide dignis, in lucem et publicum producantur res gestae Paparum Romanorum"); *VH.* In general, see A. G. Dickens and John M. Tonkin, *The Reformation in Historical Thought* (Cambridge, Mass., 1985); and Ernst Schäfer, *Luther als Kirchenhistoriker* (Gütersloh, 1897).

2. Gaillard, *Methode qu'on doit tenir en la lecture de l'histoire* (Paris, 1579), 29.

3. Barnes, *Vitae;* and see John Headley, *Luther's View of Church History* (New Haven, 1963).

4. See D. R. Kelley, *The Human Measure: Social Thought in the Western Legal Tradition* (Cambridge, Mass., 1991), 7ff, 148ff; and Walter Ullmann, *Medieval Foundations of Renaissance Humanism* (London, 1977).

5. Dante, *De monarchia,* III, 3; and see Charles Till Davis, *Dante and the Idea of Rome* (Oxford, 1957), 139ff, 195ff.

6. "Why the Books of the Pope and His Disciples Were Burned," tr. Lewis W. Spitz, *Luther's Works,* I, *Career of the Reformer,* ed. Harold T. Grimm (Philadelphia, 1957),

388; and Schäfer, *Luther,* 203, points out the significance of canon law for Luther's knowledge of history.

7. See Brian Tierney, *Foundations of the Conciliar Theory: The Contribution of the Medieval Canonists from Gratian to the Great Schism* (Cambridge, 1955).

8. "A Letter on Behalf of a Council of Peace" (1381), in *Advocates of Reform from Wyclif to Erasmus,* ed. Matthew Spinka (Philadelphia, 1953), 106–7; VH.

9. "Letter," 110.

10. See Victor Martin, *Les Origines du gallicanisme* (Paris, 1939).

11. *On Royal and Papal Power,* tr. Arthur P. Monahan (New York, 1974), 16.

12. *The Recovery of the Holy Land,* tr. Walther I. Brandt (New York, 1956), 88.

13. D. R. Kelley, *Foundations of Modern Historical Scholarship: Language, Law, and History in the French Renaissance* (New York, 1970), esp. chs. 6, 8, 10; and Orest Ranum, *Artisans of Glory: Writers and Historical Thought in Seventeenth-Century France* (Chapel Hill, 1980).

14. *The First Volume of the Ecclesiasticall History* (London, 1576), 2; VH.

15. See José Antonio Maravall, *El Concepto de España en la edad media* (Madrid, 1964).

16. *On the Vanitie and Uncertaintie of Arts and Sciences,* ed. Catherine M. Dunn (Northridge, Calif., 1974), 35ff; and see below, ch. 8 at n. 11.

17. D. R. Kelley, "Johann Sleidan and the Origins of the Profession of History," *Journal of Modern History* 52 (1980), 973–98, repr. in *The Writing of History;* and A. G. Dickens, "Johannes Sleidan and Reformation History," *Reformation Conformity and Dissent: Essays in Honour of Geoffrey Nuttall,* ed. R. Buick Knox (London, 1977), 17–43.

18. Preface to the English translation, *The General History of the Reformation of the Church* (London, 1689); VH.

19. English translation of "Preface to the History of Froissart," dedicated to Cardinal Jean Du Bellay, in Froissart, *Historiarum opus* (n.p., 1548).

20. Nicholas Gundling, *Historie der Gelahrheit* (Frankfurt, 1734), 3.

21. Seyssel, *De Republica Galliae et regum officiis libri duo* (n.p., 1562); Eng. trans., "To the Most Serene Prince, Edward VI . . ." (n.p., 1548).

22. *P. Comminaei de Carolo Octavo* (Strasbourg, 1548); Eng. trans., "The Epistle of John Sleidan" to the Protector Somerset.

23. *De statu religionis et reipublicae* (Strasbourg, 1555), preface addressed to the Elector of Saxony.

24. "John Sleidan's *Apology for His History,*" in *The General History of the Reformation.*

25. See Karl Schottenloher, "Johannes Sleidanus und Markgraf Albrecht Alcibiades," *Archiv für Reformationsgeschichte* 35 (1938): 193–202.

26. *Apology.*

27. *Apology.*

28. Letter to Nidbruch, 30 July 1555, in *Sleidans Briefwechsel,* ed. Hermann Baumgarten (Strasbourg, 1881), no. 152.

29. Sleidan, *De quatuor summis imperiis* (Geneva, 1559); *The Thre Bokes of Chronicles, which John Cario Gathered* (London, 1550); Eng. trans., *The Key to History* (London, 1631).

30. See esp. Pontien Polman, *L'Elément historique dans la controverse religieuse du XVIe siècle* (Gembloux, 1934); Emil Menke-Glückert, *Geschichtschreibung der Reformation und Gegenreformation* (Leipzig, 1912); and Peter Meinhold, *Geschichte der kirchlichen Historiographie* (Freiburg, 1967).

31. Giorgio Spini, "The Art of History in the Italian Counter-Reformation," in *The Late Italian Renaissance,* ed. Eric Cochrane (New York, 1970).

32. See Emil Clemens Scherer, *Geschichte und Kirchengeschichte an den deutschen Universitäten* (Freiburg, 1927); and, in general, François Fossier, "A propos du titre d'historiographe sous l'Ancien Régime," *Revue historique d'histoire moderne et contemporaine* 32 (1985), 361–417.

33. "De studiis linguae Graecae" (1549), *Opera quae supersunt omnia,* ed. C. G. Brettschneider and H. E. Bindsell (Halle, 1834–52), XII, col. 862; and see H. Brettschneider, *Melanchthon als Historiker* (Insterberg, 1880).

34. See Peter Fraenkel, Testimonia Patrum: *The Function of the Patristic Argument in the Theology of Philip Melanchthon* (Geneva, 1961), 82–109.

35. *Loci theologici communes,* in Wilhelm Pauck, *Melanchthon and Bucer* (Philadelphia, 1969), 63, 70; *VH.*

36. *Of the Holy Catholic Church,* in G. W. Bromley, *Zwingli and Bullinger* (Philadelphia, 1953), 309.

37. Bullinger, *Origines errorum* (Zurich, 1549).

38. *Institutes of the Christian Religion,* ed. John T. McNeill and tr. Ford Lewis Battles (Philadelphia, 1960), I, 1068ff.

39. Fraenkel, *Testimonia Patrum.*

40. *Catalogus testium veritatis, qui ante nostram aetatem reclamarunt Papae* (Basel, 1556), preface; and see Eleanor N. Adams, *Old English Scholarship in England, from 1566 to 1800* (New Haven, 1917), 14.

41. D. R. Kelley, "Martyrs, Myths and the Massacre: The Background of St. Bartholomew," *American Historical Review* 77 (1972): 1323–42; repr. in *The Massacre of St. Bartholomew,* ed. A. Soman (The Hague, 1974), 181–202, and *The Writing of History;* also Dickens and Tonkin, *The Reformation,* 739ff.

42. *Histoire des martyrs,* ed. Daniel Benoit (Toulouse, 1885–89), I, preface of 1570.

43. Tertullian, *Apology* 50.13.

44. *The Acts and Monuments of John Foxe,* ed. Stephen Reed Catley (London, 1841), 1:508ff; and see Katharine R. Firth, *The Apocalyptic Tradition in Reformation Britain* (Oxford, 1979).

45. See Heinz Scheible, *Die Entstehung der Magdeburg Zenturien* (Gütersloh, 1966).

46. See Sergio Bertelli, *Ribelli, libertini e ortodossi nella storiografia barocca* (Florence, 1973).

47. Cyriac K. Pullapilly, *Caesar Baronius, Counter-Reformation Historian* (Notre Dame, 1975), 153.

48. See Barbara Sher Tinsley, *History and Polemics in the French Reformation: Florimond de Raemond, Defender of the Church* (London, 1992).

49. *Histoire de la naissance, progrez et decadence de l'heresie de ce siecle* (Rouen, 1648 [1605]), 4.

50. *History of the Council of Trent,* tr. Peter Burke (Chicago, 1969), I, ch. 1.

51. *Prince*, ch. 26.

52. See Gerald Strauss, *Sixteenth-Century Germany: Its Topography and Topographers* (Madison, 1959).

53. "Oration in Praise of Germany," in *Manifestations of Discontent in Germany on the Eve of the Reformation*, ed. and tr. Gerald Strauss (Bloomington, 1971), 69; *VH*.

54. *Germania ad rem publicam Argentinensum* (Strasbourg, 1505), dedication.

55. Simon Schardius, *Historicorum opus*, I, *Germaniae antiquae illustrationem continet* (Basel, 1574); and see D. R. Kelley, "Tacitus Noster: The *Germania* in the Renaissance and Reformation," in *Tacitus and the Tacitean Tradition*, ed. T. J. Luce and A. J. Woodman (Princeton, 1993), 152–67, repr. in *The Writing of History*; Frank Borchardt, *German Antiquity in Renaissance Myth* (Baltimore, 1971); and Kenneth Schellhase, *Tacitus in Renaissance Political Thought* (Chicago, 1976).

56. *In libellum Cornelii Taciti . . . Scholia* (Nürnberg, 1529), 2.

57. *Rerum Germanicarum libri tres* (Basel, 1551), 3; and see John F. D'Amico, *Theory and Practice in Renaissance Textual Criticism: Beatus Rhenanus between Conjecture and History* (Berkeley, 1988).

58. Gustavo Costa, *Le antichità germaniche nella cultura italiana da Machiavelli a Vico* (Naples, 1977), 151, 186.

59. *Elegantiae latinae linguae*, I, "praefatio," in *Opera omnia* (Turin, 1962).

60. *Johann Turmairs gennant Aventinus Sämmtliche Werke* (Munich, 1886), VI, 402; and see Gerald Strauss, *Historian in an Age of Crisis: The Life and Work of Johanes Aventinus, 1477–1534* (Cambridge, Mass., 1963).

61. Borchart, *German Antiquity*, 102.

62. Bellarmino, *De translatio imperii Romani a Graecis, adversus Matthiam Flaccium Illyricum* (Antwerp, 1589).

63. *Die Verfassung des deutschen Reiches*, tr. Horst Denzer (Stuttgart, 1976).

64. See above, ch. 2 at n. 79, and below, ch. 8 at n. 22.

65. *Methodus*, 108: "in historia iuris universi pars optima est."

66. *Responses et decisions du droict françois* (Paris, 1637), *avant-propos*; and, in general, see D. R. Kelley, "Humanism and History," in *Renaissance Humanism: Its Sources, Forms and Legacy*, ed. A. Rabil (Philadelphia, 1988), III, 236–70.

67. D. R. Kelley, *Foundations of Modern Historical Scholarship* (New York, 1970); George Huppert, *The Idea of Perfect History: Historical Erudition and Historical Philosophy in Renaissance France* (Urbana, 1970); Gilbert Dubois, *La Conception de l'histoire en France, 1560–1610* (Paris, 1977); and Philippe Desan, *Penser l'histoire à la Renaissance* (Caen, 1993).

68. Roberto Bizzocchi, *Genealogie incredibile: Scritti di storia nell'Europa moderna* (Bologna, 1995); R. E. Asher, *National Myths in Renaissance France: Francus, Samothes and the Druids* (Edinburgh, 1993); and Anthony Grafton, *Defenders of the Text: Creativity and Duplicity in Western Scholarship* (Princeton, 1990).

69. See D. R. Kelley, "Clio and the Lawyers: Forms of Historical Consciousness in Medieval Jurisprudence," *Medievalia et Humanistica* n.s., 5 (1974), 25–49; repr. in *History, Law, and the Human Sciences*.

70. See Kelley, *Foundations*, ch. 7; and Elizabeth A. R. Brown, *Jean Du Tillet and the French Wars of Religion: Five Tracts, 1562–1569* (Binghamton, N.Y., 1994).

71. See Nathan Edelman, *Attitudes of Seventeenth-Century France toward the Middle Ages* (New York, 1946).

72. Kelley, *Foundations*, 241ff.

73. *Considerations sur l'histoire françoise et universelle de ce temps . . . a la Royne Mere du Roy* (Paris, 1568), and "Project ou dessein du royaume de France, pour en representer en dix livres l'estat entier, soubs le bon plaisir du Roy," in *Exhortation aux François pou vivre en concorde* (Paris, 1570); and see Werner L. Gundersheimer, *The Life and Works of Louis Le Roy* (Geneva, 1966); and see also above, ch. 3 at n. 53.

74. See above, ch. 6 at n. 96.

75. *Promesse et desseing de l'histoire de France, Au Roy* (Paris, 1571), fol. 2ᵛ.

76. *Promesse et desseing*, fol. 13.

77. *L'Idée de l'histoire accomplie* (Paris, 1599), 330–456, "Dessein de l'Histoire nouvelle des."

78. *Recueil des roys de France* (Paris, 1607), 1 ("De l'origine des François").

79. *Francogallia*, ed. Ralph E. Giesey, tr. J. H. M. Salmon (Cambridge, 1972); VH. See D. R. Kelley, *François Hotman: A Revolutionary's Ordeal* (Princeton, 1973), 238ff.

80. *Etat et succez des affaires du France* (Paris, 1570), "Preface aux lecteurs"; and cf. his *Histoire de France* (Paris, 1619), I.

81. Du Haillan, *Etat et succez*, fol. 1ff, 170; cf. his *De la fortune et vertu de la France* (Paris, 1570), and *Promesse et desseing de l'histoire de France* (Paris, 1571).

82. Dorothy Thickett, *Estienne Pasquier, 1529–1615: The Versatile Barrister of 16th-Century France* (London, 1979); and Corrado Vivanti, "Les *Recherches de la France* d'Etienne Pasquier," in *Les Lieux de mémoire*, II, pt. 1, *La Nation*, ed. Pierre Nora (Paris, 1986), 222–45.

83. In Janet Espiner-Scott (ed.), *Documents concernant la vie et les oeuvres de Claude Fauchet* (Paris, 1938), 135.

84. *Documents*, 136, 171.

85. Fauchet, *Traicté des libertez de l'eglise gallicane*, in *Oeuvres* (Paris, 1610), 532.

86. *La Bibliotheque historiale* (Paris, 1587), I, preface.

87. "Dedication to Henry IV," in John Collinson, *The Life of Thuanus, with Some Account of His Writings and a Translation of the Preface to His History* (London, 1807); VH. See esp. Samuel Kinser, *The Works of Jacques-Auguste de Thou* (The Hague, 1966).

88. Orest Ranum, *Artisans of Glory: Writers and Historical Thought in Seventeenth-Century France* (Chapel Hill, 1980).

89. Denys Hay, *Polydore Vergil* (Oxford, 1952); and, in general, Antonia Gransden, *Historical Writing in England c. 1307 to the Early Sixteenth Century* (Ithaca, 1982), 425.

90. See Rebecca W. Bushnell, "George Buchanan, James VI and Neo-Classicism," in *Scots and Britons: Scottish Political Thought and the Union of 1603*, ed. Roger A. Mason (Cambridge, 1994), 94.

91. See F. J. Levy, *Tudor Historical Thought* (San Marino, Calif., 1967).

92. T. D. Kendrick, *British Antiquity* (London, 1950), 34ff; and Arthur B. Ferguson, *Utter Antiquity: Perceptions of Prehistory in Renaissance England* (Durham, N.C., 1993), 84ff.

93. Kendrick, *British Antiquity*, 52. General background in F. Smith Fussner, *English Historical Writing and Thought, 1580–1640* (London, 1962); and Levi Fox (ed.), *En-*

glish Historical Scholarship in the Sixteenth and Seventeenth Centuries (London, 1956). *VH.*

94. See May McKisack, *Medieval History in the Tudor Age* (Oxford, 1971); and Katharine R. Firth, *The Apocalyptic Tradition in Reformation Britain* (Oxford, 1979), 41ff.

95. *Restitution of Decayed Intelligence in Antiquities* (Antwerp, 1605), 25; and see Samuel Kliger, *The Goths in England* (Cambridge, Mass., 1952).

96. *The History of the Most Renowned and Victorious Princess Elizabeth Late Queen of England,* ed. Willace T. MacCaffrey (Chicago, 1970), 6; *VH.*

97. Joseph M. Levine, *Humanism and History: Origins of Modern English Historiography* (Ithaca, 1987), 103.

98. "England's Epinomis," in *Opera omnia* (London, 1725), col. 44.

99. "Notes on Sir John Fortescue, *De laudibus legum Angliae,* in *Opera omnia*" (London, 1725), col. 1890. See also David Sandler Berkowitz, *John Selden's Formative Years: Politics and Society in Early Seventeenth-Century England* (Washington, D.C., 1988), 32ff; Paul Christianson, *Discourse on History, Law, and Governance in the Public Career of John Selden, 1610–1635* (Toronto, 1996); and D. R. Kelley, "History, English Law and the Renaissance," *Past and Present* no. 65 (1974), 24–51.

100. John Jewel, *Apology of the Church of England,* ed. J. E. Booty (Ithaca, 1963), 134.

101. *The Golden Treatise of the ancient and learned Father for the antiquitie and universalitie, of the Catholicke Religion: against the prophane novelties of all Heresies,* tr. "A. P." (n.p., 1596), "using herein rather the fidelities of a reporter, than the presumption of an author."

102. See Hooker, *Of the Laws of Ecclesiastical Polity,* ed. A. S. McGrade (Cambridge, 1989), with further bibliography.

103. Richard Helgerson, *Forms of Nationhood: The Elizabethan Writing of England* (Chicago, 1992), 22; also Arthur B. Ferguson, *Clio Unbound: Perception of the Social and Cultural Past in Renaissance England* (Durham, 1979), and D. R. Woolf, *The Idea of History in Early Stuart England: Erudition, Ideology, and "The Light of Truth" from the Accession of James I to the Civil War* (Toronto, 1990).

104. See Daniel Woolf, "Ancestral and Antiquarian: Little Crosby and Early Modern Historical Culture," in *The Historical Imagination: History and Fiction in Early Modern Britain,* ed. Donald R. Kelley and David Harris Sacks (Cambridge, 1997), which is part of a forthcoming work on historical culture in early modern Britain.

105. R. J. Smith, *The Gothic Bequest: Medieval Institutions in British Thought, 1688–1863* (Cambridge, 1987); and see Kliger, *Goths in England.*

106. *The Collection of the Historie of England* (London, 1618), 2.

107. *Poems and a Defence of Ryme,* ed. A. C. Sprague (London, 1930), 140.

108. *Collection,* 56.

109. *Collection,* 101.

110. Martine Watson Brownley, *Clarendon and the Rhetoric of Historical Form* (Philadelphia, 1985), 7; Nigel Smith, *Literature and Revolution in England, 1640–1660* (New Haven, 1994), 357ff.

111. *Selections from the "History of the Rebellion" and the "Life by Himself,"* ed.

G. Huehns (Oxford, 1978), 2; *VH*. See Philip Hicks, *Neoclassical History and English Culture from Clarendon to Hume* (London, 1996).

112. *English Scholars, 1660–1730,* 2d ed. (London, 1951).

Chapter 8: The Science of History

1. D. R. Kelley, "Humanism and History," in *Renaissance Humanism: Foundations, Forms, and Legacy,* ed. A. Rabil (Philadelphia, 1988), III, 236–70, and "The Theory of History," in *Cambridge History of Renaissance Philosophy,* ed. Charles Schmitt et al. (Cambridge, 1988), 746–62.

2. Quintilian, 1.9.1, cited, e.g., by Guarino, in Woodward, *Vittorino da Feltre and Other Humanist Educators: Essays and Versions* (Cambridge, 1921), 163.

3. "On the Study of Literature," in *The Humanism of Leonardo Bruni,* 245–46; *VH*.

4. *Opera varia* (Mainz, 1521), fo. II.

5. "Concerning Liberal Studies," in Woodward, *Vittorino da Feltre,* 107; *VH*.

6. *Epistolario,* ed. R. Sabbadini (Venice, 1915–19), II, 458.

7. *De rebus a Ferdinando rege et maioribus eius gestis,* in *Opera omnia,* ed. Eugenio Garin (Turin, 1962), II, 6.

8. Cited in Charles Trinkaus, "A Humanist's Image of Humanism: The Inaugural Orations of Bartolommeo della Fonte," *Studies in the Renaissance* 7 (1960), 90–125.

9. *De rerum inventoribus* (Basel, [1499] 1563), I, 6, 12; *VH*.

10. "Transmission of the Disciplines," in *Vives: On Education,* tr. Foster Watson (Cambridge, 1913), 236ff; *VH*.

11. *On the Vanitie and Uncertaintie of Arts and Sciences,* ed. Catherine M. Dunn (Northridge, Calif., 1974), 35ff; *VH*.

12. Johann Wolf (ed.), *Artis historiae penus octodecim scriptores* (Basel, 1579 [1576]), I, 1–407; on which see Beatrice Reynolds, "Shifting Currents in Historical Criticism," *Journal of the History of Ideas* 14 (1953), 471–92, repr. in *Renaissance Essays II,* ed. William J. Connell (Rochester, 1993).

13. Cited by Trinkaus, "Humanist's Image of Humanism," 99–100.

14. *Discourse de l'histoire* (Paris, 1604), 1–2; *VH*.

15. *Ars historica sive de historiae, et historices natura, historiaque scribendae praeceptis* (Leiden, 1623), 1.

16. *Ars historica,* 32.

17. *The Value of History,* tr. George W. Robinson (Cambridge, Mass., 1943), 14–15; *VH*.

18. See Nicholas Wickenden, *G. J. Vossius and the Humanist Concept of History* (Assen, 1993); and J. H. M. Salmon, "Example and Truth: Degory Wheare and the *Ars Historica,*" in *The Historical Imagination: History and Fiction in Early Modern Britain,* ed. Donald R. Kelley and David Harris Sacks (Cambridge, 1997).

19. Jean-Pierre Guicciardi, "Prehistoire de l'histoire: La dialectique de la vérité et de l'erreur dans quelques 'artes historicae' (fin XVIIᵉ–XVIIIᵉ siècle)," in *L'Histoire au dix-huitième siècle* (Aix-en-Provence, 1980), 3–27, summarizes six of these treatises from 1670 to 1784.

20. *A New Method of Studying History* (London, 1728), 25.

21. D. R. Kelley, "The Theory of History," 746–61, and the literature there cited; and also Guido Oldrini, *La Disputa del metodo nel rinascimento: Indagini su Ramo e sul ramismo* (Florence, 1997); and Neal Ward Gilbert, *Renaissance Concepts of Method* (New York, 1960).

22. *De institutione historiae universae et eius cum iurisprudentia coniunctione,* in *Ars historiae penus octodecem scriptores* (Basel, 1579), I, 668. See Kelley, *Foundations,* ch. 5; and Michael Erbe, *François Bauduin, 1520–1573: Biographie eines Humanisten* (Gütersloh, 1978).

23. *De institutione,* 609.

24. *Methode qu'on doit tenir en la lecture de l'histoire, vray miroir et examplaire de nostre vie* (Paris, 1579); and cf. his earlier Latin "De utilitate et ordine historiarum praefata, deprompta ex suis institutionibus historicis," *"praefixa"* to *Bap. Fulgosii Factorum dictorumque libri IX* (Paris, 1578); VH.

25. *L'Histoire des histoires, avec l'ideé de l'histoire accompli* (Paris, 1599), two works, paginated separately; and see D. R. Kelley, "History as a Calling: The Case of La Popelinière," in *Renaissance Studies in Honor of Hans Baron,* ed. A. Molho and J. Tedeschi (Florence, 1971), 771–89; repr. in *The Writing of History and the Study of Law* (London, 1997); and Erich Hassinger, *Empirisch-rationaler Historismus: Seine Ausbildung in der Literatur Westeuropas von Guicciardini bis Saint-Evremond* (Bern, 1978).

26. *Idée de l'histoire,* 37.

27. *Idée de l'histoire,* 362.

28. *De natura et proprietatibus historiae: Commentarius* (Hannover, 1610); and see Wickendon, *Vossius,* 65ff; also Kenneth McRae, "Ramist Tendencies in the Thought of Jean Bodin" and "Post Script," *Journal of the History of Ideas* 16 (1955), 306–23, 24 (1963), 569–71.

29. See Arno Seifert, *Cognitio Historica: Die Geschichte als Namengeberin der frühneuzeitlichen Empirie* (Berlin, 1976).

30. *Della "philosophia rationalis,"* in *Tutte le opere,* ed. Luigi Firpo (Milan, 1954), 1222ff.

31. *Of the Advancement of Learning,* in *The Philosophical Works,* ed. John M. Robertson (London, 1905), 95; VH.

32. *De dignitate scientiarum,* in *Works,* ed. Spedding et al. (Boston, 1816), II, 199–200.

33. *Novum Organum,* in *Works,* I, 92.

34. *Methodus ad facilem historiarum cognitionem* (1566), in *Oeuvres philosophiques,* ed. Pierre Mesnard (Paris, 1951), 109; Eng. trans. Beatrice Reynolds, *Method for the Easy Comprehension of History* (New York, 1945); VH. See Julian H. Franklin, *Jean Bodin and the Sixteenth-Century Revolution in the Methodology of Law and History* (New York, 1963); John L. Brown, *The "Methodus" of Jean Bodin* (Washington, 1939); Jean Moreau-Reibel, *Jean Bodin et le droit public comparé* (Paris, 1933); D. R. Kelley, "The Development and Context of Bodin's Method," in *Jean Bodin: Verhandlungen der internationalen Bodin Tagung in München,* ed. Horst Denzer (Munich, 1973), 123–50, repr. in *History, Law, and the Human Sciences;* and Marie-Dominique Couzinet, *Histoire et Méthode: Une lecture de la "Methodus ad facilem historiarum cognitionem de Jean Bodin"* (Paris, 1996).

35. *Method*, 15, 17.

36. La Popelinière, *Histoire des histoires* (Paris, 1599), 28.

37. *Method*, ch. 5.

38. *Method*, 113.

39. *Method*, ch. 4.

40. *Method*, 78.

41. *Method*, ch. 7.

42. Harry Levin, *The Myth of the Golden Age in the Renaissance* (Bloomington, 1969).

43. *Method*, ch. 9.

44. *Method*, ch. 8.

45. Anthony Grafton, *Joseph Scaliger: A Study in the History of Classical Scholarship*, II, *Historical Chronology* (Oxford, 1993).

46. *Method*, ch. 9.

47. *Archeologiae philosophicae sive doctrina de rerum originibus* (London, 1692), 190ff.

48. *Lives and Opinions of the Ancient Philosophers*, I, 1.

49. Vico, *La Scienza nuova seconda,* ed. Fausto Nicolini (Bari, 1953), par. 1046. Cf. Heurne, *Barbaricae philosiophiae antiquitatum libri duo* (Leiden, 1600), 5; Horn, *Historia philosophiae* (Leiden, 1655); Stanley, *The History of Philosophy* (London, 1655); Adrian Heerboord, *Meletemata philosophica* (Neomagi, 1664); Kortholt, *Tractatus de origine, progressu, et antiquitate philosophiae barbaricae* (Jena, 1660); Grau, *Historia philosophica* (Frankfurt, 1674); Buddeus, *Elementa philosophiae instrumentalis* (Halle, 1714 [1697]), 18; *Compendium historiae philosophicae* (Halle, 1731), 37; and Gundling, *Historiae philosophiae moralis pars prima* (Halle, 1706). And see John Gascoigne, "'The Wisdom of the Egyptians' and the Secularisation of History in the Age of Newton," in *The Uses of Antiquity: The Scientific Revolution and the Classical Tradition,* ed. Stephen Gaukroger (Dordrecht, 1991), 171–212.

50. See, e.g., Richard H. Popkin, *Isaac La Peyrère, 1596–1676: His Life, Work and Influence* (Leiden, 1987).

51. *An Historical Treatise of the Travels of Noah in Europe* (London, 1601), B^iv.

52. Frank Borchart, *German Antiquity in Renaissance Myth* (Baltimore, 1971), 18.

53. Peter Bietenholz, Historia and Fabula: *Myths and Legends in Historical Thought from Antiquity to the Modern Age* (Leiden, 1994).

54. Michael Greenhalgh, *The Survival of Roman Antiquities in the Middle Ages* (London, 1989).

55. Anon., *The Marvels of Rome,* tr. Francis Morgan Nicholas (London, 1889), 3, 12.

56. William McCuaig, *Carlo Sigonio: The Changing World of the Late Renaissance* (Princeton, 1989).

57. Arnaldo Momigliano, "Ancient History and the Antiquarian," *Sesto Contributo,* I, 67–106.

58. See Roberto Weiss, *The Renaissance Discovery of Classical Antiquity* (Oxford, 1969), 66ff.

59. *Two Renaissance Book Hunters: The Letters of Poggio Bracciolini to Nicolaus de Nicolis,* tr. Phyllis Walter Goodhart Gordan (New York, 1974), 168, 129.

60. *Discorsi sopra le medagli de gli antichi* (Venice, 1555); and see Francis Haskell, *History and Its Images: Art and the Interpretation of the Past* (New Haven, 1993).

61. See George Kubler, *The Shape of Time: Remarks on the History of Things* (New Haven, 1963).

62. See Erna Mandowsky and Charles Mitchell, *Pirro Ligorio's Roman Antiquities* (London, 1963).

63. See Charles L. Stinger, *The Renaissance in Rome* (Bloomington, 1985), 65ff; and Sergio Bertelli, *Ribelli, libertine e ortodossi nella storiografia barocca* (Florence, 1973), 75ff.

64. R. E. Asher, *National Myths in Renaissance France: Francus, Samothes and the Druids* (Edinburgh, 1993); Eleanor N. Adams, *Old English Scholarship in England from 1566 to 1800* (New Haven, 1917); and D. R. Kelley, "Tacitus Noster: the *Germania* in the Renaissance and Reformation," in *Tacitus and the Tacitean Tradition,* ed. T. J. Luce and A. J. Woodman (Princeton, 1993), 152–67, repr. in *The Writing of History.*

65. May McKisack, *Medieval History in the Tudor Age* (Oxford, 1971), 155–76; and F. Smith Fussner, *The Historical Revolution: English Historical Writing and Thought, 1580–1640* (London, 1962), 94ff.

66. Cited by Ira O. Wade, *The Intellectual Origins of the French Enlightenment* (Princeton, 1971), 447.

67. See the collection *Leibniz als Geschichtsforscher,* ed. Albert Heinekamp (Wiesbaden, 1982), vii; and Günter Scheel, "Leibniz und die deutsche Geschichtswissenschaft um 1700," in *Historische Forschung im 18. Jahrhundert,* ed. Karl Hammer and Jürgen Voss (Bonn, 1976), 82–101.

68. Yvon Belaval, "Leibniz comme historien," in *Leibniz als Geschichtsforscher, 33.*

69. Friedrich Meinecke, *Historism: The Rise of a New Outlook,* tr. J. E. Anderson (London, 1972), ch. 1.

70. Rudolf Pfeiffer, *History of Classical Scholarship: From the Beginnings to the End of the Hellenistic Age* (Oxford, 1968), 170.

71. *De philologia libri II* (Paris, 1532), 217; and see Antonio Bernardini and Gaetano Righi, *Il concetto di filologia e di cultura classica dal rinascimento ad oggi,* 2d ed. (Bari, 1953).

72. In *Ratio studiorum,* cited by Marjorie O'Rourke Boyle, *Erasmus on Language and Method of Theology* (Toronto, 1977), 92; and see Myron Gilmore, "*Fides et Eruditio*: Erasmus and the Study of History," in *Humanists and Jurists: Six Studies in the Renaissance* (Cambridge, Mass., 1963), 87–114.

73. Jehasse, *La Renaissance de la critique: l'essor de l'humanisme érudit de 1560 à 1614* (Saint-Etienne, 1976); and see V. A. Nordman, *Justus Lipsius als Geschichtsforscher und Geschichtslehrer* (Helsinki, 1932); and Reinhard Kosseleck, *Critique and Crisis: Enlightenment and the Pathogenesis of Modern Society* (Cambridge, Mass., 1988), 103; also *Kritik* in *Historische Wörterbuch der Philosophie.*

74. *La Renaissance de la Critique, 335.*

75. *De philosophia et philosophorum sectis libri II* (The Hague, 1658), 171.

76. *Il Diritto universale,* ed. P. Cristofolini (Florence, 1974), 387.

77. *On the Study Methods of Our Times,* tr. Elio Gianturco (Ithaca, 1990), 15.

78. "Des historiens grecs," in *Oeuvres* (Dresden, 1756), IV, ii, 4, 9, 204.

79. See Ruth Whelan, *The Anatomy of Superstition: A Study of the Historical Theory and Practice of Pierre Bayle* (Oxford, 1989).

80. *The Letters of Marsilio Ficino*, tr. Language Dept., School of Economic Science (London, 1975), I, 152.

81. Pasquier, *Recherches de la France* (Paris, 1633), 1; and Selden, "Notes on Sir John Fortescue, *De laudibus legum Angliae,*" in *Opera omnia* (London, 1725), col. 1890.

82. *Forgers and Critics: Creativity and Duplicity in Western Scholarship* (Princeton, 1990), 123.

83. See, e.g., Thomas Comber, *Roman Forgeries in the Councils during the First Four Councils, Together with an Appendix concerning the Forgeries and Errors in the Annals of Baronius* (London, 1689).

84. Walter Ullmann, *Law and Politics in the Middle Ages: An Introduction to the Sources of Medieval Political Ideas* (Ithaca, 1975), 149.

85. D. R. Kelley, *Foundations of Modern Historical Scholarship* (New York, 1970), 215–38; May McKisack, *Medieval History in the Tudor Age* (Oxford, 1971), 75–94; and F. Smith Fussner, *The Historical Revolution: English Historical Writing and Thought, 1580–1640* (London, 1962), 77.

86. David Douglas, *English Scholars, 1660–1730*, 2d ed. (London, 1951), 227.

87. David Knowles, *Great Historical Enterprises* (London, 1962); also Pierre Gasnault, "Les Travaux d'érudition des Mauristes au XVIIIe siècle," and Ludwig Hammermayer, "Die Forschungszentren der deutschen Benediktiner und ihre Vorhaben," in *Historische Forschung im 18. Jahrhundert*, 102–91.

88. Françoise Wacquet, *Le Modèle français et l'Italie savante, 1660–1750* (Rome, 1989), 177; *VH.*

89. F. W. Bierling, *De fide historica* (1707), in *Theoretiker der deutschen Aufklärungshistorie*, ed. Horst Walter Blanke and Dirk Fleischer (Stuttgart, 1990), I 154ff; also Seifert, *Cognitio historica*, 150ff; and Notker Hammerstein, *Jus und Historie: Ein Beitrag zur Geschichte des historischen Denkens an deutschen Universitäten in späten 17. und 18. Jahrhundert* (Göttingen, 1972); also D. R. Kelley, "Fides Historiae: Charles Dumoulin and the Gallican View of History," *Traditio* 22 (1966), 347–402.

90. "De fide historica, oder von der Glaubwürdigkeit in dieser Historie," in *Acta Philosophorum* (Halle, 1715), I, 381–462, citing also Johann Eisenhart, *De Fide historica*, 2d ed. (Helmstadt, 1702). Arnaldo Momigliano, "Ancient History and the Antiquarian," *[Primo] Contributo alla storia degli studi classici* (Rome, 1955), 67–106; Seifert, *Cognitio Historica*, 152; and Markus Völkel, *"Pyrrhonismus historicus" und "fides historica": Die Entwicklung der deutschen Methodologie unter dem Gesichtspunkt der historischen Skepsis* (Frankfurt, 1987), 128ff.

91. *Supplement de la Methode pour etudier l'histoire* (Paris, 1740), 17.

92. *The Court of the Gentiles or, a discourse touching the traduction of human literature both Philologie and Philosophie from the Scriptures and Jewish Church: as also the Vanity of Pagan Philosophie, and Subservience of Reformed Philosophie to Theologie* (Oxford, 1672), 7.

93. [Noel d'Argonne], *Mélanges d'histoire et de littérature*, 4th ed. (Paris, 1740), II, 166–67; and see Paul Dibon, *Régards* (1990), 154, and Adrien Baillet, *Jugements des savans sur les principaux ouvrages des auteurs* (Amsterdam, 1725), II, 65 (on phi-

losophes); and the comments of Rémy Saisselin, *The Literary Enterprise in Eighteenth-Century France* (Detroit, 1979), 19ff.

94. See Annie Barnes, *Jean Le Clerc et la République des lettres* (Paris, 1938).

95. Hubert Gillot, *Le Querelle des anciens et des moderns en France* (Paris, 1914); and Hans Baron, "The *Querelle* of the Ancients and the Moderns as a Problem for Present Renaissance Scholarship," *Journal of the History of Ideas* 20 (1959), 3–22, repr. in *In Search of Florentine Civic Humanism: Essays on the Transition from Medieval to Modern Thought* (Princeton, 1988), II, 72–100. Cf. Tacitus, *Dialogue on Oratory*, 18ff.

96. "Second meditation," in *Philosophical Writings*, tr. John Cottingham, Robert Stoothoff, and Dugald Murdoch (Cambridge, 1984), II, 16.

97. *Faust*, II, 2, 1.

98. *Origine des découvertes attribuées aux Modernes, Où l'on demonstre que nos plus célèbres Philosophes one puis de leurs connoissances dans les Ouvrages des Anciens, et que plusieurs vérités importants sur la Religion ont été connues des Sages du Paganisme*, 4th ed. (Paris, 1812), 52.

99. *The Battle of the Books*, in *The Prose Works*, ed. Temple Scott (London, 1907), I, 162.

100. Blandine Barret-Kriegel, *Les historiens et la monarchie*, 4 vols. (Paris, 1988), III, *Les Académies de l'histoire*, 222; Lionel Gossman, *Medievalism and the Ideologies of the Enlightenment: The World and Work of Lacurne de Sainte-Palaye* (Baltimore, 1968), 156–57; Muoza Raskolnikoff, *Histoire romaine et critique historique dans l'Europe des lumières* (Strasbourg, 1982); and Henri Duranton, "La Recherche historique à l'Académie des Inscriptions: l'example de l'histoire de France," *Historische Forschung im 18. Jahrhundert*, ed. Karl Hammer and Jürgen Voss (Bonn, 1976), 207–35.

101. *The European Mind, 1680–1715*, tr. J. Lewis May (New York, 1963), 183.

102. "Formal Theory of Philology," in *The Hermeneutics Reader*, ed. Kurt Mueller-Vollmer (Oxford, 1986), 139.

103. See Adelbert Klempt, *Die Säkularisierung der universalhistorischen Auffassung zum Wandel des Geschichtsdenkens im 16. und 17. Jahrhundert* (Göttingen, 1960).

104. E.g., Edu. Brerewood, *Enquiries touching the Diversity of Languages and Religions through the chief parts of the World* (London, 1614).

105. *The Ancient Ecclesiasticall Histories of the First Six Centuries after Christ*, tr. Meredith Hanmer (London, 1577), "Epistle Dedicatorie."

106. *A Compendium of Universal History* (London, 1699).

107. *The History of the World*, ed. C. A. Patrides (Philadelphia, 1971), 48–49; VH. See Patrides, *The Grand Design of God: The Literary Form of the Christian View of History* (London, 1972).

108. *Discourse on Universal History*, ed. Orest Ranum and tr. Elborg Forster (Chicago, 1976), 3–6; VH.

109. *Discourse*, 374.

110. Quoted in James Westfall Thompson, *A History of Historical Writing* (New York, 1942), II, 100; VH.

111. Philippe Briet [S. J.], *Annales Mundi, sive chronicon universale* (Paris, 1662); and see Patrides, "Renaissance Estimates of the Year of Creation," *Huntington Library Quarterly* 26 (1962–63), 315–22. Cf. Bodin, *Method*, ch. 1.

112. *Brieve chronologie ou sommaire des temps* (Paris, 1598), and *Chronologie ecclé-siastique*, rev. ed. (Paris, 1638).

113. Arno Borst, *The Ordering of Time*, tr. Andrew Winnard (Cambridge, 1993), 106; and see Grafton, *Joseph Scaliger*, II, *Historical Chronology* (Oxford, 1993).

114. *The History of the World; or, an Account of Time* (London, 1659); and see Patrides, *Grand Design of God*, 77.

115. *Confessions*, XII, xiv.

116. *Method*, ch. 8.

117. *The Measure of Times Past: Pre-Newtonian Chronologies and the Rhetoric of Relative Time* (Chicago, 1987), 214ff.

118. Ussher, *The Annals of the World* (London, 1658); *VH*.

119. La Peyrère, *Men before Adam* (London, 1656).

120. *A Theological Proposition Upon the Presupposition, That Men were before Adam* (London, 1655), and *Men before Adam*; and see Richard H. Popkin, *Isaac Le Peyrère, 1596–1676: His Life, Work and Influence* (Leiden, 1987).

121. Plutarch, *Isis and Osiris*, in *Moralia*, tr. F. Babbitt (Cambridge, Mass., 1972), V, 10; Karl Giehlow, *Die Hieroglyphenkunde des Humanismus in der Allegorie der Renaissance* (Leipzig, 1915); and Thomas Leinkauf, *Mundus Combinatus: Studien zur Struktur der barocken Universalwissenschaft am Beispiel Athanasius Kirchers SJ, 1602–1680* (Berlin, 1993).

122. *Encyclopédie*, s.v. *Egypte*: "Les prêtres égyptiens eurent tous disciples Moyse, Orphée, Linus, Platon, Pythagore, Démocrite, Thalès, en un mot tous les philosophes de la Grece."

123. John Marsham, *Canon chronicus aegyptiacus, hebraicus, graecus* (1671); John Spencer, *De Legibus hebraeorum* (1686); and see esp. Paolo Rossi, *The Dark Abyss of Time*, tr. Lydia G. Cochrane (Chicago, 1984); Frank Manuel, *The Eighteenth Century Confronts the Gods* (Cambridge, Mass., 1959); and Alan Charles Kors, *Atheism in France, 1650–1729*, I, *The Orthodox Sources of Disbelief* (Princeton, 1990).

124. *Archeologiae philosophicae sive doctrina de rerum originibus* (London, 1692), 190ff.

Chapter 9: Philosophical History

1. *Die Erziehung des Menschengeschlechts*, in *Lessings Werke* (Leipzig, n.d.), V, 340.

2. *An Essay on the History of Civil Society*, ed. Fania Oz-Salzberger (Cambridge, 1995), 10. And see Condorcet, *Sketch for a Historical Picture of the Progress of the Human Mind*, tr. June Barraclough (London, 1955).

3. *The Court of the Gentiles or, a discourse touching the traduction of human literature both Philologie and Philosophie from the Scriptures and Jewish Church: as also the Vanity of Pagan Philosophie, and Subservience of Reformed Philosophie to Theologie* (Oxford, 1672), 7.

4. *Prolegomena to Homer, 1795*, tr. Anthony Grafton et al. (Princeton, 1985), ch. 33.

5. *Elements of Philosophy*, cited by Ernst Cassirer, *The Philosophy of the Enlightenment*, tr. Fritz C. A. Koelln and James P. Pettegrove (Princeton, 1951), 3; and cf. d'Alem-

bert, *Preliminary Discourse to the Encyclopedia of Diderot,* tr. Richard N. Schwab (Indianapolis, 1963), 36, 70ff.

6. Cassirer, *Philosophy of the Enlightenment,* 197–233; and cf. Wilhelm Dilthey, "Das achtzehnte Jahrhundert und die geschichtliche Welt," in *Gesammelte Schriften* (Leipzig, 1927), III, 210–68. The d'Alembertian view is still implicit in many interpretations of Enlightenment thought which emphasize its analytical and empirical aspects, even in the "moral sciences," without attending to historical scholarship; e.g., Thomas L. Hankins, *Science and Enlightenment* (Cambridge, 1985).

7. *Cyclopedia; or an Universal Dictionary of Arts and Sciences* (London, 1728), I, 252; VH.

8. "Introduction a la lecture de l'histoire," *Les Divers Caracteres des ouvrages historiques* (Lyon, 1694), no pagination; VH.

9. *Letters on the Study and Use of History,* in *Historical Writings,* ed. Isaac Kramnick (Chicago, 1972), 9; VH.

10. See the vast survey begun by Adrien Baillet, *Jugements des savants sur les principaux ouvrages des auteurs* (Amsterdam, 1725 [1685]), on which Rémy G. Saisselin, *The Literary Enterprise in Eighteenth-Century France* (Detroit, 1979); also François Waquet, *Le Modèle français et l'Italie savante, 1660–1750* (Rome, 1989).

11. Karl Hammer and Jürgen Voss (eds.), *Historische Forschung im 18. Jahrhundert* (Bonn, 1976); Bruno Neveu, *Erudition et religion aux XVIIe et XVIIIe siècles* (Paris, 1994), *Practiques et concepts de l'histoire en Europe XVIe–XVIIe siècles* (Paris, 1990); Gioacchino Gargallo di Castel Lentini, *Storia della storiografia moderna,* I, *Il Settecento,* 3d ed. (Rome, 1990); *Leibniz als Geschichtsforscher, Studia Leibnitiana,* Sonderheft 10 (Wiesbaden, 1982); and Henri Duranton, "Le Métier d'historien au XVIIIe siècle," *Revue d'histoire moderne et contemporaine* 23 (1976), 481–500.

12. Nellie Noémie Schargo, *History in the "Encyclopédie"* (New York, 1947), 18.

13. See Lionel Gossman, *Medievalism and the Ideologies of the Enlightenment: The World and Work of La Curne de Saint-Palaye* (Baltimore, 1968); and David Knowles, *Great Historical Enterprises* (London, 1962).

14. See Joseph Levine, "Deists and Anglicans: The Ancient Wisdom and the Idea of Progress," in *The Margins of Orthodoxy: Heterodox Writing and Cultural Response, 1660–1750* (Cambridge, 1995), 219–39.

15. *Histoire philosophique et politique des Etablissements et du Commerce des Européens dans les deux Indes* (Geneva, 1781).

16. See Frank Manuel, *Isaac Newton, Historian* (Cambridge, Mass., 1963).

17. See Francis Haskell, *History and Its Images: Art and the Interpretation of the Past* (New Haven, 1993), 159–200; Chantal Grell, *L'Histoire entre érudition et philosophie: Etude sur la connaissance historique a l'âge des lumières* (Paris, 1993); and Emery Neff, *The Poetry of History: The Contribution of Literature and Literary Scholarship to the Writing of History since Voltaire* (New York, 1947).

18. *The European Mind, 1680–1715* (New York, 1963), originally entitled *La Crise de la conscience européenne* (Paris, 1935); and see Reinhard Koselleck, *Critique and Crisis: Enlightenment and the Pathogenesis of Modern Society* (Cambridge, Mass., 1988), esp. 98–126.

19. D. R. Kelley, "De Origine Feudorum: The Beginnings of an Historical Problem," *Speculum* 34 (1964), 207–28, "Ancient Verses on New Ideas: Legal Tradition and the French Historical School," *History and Theory* 26 (1987), 319–38, and *Historians and the Law in Postrevolutionary France* (Princeton, 1984), 68–69; Harold A. Ellis, *Boulainvilliers and the French Monarchy: Aristocratic Politics in Early Eighteenth-Century France* (Ithaca, 1988); and J. Q. C. Mackrell, *The Attack on "Feudalism" in Eighteenth-Century France* (London, 1973).

20. *History of the Anglo-Saxons* (London, 1799–1805); and see Thomas Preston Peardon, *The Transition in English Historical Writing, 1760–1830* (New York, 1933).

21. *Jugemens des savans* (Amsterdam, 1725), I, 31.

22. *Port-Royal*, IV, v.

23. Henri Duranton, "L'Académicien au miroir: L'historien idéal d'après les éloges de l'Académie des Inscriptions et Belles-Lettres," in *L'Histoire au dix-huitième siècle* (Aix-en Provence, 1980), 449–78.

24. "Vico and the Heritage of Renaissance Thought," *Vico: Past and Present*, ed. Giorgio Tagliacozzo (Atlantic Highlands, N.J., 1981), 104. See D. R. Kelley, "Giovanni Battista Vico," in *European Authors*, ed. George Stade (New York, 1984), III, 293–316, with further bibliography, which is kept up-to-date in *New Vico Studies*.

25. *On the Study Methods of Our Time*, tr. Elio Gianturco (Ithaca, 1990), 15, 41.

26. *Diritto universale*, I, pt. I, *De uno principio*, ch. 100.

27. *The New Science*, 2d ed. tr. Thomas Goddard Bergin and Max Harold Fisch (Ithaca, 1968).

28. *On the Most Ancient Wisdom of the Italians Unearthed from the Origins of the Latin Language*, tr. L. M. Palmer (Ithaca, 1988), 161; and see Patrick Hutton, *History as an Art of Memory* (Hanover, Vt., 1993).

29. *New Science*, 238, 147, 127.

30. *New Science*, 125, citing Diodorus Siculus, *Bibliotheca historica* 1.9.3.

31. *New Science*, 51, 202, 361.

32. *New Science*, 385, 391, 392, 393.

33. *On the Most Ancient Wisdom*, 45.

34. *New Science*, 367.

35. See Antonio Perez-Ramos, *Francis Bacon's Idea of Science and the Maker's Knowledge Tradition* (Oxford, 1988), though without discussion of Vico.

36. Machiavelli, *Il Principe*, ch. 26; and in general see Denys Hay, "Italy and Barbarian Europe," in *Italian Renaissance Studies*, ed. E. F. Jacob (London, 1960), 48–68.

37. *New Science*, 1046; and see Donald Verene, "Vico and the Barbarism of Reflection," in *History and the Disciplines: The Reclassification of Knowledge in Early Modern Europe*, ed. D. R. Kelley (Rochester, N.Y., 1997), 143–59.

38. Gustavo Costa, *Le antichità germaniche nella cultura italiana da Machiavelli a Vico* (Naples, 1977).

39. *New Science*, 470.

40. *New Science*, 337, 470, 507, 529, 556, 559, 584, 594, 671, and 992.

41. *New Science*, 173.

42. *New Science*, 314.

43. Croce, *Philosophy, Poetry, History*, tr. C. Sprigge (London, 1966), 615.

44. Intro. to *The Autobiography of Giambattista Vico,* tr. Max Harold Fisch and Thomas Goddard Bergin (Ithaca, 1975), 61 ff.

45. "Enlightenment," in *Dictionary of the History of Ideas,* 6 vols, ed. Philip P. Wiener (New York, 1973); and see Mark Lilla, *G. B. Vico: The Making of an Anti-Modern* (Cambridge, Mass., 1993).

46. See H. J. Erasmus, *The Origins of Rome in Historiography from Petrarch to Perizonius* (Assen, 1962); Walther Rehm, *Der Untergang Roms im abendländischen Denken* (Leipzig, 1930); Michel Baridou, *Edward Gibbon et le mythe de Rome: Histoire et idéologie au siècle des lumières* (Paris, 1977); and *Gibbon et Rome: A le lumière de l'historiographie moderne,* ed. Pierre Ducrey (Geneva, 1977).

47. Medieval proverb quoted by Gibbon, *Decline and Fall of the Roman Empire,* (New York, n.d.), III, 873.

48. David P. Jordan, *Gibbon and His Roman Empire* (Urbana, 1971); Rosamond McKitterick and Roland Quinault (eds.), *Edward Gibbon and Empire* (Cambridge, 1997); David Womersley, *The Transformation of "The Decline and Fall"* (Cambridge, 1988); Girolamo Imbruglia (ed.), *Ragione et immaginazione: Edward Gibbon e la storiografia europea del settecento* (Naples, 1996); Roy Porter, *Gibbon* (New York, 1988); and esp. Patricia Craddock, *Young Edward Gibbon: Gentleman of Letters* (Baltimore, 1982), and *Edward Gibbon: Luminous Historian, 1772–1794* (Baltimore, 1989); and J. G. A. Pocock, "Gibbon's *Decline and Fall* and the World View of the Late Enlightenment," in *Virtue, Commerce, and History* (Cambridge, 1985), 143–56, as well as his forthcoming book.

49. *Memoirs of My Life,* ed. George A. Bonnard (London, 1966), 65.

50. *Memoirs,* 103.

51. *Memoirs,* 99.

52. "An Address," in *Miscellaneous Works,* ed. Lord John Sheffield (London, 1796), II, 712.

53. *Essai sur l'étude de la littérature,* in *The Miscellaneous Works,* ed. John Sheffield, 5 vols. (London, 1814), IV, 66, 453, 462, 479.

54. "Essay on the Study of Literature," in *The Miscellaneous Works of Edward Gibbon,* ed. J. Walker McSpadden (New York, 1907), 1–2.

55. Arnaldo Momigliano, "Gibbon's Contribution to Historical Method," *[Primo] Contributo alla storia degli studi classici* (Rome, 1955), 195–211.

56. *Memoirs,* 97. See Jordan, *Gibbon,* ch. 2; and J. G. A. Pocock, *Edward Gibbon in History: Aspects of the Text in The History of the "Decline and Fall of the Roman Empire"* (New Haven, 1989).

57. *Memoirs,* 263. See Momigliano, "Eighteenth-Century Prelude to Mr. Gibbon," *Sesto Contributo,* I, 249–63.

58. *Memoirs,* 136.

59. *Decline and Fall,* III, 860–80.

60. *Decline and Fall,* I, n. 39.

61. *Decline and Fall,* II, 663.

62. *Decline and Fall,* III, 805, 860.

63. *Decline and Fall,* I, 277.

64. *Decline and Fall,* I, 542.

65. *Decline and Fall,* I, 340; II, 347; III, 710.

66. *Memoirs,* 155; and see Peter Gay, *Style in History* (New York, 1974), 21ff.

67. Walter Bagehot, "Edward Gibbon" (1856), *Literary Studies* (London, n.d.), II, 32.

68. Harold Bond, *The Literary Art of Edward Gibbon* (Oxford, 1960).

69. *Decline and Fall,* I, 956, n. 136.

70. *Considerations on the Causes of the Greatness of the Romans and Their Decline,* tr. David Lowenthal (New York, 1965), ch. 9.

71. See D. R. Kelley, "The Prehistory of Sociology: Montesquieu, Vico and the Legal Tradition," *Journal of the History of the Behavioral Sciences* 16 (1980), 133–44; Werner Stark, *Montesquieu: Pioneer of the Sociology of Knowledge* (London, 1960), 22; and Raymond Aron, *Main Currents in Sociological Thought,* tr. Richard Howard (New York, 1965), I, 11–56.

72. "Gibbon on Civil War and Rebellion in the Decline of the Roman Empire," in *Edward Gibbon and the "Decline and Fall of the Roman Empire,"* ed. G. W. Bowersock, John Clive, and Stephen R. Graubard (Cambridge, Mass., 1977), 27.

73. See Peter Burke, "Tradition and Experience: the Idea of Decline from Bruni to Gibbon," in Bowersock, Clive, and Graubard, *Edward Gibbon,* 87–102.

74. *Decline and Fall,* III, 880.

75. *Decline and Fall,* II, 443.

76. *Gibbon's History of the Decline and Fall of the Roman Empire . . . Reviewed* (London, 1791), 1–4.

77. *Decline and Fall,* III, 856.

78. See J. B. Black, *The Art of History: A Study of Four Great Historians of the Eighteenth Century* (New York, 1926), on Voltaire, Hume, Robertson, and Gibbon; and David Allan, *Virtue, Learning and the Scottish Enlightenment: Ideas of Scholarship in Early Modern History* (Edinburgh, 1993), mainly on Scotland; also Phillip Hicks, *Neoclassical History;* Colin Kidd, *Subverting Scotland's Past: Scottish Whig Historiography and the Creation of an Anglo-British Identity* (Oxford, 1993); and Knud Haakonssen, *Natural Law and Moral Philosophy: From Grotius to the Scottish Enlightenment* (Cambridge, 1996).

79. See John Schaeffer, Sensus Communis: *Vico, Rhetoric, and the Limits of Relativism* (Durham, N.C., 1990).

80. *Les Sciences humaines et la pensée occidentale,* 13 vols. (Paris, 1966–88), IV, *Les Principes de la pensée au siècle des lumières,* 282.

81. *The History of the Progress and Termination of the Roman Republic* (New York, 1852 [1783]), 481.

82. See Fania Oz-Salzberger, *Translating the Enlightenment: Scottish Civic Discourse in Eighteenth-Century Germany* (Oxford, 1995); Richard B. Sher, *Church and University in the Scottish Enlightenment* (Princeton, 1985), 196–99; and Karen O'Brien, *Narratives of Enlightenment: Cosmopolitan History from Voltaire to Gibbon* (Cambridge, 1997).

83. William C. Lehmann, *Adam Ferguson and the Beginnings of Modern Sociology* (Columbus, 1965).

84. *An Essay on the History of Civil Society,* ed. Fania Oz-Salzberger (Cambridge, 1995), 21.

85. *Essay,* 167.

86. Knud Haakonssen, "From Moral Philosophy to Political Economy: The Contribution of Dugald Stewart," in *Philosophers of the Scottish Enlightenment,* ed. V. Hope
(Edinburgh, 1984), 211–32; and Nicholas Phillipson, "The Pursuit of Virtue in Scottish
University Education: Dugald Stewart and Scottish Moral Philosophy in the Enlightenment," in *Universities, Society, and the Future,* ed. N. Phillipson (Edinburgh, 1983), 82–
101.

87. "Dissertation First: Exhibiting a General View of the Progress of Metaphysical,
Ethical, and Political Philosophy since the Revival of Letters in Europe," in *Works,* ed.
William Hamilton (Edinburgh, 1854), I, 14–18. The French translation by J. A. Buchon,
with additional reflections by Victor Cousin, is *Histoire abrégé des sciences meta-
physiques, morales et politiques depuis la Ren. des lettres* (Paris, 1820); the comments on
Vico (369) provided the impulse for the Vichian revival in France, culminating in Michelet's translation of the *New Science* (1827).

88. "Dissertation First," 8–9.

89. "Dissertation First," 28.

90. *Historism: The Rise of a New Historical Outlook,* tr. J. E. Anderson (London,
1972), 158.

91. Cited in Ernest Campbell Mossner, *The Life of David Hume,* 2d ed. (Oxford,
1980), 301. See also David Wootton, "David Hume, 'the Historian,' " in *The Cambridge
Companion to Hume,* ed. David Fate Norton (Cambridge, 1993), 281–312; and Nicholas Capaldi and Donald W. Livingston (eds.), *Liberty in Hume's "History of England"*
(Dordrecht, 1990). Cf. Duncan Forbes's introduction to his edition of Hume, *The History of Great Britain* (Middlesex, 1970), 8.

92. *Essays: Moral, Political, and Literary,* ed. Eugene F. Miller (Indianapolis, 1987),
203, 246.

93. *The History of England from the Invasion of Julius Caesar to the Abdication of
James the Second, 1688,* I, 1.

94. *History of England,* I, 177.

95. *History of England,* III, 21, 132, 135; IV, 115.

96. "Of the Study of History," in *Essays,* 566.

97. Robertson, *The Progress of Society in Europe,* ed. Felix Gilbert (Chicago, 1972), 4;
and see Stewart J. Brown (ed.), *William Robertson and the Expansion of Empire* (Cambridge, 1997).

98. "A Dissertation concerning the Era in which the Poet Lived," prefacing *The Poems
of Ossian,* "translated" by James MacPherson (Edinburgh, 1762), xiii.

99. Cited by Oz-Salzberger, *Translating the Enlightenment,* 70; and see Herder, "Ex-
tract from a Correspondence on Ossian and the Songs of Ancient Peoples" (1773), tr.
Joyce P. Crick, in *German Aesthetic and Literary Criticism,* ed. H. b. Nisbet (Cambridge,
1985), 154–61. On the Ossianic question, see Paul J. de Gategno, *James Macpherson*
(Boston, 1989), with further bibliography.

100. Quoted in Perreault, *Parallèle des anciens et des modernes, en ce que regarde les
arts et les sciences* (Paris, 1688), 18.

101. *Parallèle,* 986.

102. *Parallèle,* 54. In general, besides the vast bibliography on the idea of progress, see

Henry Vyverberg *Historical Pessimism in the French Enlightenment* (Cambridge, Mass., 1958).

103. *Origine des découvertes attribuées aux Modernes, Où l'on demonstre que nos plus célèbres Philosophes one puis de leurs connoissances dans les Ouvrages des Anciens, et que plusieurs vérités importants sur la Religion ont été connues des Sages du Paganisme,* 4th ed. (Paris, 1812), 52; and see Georges Canguiem, *A Vital Rationalist,* ed. F. Delaporte and tr. A. Goldhammer (New York, 1994), 50–51.

104. See esp. Jean Dagen, *L'Histoire de l'esprit humain;* Georges Gusdorf, *Les Sciences humanies,* I, *De l'histoire des sciences à l'histoire de la pensée* (Paris, 1966), 56ff; and G. Santinello (ed.), *Storia delle storie generali della filosofia,* III (Padua, 1988), 3ff.

105. *Eloges des academiciens avec l'histoire de l'academie royale des sciences* (The Hague, 1740), I, preface, xviii, xxvi; also I, 424 (on Leibniz), and II, 335 (on Newton).

106. *De l'origine des fables,* ed. J. R. Carré (Paris, 1932); and see Frank Manuel, *The Eighteenth Century Confronts the Gods* (Cambridge, Mass., 1959), 41ff.

107. *Histoire des Mathématiques* (Paris, 1758), 42.

108. *Oeuvres complètes* (Paris, 1821–22), XV, 384; and Lucien Guerci, "Condillac historien," in *Practiques et concepts de l'histoire en Europe XVIe–XVIIIe siècles* (Paris, 1990), 233–48.

109. *Treatise on Sensations,* in *Philosophical Writings,* tr. Franklin Philip (London, 1982), 393.

110. *Essai sur les moeurs et l'esprit des nations,* ed. René Pomeau (paris, 1963), II, 215; and see Jean Dagen, *L'Histoire de l'esprit humain dans la pensée françoise de Fontenelle à Condorcet* (Paris, 1977), 299ff.

111. See Anthony Pagden, "Histories of Mankind and the Identity of the Enlightenment," in *History and the Disciplines: The Reclassification of Knowledge in Early Modern Europe,* ed. D. R. Kelley (Rochester, 1997).

112. *Essai,* I, 189.

113. *The Age of Louis XIV,* tr. J. H. Brumfitt (New York, 1963), 122–23.

114. *Nouvelles études d'histoire religieuse,* in *Oeuvres complètes,* ed. Henriette Psichari (Paris, 1955), VII, 1001.

115. *Turgot on Progress, Sociology, and Economics,* tr. Ronald L. Meek (Cambridge, 1973); and see Meek, *Social Science and the Noble Savage* (Cambridge, 1976), and *Smith, Marx, and After* (London, 1977).

116. *De l'origine des arts et des sciences, et des leurs progrès chez les anciens peuples* (Paris, 1758), trans. as *Of the Origin of Laws, Arts, and Sciences and Their Progresses* (Edinburgh, 1775).

117. *Progress of the Human Mind,* introduction, 11; and see Keith Baker, *Condorcet: From Natural Philosophy to Mathematics* (Chicago, 1975).

118. *Essai,* 170.

119. See Frank Manuel, *The Prophets of Paris: Turgot, Condorcet, Saint-Simon, Fourier, Comte* (Cambridge, Mass., 1962).

120. Becker's classic work is *The Heavenly City of the Eighteenth-Century Philosophers* (New Haven, 1932), ch. 3, "The New History," ironically (?) subtitled with the classical tag, "Philosophy Teaching by Example." Peter Gay's counterclassic, *The En-*

lightenment: An Interpretation (New York, 1966), began as an essay criticizing Becker's book.

121. *Vorlesungen über die Philosophie der Geschichte,* ed. Eduard Gans (Berlin, 1837), 434.

122. Cited by Wilhelm Schmidt Biggemann, Topica Universalis: *Eine Modellgeschichte humanistischer und barocker Wissenschaft* (Hamburg, 1983), 283. See the comprehensive study by Michael Albrecht, *Eklektik: Eine Begriffsgeschichte mit Hinweisen auf die Philosophie- und Wissenschaftsgeschichte* (Stuttgart, 1993), with full bibliography.

123. See John Stroup, "Protestant Church Historians in the German Enlightenment," in *Aufklärung und Geschichte: Studien zur deutschen Geschichtswissenschaft in 18. Jahrhundert,* ed. Hans Erich Bödeker, Georg G. Iggers, Jonathan B. Knudsen, and Peter Reill (Göttingen, 1986), 169–92.

124. *Unparteyische Kirchen- und Ketzer-Historie von Anfang des Neuen Testaments biss auf das Jahr Christi 1688* (Frankfurt, 1700).

125. *An Ecclesiastical History, Ancient and Modern,* 2 vols., tr. Archibald Maclaine (New York, 1867).

126. Notker Hammerstein, *Jus und Historie: Ein Beitrag zur Geschichte des historischen Denkens an deutschen Universitäten im späten 17. und 18. Jahrhundert* (Göttingen, 1972); Peter Reill, *The German Enlightenment and the Rise of Historicism* (Berkeley, 1975); and Luigi Marino, Praeceptores Germaniae: *Göttingen 1770–1820* (Göttingen, 1995), tr. from the Italian edition (1975).

127. Horst Walter Blanke and Dirk Fleischer (eds.), *Theoretiker der deutschen Aufklärungshistorie* (Stuttgart, 1990).

128. Meinecke, *Historism;* and see, besides Reill, Horst Walter Blanke, *Historiographiegeschichte als Historik* (Stuttgart, 1991); Blanke and Jörn Rüsen (eds.), *Von der Aufklärung zum Historismus: Zum Strukturwandel des historischen Denkens* (Paderborn, 1984); Ulrich Muhlack, *Geschichtswissenschaft in Humanismus und in der Aufklärung: Die Vorgeschichte des Historismus* (Munich, 1991); Friedrich Jäger and Jörn Rüsen, *Geschichte des Historismus* (Munich, 1992); Jonathan Knudsen, *Justus Möser and the German Enlightenment* (Cambridge, 1986); Herbert Butterfield, *Man on His Past: The Study of the History of Historical Scholarship* (Cambridge, 1955); Kurt Breysig, *Die Meister der entwickelnden Geschichtswissenschaft* (Breslau, 1936), esp. on Winckelmann, Möser, and Herder.

129. See Knudsen, *Justus Möser.*

130. See Otto Dahn, "Des historische Interesse in der deutsche Gesellschaft des 18. Jahrhunderts: Geschichte und historische Forschung in der zeitgenössischen Zeitschriften," *Historische Forschung im 18. Jahrhundert,* 386–415; and Konrad H. Jarausch, "The Institutionalization of History in 18th-Century Germany," *Aufklärung und Geschichte,* 25–48.

131. "On Diligence in the Study of Several Learned Languages" (1764), and "On the Modern Usage of Mythology," in *Selected Early Works, 1764–1767,* tr. Ernest A. Menze and Karl Menges (University Park, Penn., 1992), 30 and 215.

132. "Essay on the Origin of Language," in *J. G. Herder on Social and Political Culture,* tr. F. M. Barnard (Cambridge, 1969), 142.

133. "Travel Diary," in *J. G. Herder,* 76–77.

134. *Pragmatische Staatsgeschichte Europens* (Gotha, 1762), 7.

135. On an earlier work perhaps drawn on by Herder, see P. Meinrad Alois Regli, *Isaac Iselin's "Geschichte der Menschheit": Ein Vorarbeit zu Joh. Gottfr. Herders "Ideen zur Philosophie des Menschheit"?* (Leipzig, 1919).

136. *Vorrede* to Maier, *Zur Kulturgeschichte der Völker* (Leipzig, 1798), II, iv.

137. *Yet Another Philosophy of History,* in *J. G. Herder,* 181.

138. *Ideen zur Philosophie der Geschichte der Menschheit,* in *Werke,* ed. Ernst Naumann (Berlin, n.d.), III, 51 ("Vorrede"); IV, 154; VI, 30; the only complete English translation is *Outlines of a Philosophy of the History of Man,* tr. T. Churchill (London, 1800), 230, 231.

139. *Aufklärung, Bildung,* and *Kultur* were all new words from the Enlightenment, remarks Franco Venturi, "Towards a Historical Dictionary," in *Italy and the Enlightenment,* tr. Susan Corsi (New York, 1972), 33.

140. *Ideen,* VIII, 3; IX, 1.

141. *Ideen,* XI, 5.

142. *Ideen,* XX, 4.

143. "On the Transformation of the Taste of Nations in the Course of Ages," in *Selected Early Works,* 66.

144. *Yet Another Philosophy,* 184.

145. *Ideen,* VII, 1.

146. "On the Transformation," 65.

147. *Historische Vergleichung der Sitten und Verfasssungen des Gesetz und Gewerbe, des Handels, und der Religion, der Wissenschaften, und Lehranstalten des Mittelalters mit denen unsers Jahrhunderts in Rücksicht auf die Vortheile und Nachteile der Aufklärung* (Hannover, 1793), 465.

148. See D. R. Kelley, "The Old Cultural History," in *History and the Human Sciences* (1996), 101–26.

Chapter 10: Modern Historiography

1. See above, ch. 8 at nn. 67, 88, 100, 113; ch. 9 at nn. 10, 13, 52, 130; and below, at n. 17.

2. Gottlieb Stolle, *Anleitung zur Historie der Gelahrheit,* 2d ed. (Jena, 1736), "Von de Historie," repr. in *Theoretiker der deutschen Aufklärungshistorie,* ed. Horst Walter Blanke and Dirk Fleischer (Stuttgart, 1990), I, 274; and cf. C. A. Heumann, *Conspectus Reipublicae literariae,* (Halle, 1718 [8th ed., 1791]).

3. Cellarius, *Historia antiqua* (Halle, 1685), *Historia medii aevi* (Halle, 1688), *Historia nova* (Halle, 1696); and see J. H. J. Van der Pot, *De Periodisering der Geschiedenis* (The Hague, 1951), 113ff.

4. *Methode pour étudier l'histoire, avec un catalogue des principaux historiens,* 2 vols. (Paris, 1713).

5. Georges Gusdorf, *Les Sciences humaines,* 13 vols. (Paris, 1966–88), V, *Dieu, la nature, l'homme au siècle des lumières,* 86. See Frank Manuel, *The Eighteenth Century Confronts the Gods* (Cambridge, Mass., 1959); and Emery Neff, *The Poetry of History:*

The Contribution of Literature and Literary Scholarship to the Writing of History since Voltaire (New York, 1947).

6. *Symbolik und Mythologie der alten Völker, besonders die Griechen,* 4 vols. (Leipzig, 1810–12); cf. K. O. Müller, *Introduction to a Scientific System of Mythology,* tr. J. Leitsch (London, 1844); see also Heinz Gockel, *Mythos und Poesie: Zur Mythosbegriff in Aufklärung und Frühromantik* (Frankfurt, 1981); and D. R. Kelley, "Mythistory in the Age of Ranke," in *Leopold von Ranke and the Shaping of the Historical Profession,* ed. Georg Iggers and James Powell (Syracuse, 1989), 3–20, 181–85.

7. *Prolegomenon to Homer, 1795,* tr. Anthony Grafton, Glenn W. Most, and James E. G. Zetze (Princeton, 1985).

8. *Les Sciences humaines, IV, Les Principes de la pensée au siècle des lumières,* 40.

9. See *Objects of Inquiry: The Life, Contributions, and Influences of Sir William Jones, 1746–1794,* ed. Garland Cannon and Kevin R. Brine (New York, 1995); and Raymond Schwab, *The Oriental Renaissance: Europe's Rediscovery of India and the East, 1680–1880,* tr. G. Patterson-Black and V. Reinking (New York, 1984).

10. See Michael Steinberg, "The Twelve Tables and Their Origins: An Eighteenth-Century Debate," *Journal of the History of Ideas* 43 (1982), 379–96.

11. Joseph-Marie Degérando, *The Observation of Savage Peoples,* tr. F. C. T. Mooree (Berkeley, 1969); cf. Corrado Vivanti, "Le Scoperte geografiche e gli scritti di Henri La Popelinière," *Rivista storica italiana* 74 (1962), 225–49; and, in general, see Michel Duchet, *Anthropologie et histoire au siècle des lumières* (Paris, 1995); Annemarie de Waal Malefijt, *Images of Man: A History of Anthropological Thought* (New York, 1974); and Georges Gusdorf, *Les Sciences humaines,* III, pt. 2, *La Révolution galiléenne,* 183f; V, 355ff; also Hans Erich Bödeker, "Reisebeschreibungen im historischen Diskurs der Aufklärung," in *Aufklärung und Geschichte: Studien zur deutschen Geschichtswissenschaft im 18. Jahrhundert,* eds. Hans Erich Bödeker, Georg G. Iggers, Jonathan Knudsen, and Peter H. Reill (Göttingen, 1986), 193–224.

12. See George Kubler, *The Shape of Time: Remarks on the History of Things* (New Haven, 1962); and Suzanne Marchand, *Down from Olympus: Archaeology and Philhellenism in Germany, 1750–1970* (Princeton, 1996).

13. See Alex Potts, *Flesh and the Ideal: Winckelmann and the Origins of Art History* (New Haven, 1994).

14. Jaroslav Malina and Zdenek Vasicek, *Archaeology Yesterday and Today* (Cambridge, 1990), 29; and Philip L. Kohl and Clare Fawcett (eds.), *Nationalism, Politics, and the Practice of Archaeology* (Cambridge, 1995).

15. Ulrich Muhlack, "Historie und Philologie," in *Aufklärung und Geschichte,* 49–81.

16. Anthony Grafton, " 'Mas muss aus der Gegenwart heraufsteigen': History, Tradition, and Traditions of Historical Thought in F. A. Wolf," in *Aufklärung und Geschichte,* 416–29.

17. See Gabriella Valera, "Statistik, Staatengeschichte, Geschichte im 18. Jahrhundert," and Pasquale Pasquino, "Politische und historische Interesse: Statistik und historische Staatslehre bei Gottfried Achenwall, 1719–1772," in *Aufklärung und Geschichte,* 193–68. And see Arno Seifert, Cognitio Historica: *Die Geschichte als Namengeberin der frühneuzeitlichen Empirie* (Berlin, 1976).

18. See, e.g., C. T. G. Schönemann, "Grundriss einer Encyclopädie der historischen

Wissenschaften" (1799), in Blanke and Fleischer, *Theoretiker*, I, 350; II, 369, 379; also Luigi Marino, *Praeceptores Germaniae Göttingen, 1770–1820* (Göttingen, 1995), 246ff, and Blanke, *Historiographiegeschichte als Historik* (Stuttgart, 1991), 128.

19. Glyn Daniel and Colin Renfrew, *The Idea of Prehistory*, 2d ed. (Edinburgh, 1986), 22ff.

20. See J. D. Michaelis, *A Dissertation on the influence of opinion on language, and of language on opinions* (London, 1769); Adolph Harnack, *Geschichte der königlich preussisschen Akademie der Wissenschaften zu Berlin* (Berlin, 1900), I, 409, 416; and see Robert S. Leventhal, *The Disciplines of Interpretation: Lessing, Herder, Schlegel and Hermeneutics, 1750–1800* (Berlin, 1994), 214.

21. *Essai sur l'esprit et l'influence de la Réformation de Luther*, 5th ed. (Paris, 1851), 50, 36–37.

22. *The Fortunes of Inquiry* (Oxford, 1986), and *The Scenes of Inquiry* (Oxford, 1991).

23. See above, n. 1.

24. *Geschichte der Luxus der Athenienses von der ältesten Zeiten bis auf den Tod Phillips von Makedonien* (Lemgo, 1782).

25. Otto Henne am Rhyn, *Die Kultur der Vergangenheit, Gegenwart und Zukunft* (Danzig, 1890), 210.

26. See Frank Manuel, *The Prophets of Paris: Turgot, Condorcet, Saint-Simon, Fourier, Comte* (Cambridge, Mass., 1962); and Brian William Head, *Ideology and Social Science: Destutt de Tracy and French Liberalism* (Dordrecht, 1985), 114.

27. See D. R. Kelley, "The Old Cultural History," *History of the Human Sciences* 9 (1996), 101–26, with further bibliography.

28. Friedrich Creuzer, *Die historische Kunst der Griechen* (Leipzig, 1803); and Ludwig Wachler, *Geschichte der historischen Forschung und Kunst seit der Wiederherstellung der litterarische Cultur in Europa* (Göttingen, 1812); and see Josef Engel, "Die deutschen Universitäten und die Geschichtswissenschaft," *Historische Zeitschrift* 189 (1959), 223–378.

29. Creuzer, *Die historische Kunst;* Wegele, *Geschichte der deutschen Historiographie seit dem Auftreten des Humanismus* (Munich, 1885), reviewed by Acton in "German Schools of History," in *Selected Writings of Lord Acton*, II, *Essays in the Study and Writing of History*, ed. J. Rufus Fears (Indianapolis, 1985), 325; and see Blanke, *Historiographiegeschichte*, 194ff.

30. *Geschichte der neueren Historiographie*, 2d ed. (Munich, 1936), with translations into French and Italian but not English.

31. *Reflections on the Revolution in France* (New York, 1969), 193–94, 247.

32. *Lectures on the French Revolution* (Cambridge, 1910), 345.

33. See D. R. Kelley, *Historians and the Law in Postrevolutionary France* (Princeton, 1984), 68ff, and "Ancient Verses on New Ideas: Legal Tradition and the French Historical School," *History and Theory* 26 (1987), 319–38; also E. Carcassonne, *Montesquieu et le problème de la constitution française au XVIIIe siècle* (Paris, 1927).

34. *L'Institution des sciences morales, 1795–1850* (Paris, 1995), 37.

35. Jacques Godechot, *Les institutions de la France sous la Révolution et l'Empire* (Paris, 1951), 391.

36. See Dominique Puolot, *"Surveiller et s'instruire"*: *La Révolution française et l'intelligence de l'héritage historique* (Oxford, 1996), and Dieter Gembicki, "Das 'Dépot des chartes' (1762–1790): Ein historisches Forschungszentrum," *Historische Forschung im 18. Jahrhundert,* 192–206.

37. "Geschichte und Naturwissenschaft," in *Präludien* (Tübingen, 1924), II, 145; discussion continued by Heinrich Rickert, *The Limits of Concept Formation in Natural Science,* tr. Guy Oakes (Cambridge, 1986).

38. See Reinhart Koselleck, *"Historia Magistra Vitae:* The Dissolution of a Historical Topos into the Perspective of a Modernized Historical Process," in *Futures Past: On the Semantics of Historical Time,* tr. Keith Tribe (Cambridge, Mass., 1985), 21–38; and Frank Manuel, *Shapes of Philosophical History* (London, 1965).

39. The great omission in Kant's system, a "critique of historical reason," was the challenge taken up later within the Kantian tradition by Wilhelm Dilthey and others.

40. See Martin Haeussler, *Das Ende der Geschichte in der mittelalterlichen Weltchronistik* (Cologne, 1980).

41. *Historische Vergleichung der Sitten und Verfassungen, der Handels und des Gewerbe, des Handels und der Religion, der Wissenschaften und Lehranstalten des Mittelalters mit denen unsres Jahrhunderts in Rücksicht auf die Vortheile, und Nachtheile der Aufklärung* (Hanover, 1793), 585.

42. *Sketch for a Historical Picture of the Progress of the Human Mind,* tr. June Barraclough (London, 1955), 188.

43. Ernst Cassirer, *The Philosophy of the Enlightenment,* tr. Fritz C. A. Koelln and James P. Pettigrove (Princeton, 1951), ch. 7.

44. *Critical Reflections on Poetry, Painting and Music,* tr. Thomas Nugent (London, 1748), 56–95.

45. Henry Caraway Hatfield, *Winckelmann and His German Critics, 1755–1781* (New York, 1943), 93.

46. Erich Auerbach, "Vico and Aesthetic Historicism," in *Scenes from the Drama of European Literature* (New York, 1959), 183–98.

47. *The Great Chain of Being: A Study in the History of an Idea* (Cambridge, Mass., 1950), ch. 9.

48. Friedrich Meinecke, *Historism: The Rise of a New Outlook,* tr. J. E. Anderson (London, 1972), 67; Jonathan B. Knudsen, "Justus Möser: Local History as Cosmopolitan History," in *Aufklärung und Geschichte,* 324–43; and see Geertz, *Local Knowledge* (New York, 1983).

49. See, e.g., *Philosophical Interventions in the Unfinished Project of Enlightenment,* ed. Axel Honneth et al. (Cambridge, Mass., 1992).

50. Cited by Blanke, *Historiographiegeschichte,* 159.

51. For example, in his essay "Enlightenment" for the *Dictionary of the History of Ideas,* ed. Philip P. Wiener, 6 vols. (New York, 1973).

52. In a vast literature, see *The Hermeneutic Tradition from Ast to Ricoeur,* ed. Gayle L. Ormiston and Alan D. Schrift (Albany, 1990); and also Michael Ermarth, "Hermeneutics and History: The Fork in Hermes's Path through the 18th Century," in *Aufklärung und Geschichte,* 193–224.

53. See Notker Hammerstein, "Der Anteil der 18. Jahrhunderts an der Ausbildung der

historischen Schulen des 19. Jahrhunderts," Karl Hammer and Jürgen Voss (eds.), *Historische Forschungen im 18. Jahrhundert* (Bonn, 1976), 432–50.

54. See above ch. 5 n. 1.

55. *Allgemeine Geschichtswissenschaft worinnen des Grund zu einen Einsicht in allen Arten der Gelahrheit gelegt wird* (Leipzig, 1752), 104ff; also Blanke and Fleischer, *Theoretiker*, I, 237ff, with other texts by Chladenius, and "On the Concept of Interpretation," in *The Hermeneutics Reader*, ed. Kurt Mueller-Voellmer (Oxford, 1985), 55ff; see also Peter Szondi, *Introduction to Literary Hermeneutics*, tr. Martha Woodmansee (Cambridge, 1995), 14–66; and Reinhart Koselleck, "Perspective and Temporality: A Contribution to the Historiographical Exposure of the Historical World," in *Futures Past*, 130–55.

56. Chladenius, "On the Interpretation of Historical Books and Accounts," in *Hermeneutics Reader*, 70.

57. *Das Verstehen: Grundzüge einer Geschichte der hermeneutischen Theorie im 19. Jahrhundert*, 3 vols. (Tübingen, 1926–33).

58. See Robert S. Leventhal, *The Disciplines of Interpretation: Lessing, Herder, Schlegel and Hermeneutics in Germany, 1750–1800* (Berlin, 1994), 258ff.

59. Hans Robert Jauss, *Question and Answer: Forms of Dialogic Understanding*, tr. Michael Hays (Minneapolis, 1989), 30.

60. "A Definition of the Concept of History," in *Philosophy and History: Essays Presented to Ernst Cassirer*, ed. R. Klibansky and H. J. Paton (Oxford, 1936), 6.

61. See, e.g., Robert Berkhofer, *Beyond the Great Story* (Cambridge, Mass., 1995).

62. Quintilian, *Institutes of Oratory*, 6.2.15; 8.6.54; and see Dilwyn Knox, Ironia: *Medieval and Renaissance Ideas of Irony* (Leiden, 1989). More recent discussions — beyond the huge literature on romantic irony — center on Kenneth Burke, *A Grammar of Motives* (New York, 1954), 514–17; and Hayden White, *Metahistory: The Historical Imagination in Nineteenth-Century Europe* (Baltimore, 1973).

63. Schleiermacher, *General Hermeneutics*, in *Hermeneutics Reader*, 83; and see Ernst Behler, "What It Means to Understand an Author Better than He Understood Himself: Idealistic Philosophy and Romantic Hermeneutics," in *Literary Theory and Criticism: Festschrift Presented to René Wellek*, ed. Joseph P. Strelka (Bern, 1984), I, 69–92.

64. Nietzsche, *Twilight of the Idols*, tr. R. J. Hollingdale (New York, 1968), 25.

65. "Hermeneutics and the Critique of Ideology," in *Hermeneutics and the Human Sciences*, tr. John B. Thompson (Cambridge, 1981), 63–100.

66. *Essays*, II, 326, 526, 543; and see above, ch. 9 at n. 128.

67. "Zur Philologie I," in *Fragmente zur Poesie und Literatur, Kritische-Friedrich-Schlegel-Ausgabe*, ed. Ernst Behler, XVI (Paderborn, 1981), 35. Conventional German usage has settled on *Historismus*, while Italian insists on *storicismo*, and English vacillates between the two forms (*historism, historicism*).

68. *Schriften*, ed. J. Minor (Jena, 1907), III, 118 ("Fragmenta").

69. See Erich Rothacker, "Das Wort 'Historismus,'" *Zeitschrift für deutsche Wortforschung* 16 (1960), 3–6; Gunter Scholz, *"Historismus" als speculative Geschichtsphilosophie: Christlieb Julius Braniss, 1792–1873* (Frankfurt, 1973); and Georg Iggers, "Historicism: The History and Meaning of the Term," *Journal of the History of Ideas* 56 (1995), 129–52.

70. *Historism*, lv, 122. The notion of "individualizing" is no doubt drawn from the earlier discussion by Wilhelm Windelband, "Geschichte und Naturwissenschaft," in *Präludien*, 8th ed. (Tübingen, 1921), II, 142–45, and Heinrich Rickert, *Kulturwissenschaft und Naturwissenschaft*, 5th ed. (Tübingen, 1921).

71. David Womersley, *The Transformation of The Decline and Fall of the Roman Empire* (Cambridge, 1988), sees a failure of Meinecke's own individualizing vision in his indiscriminate application of the concept of "historism" to the English, Scotch, French, and German historians alike — and all under the shadow of a nonhistorian, Goethe.

72. *Historism*, 311.

73. *Historism*, 324.

74. Erich Hassinger, *Empirisch-rationaler Historismus: Seine Ausbildung in der Literatur Westeuropas von Guicciardini bis Saint-Evremond* (Bern, 1978); and see my review of this and other related works in *Journal of Modern History* 54 (1982), 320–26.

75. *Geschichtswissenschaft im Humanismus und in der Aufklärung: Die Vorgeschichte des Historismus* (Munich, 1991). I suggested a similar argument in my *Foundations of Modern Historical Scholarship* (1970), also referring to Thomas Kuhn.

76. *Historiographiegeschichte*, 25–36. Blanke's book is dedicated "Dem Andenken Eduard Fueters, 1876–1928."

77. For example, Michael Allen Gillespie, *Hegel, Heidegger, and the Ground of History* (Chicago, 1984), which totally divorces historicism from any associations with historical learning.

78. See the entry in *Historisches Wörterbuch der Philosophie*, ed. J. Ritter, 9 vols. (Basel, 1968–).

79. "Hegel's Historicism," in *The Cambridge Companion to Hegel*, ed. Beiser (Cambridge, 1993), 270ff.

80. See D. R. Kelley, *Historians and the Law in Postrevolutionary France* (Princeton, 1984), and *The Human Measure: Social Thought in the Western Legal Tradition* (Cambridge, Mass., 1991), ch. 13.

81. *The Life of Jesus Critically Examined*, tr. George Eliot (London, 1892).

82. *The Idea of History* (rev. ed.; Oxford, 1993), 9, 10.

83. See Edward Said, *Beginnings: Intention and Method* (Baltimore, 1975), with many invocations of Vico.

84. Yirmiahu Yovel, *Kant and the Philosophy of History* (Princeton, 1980), 225.

85. Cited by Lutz Geldsetzer, *Die Philosophie der Philosophiegeschichte* (Mersenheim, 1968), 30.

86. *The Philosophy of History*, tr. J. Sibree (New York, 1944), 442; and see Joachim Ritter, *Hegel and the French Revolution*, tr. R. D. Winfield (Cambridge, 1982).

87. See D. R. Kelley, "The Science of Anthropology: An Essay on the Very Old Marx," *Journal of the History of Ideas* 45 (1984), 245–62; repr. in *History, Law, and the Human Sciences* (London, 1984).

88. *The Archaeology of Knowledge*, tr. A. M. Sheridan Smith (New York, 1972), 21ff.

89. *The Order of Things: An Archaeology of the Human Sciences*, tr. A. M. Sheridan Smith (New York, 1970), 131.

90. See Hervé Contau-Begarie, *Le Phenomène "nouvelle histoire"* (Paris, 1983); and

Ignacio Olábarri Gortázar, " 'New' New History: A *Longue Durée* Structure," *History and Theory* 34 (1995), 1–29.

91. Lynn Hunt, *The New Cultural History* (Berkeley, 1989).

92. *The New Historicism and Other Old-Fashioned Topics* (Princeton, 1991), 44.

93. "Renaissance Literary Studies and the Subject of History," *English Literary Renaissance* 16 (1986), 8.

94. *A Treatise of Human Nature,* I, iv, 6.

95. *Archaeology of Knowledge,* 12.

96. Posthistoire: *Has History Come to an End?* tr. Patrick Camiller (London, 1989); and Francis Fukuyama, *The End of History and the Last Man* (London, 1992), with his ironic afterthoughts, "The End of History, Five Years Later," *History and Theory* Theme Issue 34 (1995), 27–43.

Index

Abraham, 87, 89, 190
Accolti, Benedetto, 140
Achenwall, Gottfried, 246
Acton, John Emerich Edward Dahlberg,
   Lord, 4, 16, 257, 265, 273
Adam, 8, 73, 77–78, 89, 92, 107–8, 113,
   166, 202, 211, 215, 252
Adam of Bremen, 116, 184
Adelung, Johann Christoph, 238, 245, 247
Aeneas, 39–40, 55, 57, 94, 111, 112, 137
Aeschylus, 31
Africanus, Julius, 87–88, 100
Agamemnon, 16, 30, 257, 273
Agarde, Arthur, 208
Agricola, Rudolf, 136
Agrippa of Nettesheim, Henry Cornelius,
   167, 190–91
Aimon of Fleury, 110, 114, 178
Alaric, 90, 104, 109
Alciato, Andrea, 184
Alembert, Jean Le Rond d', 218, 221,
   228, 230, 235

Alexander of Roes, 127–28
Alexander the Great, 20, 26, 33, 35, 44,
   73, 93, 106, 107, 115, 132, 228, 242
Alexandrine school, 42, 43, 96, 205, 267
Alfonso III, king of Leon, 118
Alfonso X, king of Castile, 118, 157
Alfred the Great, 113
Althamer, Andreas, 175, 200
Ambrose, 69–70
Ammonius Saccus, 83
Ancients and Moderns, 11, 12, 155–56,
   160, 175, 200, 209–10, 222–23, 238–
   39, 248, 267, 274
Annales Maximi, 66
Anselm of Havelberg, 126
Antichrist, 92, 124, 126, 128, 173
Antoninus, 85
Apocalypse, 87
Appian, 144
Aquinas, Thomas, 99, 170
Aratus, 85
archaeolatry, 7, 49–56, 201, 252